COGNITIVE APPROACHES TO ANCIENT RELIGIOUS EXPERIENCE

For some time interest has been growing in a dialogue between modern scientific research into human cognition and research in the humanities. This ground-breaking volume focuses this dialogue on the religious experience of men and women in the ancient Greek and Roman worlds. Each chapter examines a particular historical problem arising from an ancient religious activity, and the contributions range across a wide variety of ancient contexts and sources, exploring and integrating literary, epigraphic, visual, and archaeological evidence. In order to avoid a simple polarity between physical aspects (ritual) and mental aspects (belief) of religion, the contributors draw on theories of cognition as embodied, emergent, enactive, and extended, accepting the complexity, multimodality, and multicausality of human life. Through this interdisciplinary approach, the chapters open up new questions around and develop new insights into the physical, emotional, and cognitive aspects of ancient religions.

ESTHER EIDINOW is Professor of Ancient History at the University of Bristol. She works on ancient Greek culture, specializing in magic and religion. She is a distinguished fellow of the Religion, Cognition, and Culture Unit of Aarhus University, and a founder of the *Journal of Cognitive Historiography*. She is currently leading a project funded by the UK's Arts and Humanities Research Council to develop a virtual reality experience of consultation of the oracle of Zeus at Dodona.

ARMIN W. GEERTZ is Emeritus Professor in the History of Religions at Aarhus University. He works on the cognitive science of religion, evolutionary theory, and the psychology of religious experiences. He is co-founder/editor of the *Journal for the Cognitive Science of Religion* and *Advances in the Cognitive Science of Religion*.

JOHN NORTH is Emeritus Professor of History at University College London. He has worked on the religious history of Rome and the changing character of religious life in the Roman Empire down to the rise of Christianity. He is a co-author of the two-volume history and sourcebook *Religions of Rome* (Cambridge 1998).

ANCIENT RELIGION AND COGNITION

Series Editors

Esther Eidinow, *University of Bristol*
Thomas Harrison, *University of St Andrews*

This series seeks to take advantage of a critical moment in the development of the study of ancient religion. This is one in which previous models (especially the sharp oppositions frequently drawn between ritual and belief, or between the social and the individual) are increasingly being questioned, and in which scholars of the ancient world are more and more drawing on cognitive approaches in the search for new paradigms. The 'cognitive science of religion' draws on insights developed in a wide range of fields: cognitive and evolutionary psychology, cognitive anthropology, and neurobiology, amongst others. In essence, however, it seeks to understand religious experience as rooted in the ordinary cognitive capacities of the human brain. The series covers not only Greek and Roman religion but a range of ancient cultures from the Mediterranean and Near East, including Greece, Rome, Egypt, Babylonia, Persia, and Phoenicia, as well as cultures from Iron Age Europe. It will also explore the implications for the study of these cultures of a range of different cognitive approaches to religion and will include work by scholars from a wide range of disciplines in anthropology, the study of religion, evolutionary psychology, and neuroscience in addition to that by historians and archaeologists of the ancient world.

COGNITIVE APPROACHES TO ANCIENT RELIGIOUS EXPERIENCE

EDITED BY

ESTHER EIDINOW
University of Bristol

ARMIN W. GEERTZ
Aarhus University

JOHN NORTH
University College London

Shaftesbury Road, Cambridge CB2 8EA, United Kingdom

One Liberty Plaza, 20th Floor, New York, NY 10006, USA

477 Williamstown Road, Port Melbourne, VIC 3207, Australia

314–321, 3rd Floor, Plot 3, Splendor Forum, Jasola District Centre, New Delhi – 110025, India

103 Penang Road, #05–06/07, Visioncrest Commercial, Singapore 238467

Cambridge University Press is part of Cambridge University Press & Assessment, a department of the University of Cambridge.

We share the University's mission to contribute to society through the pursuit of education, learning and research at the highest international levels of excellence.

www.cambridge.org
Information on this title: www.cambridge.org/9781009011600
DOI: 10.1017/9781009019927

© Cambridge University Press & Assessment 2022

This publication is in copyright. Subject to statutory exception and to the provisions of relevant collective licensing agreements, no reproduction of any part may take place without the written permission of Cambridge University Press & Assessment.

First published 2022
First paperback edition 2023

A catalogue record for this publication is available from the British Library

Library of Congress Cataloging-in-Publication data
NAMES: Eidinow, Esther, 1970– editor. | Geertz, Armin W., 1948– editor. | North, John, 1938– editor.
TITLE: Cognitive approaches to ancient religious experience / edited by Esther Eidinow, Armin W. Geertz, John North.
DESCRIPTION: Cambridge; New York, NY: Cambridge University Press, 2022. | Series: Ancient religion and cognition | Includes bibliographical references and index.
IDENTIFIERS: LCCN 2021061903 (print) | LCCN 2021061904 (ebook) | ISBN 9781316515334 (hardback) | ISBN 9781009011600 (paperback) | ISBN 9781009019927 (epub)
SUBJECTS: LCSH: Experience (Religion) | Cognition and culture–Greece. | Cognition and culture–Rome. | Civilization, Ancient. | Greece–Religious life and customs. | Rome–Religious life and customs. | BISAC: HISTORY / Ancient / General
CLASSIFICATION: LCC BL785 .C64 2022 (print) | LCC BL785 (ebook) | DDC 292–dc23/eng20220314
LC record available at https://lccn.loc.gov/2021061903
LC ebook record available at https://lccn.loc.gov/2021061904

ISBN 978-1-316-51533-4 Hardback
ISBN 978-1-009-01160-0 Paperback

Cambridge University Press & Assessment has no responsibility for the persistence or accuracy of URLs for external or third-party internet websites referred to in this publication and does not guarantee that any content on such websites is, or will remain, accurate or appropriate.

Contents

List of Figures and Tables	*page* vii
List of Contributors	viii
List of Abbreviations	xiii
Funder Acknowledgement	xiv

Introduction   1
Esther Eidinow, Armin W. Geertz, Quinton Deeley, and John North

PART I RITUAL

1 A Cognitive Approach to Ancient Greek Animal Sacrifice   19
  Hugh Bowden

2 To the Netherworld and Back: Cognitive Aspects of the Descent to Trophonius   44
  Yulia Ustinova

PART II REPRESENTATION

3 Ancient Greek Smellscapes and Divine Fragrances: Anthropomorphizing the Gods in Ancient Greek Culture   69
  Esther Eidinow

4 Belief, Make-Believe, and the Religious Imagination: The Case of the *Deus Ex Machina* in Greek Tragedy   96
  Felix Budelmann

5 Chanting and Dancing into Dissociation: The Case of the Salian Priests at Rome   118
  Maik Patzelt

PART III GENDER

6 The Bacchants Are Silent: Using Cognitive Science to
Explore the Experience of the *Oreibasia*   145
Vivienne McGlashan

7 Who Is the *Damiatrix*? Roman Women, the Political Negotiation
of Psychotropic Experiences, and the Cults of Bona Dea   167
Leonardo Ambasciano

PART IV MATERIALITY

8 Walls and the Ancient Greek Ritual Experience: The Sanctuary
of Demeter and Kore at Eleusis   193
Michael Scott

9 Identifying Symptoms of Religious Experience from Ancient
Material Culture: The Example of Cults of the Roman Mithras   218
Luther H. Martin

PART V TEXTS

10 Bridging the Gap: From Textual Representations to the
Experiential Level and Back   245
Anders Klostergaard Petersen

11 A Relevant Mystery: Intuitive and Reflective Thought in
Gregory of Nyssa's Representations of Divine Begetting in
the *Against Eunomius*   266
Isabella Sandwell

Index   290

Figures and Tables

Figure

8.1 Plan of the sanctuary of Demeter and Kore at Eleusis by J. Travlos 'The Topography of Eleusis' *Hesperia* 1949 (18.1) pp. 138–147, adapted by M. Scott. *page* 196

Tables

7.1 Ritual form hypothesis (adapted from Larson 2016). 179
7.2 Ritual form hypothesis applied to the Bona Dea cults. 181
7.3 Theory of the modes of religiosity (adapted from Whitehouse 2002: 309). 182
7.4 Organization and experiences of the Bona Dea cults and Roman state religion (*sacra publica*) according to the theory of the modes of religiosity. 183

Contributors

LEONARDO AMBASCIANO earned his PhD in historical studies at the University of Turin, Italy, in 2014 with a cognitive, evolutionary, and gender and sexuality analysis of the ancient Roman cult of Bona Dea. In 2016, he was Visiting Lecturer in Religious Studies at Masaryk University, Brno, Czech Republic. He also served as Editorial Assistant and Managing Editor of the *Journal of Cognitive Historiography* from 2014 to 2021. Ambasciano is the author of *Sciamanesimo senza sciamanesimo* (Nuova Cultura 2014) and *An Unnatural History of Religions: Academia, Post-Truth, and the Quest for Scientific Knowledge* (Bloomsbury 2019). Among his most recent articles are 'The Trials and Tribulations of Luke Skywalker: How the Walt Disney Co. and Lucasfilm Have Failed to Confront Joseph Campbell's Troublesome Legacy,' *Implicit Religion* 23(3): 251–276, and 'An Evolutionary Cognitive Approach to Comparative Fascist Studies: Hypermasculinization, Supernormal Stimuli, and Conspirational Beliefs,' *Evolutionary Studies in Imaginative Culture* 5(1): 23–39.

HUGH BOWDEN is Professor of Ancient History at King's College London. He has been involved in a series of national and international research projects focused on cognitive approaches to Greek religion, working with neuroscientists and anthropologists alongside classical scholars. He has written extensively in the field of ancient religion, with a particular focus on oracles and divination, and on mystery cults. His books include *Classical Athens and the Delphic Oracle: Divination and Democracy* (Cambridge University Press 2005) and *Mystery Cults in the Ancient World* (Thames and Hudson/Princeton University Press 2010).

FELIX BUDELMANN is Professor of Classics at the University of Groningen. He works on Greek literature and has a special interest in the interface of literature and cognition. A volume on cognitive approaches to Greek tragedy, jointly edited with Ineke Sluiter, is forthcoming. Earlier books, authored or (co-)edited, include *The Language of Sophocles* (2000), *The Cambridge Companion to Greek Lyric* (2009), *Choruses Ancient and Modern* (2013), *Textual Events* (2018), and *Greek Lyric: A Selection* (2018). He is currently working on a monograph about configurations of the 'now' in Greek literature.

QUINTON DEELEY is Senior Lecturer in Social Behaviour and Neurodevelopment at the Institute of Psychiatry, Psychology, and Neuroscience (IOPPN), King's College London. He is also Consultant Neuropsychiatrist in the National Autism Unit and Neuropsychiatry Brain Injury Clinic at the Maudsley and Bethlem Hospitals. He chairs the Maudsley Philosophy Group, and the Social and Cultural Neuroscience Group at the IOPPN. Dr Deeley has researched the relations between culture, cognition, and brain function since his qualifications in Theology and Religious Studies from the University of Cambridge, and later medicine at Guys and St Thomas' Medical School, London, and psychiatry at the Maudsley and Bethlem Hospitals. He brings cognitive neuroscience research methods into dialogue with humanities scholarship to improve understanding of religious cognition, experience, and behaviour. Current research topics include researching voice hearing in patient groups and cultural practitioners, and how cognitive and brain processes involved in the formation of beliefs and experiences can be influenced by cultural practices such as ritual.

ESTHER EIDINOW is Professor of Ancient History at the University of Bristol. Her research explores ancient Greek culture, with particular focus on religion, magic, and myths; she also works on risk and futures thinking, both ancient and modern. Her books include *Oracles, Curses, and Risk among the Ancient Greeks* (2007); *Fate, Luck and Fortune: Antiquity and Its Legacy* (2011); *Envy, Poison, and Death: Women on Trial in Classical Athens* (2016). From 2014 to 2016, she was primary investigator on the UK's Arts and Humanities Research Council (AHRC)-funded network 'Cognitive Approaches to Ancient Religious Experience', with Armin W. Geertz (Aarhus University). She is currently leading a project, funded by the AHRC, which is building a virtual reality experience of consultation at the ancient oracle of Zeus at Dodona, north-western Greece (see www.vroracle.co.uk).

ARMIN W. GEERTZ is Emeritus Professor in the History of Religions at the Department of the Study of Religion, Aarhus University, Denmark. He has served as partner and co-investigator of the Arts and Humanities Research Council-funded network, 'Cognitive Approaches to Ancient Religious Experience'. He was co-founder and director of the Religion, Cognition and Culture Research Unit (2009–2016) and co-founder and member of the board of MINDLab (2009–2014) in Aarhus. He is editor of the *Journal for the Cognitive Science of Religion* and *Advances in the Cognitive Science of Religion* at Equinox. His interests and publications include the cognitive science of religion, evolutionary theory, psychology of religion, neuropsychology of religious experiences, ritual embodiment, method and theory in the study of religion, contemporary spirituality, and the religions of indigenous peoples. He recently co-authored *The Emergence and Evolution of Religion: By Means of Natural Selection* (Routledge 2018).

LUTHER H. MARTIN is Professor of Religion Emeritus, University of Vermont. He is the author, editor, or co-editor of eighteen books in his historical specialty, including *Hellenistic Religions* (1987), *The Mind of Mithraists* (2015), and *Studies in Hellenistic Religions* (2018). He has also published widely in the field of theory and method in the study of religion, collected in *Deep History, Secular Theory* (2014). Martin is a founder and past Executive Secretary of the North American Association for the Study of Religion, and a founder and past President of the International Association for the Cognitive Science of Religion. He has been a fellow at the American School of Classical Studies in Athens (1982) and the American Academy in Rome (1987), Distinguished International Fellow at Queen's University Belfast (2005–2007), Visiting Professor at Masaryk University, Brno, Czech Republic (2010), and recipient of an Honorary Medallion from that university (2012). He has been recognized as an Honorary Life Member by the International Association for the History of Religions.

VIVIENNE MCGLASHAN gained her undergraduate and master's degrees at the Open University and King's College London before embarking on her PhD, which examined the experience of maenadic ritual through the lens of the interplay of cognitive functions and physiological ritual effects. She successfully defended her thesis in 2021 in the department of Classics and Ancient History at the University of Bristol.

JOHN NORTH taught ancient Greek and Roman history in the History Department of UCL from 1963 until 2003 when he retired, having been Professor of History since 1992. On retirement, he became

Emeritus Professor and an Honorary Fellow of UCL. He acted as the Director of London University's Institute of Classical Studies from 2012 to 2014, and subsequently, together with Peter Mack, edited a number of the Institute's Reception Studies. His research interest has been primarily in the religious history of Rome in the Republican period and in the changing character of religious life in the Roman Empire down to the fourth century CE and the rise of Christianity. More recently, he has been working on the significance of religious activities in the lives of the slaves 'owned' by Romans. Currently, he is focused on the important interdisciplinary issues – between religious history and cognitive science – raised by the essays in this book.

MAIK PATZELT is Lecturer in Ancient History at the University of Freiburg. During his PhD studies he specialized in the religious history of the early Roman Empire, which concluded in his book *Über das Beten der Römer* (2018) as well as a number of articles that investigate Roman prayers through the lens of emotion theory, cognitive science, and theory of practice. He was Research Fellow (2019–2020) at the History Department of the University of Sheffield, where he started his new project on inheritance hunting, flattery, and gossip in Late Antiquity. For minor studies, he also investigates corruption, gendered agency, and early medieval convent rules.

ANDERS KLOSTERGAARD PETERSEN is senior lecturer in Science of Religion, Aarhus University, specializing in formative Christ-religion, Judaic religion of the Second Temple period, Graeco-Roman philosophy, intellectual history of scholarship in theology, study of religion, anthropology, and related fields, and greater matters pertaining to philosophy of science. In recent years, he has worked extensively on bio-cultural evolutionary questions, especially with respect to the shift from urban types of religion to the *kosmos* form of religion (or *Achsenzeit* discussion). He has recently co-authored with Jonathan H. Turner, Alexandra Maryanski, and Armin Geertz, *The Emergence and Evolution of Religion: By Means of Natural Selection*. He holds a list of publications of 600 items. He has lectured across the world and is a member of several boards of leading international journals. His most recent publication is *Theoretical and Empirical Investigations of Divination and Magic: Manipulating the Divine* (Brill 2021), co-edited with Jesper Sørensen.

ISABELLA SANDWELL is Senior Lecturer at the University of Bristol. She is author of a number of articles and chapters on John Chrysostom, Basil of Caesarea, and Libanius as well as the monograph *Religious Identity in Late Antiquity: Greeks, Jews and Christians in Antioch* (Cambridge 2007). She has also edited a number of volumes on preaching, Antioch, and late-antique religion. Her recent work uses the cognitive science of religion and cognitive linguistics to understand the transmission of Christian doctrine and the impact of Christian preaching in late antiquity. She has published articles on John Chrysostom and Gregory of Nyssa exploring these ideas. She is currently writing a monograph exploring how the cognitive science of religion and cognitive linguistics can be used to explore the success of Nicene Trinitarian doctrine in the late fourth century CE, using Gregory of Nyssa's *Against Eunomius* as a case study.

MICHAEL SCOTT is Professor in Classics and Ancient History at the University of Warwick and Director of the Warwick Institute of Engagement. He has written extensively on ancient Greek sanctuaries and religious practice, holding an honorary citizenship of Delphi in recognition of his work. He has taught widely in the UK and Greece and is a National Teaching Fellow and Principal Fellow of the Higher Education Academy. He has written for wider public audiences on a range of ancient Greek, Roman, and ancient global history topics, and has written and presented a range of TV and radio documentaries for National Geographic, History Channel, ITV, and the BBC. He is a Trustee and Director of Classics for All and President of the Lytham Saint Annes Classical Association. www.michaelscottweb.com @profmcscott

YULIA USTINOVA is Professor at the Department of General History and incumbent of the Anna and Sam Lopin Chair in History at Ben-Gurion University of the Negev, Israel. Her current research focuses on ancient Greek religion and culture, in particular on alteration of consciousness and insanity, healing practices, biased thinking, and cults in the colonial milieu. She is the author of many publications on ancient religion and culture, among them *The Supreme Gods of the Bosporan Kingdom: Celestial Aphrodite and the Most High God* (Brill 1999), *Caves and the Ancient Greek Mind: Descending Underground in the Search for Ultimate Truth* (Oxford University Press 2009), and *Divine Mania: Alteration of Consciousness in Ancient Greece* (Routledge 2018).

Abbreviations

This volume uses the abbreviations found in Hornblower, S., Spawforth, A., and Eidinow, E. 2012. *The Oxford Classical Dictionary*. Oxford; this is also available online.

Additional abbreviations:

1 Cor	1 Corinthians
CGRN	J.-M. Carbon; V. Pirenne-Delforge, *Collection of Greek Ritual Norms* (Liège 2016–)
CIMRM	M. J. Vermaseren, *Corpus Inscriptionum et Monumentorum Religionis Mithraicae*, 2 vols (The Hague, 1956, 1960)
Hom. Hymn Apollo	Homeric Hymn to Apollo
Hom. Hymn Dionysus	Homeric Hymn to Dionysus
Hom. Hymn Hermes	Homeric Hymn to Hermes
IMilet	P. Herrmann, W. Günther, N. Ehrhardt, *Inschriften von Milet* VI, 3, in the series *Milet: Ergebnisse der Ausgrabungen und Untersuchungen seit dem Jahr 1988* (Berlin 1899–2006)
LfgrE	B. Snell and H. Erbse, *Lexikon des frühgriechischen Epos* (Göttingen 1955–)
MV	Marrucini, Vestini
ST	H. Rix, *Sabellische Texte: die Texte des Oskischen, Umbrischen und Südpikenischen*. Handbuch der italischen Dialekte vol. 5 (Heidelberg 2002).

Funder Acknowledgement

This publication is the result of a project funded by the Arts and Humanities Research Council (AH/M006352/1).

Introduction

Esther Eidinow, Armin W. Geertz, Quinton Deeley, and John North

Religious Experience

This volume arises from a project that brought together cognitive scientists of religion (CSR) in face-to-face contact with historians and other scholars in the humanities concerned with the religious history of antiquity in a series of meetings and conferences, some held in the UK, some in Denmark. The objective was to provide up-to-date historical data for cognitive scientists to analyze, up-to-date theories about cognition for historians to exploit, and an opportunity for both groups to discuss the contributions they could offer one another, through bringing the two disciplines (traditionally quite separate) together. This volume seeks to extend this project through a collection of essays mostly by those scholars. Each chapter reports on a problem of understanding that arises from some ancient religious activity and seeks to bring together the different insights of the two disciplines.

The notion of 'religious experience' has been, since the very early years of the nineteenth century, of key importance to any discussion of the individual's relationship to the powers they worship, in any religion. In order to carry these ideas further, we need to explore and, if possible, define the terms of the debate and crucially the phrase itself – 'religious experience'. This may seem at first sight a reasonably undemanding requirement: an experience is a happening of which an individual or group is aware. 'Religious', like 'religion' and 'religions', is notoriously difficult to define, but does at least allow the giving of examples to illustrate what is to be understood: presence at a sacred event, a message understood to be from the gods, the reading out of holy texts, and so on.

Scholars have sometimes claimed that the very notion of 'religious experience' is laden with ideological and political significance. One suggestion is that the notion of religious experience leads to and supports the idea that there are universal religious phenomena.[1] The notion of 'mystical experience', for instance, and its acceptance as a 'core' religious experience, has been taken to provide an instance of an experience that is unmediated by any 'linguistic, cultural, or historical contingencies'.[2] This is one kind of universalization, one that, over time, and across different writers, using a variety of evocative vocabulary, has embraced the possibility of a direct encounter with the divine. But we can also note that a paradigm of universalization may remain, even when scholars introduce naturalizing explanations: for example, Ann Taves has explored how, as new frameworks for the interpretation of mental states developed, such as psychology and psychiatry, religious explanations persisted.[3] Others have drawn attention to the same phrase working as a divisive term: how, over time, it has become 'freighted with the politics of true and false religion, . . . caught up in "tangled reciprocities" that undermine the distinction between the authentic and the simulated'.[4]

In many of these examples, there is an implicit claim that experience is somehow a thing separate from us, with which we come into contact; it is based on an understanding of the self as an object that can be analyzed, and that interacts with phenomena external to itself. We might re-describe this using the approach suggested in Ann Taves' examination of religious experience. She suggests that we re-identify 'religious experiences' as 'experiences deemed religious',[5] an insight which the participants in this volume have found very helpful. This key observation shapes her discussion of both top-down and bottom-up processes or accounts of those experiences. Top-down processes occur when thoughts trigger feelings or when thoughts and feelings trigger perceptions; all such experiences vary with culture and context and are often influenced by cultural and social values, norms, and assumptions. Bottom-up processes occur when thoughts and feelings are triggered by physiological processes or perceptions; these have often been considered to be unvarying.[6]

However, recent work in computational neuroscience understands perception and cognition to involve prediction across different levels of information processing in the brain based on prior learning or

---

[1] With Proudfoot (1985: xiii); he questioned the assertion that such experience is a 'universal' phenomenon that spans all of the major religious traditions, and suggested instead that it arose as an uneasy bridge between Christian and non-Christian camps, a means of preserving (p. 134) 'the validity of Christian revelation without . . . impugning . . . non-Christian rivals'.
[2] Sharf 1998: 96.   [3] Taves 1999: 4–12.   [4] Hall 2003: 249.   [5] Taves 2009: xiii.
[6] Taves 2009: 99.

assumptions – so-called priors[7] The priors weight information processing in the brain to produce different outcomes in what the behavioural neurologist Marcel Mesulam described as our 'highly edited subjective version of the world'.[8] This paradigm, known as predictive processing (or 'active inference'), is essential to our ability to navigate the physiological, natural, social, and cultural environments that we are embedded in. Cognition proceeds on the basis of maps that are configured by prior experience, brain and body processes, and cultural and social models of behaviour that are continually updated throughout life.[9] In this view, cultural learning (or culturally embedded learning) potentially has marked effects on seemingly spontaneous or automatic responses to the world – including habitual cognitive-affective responses and accompanying behavioural as well as autonomic and endocrine responses (such as frenzied compared to quiescent 'trance'[10]). Consequently, 'bottom-up' or automatic neurophysiological processes should not be thought of as unvarying but as also constrained by shared learning and contexts in the course of development and enculturation.[11] How a species-typical repertoire of cognitive and brain systems is differentiated by individual and shared learning is a matter of ongoing research within developmental and cultural neuroscience.[12]

The links between these complex processes are difficult to delineate in terms of simple causality. As Ann Taves insightfully notes, '... constructivist theories have been insensitive to the distinction between top-down and bottom-up processing and the differential role of cultural input along the gradient that interrelates them'.[13] The editors and contributors to this volume accept the complexity, multimodality, and multicausality of human life, for while we as social creatures construct social and cultural worlds – including how we 'experience' our bodies in those worlds – as Thomas Csordas, drawing on Merleau-Ponty and Bourdieu, has argued,[14] our brains and bodies are also constructing those very same worlds.[15] Indeed, today philosophers, neurologists, and cognitive scientists are actively promoting a much broader, more embodied, emergent, enactive,

---

[7] Andersen 2019; Andersen et al. 2019; Clark 2013; van Elk 2017; Frith 2007; Schjødt et al. 2013; Schjødt 2019.
[8] Mesulam 1998: 1013.
[9] Andersen 2019; Andersen et al. 2019; Clark 2013; van Elk 2017; Frith 2007; Schjødt et al. 2013; Schjødt 2019.
[10] Rouget 1985.   [11] Deeley 2004 and 2018.   [12] Johnson and De Haan 2015; Deeley 2018.
[13] Taves 2009: 99.   [14] Csordas 1990: 15.
[15] Frith and Frith 2010; Roepstorff and Frith 2004; Roepstorff et al. 2009.

and extended understanding of cognition.[16] We may be constructing social reality, as noted by Searle,[17] but we are not constructing fundamental physiological processes produced by the body systems, such as the endocrine system, the digestive system, the brain and nervous system, etc. Our cultural practices may influence these systems and help us interpret their effects, but they do not construct them. Most of the physiological processes are unconscious, and they can give rise to background emotions and experiences that individuals cannot explain.[18]

Taves' re-description of 'religious experience' (as 'experiences deemed religious') allows us to analytically differentiate between the 'experience' and its implied religiousness, thus avoiding the implication that religiousness constitutes an unchanging, unarguable characteristic built into a particular experience. But the word 'deemed', of course, raises the question of who would be the postulated doer of the deeming. At one extreme, it might be deemed by the person having the experience; at the other extreme, it might be deemed by a whole religious hierarchy, in which case the person having the experience would be constrained by that authority. In practice, claims to 'experience' might seem to offer an authoritative note of subjectivity and authenticity; in historiography, the use of material that apparently describes direct experience in this sense might be contrasted with interpretations that are objective or empirical.[19] Both within and outside academia, such claims to experience may be wielded as banners of a particular type of truth.[20] This underscores the importance of considering the implicit epistemology and truth claims associated with reports of 'religious experience' – whether they are presented within the 'emic' terms of a tradition, or the 'etic' terms of academic or other specialist discourse.

This question of the extent to which any physiological symptom or feeling in the body, or perception in the mind is mediated or interpreted is, of course, highly relevant to this volume. Because of the nature of our focus, historians of ancient cultures must explore these questions not only with regard to the content of our evidence, but also with relation to the identification of that evidence in the first place. We are largely dealing with

---

[16] Clark 1997 and 2008; Donald 2002, 2011, and 2019; Geertz 2010a; Kundtová Klocová and Geertz 2019; Newen et al. 2018; Rowlands, 2003.
[17] Searle 1995 and 1998; see also Berger and Luckmann 1966.
[18] Damasio 2000; Gallagher 2006.
[19] Although from a phenomenological perspective, a claim to experience can be considered 'empirical' even if its claim to truth is not accepted at face value.
[20] Sharf (1998: 96) argued that such approaches can serve 'to legitimise certain vested social, institutional, and professional interest[s]'.

sources that offer glimpses of events, rather than first-person descriptions of inner processes: of the two definitions of experience that Sharf offers, our material tends to be closer to the first – that of 'living through' or 'participating in', which appears to imply social contexts – than the second, which describes 'experience as a subjective "mental event" or "inner process" that eludes public scrutiny'.[21]

At first sight, this might seem to preclude the objectives of a cognitive approach, but in fact it is a crucial methodological insight. These essays are not (or not only) intended to make the experience or experiences of our ancient subjects visible, but aim rather, recalling Joan Scott's analysis of experience, to try to understand their 'inner workings or logics' – as revealed in textual evidence or material representations – as constraints on experiences.[22] As this may in turn suggest, the editors of and contributors to this volume see broader ramifications arising from these investigations. Rather than assuming that the term 'experience' means taking the existence of individuals for granted, we note, with Scott, how talking about experience prompts questions about 'how conceptions of selves (objects and their identities) are produced'. As Scott notes, 'It is not individuals who have experience, but subjects who are constituted through experience.'[23]

For the ancient subjects of our investigation, part of that constitution consisted of their (perceived) interrelationships with the world of supernatural entities, conceived as generally being inaccessible except through culturally specific means of communication (although, importantly, the gods themselves were understood to be capable of interacting with mortals through their own initiative outside such ritual practices). As this suggests, not only are we concerned about the notion of 'experience', we must also underline the meaninglessness of the notion of 'religious', or perhaps rather its meaning-fullness. As Jonathan Z. Smith notes, this 'second-order, generic concept' sets a disciplinary horizon for scholars for their own intellectual purposes, 'and therefore is theirs to define'.[24] This has tremendous resonance for ancient historians, since, for those who talk about religion in ancient Greece and Rome, it is something of a trope to observe that there were no contemporary terms for this; in Classical Greek, there simply was no equivalent word; while the Latin term – *religio* – from

---

[21] Sharf 1998, 104; Proudfoot 2010.   [22] Scott 1991: 779.
[23] Scott 1991: 780; see Ochs and Capps 1996.
[24] Smith 1998: 281. For a discussion of CSR definitions of religion see Geertz 2016b.

which our 'religion' is ultimately derived, has a rich variety of usages, none of them corresponding to the modern sense of the word 'religion'.[25]

The use of the terms 'religious' or 'religion' in this volume must be regarded as being for our hermeneutic convenience. For the most part, they are used to describe interactions that include the gods (or other supernatural entities), and that are found in a wide range of both evidence and contexts. The contributions range across a wide variety of both ancient contexts and sources, exploring and integrating literary, epigraphic, visual, and archaeological evidence. Each chapter's investigation draws attention to a different theme, which we have highlighted in our grouping of the chapters, but these are, obviously, not the only ways of viewing these contributions.

Similarly, across this volume, there is no single definition of 'experience'; instead, the authors explore the question of its meanings, rooting their investigations in broader dimensions of Greek and Roman cultures, and in the interactions between individuals and the wider societies in which they lived. Their contributions analyze not only the emotional, sensory, and mental dimensions from which 'experience' emerges, but also the generative role played both by space and the shaping of space, and by material culture. They use a wide range of theoretical approaches, although most involve an embodied approach, to explore a broad range of evidence.

The Context

The essays were largely developed during or as a result of the Cognitive Approaches to Ancient Religious Experience (CAARE) network, by participants in the network's events (these are described in more detail below). We have also commissioned two further essays from scholars who did not participate directly in the events, but became part of the larger network that CAARE developed.

Funded by the Arts and Humanities Research Council (AHRC) in the UK, CAARE ran from 2014 to 2016, developing out of a previous small project, led by Esther Eidinow and Thomas Harrison, which was funded by the British Academy. The first project brought together scholars of diverse ancient cultures to examine: (i) how authority may be imposed in ritual beliefs and practices, and by what means it is maintained and (ii) how ideas and concepts of religious belief and ritual practice move across time, and/or between generations and through space. These initial

---

[25] See North 2014. For an in-depth discussion see Platvoet and Molendijk 1999 and Streeter 2020.

thematic explorations identified a clear interest among scholars for pursuing a dedicated and interdisciplinary network of the kind described here, with a closer focus on ancient Greek and Roman cultures. It also led to partnership with Professor Armin W. Geertz and the opportunity for the network to hold one of its workshops at the Religion, Cognition and Culture Research Unit (RCC) and the MIND*Lab* at Aarhus University, Denmark.

CAARE's participants were exploring new approaches to ancient religions. Previous scholarship on ancient religions has often (implicitly) served an ideological purpose, designating ancient cultures as 'other', and reinforcing preconceptions about the differences between ancient and modern religious experience, and, more particularly, the distinctive nature of Christianity. More specifically, previous scholarship on ancient religion had focused on the external activities of historical subjects, and stressed the role of ritual and practice. While more recent research was arguing for a more prominent place to be given to the role and experience of individuals, this was chiefly being done by questioning the existing, central place of *polis* religion in scholarship on ancient Greek religion, rather than successfully introducing (or even suggesting) new models.[26] Inevitably, scholars of ancient religion had been engaging in rather piecemeal fashion with cognitive approaches, but these approaches were yet to be established.[27] The developing discussion risked being drawn into a simple polarity between physical aspects (ritual) and mental aspects (belief).

One ongoing ambition of CAARE has been to try to address this context, and to show that cognitive approaches have the potential, not perhaps to generate a ruling model like that of the *polis*, which is perhaps not anyway desirable, but to breathe significant new life into these fields of study. In general, the participants have felt that a more theoretically sophisticated approach is needed that will open up questions around the physical, emotional, and cognitive aspects of ancient religions, which includes the meaning of ritual and the significance of practice. In order to develop understanding of ancient religions, both in academic and public arenas, research is needed that will cross disciplinary divides, providing data to test scientific models, and offering new methodologies to consider historical paradigms used to think about religion and society.

---

[26] See for a summary of these approaches, Harrison 2015.
[27] And we may be turning a corner as these approaches become more familiar. Thus, for example, Jennifer Larson's admirable survey volume, *Understanding Greek Religion* (2016), has been praised for the lucidity of its presentation of CSR as well as its skillful synthesis of recent and relevant scholarship, e.g. Pirenne-Delforge 2017: 48 and Geertz 2017: 44–45.

We might add that these insights seem also to hold true for the cognitive study of religions, where a similarly reductive approach threatens, which aims to construct cross-cultural, diachronic models to explain religious practice and belief, but lacks complex examples of historical evidence. As has been argued: 'The current multidisciplinary conversation is in a moment of pitched debate, when the role of neuroscientific methods and findings in understanding religious experience is affected by intersecting political struggles over which ideology drives the narration of what it means to experience and participate in "religion" or "spirituality".'[28] The focus of this research tends to be on current subjects and contemporary religious practices, which risks leading to universalist claims that are often untested by historical or cross-cultural data. Where historical evidence is included in the data under examination, a quantitative approach may ignore crucial qualitative aspects and the essential role of contextual interpretation – 'differences that make a difference' – to the formation and significance of experience. Cognitive scientists have stated their belief that greater collaboration is needed, not only between cognitive scientists and anthropologists, but also between these scholars and historians.[29]

The Process

CAARE was intended to build on this initial work to address a new area – the experience of religion – using a new approach, identifying transhistorical, transcultural 'symptoms of religion', bringing together scholars from the ancient history of religions on the one hand and the cognitive science of religion on the other, to investigate the nature of individual religious experience. It allowed the scholars systematically to examine a set of evidence and questions in a collaborative environment, providing an unusual opportunity to develop a sustained and interdisciplinary research focus. The network aimed to develop a new agenda for interdisciplinary research, testing cognitive approaches to religion with evidence from the ancient world, and investigating whether and how scholars of ancient religions could use cognitive theories to develop insights into ancient religious experience.

---

[28] Kime and Snarey 2018: 309.
[29] See Eidinow and Martin 2014; Geertz 2010b, 2016a, and 2017; Martin and Sørensen 2011; Slingerland 2008 and 2014; Slingerland and Bulbulia 2011; Slingerland and Chudek 2012; Turchin et al. 2012; Whitehouse 2007 and 2009; Whitehouse and Martin 2004.

To achieve these goals, the network ran two interdisciplinary workshops. Both workshops featured presentations from key speakers, introducing data and approaches for participants to work with:

- Workshop 1 'Symptoms of Religious Experience' aimed to identify and examine 'symptoms' of religious experience in ancient Greek/Roman evidence. This was intended to provide all participants with data, both extensive and nuanced, that offered examples of cultural interactions, tradition, innovation, and transmission.
- Workshop 2 'Symptoms of Current Experience' brought to bear relevant cognitive approaches in the analysis of these 'symptoms'. It was intended to provide scholars of ancient religion with heuristic tools to investigate the evidence for individual religious experience in ancient cultures, dismantling current assumptions about the nature of ancient religious experience and the limits of evidence.

The first meeting of the project (held in London, with the generous support of the Institute of Classical Studies) was designed to provide participants with an initial body of ancient evidence. Topics were selected that reflected different contexts of religious experience – moving from external physical spaces to internal phenomena. Those giving papers were asked to think about a topic and then present key sources that, in their opinion, offered evidence for a particular 'symptom' of religious experience in that context. Discussions focused as far as possible on drawing out details of both the nature of the symptom (physical and mental) and its context. Themes and questions that emerged concerned the transmission of knowledge and/or understanding – how and why certain religious 'cultures' die and others take over and spread – and in particular the roles of social learning, social scripts or schemas, and charismatic authority. Participants were also interested in the relationship between ancient religious experience and modern interpretations of certain experiences as pathologies, and asked, for use in the next workshop, that relevant participants share information about current research into religious systems as cognitive governance systems; new methods using big data sites, which enable the modelling of discourse over time; explorations of the impact of certain experiences, including sensory experiences, the impact of discourse (written and spoken), perceptual illusions, and anthropomorphism; and experimental approaches and how they might contribute to approaches and theories in historical studies. On the question of 'religious experience', the workshop concluded that we needed to think in terms of experiences deemed religious, rather than 'religious experience', and in that context consider the role of the senses and emotions in those attributions; the interplay of local knowledge and/or understanding with experience, including space and the shaping of space; and the ways in which we attempt to explain rituals, ancient and modern.

The second meeting of the network, which took place in Aarhus, was designed to provide participants with papers on methodology, as well as case studies of research and work-in-progress in the cognitive science of religion, including papers on embodied cognition, the methodological issues that arise in experimental anthropological studies of religious behaviour and experience in real-life settings, the role of the experimental method, modern clinicopathological explanations of 'symptoms' of revelatory experience that explored the interaction between experiences and behaviour and brain activity, and data-intensive knowledge discovery in the study of religious textual traditions.

Several themes emerged from this workshop, which illustrated for participants the value and indeed necessity of interdisciplinary engagement to improve understanding of religiously interpreted experience and its relationship to the biographical and cultural contexts within which it occurs.

Contributors reflected in particular on how cognitive and neuroscience accounts have viewed religiously interpreted experience with an appeal to universal mechanisms (and often through the lens of psychopathology in the case of neuroscience). These accounts have, however, tended to be insensitive to the influence on experience of local attributions of meaning. This partly reflects the practice of seeking universal mechanisms, but also occurs because of the absence of a widely accepted framework for understanding how attributions can influence cognition and brain function. A relative lack of detailed knowledge of religions of some practitioners, and perhaps also the range of cross-civilizational phenomena that can be understood as religious, may also motivate a search for universal mechanisms that are insensitive to local variation. By contrast, humanities and social science accounts have located experience and its meanings within their social and cultural context. Also, the understanding of ancient societies provided by classics and related disciplines has extended the range of phenomena that any adequate account of religion and religiously interpreted experience must account for. Yet humanities and social science accounts have not in general informed attempts to identify the cognitive and brain processes underlying variations in experience – in other words, the full set of processes by which religiously interpreted experience arises within specific human contexts.

The advent of predictive coding accounts in the cognitive sciences – as discussed above – has emphasized the role of prior information in constraining experience and behaviour. This theoretical emphasis has in effect restored the human subject to the social world, and underlines the importance of humanities scholarship in revealing the 'ecology of mind' of ancient people as the basis for differentiating cognition into locally meaningful forms. The reconstruction of the systems of ideas, symbols, practices, social relations, and sensory and material settings within which religiously interpreted experience occurs reveals its influences.[30] The effects of this 'tipping point' in the cognitive sciences – a recognition of the centrality of beliefs, expectations, and other meaningful attributions to the formation of experience – are likely to persist even as the details of predictive coding and other computational theories of cognition evolve. In other words, the ideational, movement, and sensory contexts of ancient people are not surface-level phenomena to be accounted for by uniformly operating cognitive and brain processes, but necessary components of the network of constraint that contributes to locally distinctive sensibilities and their interpretation. In this respect, cognitive and brain accounts, and humanities and social science accounts, need each other to deepen understanding of religious experience.

The power of belief in shaping experience through effects on brain function is illustrated by experiments using suggestion to reproduce aspects of altered self-experience in religious settings as well as psychopathology – potentially revealing cognitive and brain processes contributing to 'real-world' instances of religiously interpreted experience. This raises the question of how research on contemporary populations – whether experimental, qualitative, or ethnographic – can be used to inform understanding of ancient religiously interpreted experience.[31] Extant information from ancient religions – whether textual or material – can suggest family resemblances with contemporary phenomena. On this basis similar phenomena can be understood as members of an overarching category of religious phenomena with shared characteristics, such as mediumistic or divinatory possession.[32] Each member of an overarching category can be regarded as an analogue of the others, and can potentially include ethnographic examples as well as experimental models that reproduce relevant characteristics of the larger category of phenomena. This does not mean

---

[30] Deeley 2019.   [31] Summarized in Deeley 2019 and Deeley 2016.
[32] Deeley 2019; see also Harré 2002 for a formal consideration of the use of analogy in cognitive explanation.

that all members of a presumed overarching category should be regarded as identical: differences do make a difference, and there may be disanalogies as well as analogies between ostensibly similar phenomena. Nevertheless, triangulation of research methods and populations can add weight to hypotheses about aspects of an ancient phenomenon that may be less well understood – in terms of phenomenology, attributed significance, or indeed underlying mechanisms given that similar phenomena have similar causes. This approach has been implicit in previous attempts to understand ancient religion in light of contemporary phenomena,[33] although raising its presuppositions to awareness compels us to consider how the past can and cannot be understood in terms of the present.

At a final conference, the project brought together participants to share their insights into cognitive approaches to experiences identified by their subjects as religious. We organized the final event in themed panels on Ritual, Divination, Music, Sensing Gods, Material Evidence, and Text and Rhetoric. And we thank all the speakers who gave their time and insights to this project across all these events: Ralph Anderson, Hugh Bowden, Felix Budelmann, Quinton Deeley, Merlin Donald, Thomas Harrison, Jeppe Sinding Jensen, Radek Kundt, Eva Kundtová Klocová, Katherina Lorenz, Luther Martin, Kristoffer Nielbo, Olympia Panagiotidiou, Robert Parker, Maik Patzelt, Anders Klostergaard Petersen, Bella Sandwell, Uffe Schjødt, Maria Sommer and Dion Sommer, Jesper Sørensen, Yulia Ustinova, Lieke Wijnia, and Dimitris Xygalatas. At the final conference, we were grateful to explore religious experience in a discussion led by Rowan Williams and to hear some final responsive thoughts on the network from Istvan Czachesz. As well as this volume, and the myriad individual pieces of work that it helped to stimulate and inspire, the CAARE network also produced a series of podcasts on religious ritual published on the website of the Historical Association, along with a suggested scheme of work for their use in classrooms (www.history.org.uk/secondary/module/8658/podcast-series-associated-scheme-of-work-an-int). Our thanks go to the Historical Association, especially Simon Brown, for all his support in creating the podcasts.

Conclusion

In an analysis of interdisciplinary work, it has been argued that 'the fundamental evaluation criterion of a branch of intellectual work is its

---

[33] E.g. Dodds 1951.

applicability to things we care about'.[34] For the participants, CAARE did this: we began with the aim of better understanding ancient religious experience; we found some of the ways in which *ordinary*, embodied cognitive capacities may, in particular historical cultural contexts, have generated experiences that their ancient subjects would have associated with some kind of interaction with the supernatural, which modern interpreters may interpret as 'religious'. We hope that this volume captures something of that learning and continues to provide stimulation for further discussion.

Our aim was not only to produce new insights but also to advance methods by which scholars from these different disciplines could learn to collaborate to develop new approaches to, and understandings of, their own and others' data, as presented across these workshops. As Jeppe Sinding Jensen observed, by the end of the second workshop of the CAARE network, our collaboration had revealed a common nature between two cultures of scholarship – scientific and humanities – in terms of the studies of humans and what they do. Cultures are cognitive networks, he argued; in terms of interrogating our historical subjects, we can formulate the usual questions differently and we can ask, not only, are they like us, but also, what are we?

BIBLIOGRAPHY

Andersen, M. 2019. 'Predictive Coding in Agency Detection', *Religion, Brain & Behavior* 9 (1): 65–84.

Andersen, M., Pfeiffer, T., Müller, S., and Schjoedt, U. 2019. 'Agency Detection in Predictive Minds: A Virtual Reality Study', *Religion, Brain & Behavior* 9 (1): 52–64.

Berger, P. L. and Luckmann, T. 1966. *The Social Construction of Reality: A Treatise in the Sociology of Knowledge*. Harmondsworth.

Cho, F. and Squier, R. K. 2008. 'Reply to Slingerland', *Journal of the American Academy of Religion* 76 (2): 455–456.

Clark, A. 1997. *Being There: Putting Brain, Body, and World Together Again*. Cambridge and London.

    2008. *Supersizing the Mind: Embodiment, Action, and Cognitive Extension*. Oxford and New York, NY.

    2013. 'Whatever Next? Predictive Brains, Situated Agents, and the Future of Cognitive Science', *Behavioral and Brain Sciences* 36 (3): 181–204.

Csordas, T. 1990. 'Embodiment As a Paradigm for Anthropology', *Ethos* 18 (1): 5–47.

---

[34] Cho and Squier 2008: 456.

Damasio, A. R. 2000. *The Feeling of What Happens: Body, Emotion and the Making of Consciousness*. London.

Deeley, P. Q. 2004. 'The Religious Brain: Turning Ideas into Convictions', *Anthropology & Medicine* 11(3): 245–267.

2016. 'Hypnosis As a Model of Functional Neurologic Disorders', *Handbook of Clinical Neurology* 139: 95–103.

2018. 'Neuroanthropology: Exploring Relations between Brain, Cognition, and Culture', in A. K. Petersen, I. S. Gilhus, L. H. Martin, J. S. Jensen, and J. Sørensen, eds., *Evolution, Cognition, and the History of Religions: A New Synthesis. Festschrift in Honour of Armin W. Geertz*, 380–396. Leiden and Boston, MA.

Deeley, Q. 2019. 'The Pythia at Delphi', in L. Driediger-Murphy and E. Eidinow, eds., *Ancient Divination and Experience*, 226. Oxford.

Dodds, E. R. 1951. *The Greeks and the Irrational*. Berkeley and Los Angeles, CA.

Donald, M. 2002. *A Mind So Rare: The Evolution of Human Consciousness*. London and New York, NY.

2011. 'The First Hybrid Minds on Earth', in A. W. Geertz and J. S. Jensen, eds., *Religious Narrative, Cognition and Culture: Image and Word in the Mind of Narrative*, 67–96. Sheffield and Oakville.

2019. 'Self-programming and the Self-domestication of the Human Species: Are We Approaching a Fourth Transition?' in A. K. Petersen, I. S. Gilhus, L. H. Martin, J. S. Jensen, and J. Sørensen, eds., *Evolution, Cognition, and the History of Religions: A New Synthesis. Festschrift in Honour of Armin W. Geertz*, 159–174. Leiden and Boston, MA.

Eidinow, E. and Martin, L. H. 2014. 'Editors' Introduction: *Journal of Cognitive Historiography*', *Journal of Cognitive Historiography* 1 (1): 5–9.

Frith, C. 2007. *Making Up the Mind: How the Brain Creates Our Mental World*. Oxford.

Frith, U. and Frith, C. D. 2010. 'The Social Brain: Allowing Humans to Boldly Go Where No Other Species Has Been'. *Philosophical Transactions of the Royal Society B. Biological Sciences* 365: 165–176.

Gallagher, S. 2006. *How the Body Shapes the Mind*. Oxford and New York, NY.

Geertz, A. W. 2010a. 'Brain, Body and Culture: A Biocultural Theory of Religion', *Method and Theory in the Study of Religion* 22 (4): 304–321.

2010b. 'Too Much Mind and Not Enough Brain, Body and Culture: On What Needs to Be Done in the Cognitive Science of Religion', *Historia Religionum. An International Journal* 2: 21–37.

2016a. 'Cognitive Science', in M. Stausberg and S. Engler, eds., *The Oxford Handbook of the Study of Religion*, 97–111. Oxford.

2016b. 'Conceptions of Religion in the Cognitive Science of Religion', in P. Antes, A. W. Geertz and M. Rothstein, eds., *Contemporary Views on Comparative Religion in Celebration of Tim Jensen's 65th Birthday*, 127–139. Sheffield and Bristol, CT.

2017. 'Religious Bodies, Minds and Places: A Cognitive Science of Religion Perspective', in L. Carnevale, ed., *Spazi e luoghi sacri espressioni ed esperienze di vissuto religioso*, 35–52. Bari.

Hall, D. 2003.'What Is the Place of "Experience" in Religious History?', *Religion and American Culture: A Journal of Interpretation* 13 (2): 241–250.
Harré, R. 2002. *Cognitive Science: A Philosophical Introduction*. London and Thousand Oaks, CA.
Harrison, T. 2015. 'Beyond the Polis? New Approaches to Greek Religion', *Journal of Hellenistic Studies* 135: 165–180.
Johnson, M.H. and De Haan, M. 2015. *Developmental Cognitive Neuroscience: An Introduction*. London.
Kime, K. G. and Snarey, J. R. 2018. 'A Jamesian Response to Reductionism in the Neuropsychology of Religious Experience', *Archive for the Psychology of Religion* 40 (2–3): 307–325.
Kundtová Klocová, E. and Geertz, A. W. 2019. 'Ritual and Embodied Cognition', in R. Uro, J. J. Day, R. E. DeMaris, and R. Roitto, eds., *The Oxford Handbook of Early Christian Ritual*, 74–94. Oxford.
Larson, J. 2016. *Understanding Greek Religion: A Cognitive Approach*. London and New York, NY.
Martin, L. H. and Sørensen, J. 2011. *Past Minds: Studies in Cognitive Historiography*. London and Oakville.
Mesulam, M. M. 1998. 'From Sensation to Cognition', *Brain: A Journal of Neurology* 121 (6): 1013–1052.
Newen, A., de Bruin, L. and Gallagher, S., eds. 2018. *The Oxford Handbook of 4E Cognition*. Oxford.
North, J. 2014. 'Caesar on *religio*' in J. Rüpke, ed., *Gods of the Others, Archiv für Religionsgeschichte* 15: 167–200.
Ochs, E. and Capps, L. 1996. 'Narrating the Self', *Annual Review of Anthropology* 25: 19–43.
Pirenne-Delforge, V. 2017. 'Greek Gods and Cognitive Sciences: About Jennifer Larson's *Understanding Greek Religion*', *Journal of Cognitive Historiography* 4 (1): 47–52.
Platvoet, J. G. and Molendijk, A. L. 1999. *The Pragmatics of Defining Religion: Contexts, Concepts and Contests*. Leiden.
Proudfoot, W. 1985. *Religious Experience*. Berkeley and Los Angeles, CA.
   2010. 'Attribution and Building Blocks: Comment on Ann Taves's *Religious Experience Reconsidered*', *Religion* 40 (4): 308–310.
Roepstorff, A. and Frith, C. 2004. 'What's at the Top in the Top-Down Control of Action? Script-sharing and "Top-Top" Control of Action in Cognitive Experiments', *Psychological Research* 68: 189–198.
Roepstorff, A., Frith, C., and Frith, U. 2009. 'How Our Brains Build Social Worlds', *New Scientist* (2737): 1–3.
Rouget, G. 1985. *Music and Trance: A Theory of the Relations between Music and Possession*. Chicago.
Rowlands, M. 2003. *Externalism: Putting Mind and World Back Together Again*. Montreal.
Schjødt, U. 2019. 'Predictive Coding in the Study of Religion: A Believer's Testimony', in A. K. Petersen, I. S. Gilhus, L. H. Martin, J. S. Jensen,

and J. Sørensen, eds., *Evolution, Cognition, and the History of Religions: A New Synthesis. Festschrift in Honour of Armin W. Geertz*, 364–379. Leiden and Boston, MA.

Schjoedt, U., Sørensen, J., Nielbo, K. L., Xygalatas, D., Mitkidis, P., and Bulbulia, J. 2013.'The Resource Model and the Principle of Predictive Coding: A Framework for Analyzing Proximate Effects of Ritual', *Religion, Brain & Behavior* 3 (1): 79–86.

Scott, J. 1991. 'The Evidence of Experience', *Critical Inquiry* 17 (4): 773–797.

Searle, J. R. 1995. *The Construction of Social Reality*. Harmondsworth.

1998. *Mind, Language and Society: Philosophy in the Real World*. New York, NY.

Sharf, R. 1998. 'Experience', in M. C. Taylor, ed., *Critical Terms in Religious Studies*, 94–115. Chicago, IL.

Slingerland, E. 2008. *What Science Offers the Humanities: Integrating Body and Culture*. Cambridge.

2014. 'Toward a Second Wave of Consilience in the Cognitive Scientific Study of Religion', *Journal of Cognitive Historiography* 1 (1): 121–130.

Slingerland, E. and Bulbulia, J. 2011. 'Introductory Essay: Evolutionary Science and the Study of Religion', *Religion* 41 (3): 307–328.

Slingerland, E. and Chudek, M. 2012. 'The Challenges of Quantitatively Coding Ancient Texts', *Cognitive Science. A Multidisciplinary Journal* 36: 183–186.

Smith, J. Z. 1998. 'Religion, Religions, Religious', in M. C. Taylor, ed., *Critical Terms in Religious Studies*, 269–284. Chicago, IL.

Streeter, J. 2020. 'Should We Worry about Belief?', *Anthropological Theory*, 20 (2): 133–156.

Taves, A. 2009. *Religious Experience Reconsidered: A Building-Block Approach to the Study of Religion and Other Special Things*. Princeton, NJ.

Turchin, P., Whitehouse, H., Francois, P., Slingerland, E., and Collard, M. 2012. 'A Historical Database of Sociocultural Evolution', *Cliodynamics: The Journal of Theoretical and Mathematical History* 3(2): 271–293.

van Elk, M. 2017. 'Predictive Processing and Situation Models: Constructing and Reconstructing Religious Experience', *Religion, Brain & Behavior* 7 (1): 85–87.

Whitehouse, H. 2007. 'Towards an Integration of Ethnography, History, and the Cognitive Science of Religion', in H. Whitehouse and J. Laidlaw, eds., *Religion, Anthropology and Cognitive Science*, 247–280. Durham.

2009. 'Introduction I: Graeco-Roman Religions and the Cognitive Science of Religion', in L. H. Martin and P. Pachis, eds., *Imagistic Traditions in the Graeco-Roman World: A Cognitive Modeling of History of Religions Research. Acts of the Panel Held during the XIX Congress of the International Association for the History of Religions (IAHR), Tokyo, Japan, March 2005*, 1–13. Thessaloniki.

Whitehouse, H. and Martin, L. H. 2004. *Theorizing Religions Past: Archaeology, History, and Cognition*. Walnut Creek, CA.

PART I

Ritual

CHAPTER I

A Cognitive Approach to Ancient Greek Animal Sacrifice

Hugh Bowden

Introduction

One of the useful achievements of the cognitive science of religion (CSR) has been to make it possible to ask new questions about much-discussed topics, or perhaps to return to some of the questions that were asked in times past but then abandoned as unanswerable. In the words of Jesper Sørensen,

> Influenced by information science, neuroscience, cognitive science and theoretical biology, the last couple of decades have borne witness to renewed attempts to understand human behavior in general and religion in particular in terms of explanatory principles uniting into a single framework cases from different cultural and historical backgrounds. It is, once again, acceptable to propose wide-ranging theories of human phenomena based on reductive methods and general laws ... Advances in neighboring fields, technological developments, and a surge towards consilience amongst the sciences have allowed scholars to address once again the big questions posed more than a hundred years ago, such as the relation between religion and sociality, why religion exists at all, how rituals influence the transmission of religious ideas, why religions take anthropomorphic forms, or why magic prevails.[1]

One such topic is animal sacrifice, which has frequently been described as 'the central ritual [action] of [ancient] Greek religion'.[2] And in the spirit of CSR, instead of asking 'What is the significance of "sacrifice" from the Archaic to the Hellenistic periods?',[3] we might ask 'What made "sacrifice" memorable enough to be regularly repeated, and transmitted from

---

[1] Sørensen 2021: 248–249. See also Parker 2014: 190: 'CSR brings the 19th century questions into the 21st century'.
[2] E.g. Parker 2011: 124, Naiden 2015: 464, Georgoudi 2017: 105, Ekroth 2019: 226.
[3] Naiden 2015: 464.

generation to generation over many centuries?'.[4] Having said this, we should note that while attempts have been made to analyse animal sacrifice using the methods of CSR, the results have not been generally convincing.[5] One explanation for this is that sacrifice has been treated as a single ritual act, which should therefore have a single explanation. This is a feature also of earlier theories of sacrifice. In this chapter I argue that Greek animal sacrifice should be treated as a sequence of distinct rituals, which may be performed with very different emphases, depending on the needs of the person or group performing them. This approach will be supported by comparison with sacrificial ritual from the southern Levant, as described in the Hebrew Bible. I will then draw attention to the significance of one of these rituals, burning on the altar, and suggest that it had a particular emotive power and should be considered as a key element in explaining the appeal of sacrifice.

Until recently, theoretical approaches to Greek sacrifice have been dominated by the work of two scholars, Walter Burkert and Jean-Pierre Vernant.[6] The influences on them, their contrasting approaches, and the limitations of their interpretations have been much debated.[7] Here is not the place to rehearse these arguments or to consider the rich vein of more recent scholarship on sacrifice to be found in a number of edited volumes.[8] Instead, I want to consider cognitive approaches to sacrifice, which have come generally from scholars from outside the field of ancient history or classical studies. CSR, drawing as it does on methods and theories from evolutionary science, cognitive anthropology, and cognitive psychology amongst others, generates hypotheses that are universal rather than specific to particular societies. In this they resemble Burkert's theories, which were also grounded in evolutionary ideas.

Work on ritual by Harvey Whitehouse on the one hand, and Robert N. McCauley and E. Thomas Lawson on the other, suggests that the forms of ritual practices tend towards two 'attractor positions'.[9] To use the terms

---

[4] See Veyne 2000: 21 (as translated in Parker 2011: 126): 'sacrifice is widely distributed across centuries and across societies because this practice is sufficiently ambiguous for everyone to find in it their own particular satisfaction'. Veyne here is rejecting the search for 'the true meaning' of sacrifice, but he is not providing an explanation of the form of the ritual.

[5] Larson 2016: 196–198.

[6] The key works are Burkert 1972 (English translation Burkert 1983) and Detienne and Vernant 1979 (English translation Detienne and Vernant 1989).

[7] E.g. Graf 2012, Naiden 2013: 3–15 and 2015, Larson 2016: 200–204, Murray 2016, Hitch and Rutherford 2017.

[8] E.g. Mehl and Brulé 2008, Knust and Várhelyi 2011, Faraone and Naiden 2012.

[9] Lawson and McCauley 1990, Whitehouse 2000, McCauley and Lawson 2002, Whitehouse 2004.

of McCauley and Lawson, rituals are performed either with low frequency and high sensory pageantry or else with high frequency but low sensory pageantry. An example of the former might be certain types of initiation ritual, and an example of the latter might be a weekly spoken church service. Whitehouse identifies these as representing two 'modes of religiosity' – the former being the 'imagistic mode' and the latter the 'doctrinal mode' – and he proposes that the former was the earlier to develop and is characteristic of small-scale communities, while the latter is found in larger, more hierarchical societies and was enabled by the development of literacy. McCauley and Lawson offer an alternative interpretation – the 'ritual form hypothesis'. They argue that the form of ritual is determined by the assumed role within it of a superhuman being. Rituals where the supernatural being is the recipient of the action, for example a worship service, are classified as 'special patient rituals', and those where the supernatural being is considered to be acting, for example in baptism, are 'special agent rituals'. They propose that the former will be high-frequency, low-sensory pageantry, while the latter will be low-frequency, high-sensory pageantry.

Memory is central to the work of both Whitehouse and Lawson and McCauley.[10] They use the distinction identified by Endel Tulving between semantic and episodic (or autobiographical) memory,[11] showing how these two different types of explicit memory are engaged by the two modes or ritual forms. Low-frequency rituals with high sensory pageantry (Whitehouse's imagistic mode) trigger a particular form of episodic memory, commonly referred to as 'flashbulb memory': this is the kind of memory created by significant world events (examples might include the memory of what a person was doing when they first learned about the terrorist events of 9/11).[12] The emotional arousal that such events trigger is also stimulated by certain kinds of ritual activity, for example intense initiation rituals. In contrast, rituals with low sensory pageantry (Whitehouse's doctrinal mode) engage semantic memory:

> If people experience events of the same type frequently, they tend to remember that type of event well, though not necessarily the details of

---

[10] McCauley and Lawson 2002: 38–88, Whitehouse 2004: 64–84. On the ritual form hypothesis, and theory of modes of religiosity, see also Ambasciano, Chapter 7 in this volume.
[11] Tulving 1983. See also Schachter 1996.
[12] McCauley and Lawson 2002: 56: 'Prototypical flashbulb memories concern our recall for the *circumstances* in which we learned of some significant event that, usually, was unexpected – rather than the event itself, which we may *not* have experienced *even indirectly* (by way of some electronic medium)' (emphases in the original).

any of the particular instances of that type. Their discursive knowledge of these matters is stored in semantic memory, i.e., our store of general knowledge about the world, the recollection of which does not turn on the retrieval of information about specific episodes from our lives.[13]

As Whitehouse notes, these rituals also activate implicit memory, that is, the type of memory that 'deals with things we know without being aware of knowing'.[14]

But the role of memory in the maintenance and transmission of sacrificial ritual may be more varied than the characterization by Lawson and McCauley suggests. In earlier work, Lawson and McCauley discuss how sacrifice fits into their schema, using Vedic rituals as examples.[15] Sacrifice is treated as a special patient ritual: 'Participants give their sacrifices and offerings to the gods. The involvement of superhuman agents in these rituals is minimal compared with their actions in those rituals whose effects are super-permanent.'[16] As we will see, this is to oversimplify the way that sacrifice was considered to function in the ancient Mediterranean world, where there clearly was some notion of two-way communication between sacrificer and god.

While McCauley and Lawson maintain the universal applicability of the ritual form hypothesis, Whitehouse has adapted his theory of 'modes of religiosity', distinguishing between the 'cognitively costly' practices that characterize both 'modes', and what he calls 'cognitively optimal religion', which he characterizes as a third attractor position.[17] He uses ideas drawn particularly from the work of Pascal Boyer and others on the naturalness of both religious beliefs and religious rituals.[18] According to this view, evolution has made the human brain particularly susceptible to certain ideas and ritual practices, which trigger emotional and instinctive responses rather than intellectual ones. On the naturalness of ritual, Whitehouse suggests, 'Simple ritual procedures are easily and naturally acquired for two main reasons: The first is that they activate some rather powerful mechanisms dedicated to protection against contaminants. Second, whenever rituals are addressed to supernatural agents, they are capable of triggering tacit intuitive judgments about the appropriate forms that these rituals

---

[13] McCauley and Lawson 2002: 86.
[14] Whitehouse 2004: 66. He gives the example of knowing how to ride a bicycle.
[15] Lawson and McCauley 1990: 102–136, McCauley and Lawson 2002: 26.
[16] Lawson and McCauley 1990: 134.   [17] Whitehouse 2004: 36–52.
[18] E.g. Boyer 1994 and 2001, Barrett 2004, Fiske and Haslam 1997. For an example of the application of some of these ideas to the Greek world, see Bowden 2008.

should take.'[19] In contrast to its centrality in the 'cognitively costly' modes of religiosity, explicit memory does not play a significant role in 'cognitively optimal religion', as presented by Whitehouse. And while it is easy to see how certain types of ritual practice – most obviously those relating to ritual purification – fit this explanation, it is less obvious in other cases, including those related to animal sacrifice.

We may now turn to Greek animal sacrifice. There are two issues that need to be considered. The first is whether it is helpful to consider sacrifice as a single ritual, with a single purpose, or rather as a sequence of rituals that may take place independently of each other. The second is to what extent and in what ways this sequence of rituals was understood to involve superhuman beings: were the gods the agents or the patients of ritual, or even involved in all aspects of it? If some parts of the ritual sequence were not related to the gods, they were not religious rituals at all, in the understanding of Lawson and McCauley.

Greek Animal Sacrifice: Four Examples

We may start by examining four texts dealing with ritual practices that would generally be recognized as examples of sacrifice. The first account is taken from the end of the first book of the *Iliad*. Odysseus has sailed from the Greek camp outside Troy to return Chryseis to her father Chryses, and to offer a 'sacred hecatomb' to Apollo. The sacrificial victims are lined up around an altar near the harbour, and then Chryses prays to Apollo asking him to bring an end to the plague that has afflicted the Greeks. After this the sacrificial victims are slaughtered and skinned, and after some of the meat is burned, the rest is roasted and eaten by the participants. Once the meal is over, wine is served, and the Greek men spend the rest of the day singing a hymn to Apollo.

> And the men arranged the sacred hecatomb
> for the god in orderly fashion around the strong-founded altar.
> Next they washed their hands and took up the scattering barley.
> Standing among them with lifted arms Chryses prayed in a great voice:
> 'Hear me, lord of the silver bow, who set your power about
> Chryse and Killa the sacrosanct, who are lord in strength over
> Tenedos; if once before you listened to my prayers
> and did me honour and smote strongly the host of the Achaians,

[19] Whitehouse 2004: 39. On the relevance of this for ancient Greece, see Larson 2016: 195. See also Sandwell, Chapter 11 in this volume.

> so one more time bring to pass the wish that I pray for.
> Beat aside at last the shameful plague from the Danaans.'
> So he spoke in prayer, and Phoibos Apollo heard him.
> And when all had made prayer and flung down the scattering barley
> first they drew back the victims' heads and slaughtered them and skinned them,
> and cut away the meat from the thighs and wrapped them in fat,
> making a double fold, and laid shreds of flesh upon them.
> The old man burned these on a cleft stick and poured the gleaming
> wine over, while the young men with forks in their hands stood about him.
> But when they had burned the thigh pieces and tasted the vitals,
> they cut all the remainder into pieces and spitted them
> and roasted all carefully and took off the pieces.
> Then after they had finished the work and got the feast ready
> they feasted, nor was any man's hunger denied a fair portion.
> But when they had put away their desire for eating and drinking,
> the young men filled the mixing bowls with pure wine, passing
> a portion to all, when they had offered drink in the goblets.
> All day long they propitiated the god with singing,
> chanting a splendid hymn to Apollo, these young Achaians,
> singing to the one who works from afar, who listened in gladness.[20]

The second passage is from Book 14 of the *Odyssey*, and describes a meal prepared by Eumaios and his fellow swineherds on Ithaka for themselves and their guest, Odysseus, who has returned from Troy and is on the island in disguise. A fine pig is brought to the fireplace (no altar is mentioned) and hair is cut from its head and thrown on the fire, accompanied by a prayer for the homecoming of Odysseus. The pig is then killed and cut up, and, as in the previous case, a small amount is burned, and the rest roasted on spits. The meat is then divided into seven portions, one of which is set aside for the god Hermes and the nymphs, while the rest are given to the human participants, with Odysseus, as guest of honour, receiving the best parts.

> So he spoke, and with the pitiless bronze split kindling,
> and the men brought in a pig, five years old and a very fat one,
> and made it stand in front of the fireplace, nor did the swineherd forget
> the immortal gods, for he had the uses of virtue;
> but he cut off hairs from the head of the white-toothed pig, and threw them
> into the fire as dedication, and prayed to all the gods
> that Odysseus of the many designs should have his homecoming.
> He hit the beast with a split of oak that he had lying by him. The breath
> went out of the pig; then they slaughtered him and singed him,

---

[20] Hom. *Il.* 1.447–476 (trans. Lattimore).

then jointed the carcass, and the swineherd laid pieces of raw meat
with offerings from all over the body upon the thick fat,
and sprinkled these with meal of barley and threw them in the fire, then
they cut all the remainder into pieces and spitted them, and roasted all
carefully and took off the pieces,
and laid it all together on platters. The swineherd
stood up to divide the portions, for he was fair minded,
and separated all the meat into seven portions.
One he set aside, with a prayer, for the nymphs and Hermes, the son of
Maia, and the rest he distributed to each man,
but gave Odysseus in honour the long cuts of the chine's portion
of the white-toothed pig, and so exalted the heart of his master.
Then resourceful Odysseus spoke to him and addressed him:
'I wish, Eumaios, you could be as dear to our father Zeus as to me, when I
am so poor, but you grace me with good things.'
Then, O swineherd Eumaios, you said to him in answer:
'Eat, my guest, strange man that you are, and take your pleasure
of what is here now; the god will give you such, or will let it
be, as in his own mind he may wish. He can do anything.'
He spoke, and sacrificed first-offerings to the immortal gods, then
poured bright wine for Odysseus, sacker of cities,
and put the cup in his hands, and sat down to his own portion.
Mesaulios served the bread to them, a man whom the swineherd
owned himself by himself and apart from his absent master, and
independently of his mistress and aged Laertes,
having bought him from the Taphians with his own possessions.
They put forth their hands to the good things that lay ready before them.
But when they had put away their desire for eating and drinking,
Mesaulios took the food away again, and they made haste to go to bed,
filled with bread and meat to repletion.[21]

The third text is an extract from a 'sacred calendar'. It is a list of all the animals that the deme of Thorikos is responsible for sacrificing in the months Boedromion to Maimakterion, that is roughly mid-September to mid-December. In most cases the document lists only the name of the god and the type of animal to be sacrificed, for example 'for Apollo a choice one-year-old goat', although in the case of Poseidon the location of the sacrifice is specified. We can assume that the sacrifices were performed at sanctuaries dedicated to the various gods usually within the territory of the deme. This document gives less information about the sacrifices than most other 'sacred calendars': it does not record the cost of victims or the precise date of the rituals.

[21] Hom. *Od.* 14.418–456 (trans. Lattimore).

> During Boedromion: the Proerosia: for Zeus Polieus, | a choice sheep, a choice piglet; at Automenai | a piglet, bought, to be burnt whole, the priest to | provide lunch for the acolyte; for Kephalos | a choice sheep; for Prokris an offering-table; | for Thorikos a choice sheep; for the Heroines of Thorikos an offering-table; | at Sounion for Poseidon a choice lamb; | for Apollo a choice one-year-old goat; | for Kourotrophos a choice female piglet; for Demeter a full-grown victim; | for Zeus Herkeios a full-grown victim; for Kourotrophos a piglet; | for Athena a sheep, to be sold;[22] at the Salt Pan for Poseidon | a full-grown victim; for Apollo a piglet. | During Pyanopsion: for Zeus Kataibates in Philomelidai, a full-grown victim, to be sold; on the sixteenth a full-grown victim for Young Man; at the Pyanopsia —— | <for Apollo, a full-grown victim at the Pyanopsia>[23] | During Maimakterion: for Thorikos a cow worth not less than 40-50 | drachmas; for the Heroines of Thorikos an offering-table.[24]

The fourth passage describes the actions Xenophon took when he was offered the chance to become a leader of the army of mercenaries in which he was serving. He provides little detail about what he actually did, but it is clear that he killed two victims, presumably sheep, at an altar and examined their entrails. On the basis of what he saw, he decided not to accept any command that was offered to him.

> Hesitating as he was over his decision, he decided that the best thing to do was to put the matter before the gods; so he brought two victims to the altar and made a sacrifice to Zeus the King, who had been declared by the oracle of Delphi to be the god whom he ought to consult ... When Xenophon sacrificed the god made it plain to him that he was not to seek an additional command and not to accept it if they elected him. This then was the end of the matter.[25]

The aims of the participants in these four examples are all significantly different. The Greeks at Troy are concerned to propitiate Apollo, in order to bring an end to the plague that has spread through their camp. The Greek verb for their motivation is *hilaskomai*: the same verb is used by Nestor to explain his purpose in sacrificing to Athene in the *Odyssey*, although there is no suggestion of divine anger against Nestor.[26] Eumaios' aim is to provide an evening meal: the key word is *dorpon*;[27] although there are rituals directed towards the gods, these appear incidental, and the focus of the passage is very much on humans eating. The calendar from Thorikos provides no indication of motivation. Nor can we

---

[22] This entry is cancelled on the inscription. [23] This entry is on the left side of the stone.
[24] As translated in Osborne and Rhodes (*OR*) 2017, 146.13–30.
[25] Xen. *Anab.* 6.1.22–24 (trans. Warner). [26] Hom. *Od.* 3.419. [27] *Od.* 14.407–8.

assume that there existed any documents that would provide a motivation. Epigraphic evidence about rituals of this kind can provide much evidence about how they should be performed, but not why. What we can say is that the rituals listed on documents of this sort imply an inherited obligation to perform them. It is possible that stories might have been told about the origins or meanings of some of these actions. For example, Xenophon offers an explanation for why the Athenians made the substantial and unusual offering of 500 goats every year to Artemis Agrotera: when the Athenians went to fight the Persians at Marathon, they vowed that if they were victorious they would offer Artemis a goat for every Persian soldier they killed. After the battle they could not find enough animals to fulfil the vow, and so determined instead to offer the goddess 500 goats a year in perpetuity.[28] It is unlikely that many of the much more modest offerings made at Thorikos had similar stories attached, and it is not obvious that such stories would continue to provide a clear motivation for the men who carried out the rituals. Xenophon's motivation for his own actions in the last example is to gain advice from the gods, so it is an act of divination.

This is not to deny that there were connections between these different aims. Xenophon states more than once that the gods are more likely to communicate with men who sacrifice to them regularly.[29] In *Cyropaedia* he says 'when men consult them, they announce to those to whom they are propitious (*hilaos*) what they are to do and what they are not to do',[30] using a word cognate with the verb *hilaskomai* used by Homer to describe the aim of the sacrifice in Book 1 of the *Iliad* discussed above. Thus, Xenophon's divinatory sacrifice is supported by the presumably numerous and regular other sacrifices he has carried out before it. In the Thorikos calendar, when the sacrifice takes place away from the deme centre, the victim may be listed as 'to be sold', presumably because there was nowhere suitable for eating it at the site of sacrifice,[31] but normally it would have been eaten by those who took part in the sacrifice, in the sanctuary, as a substantial and probably convivial meal, not too dissimilar from the meal described in *Odyssey* 14.[32] It remains the case, however, that the intentions of those performing the rituals were different in each of these cases and, in as far as the intentions of those who performed the rituals gave them

---

[28] Xen. *Anab.* 3.2.11–12. [29] Xen. *Eq. mag.* 9.8–9 and *Mem.* 1.4; see Bowden 2004.
[30] Xen. *Cyr.* 1.6.46. [31] Osborne and Rhodes 2017: 273.
[32] Where the victim was small, the meal may have been bulked out by the addition of other, non-sacrificial meat, sometimes of questionable quality: Ekroth 2014: 339–341. We may also note that when the animal is completely burnt, a separate meal is provided for the acolyte: *OR* 146.16.

meaning, we can say that these examples demonstrate that there was no single meaning of animal sacrifice in ancient Greece.

We can also see that the role of the gods in the different sacrifices varied. In the first example the poet states that Apollo heard Chryses' prayer, and we can take from this that he acted, bringing the plague to an end.[33] In a description of a similar sacrifice in the *Odyssey*, this time to Athena, the poet states that the goddess was actually present to take part in the sacrifice.[34] In Lawson and McCauley's terms, these would appear to be straightforwardly 'special patient rituals'. In the second case a portion is set aside for the nymphs and Hermes, but it is not mentioned whether they came.[35] This is again a 'special patient' ritual, but here the ritual appears much more marginal to the whole event. In the third case we are told nothing, although the inscription makes clear that the gods are the intended beneficiaries of the sacrifices, so this would be categorized again as a 'special patient' ritual. The fourth case is rather different: the aim of the exercise is to receive information from the god, which implies the active intervention of the god in the activity. McCauley and Lawson identify divination as a 'special instrument ritual', which on their hypothesis has the same characteristics as a 'special patient ritual' (high frequency, low sensory pageantry).[36] This assumes a form of divination that uses some form of tool that has at some point in the past been given powers by a superhuman agent, such as the bones used in Zulu divination.[37] The ritual that imparts the special qualities to the instrument would be considered a 'special agent ritual' (low-frequency, high-sensory pageantry). In extispicy, the form of divination associated with sacrifice, by contrast, the 'instrument' is the sacrificed animal, and it is given its special status at the time of the sacrifice. This makes it difficult to fit extispicy into the schema of the ritual form hypothesis. There is no space in this chapter to pursue this issue further, but it is worth further investigation.[38]

We have so far been treating each of the four examples as referring to single rituals, labelled 'sacrifice'. We need at this point to consider whether we can gain a deeper understanding by considering sacrifice not as a single ritual, but as a sequence of distinct ritual actions.

---

[33] Hom. *Il.* 1.457.   [34] Hom. *Od.* 3.435–436.   [35] Hom. *Od.* 14.435–436.
[36] McCauley and Lawson 2002: 26.
[37] E.g. McCauley and Lawson 2002: 29. A fuller discussion of special instrument rituals can be found in McCauley and Lawson 2007.
[38] See Koch 2010.

The Rituals of Sacrifice

Naiden, in his analysis of a passage of Homer, states that 'animal sacrifice included half a dozen phases', thereby emphasizing that, for him, sacrifice is one extended ritual.[39] Naiden's six phases are not entirely easy to identify from his account (which is based mainly on the narrative in *Odyssey* Book 3) but appear to be: (i) procession, (ii) purification of worshippers, (iii) *aparchê* (which is taken to cover throwing barley groats on the altar, and/or cutting and burning hair from the victim) and prayer, (iv) the disposition of the victim (this includes, but is not limited to, killing the animal), (v) the priest or celebrants observing and eating the entrails and creating smoke by pouring alcohol (in the form of wine) on the fire, and (vi) the meal. Jan Bremmer gives a similar detailed account, dividing the sequence into two sections: 'before the kill' and 'the kill'.[40] These accounts are intended to be maximalist, and include elements that were not always present. For example, while even small family-organized sacrifices may have included a procession,[41] we have no suggestion of one in my second example, and may reasonably doubt that it was part of the fourth. I will also say nothing more about the initial purification of worshippers, taking it to be required for all forms of religious ritual, not only sacrifice.

For my purposes I want to offer a simpler sequence of actions: (i) burning of barley groats and animal hair on the altar, (ii) killing the victim, (iii) examining the entrails of the victim, (iv) pouring libations and burning parts of the victim's flesh on the altar, and (v) cooking and eating the remaining meat. The distinction I have made between rituals (i) and (iv) should not be exaggerated: obviously the burning of parts of the victim can only be carried out after it has been killed, but the burning of the barley groats may be delayed until this point too, as is the case with Eumaios' sacrifice, my second example above. Prayers are generally described as accompanying both sets of actions, as in Naiden's account. Similarly, the behaviour of the animal before it is killed might be considered ominous, as well as whatever might be read in the animal's entrails.[42] A further practice that should be mentioned as belonging to the same

---

[39] Naiden 2013: 15–25, quotation from 15. This comes in a chapter entitled 'invention of *a ritual*' (emphasis mine).
[40] Bremmer 2007: 133–138.
[41] See for example the depiction of a sacrifice on the Pitsa Panel (Athens National Archaeological Museum no. 16464). See also Ar. *Ach.* 237–279.
[42] For examples see Naiden 2013: 83–90.

point of the sequence as the burning of the flesh is the smearing of the altar with blood. This is not explicitly described in the Homeric narratives but is a feature in particular of depictions of sacrifice in Greek painting from the Archaic and Classical period.[43] We might therefore identify sacrifice as made up of four distinct elements: killing, divination, the activities at the altar (smearing with blood, burning materials, pouring libations), and eating. We should consider each in turn.

Killing

There are occasions when the killing of an animal appears to be considered a complete ritual in itself. Xenophon describes an occasion where this happened after a group of soldiers was caught by the enemy while out foraging:

> And Xenophon, inasmuch as the sacrifices had not proved favourable on that day, took a bullock that was yoked to a wagon – for there were no other sacrificial animals – and, having slaughtered it (*sphagiasamenos*), set out to the rescue, as did all the rest who were under thirty years of age, to the last man.[44]

The issue here is that the leaders of the army had already sacrificed a number of animals, and examined their entrails, in order to establish whether the army could advance. Those sacrifices, it may be assumed, had involved a number of preparatory rituals. In this case there is no consultation of the entrails because there is no question to ask the gods: the need to rescue the soldiers is paramount. Xenophon is describing his own actions, and for him it is the killing alone that is worth reporting. Robert Parker has argued that this kind of action represents a specific form of sacrifice, *sphagion*, to be contrasted with the more 'normal' *thusia*:

> Greeks tend to make such a distinction linguistically, calling the one rite *thusia* and the other *sphagion*, slaughter offering. But we find Herodotus blithely applying the verb *thuô* to a *sphagion* offering.[45]

However, as the case of Herodotus indicates, it is not clear that this is a helpful distinction. We have cases where animals are slaughtered and then thrown into rivers or the sea, rather than being burned, and these have been associated with *sphagia*. However, these are generally sacrifices to river or sea gods, and throwing the victims into the water is functionally a

---

[43] Bremmer 2007: 137.   [44] Xen. *Anab.* 6.4.25.
[45] Parker 2011: 154. See Jameson 1991 for a discussion of the relationship between *sphagia* and *thusia*: the discussion in the present chapter takes a different view on various points.

way of putting them beyond human access, symbolically passing them to the gods.[46] This is equivalent to holocaust sacrifice, where the animal is completely burned.[47] The action Xenophon describes is distinct from this. We are not told what happened to the slaughtered ox, but it would be reasonable to assume that it was subsequently butchered and cooked and eaten:[48] shortage of food was one of the dangers facing the men, and the alternative to using the meat would have been to see it scavenged by animals or by other people.

If we set to one side these exceptional events, and consider the act of killing in the context of Greek sacrifice, we might conclude that in Lawson and McCauley's terms it was not a religious ritual at all. To slaughter a large animal efficiently required skill and practice but no special status or special tools: Eumaios kills his boar with an ordinary piece of wood that was presumably cut to be burned on the fire. The killing might be accompanied by the shout of women, the *ololugê*, but it is not clear what this shout meant – it is not described as directed towards the gods.[49] This was therefore a stage in the sequence in which there were no superhuman participants – the basic requirement for a religious ritual.

Divination

It is obviously the case that divination through the examination of an animal's entrails could not take place without the animal being killed. However, as it is presented in our sources, both literary and material, not all aspects of the craft of divination are closely related to the rest of the ritual. It is said that the curling of the tail of a victim as it was burned was taken as a sign that the gods accepted the sacrifice, and there are other phenomena that have been considered as omens.[50] Such events are part of a wider pattern of recognizing meaning in apparently chance events, a pattern that extends beyond the context of sacrifice.[51] Asking a specific question, and seeking an answer by the examination of an animal's entrails, was a different kind of divinatory practice. It could be taught and learned, as the existence of model livers from Etruria and Mesopotamia indicates.[52] The liver was a favoured organ for examination, arguably because, being essentially dark

---

[46] Parker 2011: 155–156, esp. n. 121.   [47] On holocausts, see Ekroth 2017.
[48] Contra Jameson 1991: 201.   [49] Bremmer 2007: 136–137.
[50] For a discussion of the tail and related elements depicted on vases: Van Straten 1995: 118–144.
[51] E.g. sneezing: Hom. *Od.* 17.541–545, Xen. *Anab.* 3.2.9, Ar. *Av.* 719–721. See van der Horst 2013.
[52] For the bronze liver from Piacenza, dated to c. 100 BCE, see Bouke van der Meer 1987. On Mesopotamia see e.g. Koch 2011. On Greek practice see e.g. Collins 2008.

and dome-shaped, it could be seen to be a model of the heavens (which would have been unreadable in the daytime, when this form of divination usually took place).[53] While an animal had to be killed to provide a fresh liver, no other aspect of the rituals surrounding the killing would necessarily have had an impact on the reading of the liver. Scenes on vases depicting a hoplite leaving home to go to war sometimes show him examining a liver, with no other indication of sacrificial activity, indicating that this action was something that could receive focus in its own right.[54]

We have already noted that there is more work to be done on cognitive approaches to extispicy. For a practised diviner this would be a frequent activity, with low sensory pageantry, but its aim – to gain information from a superhuman agent – does not seem to make it clearly a special patient ritual.

Activities at the Altar

The pouring of libations of wine was a normal part of sacrifice and is mentioned in the episode from the *Iliad* already discussed, but libations could take place outside the context of animal sacrifice. Notably, the use of the word *spondai* to mean 'treaty' indicates that the pouring of libations was the central ritual of diplomatic negotiation. Libations play an important role in their own right on other occasions too, for example at a symposium,[55] before the performance of plays at the City Dionysia in Athens,[56] and in rituals associated with the dead, and divinities associated with the underworld.[57] Naiden offers a rationalizing explanation for the function of libations which attempts to link it directly to other aspects of sacrifice. In his discussion of the story in the *Odyssey* of Odysseus' companions sacrificing the cattle of the Sun, he suggests that libations would normally have increased the fire.[58] This seems unlikely, as pouring wine on a fire (in contrast to, say, whiskey) would have had essentially the same effect as pouring on water. In contrast, Diodorus offers a mythological story to explain the origins of pouring libations as part of treaty-making that has no link to sacrifice. He tells of how Dionysus, in his war against the Titans, invited a group of prisoners of war to join his side, and poured

---

[53] Bouke van der Meer 1987.   [54] See Durand and Lissarrague 1979.
[55] E.g. Pl. *Sym.* 176a: here libations are associated with singing a hymn and other customary acts and take place between dining and drinking.
[56] Plut. *Cim.* 8.7.
[57] Sophocles describes an elaborate libation ritual in honour of the Eumenides: *OC.* 466–506. See Johnston 1999: 46–47, 117–118.
[58] Naiden 2013: 29.

a libation of wine for each of them while they swore allegiance to him.[59] It is not clear how widely shared this *aition* was. Whatever the context, libations certainly meet the requirements of Lawson and McCauley's 'special patient' rituals: low sensory pageantry and high frequency.

Prayers and hymns are mentioned in many accounts of sacrifices, and these might also be performed outside that context.[60] Hymns were on occasion described as sacrifices themselves, suggesting that they could be offerings to the gods in their own right.[61] The choral performance of hymns to the gods took place in the context of sacred embassies (*theôria*) and in competitions in festivals. And while sacrifice might also be an element of these festivals and journeys, it would be the choruses that were at the centre.[62] While it was common for prayers to make reference to sacrifice, as the one who prayed might promise to sacrifice to the god if the prayer was answered, this was not always the case; those prayers that did promise a future sacrifice were generally not performed as part of sacrificial ritual.[63] Again, prayers and hymns clearly belong to the category of low-intensity, high-frequency, special patient rituals, and, given that they are verbal, they fit very much into Whitehouse's doctrinal mode of religiosity.

Of all the ritual activities that we are considering here, burning material is possibly the most overlooked, and yet most important. The verb most commonly associated with sacrifice is *thuein*, and the cognate noun is *thusia*. Although the word is used to refer to a variety of ritual actions, at its root is the notion of burning.[64] Vegetable matter, including barley grains, cakes, and incense, might be burned as preliminaries to animal sacrifice. However, vegetable matter might be burned on its own without further offering, for example most spectacularly the burning by the Persian general Datis of 300 talents of incense on the altar of Apollo on Delos.[65] While this kind of activity might seem similar to pouring libations, and might be classifiable as another typical 'special patient' ritual, I will argue that this does not do full justice to the phenomenon of burning.

Eating

A previous orthodoxy, that the only source of meat was from sacrificial victims, is no longer widely held.[66] Even when meat from sacrificed

---

[59] Diod. 3.71.6.   [60] *Pace* Furley 2007: 119–122.   [61] Pulleyn 1997: 49–50.
[62] On this see Kowalzig 2007.   [63] Pulleyn 1997: esp. 56–69.   [64] LSJ sv. *thuô*.
[65] Hdt. 6.97.2.
[66] Naiden 2013: 233–275; Ekroth 2007; countering Detienne and Vernant 1989: 3, 25.

animals was eaten, this might happen at a time and place distant from where the animal was killed. We have seen that the meat from some of the sacrifices in Thorikos was sold rather than eaten on the spot. Theophrastus' *Characters* contain a number of references to the practice of sending portions of meat to individuals who could not attend, or of salting and storing meat for future consumption, or of selling it.[67] While those who ultimately consumed this meat might be aware that the animal had been killed as part of a religious ritual, it does not follow that this would have a significant impact on their experience of eating it. As we have seen, for Detienne and Vernant, the communal meal was at the heart of sacrifice. Hesiod, in his *Theogony*, tells the story of the origins of sacrificial ritual, where Zeus was offered the choice between receiving the fat and bones, or the flesh of the sacrificed ox.[68] Vernant says about this story, 'In the distinction between the shares allocated to men and gods in the sacrifice, it stresses the difference that now separates them, their membership in two distinct races.'[69] But it is not only the content of the two 'shares' that differentiates them, it is also their treatment. The god's share, as Hesiod would have it, is burned on the altar, while the mortal's share is cooked afterwards, often by boiling, and frequently consumed away from the altar. This makes it difficult to see the eating itself as having 'a religious intentionality'.[70] Indeed, as Naiden notes, 'The last phase of a sacrifice, the meal, would seem to be a human affair.'[71] Thus, like killing, eating should not, on Lawson and McCauley's terms, be considered a religious ritual.

Interim Conclusions

This discussion of the rituals that together made up what scholars call 'Greek sacrifice' suggests, perhaps provocatively, that earlier studies have put the emphasis in the wrong place. A cognitive approach to Greek animal sacrifice should focus neither on the act of killing, nor on the act of eating, but on the rituals that come in between. That is to say that it should focus on the activities that take place at the altar or, in the absence of an altar, the hearth. These include above all the action of burning, which gives its name to the ritual sequence as a whole. Some of these activities conform well to the Ritual Form Hypothesis, and can be classified as 'special patient' rituals, which is how Lawson and McCauley

---

[67] Theophr. *Char.* 9.3, 17.2, 22.3. [68] Hes. *Theog.* 521–569.
[69] Detienne and Vernant 1989: 24. [70] Detienne and Vernant 1989: 24.
[71] Naiden 2013: 22.

A Cognitive Approach to Ancient Greek Animal Sacrifice

themselves classify sacrifice, treated as a single ritual. However, there are some ritual elements that do not fit so well. We have already briefly discussed one of these, divination; in the next part of this chapter I want to examine the other, burning, in more detail. We will start by turning to evidence for sacrificial practice in another part of the eastern Mediterranean world from the same period as Xenophon and the Thorikos calendar – the southern Levant and, specifically, Jerusalem.

Sacrifice in the Hebrew Bible

Sacrifice was an important element in ritual practice in Jerusalem in the Second Temple Period.[72] The fullest description of the range of sacrificial offerings comes in the first seven chapters of Leviticus. Although the setting of the work is the Israelite camp in the desert of Sinai, the practice is assumed to relate to the fifth or fourth century BCE, and to reflect what took place in the Jerusalem temple.[73] The explanations of the rituals in Leviticus should not be taken as authoritative: the text is a contribution to debate about cult practice in the south Levant in the period.[74] The text describes a series of offerings, the names of which may be related either to the content of offering, the physical actions involved, or the supposed purpose of the action:[75] the burnt-offering (which may be a bull, a male sheep or goat, or a pigeon); the grain-offering (which may be of flour, unleavened cakes or wafers, or grain mixed with oil cooked on a griddle or fried); the offering of well-being (a bull or cow, or a sheep or goat, male or female); the sin-offering (a bull, or male goat, or female goat or sheep, or a pair of doves or pigeons, or a quantity of flour, depending on the status and wealth of the person or group who is making atonement); and the guilt-offering (a ram).[76]

The text then provides instructions to the priests on how to perform elements of the rituals, with a particular concern for ritual purity, and also indicates which parts of the offering are taken by the priest. The priests receive the skins of animals in the case of burnt-offerings, and the right

---

[72] Sanders 2016: 171–195. [73] On dating and context of the text see Watts 2007, Leuchter 2010.
[74] On Leviticus more generally see Douglas 1999, Rendtorff and Kugler 2003, Milgrom 2004, Watts 2007.
[75] The translation used here is the New Revised Standard Version.
[76] These categories are complicated further in chapter 7, which divides offerings of well-being into thank-offerings and votive or freewill-offerings (11–18), and identifies part of the procedure, in which the breast of the animal is lifted up, as an elevation-offering (30–35). An additional ritual, the offering of ordination, is mentioned in verse 37, and then described in chapter 8, which resumes a narrative about Moses' actions from Exodus 40, the last chapter of the previous book.

thigh and right breast of an offering for well-being; they also are able to eat the meat of sin- and guilt-offerings, and whatever parts of a grain offering are not burnt. Certain of the perquisites belong specifically to the priest performing the sacrifice, while others are shared amongst all the priests.[77]

If we look at the ritual actions outlined in Leviticus 1–7, we can see that they are essentially similar to Greek practice. Animals are either completely burned, or partly burnt and partly eaten. In the latter case, if it is an offering of well-being it is to be eaten by the people who brought the victim: under some circumstances the meat could be kept until the following day, although in others it had to be eaten on the day of the sacrifice.[78] If it is a sin- or guilt-offering, it is to be eaten by the priests as a group.[79] And while in Leviticus there is a clear attempt to distinguish between different types of offering, and to present them in isolation from each other, elsewhere in the Bible it is clear that they could be combined, and a normal act of offering would include meat, grain, and wine.[80] There is no mention of examining the entrails of sacrificial victims as a form of divination in the Hebrew Bible. Indeed, divination is forbidden in Leviticus, although it is not clear precisely what is covered by the ban.[81] Other than this, however, we may see in the Hebrew Bible a set of practices that resemble Greek sacrificial practice.

It is striking that in Leviticus the grain-offering is described second in a list of offerings in which all the others involve animals. Theories of sacrifice that focus on killing, or on meat-eating, cannot straightforwardly accommodate vegetal offerings, while the author of Leviticus appears to see no inconsistency. What is common to all the types of offering in Leviticus is the burning of at least part of the offering on the altar, whether it is animal or vegetable, and whether it is wholly burnt on the altar, partly eaten by the participants, or taken outside the settlement and burnt there.[82] This suggests that the focus on burning in our examination of Greek sacrifice is not misplaced. The evidence from the Hebrew Bible can also help us to understand what is significant about burning, which is its sensory impact.

---

[77] Leviticus 7.6–10, 7.31–35.   [78] Leviticus 7.15–17.   [79] Leviticus 6.26, 6.29, 7.6.
[80] Numbers 15.1–12, 28–29: the latter chapters form a sacrificial calendar. These passages belong to the 'Priestly Writings' (P) in the Pentateuch.
[81] Leviticus 19.26. This passage may however be more concerned with oracles of the dead rather than extispicy: Houston and Dunn 2003: 18, Milgrom 2004: 240–241.
[82] See Eberhart 2004.

The Importance of Smell

In Leviticus and Numbers the act of burning offerings on the altar is said to create a 'pleasing odour' for the Lord.[83] This term is used in descriptions of the grain-offering as well as of offerings of meat. Significantly, while it is frequently used to describe what might be considered the happier offerings, that is, the first three in Leviticus (burnt-offering, grain-offering, offering for well-being), it is much rarer in the descriptions of the sin- and guilt-offerings. It is notable that if flour is offered as a grain-offering, oil and frankincense are added to it before burning, but if it is offered as a sin-offering, neither may be added.[84] As we will see, this is effectively a way of making such an offering less pleasant-smelling, but other sin- and guilt-offerings would not have smelled any different from the offerings for well-being, so the notion of the odour being pleasing to God would appear to reflect the broader context of the sacrifice.

We can find the same notion of the smell (*knisê*) of sacrifice being attractive to the gods in the *Iliad* and in some later texts.[85] On two occasions in the *Iliad* Zeus explicitly describes the *knisê*, along with the drink-offering (*loibê*), as the 'gift of honour' (*geras*) that was the gods' portion at a feast.[86] The word is also used by association to refer to fat that was wrapped around bones for burning.[87] For Naiden, *knisê* is essentially a visual phenomenon, to be understood intellectually: 'The *knisê* rose parallel to the words of prayer. Going up and out, it moved from the scene of the rite to the larger scene ... The worshippers followed it, gazing upwards, towards the god and not each other.'[88] We will be able to appreciate the significance of burning more fully if we recognize that *knisê* appealed to the senses more widely, and with emotional rather than intellectual impact.

Of course, the people who were present at a sacrifice would also have been beneficiaries of the smells it produced. The smell of meat cooked on an open fire is usually reckoned to be particularly appetizing. It is the result of a particular chemical process, the Maillard reaction, which involves reactions between sugary carbohydrates and amino acids, and occurs at temperatures of around 115°C. The Maillard reaction generates a range of complex savoury odours that generally have a low odour detection

---

[83] The Hebrew phrase is *reakh nikhoakh*: Leviticus 1.9, 1.13, 2.2, 2.9, 2.12, 3.5, 3.16, 4.31, 6.15, 6.21, 17.6; Numbers 18.17, 23.13, 28–29 passim.; cf. Genesis 8.21.
[84] Leviticus 2.1–2, 5.11. [85] E.g. Hom. *Il.* 1.66, 1.317, 8.548, 9.500.
[86] Hom. *Il.* 4.49, 24.70. [87] E.g. Hom. *Il.* 1.460, 2.423, 21.363. [88] Naiden 2013: 21.

threshold, which means that they are perceivable by the human sense of smell when they are present in only relatively small quantities, and can have a profound impact at higher levels. Alongside the Maillard reaction, cooking meat on an open fire would also lead to caramelization when the temperature reached around 165°C, adding a further set of odours.[89] These odour-producing reactions would occur when baked goods were burned, which is why the grain-offerings in Leviticus could be described as generating a 'pleasing odour'. On the other hand, raw flour, in which the carbohydrate is more starch than sugar, would not produce these odours to a noticeable effect, and this may well be why when the grain-offering takes the form of flour, oil and frankincense are added to it for burning (but not when it is used for a sin-offering, when a pleasant smell is not required).[90] When meat is boiled, as it was for distribution to the *dêmos* at major Athenian festivals, and elsewhere, the temperature of the water never exceeds 100°C. As a result Maillard and caramelization reactions do not take place, and there would have been no pleasant smell around the boiling cauldrons. The 'pleasing odour' associated with sacrifice was therefore something to be found specifically in the area near the altar.

Smell and Memory

As we have seen, McCauley and Lawson use the term 'sensory pageantry' to characterize the form of rituals. This is a deliberately chosen multisensory term, as they point out. 'Religious rituals are replete with the smells of burning incense and the tastes of special foods, the sound of chant and the sights of ornate attire, the kinaesthetic sensations of the dancer and the haptic sensations of the fully immersed.'[91] Whether they would recognize the powerful aromas created by the burning on the altar as being an example of 'high sensory pageantry' is open to question, as smell is only mentioned in the book three times, always as part of a depiction of general sensory overload. It is clear, however, that smell is strongly linked to memory, and in particular to autobiographical or semantic memory, the type of memory associated with McCauley and Lawson's special agent rituals.[92] This is a phenomenon that is much more powerful in olfactory memory than in other sensory experiences: according to Herz, 'autobiographical memories triggered by odors feel much more emotional, activate

[89] McGee 2004: 777–779. [90] Grossman 2019.
[91] McCauley and Lawson 2002: 102. Smell is also mentioned on pp. 1 and 111.
[92] Herz 2016, Verbeek and van Campen 2013.

the neurobiological substrates of emotional processing, and ... people are more brought to the original time and place of their memories compared to when the same events are recalled through other modalities'.[93] That is to say that the smell of sacrifice is likely to bring back to a person memories of their earliest experiences of sacrifice.[94] This contrasts with the way in which repeated experiences of most rituals have their effect. As we have seen, these normally become part of semantic memory, and participants do not retain specific memories of particular occasions. This would suggest the possibility that the experience of sacrifice, despite the fact that it was often repeated, can be better understood as a special agent ritual than a special patient one: the god is felt to be an active participant rather than a passive recipient. This is perhaps what is being hinted at when Athena and Apollo are depicted as present at sacrifices in the Homeric poems. And, as Anne Katrine de Hemmer Gudme puts it when discussing the material from Leviticus, 'the Hebrew Bible's olfactory cultic theology impresses upon us that Yahweh the king is present in his sanctuary and that he accepts the smoke from sacrifices as "pleasing odours" exactly because he is a god'.[95]

Conclusion

In her assessment of the value of Lawson and McCauley's work to the study of Greek sacrifice, Jennifer Larson has noted that 'more work is needed in order to pinpoint how ritual form is related to sensory arousal, individual experience and emotionality, and how these factors are affected by participation versus observation'.[96] In this chapter I have attempted to address these points, and to show how a slightly more complicated understanding of the relationship between ritual and memory, that recognizes the distinctive features of olfactory memory in particular, can resolve some of the concerns ancient historians may have with the application of the cognitive science of religion to the ancient world.[97] I am under no illusion that Thomas Lawson or Bob McCauley would be persuaded that I have come up with an acceptable solution, or that they would recognize the problems Larson identifies. At the same time I have attempted an analysis of Greek animal sacrifice, drawing in part on comparison with accounts of sacrifice from the Hebrew Bible, from which I conclude that

---

[93] Herz 2016: 2.
[94] On this point and on smell, ritual, memory and the gods, see Eidinow's in Chapter 3 in this volume.
[95] Gudme 2018: 19.   [96] Larson 2016: 198.   [97] E.g. Parker 2014.

the focus of previous theories of sacrifice has been misdirected. In concentrating on the word 'sacrifice', even while acknowledging that this is not a Greek term, and problematizing its use, scholars may have missed the significance of the word most commonly used by the Greeks, *thusia* (and its cognate *thuein*). Whatever else was involved, the central act of Greek sacrifice was the burning of substances on the altar to create attractive billowing smoke, but above all a set of odours so pleasant and so powerful that the people who experienced them might think that they were in the presence of the gods.

BIBLIOGRAPHY

Barrett, J. 2004. *Why Would Anyone Believe in God?* Walnut Creek, CA: AltaMira.
Bouke van der Meer, L. 1987. *The Bronze Liver of Piacenza: Analysis of a Polytheistic Structure*. Leiden: Brill.
Bowden, H. 2004. 'Xenophon and the scientific study of religion'. In C. Tuplin, ed. *Xenophon and His World*. Stuttgart: Steiner: 229–246.
  2008. 'Before superstition and after: Theophrastus and Plutarch on Deisidaimonia.' *Past & Present* 199 supplement 3: 56–71.
  2022. 'Sensory approaches to divine epiphany'. In S. Deacy & E. Eidinow, eds. *Problems with Greek Gods*. London: Institute of Classical Studies.
Boyer, P. 1994. *The Naturalness of Religious Ideas: A Cognitive Theory of Religion*. Berkeley, CA: University of California Press.
  2001. *Religion Explained: The Human Instincts That Fashion Gods, Spirits and Ancestors*. London: Heinemann.
Bremmer, J.N. 2007. 'Greek normative animal sacrifice'. In D. Ogden, ed. *A Companion to Greek Religion*. Malden, MA: Wiley Blackwell: 132–144.
Burkert, W. 1972. *Homo Necans: Interpretationen altgriechischer Opferriten und Mythen*. Berlin: de Gruyter.
  1983. *Homo Necans: The Anthropology of Ancient Greek Sacrificial Ritual and Myth*. Berkeley, CA: University of California Press.
Collins, D. 2008. 'Mapping the entrails: The practice of Greek hepatoscopy.' *American Journal of Philology* 129: 319–345.
Detienne, M. & Vernant, J.-P. eds. 1979. *La cuisine du sacrifice en pays grec*. Paris: Gallimard.
  1989. *The Cuisine of Sacrifice among the Greeks*. Chicago: University of Chicago Press.
Douglas, M. 1999. *Leviticus As Literature*. Oxford: Oxford University Press.
Durand, J.L. & Lissarrague, F. 1979. 'Les entrailles de la cite. Lectures de signes: Propositions sur la hiéroscopie.' *Hephaistos* 1: 92–108.
Eberhart, C.A. 2004. 'A neglected feature of sacrifice in the Hebrew Bible: remarks on the burning rite on the altar.' *Harvard Theological Review* 97: 485–493.

Ekroth, G. 2007. 'Meat in Ancient Greece: Sacrificial, sacred, or secular.' *Food and History* 5: 249–272.
    2014. 'Animal sacrifice in antiquity'. In G.L. Campbell, ed. *The Oxford Handbook of Ancient Animals*. Oxford: Oxford University Press: 324–354.
    2017. 'Holocaustic sacrifices in ancient Greek religion: Some comments on practice and theory'. In K. Bielawski, ed. *Animal Sacrifice in Ancient Greece*. Proceedings of the first international workshops in Kraków. Warsaw: no named publisher: 45–66.
    2019. 'Why does Zeus care about burnt thighbones from sheep? Defining the divine and structuring the world through animal sacrifice in ancient Greece.' *History of Religions* 58: 225–250.
Faraone, C.A. & Naiden, F.S. eds. 2012. *Greek and Roman Animal Sacrifice: Ancient Victims, Modern Observers*. Cambridge: Cambridge University Press.
Fiske, A.P. & Haslam, N. 1997. 'Is obsessive-compulsive disorder a pathology of the human disposition to perform socially meaningful rituals? Evidence of similar content.' *Journal of Nervous and Mental Disease*, 185: 211–222.
Furley, W.D. 2007. 'Prayers and hymns'. In D. Ogden, ed. *A Companion to Ancient Greek Religion*. Malden, MA: Wiley Blackwell: 117–131.
Georgoudi, S. 2017. 'Reflections on sacrifice and purification in the Greek world'. In *Hitch & Rutherford* 2017, 105–135.
Graf, F. 2012. 'One generation after Burkert and Girard: Where are the great theories'. In *Faraone & Naiden* 2012, 32–52.
Grossman, J. 2019. 'The significance of frankincense in grain offerings.' *Journal of Biblical Literature* 138: 285–296.
Gudme, A.K. de H. 2018. 'A pleasing odour for Yahweh: the smell of sacrifices on Mount Gerizim and in the Hebrew Bible.' *Body and Religion* 2: 7–24.
Herz, R. 2016. 'The role of odor-evoked memory in psychological and physiological health.' *Brain Sciences* 6, 22: 1–13.
Hitch, S. & Rutherford, I. eds. 2017. *Animal Sacrifice in the Ancient Greek World*. Cambridge: Cambridge University Press.
Houston, W.J. & Dunn, J.D.G. 2003. *Eerdmans Commentary on the Bible: Leviticus*. Grand Rapids, MI: Eerdmans.
Jameson, M.H. 1991. 'Sacrifice before battle'. In V.D. Hanson, ed. *Hoplites: The Classical Greek Battle Experience*. London: Routledge: 197–227.
Johnston, S.I. 1999. *Restless Dead: Encounters between the Living and the Dead in Ancient Greece*. Berkeley, CA: University of California Press.
Knust, J.W. & Várhelyi Z. eds. 2011. *Ancient Mediterranean Sacrifice*. Oxford: Oxford University Press.
Koch, U.S. 2010. 'Three strikes and you're out! A view on cognitive theory and first-millennium extispicy ritual'. In A. Annus, ed. *Divination and Interpretation of Signs in the Ancient World*. Chicago: Oriental Institute: 43–59.
    2011. 'Sheep and sky: Systems of divinatory interpretation'. In K. Radner & E. Robson, eds. *The Oxford Handbook of Cuneiform Culture*. Oxford: Oxford University Press: 447–469.

Kowalzig, B. 2007. *Singing for the Gods: Performances of Myth and Ritual in Archaic and Classical Greece*. Oxford: Oxford University Press.

Larson, J. 2016. *Understanding Greek Religion: A Cognitive Approach*. London: Routledge.

Lawson, E.T. & McCauley, R.N. 1990. *Rethinking Religion: Connecting Cognition and Culture*. Cambridge: Cambridge University Press.

Leuchter, M. 2010. 'The politics of ritual rhetoric: a proposed sociopolitical context for the redaction of Leviticus 1-16.' *Vetus Testamentum* 60: 345–365.

McCauley, R.N. & Lawson, E.T. 2002. *Bringing Ritual to Mind: Psychological Foundations of Cultural Forms*. Cambridge: Cambridge University Press.

2007. 'Cognition, religious ritual, and archaeology'. In E. Kyriakidis, ed. *The Archaeology of Ritual*. Los Angeles: Cotsen Institution of Archaeology: 209–253.

McGee, H. 2004. *On Food and Cooking: The Science and Lore of the Kitchen*. Revised edition. New York: Scribner.

Mehl, V. & Brulé, P. eds. 2008. *Le sacrifice antique: Vestiges, procedures et strategies*. Rennes: Presses Universitaires de Rennes.

Mikalson, J.D. 2010. *Ancient Greek Religion*. Second Edition. Chichester: Wiley.

Milgrom, J. 2004. *Leviticus: A Book of Ritual and Ethics*. Minneapolis, MN: Fortress Press.

Murray, C.A. ed. 2016. *Diversity of Sacrifice: Form and Function of Sacrificial Practices in the Ancient World and Beyond*. Albany, NY: State University of New York Press.

Naiden, F.S. 2013. *Smoke Signals for the Gods: Ancient Greek Sacrifice from the Archaic through Roman Periods*. New York: Oxford University Press.

2015. 'Sacrifice'. In E. Eidinow & J. Kindt, eds. *The Oxford Handbook of Ancient Greek Religion*. Oxford: Oxford University Press: 463–475.

Osborne, R. & Rhodes, P.J. eds. 2017. *Greek Historical Inscriptions 478-404 BC*. Oxford: Oxford University Press.

Parker, R. 2011. *On Greek Religion*. Ithaca, NY: Cornell University Press.

2014. 'Commentary on *Journal of Cognitive Historiography*, Issue 1.' *Journal of Cognitive Historiography* 1: 186–192.

Pulleyn. D. 1997. *Prayer in Greek Religion*. Oxford: Clarendon Press.

Rendtorff, R. & Kugler, R.A. eds. 2003. *The Book of Leviticus: Composition and Reception*. Leiden: Brill.

Sanders, E.P. 2016. *Judaism: Practice and Belief, 63 BCE-66 CE*. New edition. Minneapolis, MN: Fortress Press.

Schachter, D.L. 1996. *Searching for Memory: the Brain, the Mind, and the Past*. New York: Basic Books.

Sørensen, J. 2021. 'Force and categorization: reflections on Marcel Mauss and Henri Hubert's *Esquisse d'une théorie general de la magie*'. In J. Sørensen & A.K. Pedersen, eds. *Theoretical and Empirical Investigations of Divination and Magic: Manipulating the Divine*. Leiden: Brill: 246–273.

Tulving, E. 1983. *Elements of Episodic Memory*. Oxford: Clarendon Press.

van der Horst, P.W. 2013. 'The omen of sneezing in pagan antiquity.' *Ancient Society* 43: 213–221.
Van Straten, F.T. 1995. *Hierà kalá: Images of Animal Sacrifice in Archaic and Classical Greece*. Leiden: Brill.
Verbeek, C. & van Campen, C. 2013. 'Inhaling memories.' *The Senses and Society* 8: 133–148.
Veyne, P. 2000. 'Inviter les dieux, sacrifice, banqueter: Quelques nuances de la religiosité gréco-romaine.' *Annales* 55: 3–42.
Watts, J.W. 2007. *Ritual and Rhetoric in Leviticus: From Sacrifice to Scripture*. Cambridge: Cambridge University Press.
Weddle, C.C. 2013. 'The sensory experience of blood sacrifice in the Roman imperial cult'. In J. Day, ed. *Making Sense of the Past: Toward a Sensory Archaeology*. Carbondale, IL: University of Southern Illinois Press: 137–159.
  2017. 'Blood, fire and feasting: The role of touch and taste in Graeco-Roman animal sacrifice'. In E. Betts, ed. *Senses of the Empire: Multisensory Approaches to Roman Culture*. London: Routledge: 104–119.
Whitehouse, H. 2000. *Arguments and Icons: Divergent Modes of Religiosity*. Oxford: Oxford University Press.
  2004. *Modes of Religiosity: A Cognitive Theory of Religious Transmission*. Walnut Creek, CA: AltaMira.

CHAPTER 2

To the Netherworld and Back
Cognitive Aspects of the Descent to Trophonius

Yulia Ustinova

Cognitive scientists of religion require 'rich evidence' for in-depth analysis of religious experiences, but first-hand information on the thoughts and feelings of ancient participants in activities that may be defined as religious rites is very rarely available. We are fortunate to have detailed descriptions of both the ritual and the suppliant's experience at the sanctuary of Trophonius at Lebadeia in Boeotia by two Greek authors, Plutarch (c. 46–120 CE) and Pausanias (died in 180 CE). Even if these accounts lack the precision required by modern standards, they provide an exceptional opportunity for a case study combining ancient evidence with the results of modern research in cognitive science. Using this approach, this chapter explores likely changes in the suppliant's body and mind experienced during his stay in the sanctuary, and applies the analysis of these phenomena to the construal of the nature of the ritual at the Trophonium.

Trophonius supposedly vanished beneath the earth at Lebadeia and lived in a cave under a hill as an oracular god.[1] The son of a human mother, and therefore a mortal in the eyes of the Greeks, he however did not die and was regarded as a god rather than a hero.[2] The liminal status of Trophonius, an immortal subterranean dweller who did not fit into any of the usual Greek categories, allowed his role as a mediator between three worlds: of the living, the dead, and the gods.[3]

I am very grateful to the editors of the volume, and to the two anonymous reviewers, for their most helpful comments and suggestions, which have greatly improved the chapter. The remaining shortcomings are my responsibility.

[1] The most systematic and profound research on Trophonius was conducted by Pierre Bonnechere: Bonnechere 2003a, as well as a series of papers, Bonnechere and Bonnechere 1989, Bonnechere 1998a, 1998b, 1999, 2003b, and 2010. See also Schachter 1967, 1981–1994: 3, 66–89, and 1984, Clark 1968, Ustinova 2002: 269–274, 2009: 90–96, and 2018: 67–71.

[2] Schol. Ar. *Nub.* 508; Schachter 1981–1994: 3, 75; for Trophonius' genealogy see Bonnechere 1999: 290–297.

[3] For a detailed discussion of the status of Trophonius and similar immortal subterranean daemons see Ustinova 2002 and 2009: 108–109. Their strange mode of life under the earth appears to stem from their function as revealers of the hidden truth to men: these mythological figures were needed to

The main rite was a descent into the artificial subterranean cave of Trophonius, who was believed to appear to the suppliants in person. The oracle was active from the sixth century BCE[4] to the Roman Imperial period. In both literary and epigraphic sources, the act of consultation of the oracle is described as a descent, *katabasis*, to the god's underground dwelling.[5]

The most concise definition of *katabasis* is given by Alberto Bernabé: 'The *katabasis* has to be defined as a specific type of narrative characterized by the following features: an extraordinary protagonist that is better off with the assistance of a god, who travels alive to the subterranean world of the dead with a well defined purpose and with the intention to return (irrespectively of whether his purposes or the return are fulfilled).'[6] The most prominent Greek heroes, including Orpheus, Heracles, and Theseus, were able to descend to Hades and return to the realm of the living.[7] The long sequence of actions performed by the suppliant at the sanctuary of Trophonius was modelled on mythical narrations of *katabaseis* accomplished by these famous heroes, but also served the practical aim of securing the desired results, the most important of which was obtaining prophetic visions.

My analysis of the cognitive aspects of a suppliant's experience in the Trophonium will be based on an examination of culturally conditioned notions that were involved in the rite, juxtaposed with consideration of the physical factors that affected the suppliant's body and also had an impact on his mind. This is a case study, aiming to demonstrate the potential of the combination of top-down and bottom-up perspectives on religious experiences, as outlined in the Introduction to the volume, and suggesting that this approach may produce new insights into ancient cults.[8]

Preparation for the *Katabasis*

The induction process leading to the principal stage of the ritual was complex and would have affected multiple channels of perception. Some

---

explain the practice of descent into caves and grottoes in order to attain visions, interpreted as prophetic.

[4] The dates are BCE, unless indicated otherwise.
[5] Ar. *Nub.* 508, Hdt. 8. 134, Semus of Delos, *FGrH* 396 F10 (in Ath. 14. 614A), Paus. 9.39, *IG* VII 4136. Dicaearchus: Wehrli 1944–1969, fr. 13–22, Ath. 13. 594EF and 14. 641EF; cf. Schachter 1981–1994: 3. 80, Bonnechere 1998a: 445, Clark 1968 and 1979: 56.
[6] Bernabé 2015: 3. For the phenomenon of *katabasis* see most recently Bonnechere and Cursaru 2015–2016, Ekroth and Nilsson 2018.
[7] For these underworld journeys see Clark 1979.
[8] For further use of top-down and bottom-up analysis see also McGlashan, chapter 6, and Scott chapter 8, in this volume.

factors involved in this process may seem self-evident, but probably because of their triviality, they tend to be neglected in the research focusing on the 'main rite'. I include them here because this main rite cannot be comprehended in isolation from its background.

Ancient sources refer to inquirers at the Trophonium exclusively as men, but offer neither mythological nor cultic explanations of the segregation of women.[9] In other oracular centres involving direct interaction between the suppliant and the deity, most notably in the sanctuaries of Asclepius, women have left numerous testimonies of their consultations.[10] In contrast, the descent to Trophonius, discussed in detail in what follows, was perhaps considered too stressful for feeble female worshippers.

A suppliant's preparation began before his arrival at Lebadeia. Pilgrimage was a complex project even for well-to-do people who lived not very far from their destination.[11] Since the Trophonium is mentioned by many fifth-century non-Boeotian authors, its fame must have reached far beyond the boundaries of Boeotia, the land where the sanctuary of Trophonius was located. Many pilgrims therefore came from distant places. Before he undertook the journey, a potential pilgrim already knew enough about Trophonius and his powers to wish to invest time and a considerable sum of money in an extraordinary and risky adventure. The suppliant also knew that he would have to pay a considerable sum as a fee for consulting the god, and to buy animals for multiple sacrifices he was to offer (to be discussed shortly).[12] Modern research demonstrates that customers and patients who pay a higher price for a product derive more benefit from it, which implies an important role of expectancies in conditioning the placebo effect.[13] Sea and land travel had to be planned beforehand, which implies prolonged expectation of an awesome experience, including hope and fear, and a building up of both anxiety and eagerness to face Trophonius. Thus, when the suppliant finally reached Lebadeia, the more effort he had made and the higher his expenses, the easier it was for him to experience emotions and visions that he passionately desired to attain.

---

[9] Bonnechere 2003a: 61.   [10] Edelstein and Edelstein 1948.
[11] For pilgrimage in the Greek world see Dillon 1997, Rutherford 2013, esp. 178–187 on technicalities and dangers of the journey.
[12] The fee: *LSCG* 74, fourth century; Dillon 1997: 167 discusses fees for consulting other oracles, and the sum requested in Lebadeia, which was higher than in most other sanctuaries, including Delphi.
[13] Shiv, Carmon, and Arieli 2005, Kaptchuk 2002.

Myths of Trophonius

The inquirer descended to Trophonius' abode only when mentally prepared for the experience. His acquaintance with myths of Trophonius may be taken for granted, and some details were of particular significance. Trophonius and his brother Agamedes were legendary architects, whose works included the lower courses of Apollo's first temple at Delphi and other mythical buildings.[14] Most of them were secret chambers, where encounters between men and gods took place. Supernatural features of these constructions disclose their builders' similarity to magicians.[15]

Pausanias tells the story of a stratagem used by the brothers while building the treasury of the Boeotian king Hyrieus, which proved fatal for them.[16] By employing this stratagem, they were able to repeatedly enter the treasury and steal from it. When Agamedes was trapped, Trophonius was forced to kill him, lest the identity of the thieves be disclosed. The earth swallowed up Trophonius in Lebadeia. In another version of the tale Trophonius descended to a subterranean dwelling because of his ambition or vanity, wishing to hide his remains and thus make people believe that he had become a god.[17] These strange and unflattering foundation myths seem to have been necessary in order to account for a pre-existing notion of Trophonius' presence beneath the earth. In Pausanias' days, the place where Trophonius vanished was marked with a slab, serving to remind visitors of the myth and the physical presence of the immortal subterranean dweller under the earth of the sanctuary at which they had arrived.

The First Impression of the Sanctuary

The suppliant's admiration for Trophonius grew when he toured the imposing sanctuary. It was located on a picturesque mountain gorge above the river Hercyna, boasted several temples, of Trophonius, Hercyna, Zeus, Demeter, and Apollo, and was embellished with sculptures, including the statue of Trophonius by Praxiteles.[18] Pausanias reports that 'those who have descended into the shrine of Trophonius are obliged to dedicate a

---

[14] Paus. 9. 37.5–7; Bonnechere 1999: 269–275 and 2003a: 71–75.
[15] Paus. 9.11.1; Bonnechere 1999: 280.
[16] Paus. 9.37.3; Bonnechere 2003a: 75–78, Ustinova 2009: 94–95.
[17] Charax of Pergamon, *FGrH* 103 F5; Bonnechere 1999: 276, 289; additional versions of Trophonius' descent: Schol. in Ar. *Nub.* 508, Schol. in Lucian *Dial. mort.* 10.
[18] Paus. 9. 39. 1–4. Schachter 1981–1994: 3, 72–79, Bonnechere 1998b: 91–96 and 2003a: 7–26.

tablet on which is written all that each has heard or seen'.[19] No such tablet set in the Trophonium has survived,[20] but hundreds of inscriptions discovered in various sanctuaries of Asclepius attest to visions sent by the god and miracles that he allegedly performed, and there is no reason to doubt that the inquirers at the sanctuary of Trophonius described their astonishing experiences following a similar pattern.[21] The tablets fed the hope of the new inquirers to be endowed with the privilege of meeting supernatural entities, and supplied them with a template of emotions and visions they could expect. In the past, like today, people's hypnotizability varied, but the impact of reading accounts of encounters with Trophonius on a significant proportion of individuals, those categorized nowadays as easily hypnotizable, was probably considerable.[22] The importance of acquaintance with the experiences of other suppliants was fully appreciated in antiquity.[23]

Priming is presentation of stimuli that are supposed to produce responses in other domains, and it affects substantially the behaviour of individuals who participate in cultic activities.[24] The impact of the first acquaintance with the sanctuary, its buildings, and the dedications, was multifarious: the visitor was moved aesthetically, impressed by the wealth that presumably attested to the importance of the god, fascinated by the testimonies of his predecessors, and orientated to anticipate similar awe-inspiring experiences. His attention was also stimulated and it plays an important role in regulating cognition and hypnotizability,[25] which was crucial at the subsequent stages of preparation for the descent to Trophonius.

Thus, induction was under way even before the preparatory rituals began. It included the knowledge of the myth, which persuaded the inquirer that Trophonius was actually present beneath the earth in the very place where he arrived, and the impact of the tour of the sanctuary. Priming and firm belief in the possibility of a positive result are known to enhance placebo effects in modern patients treated by hypnotherapy, and social psychological factors alter their expectancies.[26] The promenade

---

[19] Paus. 9. 39. 14, trans. W. H. S. Jones.
[20] For other inscriptions discovered in Lebadaia, and a list of consulters at the Trophonium see Bonnechere 2003a: 59–60, 364–367.
[21] Inscriptions from the temples of Asclepius: Edelstein and Edelstein 1948.
[22] On variation in hypnotizability see Cardeña and Krippner 2010.
[23] On the cognitive effect on the suppliant, produced by the acquaintance with inscriptions in the sanctuaries of Asclepius, see Panagiotidou 2014.
[24] Shariff et al. 2016.   [25] Raz 2007.   [26] Benedetti 2009, Sliwinski and Elkins 2013.

through the sanctuary enhanced the ability of the suppliant to respond to the following stages of the rite in the desirable manner.

The Preliminary Stage of the Ritual

Pausanias offers some precious details on the preparatory stage of the ritual in the Trophonium. He describes the traditional ceremonies:

> When a man has made up his mind to descend to the oracle of Trophonius, he first lodges in a certain building for an appointed number of days, this being sacred to the good Spirit and to good Fortune. While he lodges there, among other regulations for purity he abstains from hot baths, bathing only in the river Hercyna. Meat he has in plenty from the sacrifices, for he who descends sacrifices to Trophonius himself and to [his children and five other gods]. At each sacrifice a diviner is present, who looks into the entrails of the victim, and after an inspection prophesies to the person descending whether Trophonius will give him a kind and gracious reception. The entrails of the other victims do not declare the mind of Trophonius so much as a ram, which each inquirer sacrifices over a pit on the night he descends, calling upon Agamedes. Even though the previous sacrifices have appeared propitious, no account is taken of them unless the entrails of this ram indicate the same; but if they agree, then the inquirer descends in good hope.[27]

Seclusion was an essential requirement for prophetic officials in Greek oracular centres such as Delphi, Didyma, and Claros, and is common cross-culturally in preparation for vision quest.[28] Hefty daily portions of meat, purification rites, and bathing in a river created a break from the normal regimen and hence a feeling that something odd was going on and even more extraordinary events could be expected. This feeling was boosted by music: piping in the Trophonium is mentioned in a comedy by Cratinus.[29] Several days spent in ways different from the usual daily regimen enhanced the inquirer's sense of anticipation. These days also gave the experienced temple officials time to observe his behaviour and evaluate his ability to attain alteration of consciousness: the suppliant's request to descend to Trophonius could be declined on no less than eight occasions if his sacrifices appeared to be rejected by the gods. The preliminary stage of the ritual played therefore a double role. On the one hand, it manipulated the state of the suppliant's body and mind, making him receptive to the

---

[27] Paus. 9. 39. 5–6, trans. W. H. S. Jones.
[28] Delphi: Plut. *Mor.* 438C. Claros and Didyma: Iambl. *Myst.* 3. 11; Ustinova 2018: 59, 63–65.
[29] For the ceremony at the Trophonium, see Bonnechere 2003a: 32–61, esp. 40–41, 139–164, 236–248 and 2007: 34–36. Cratinus on Trophonius: Quaglia 2000.

effects of the great ceremony. On the other hand, the early stage of the ritual allowed careful selection of suppliants who were likely to obtain visions and therefore sustain the fame of the sanctuary.

The Descent to Trophonius: The Route to the Grotto

Pausanias' description of the preliminary ritual leads to a lengthy account of the central procedure:

> First, during the night he is taken to the river Hercyna by two boys of the citizens about thirteen years old, named Hermae, who after taking him there anoint him with oil and wash him. ... After this he is taken by the priests, not at once to the oracle, but to fountains of water very near to each other. Here he must drink water called the water of Forgetfulness (Lethe), that he may forget all that he has been thinking of hitherto, and afterwards he drinks of another water, the water of Memory (Mnemosyne), which causes him to remember what he sees after his descent. After looking at the image which they say was made by Daedalus (it is not shown by the priests save to such as are going to visit Trophonius), having seen it, worshipped it and prayed, he proceeds to the oracle, dressed in a linen tunic, with ribbons girding it, and wearing the boots of the country.[30]

The imagery of this trip is that of the netherworld. The direction of the nocturnal promenade down the hill, and the terms used to describe it, invoked the notion of *katabasis*, heroic descent into the land of the dead. The river Hercyna, its rocky banks covered in vegetation, and the sounds of the night were reminiscent of the murky landscapes surrounding the entrance to Hades and depicted in numerous texts, starting from the terrifying scene of Odysseus' visit to the netherworld in Homer's *Odyssey*.[31]

In the darkness of the night, the inquirer was first led by two boys personifying Hermes the Conductor of Souls to Hades (*Hermes Psychompos*), and without doubt costumed accordingly, which made him feel as if he were already dead. In the night-time coolness, the suppliant was washed in the river and anointed. Bathing in the water of Hercyna was not a regular purification rite: the entire mise-en-scène indicated to the inquirer that he was washed in a netherworld river.[32] Feeling the chilly touch of water and being rubbed by the hands of the two Hermae added a tactile aspect to the suppliant's perception of the scene.

---

[30] Paus. 9.39.7–8, trans. W. H. S. Jones.
[31] Hom. *Od.* 11. 12–25; for a survey of such descriptions see Leclerc 2015, Macías Otero 2015.
[32] Purification rites normally preceding oracular consultations: Dillon 1997: 158–160.

The next leg of the journey resembled the images of the netherworld even more: the inquirer was brought to a fountain gushing with the water of Lethe, the horrifying river of oblivion flowing in Hades. The inquirer knew that having drunk from this fountain he would forget whatever he had thought before. When he felt the cold liquid, first in his mouth, then sinking inside his body, he could imagine his memories obliterated by the physical contact with the water from the netherworld river. Thus, the inquirer's complex experience of Hades comprised visual, auditory, tactile, gustatory, and kinaesthetic sensations. As a result, he was induced to feel like the dead souls depicted in the Homeric scene of Odysseus' descent into Hades: a shadow of a human being, deprived of memory and hence of identity, since death was believed to be 'the field of Lethe' (*lêthês pedion*), that is, the land of oblivion.[33]

The proximity of the fountains of Lethe and Mnemosyne, topographical and ritual, to the Trophonium is immediately reminiscent of the gold tablets that accompanied deceased Bacchic-Orphic initiates to their graves.[34] Several tablets refer to the two springs located in Hades, one of them presenting dire dangers to the souls of the dead initiates, and the other promising them the gift of Mnemosyne.[35] A soul that forgets is bereft of its consciousness and thus is doomed; the soul that has drunk from the source of memory sustains itself and acquires immortality.[36] These texts demonstrate the remarkable significance of correct actions regarding both sources of magic water, to be performed by the initiate's soul on its arrival in Hades. In the Trophonium, the motif of the two sources was used as a part of the netherworld imagery, to be perceived by a supplicant who was mortally terrified, although still alive.

Yet there is more to learn from Pausanias' passage. The succession of ritual death, through erasing the person's identity, and rebirth as a new person is prominent in initiation rites.[37] In particular, symbolic death and rebirth constitute the core of Greek mystery initiations, which may be

---

[33] Hom. *Od.* 11, Ar. *Ran.* 186; Ustinova 2012: 116.   [34] For a discussion see Ustinova 2012.
[35] Graf and Johnston 2013: Nos 1, 2, 8, 25. Mnemosyne: Bernabé and Jiménez San Cristóbal 2008: 15–19.
[36] Bernabé and Jiménez San Cristóbal 2008: 17.
[37] In the rites articulating the initiation into a new status, the opposition dying–rebirth is a particularly strong symbol of transition; cross-culturally, dying and rebirth are used in initiations as a pair, emphasizing the irreversibility of changes undergone by an individual (Schjødt 1986: 98; for a classicist's perspective on initiation rites see Calame 1999, Turcan 1998). 'Mystery initiation' is a common rendering of the Greek term *teletê* (rite of fulfilment). Notwithstanding the critical approach to the use of the term 'initiations' (Dodd and Faraone 2003), it is still applied to mystery initiations and is in my opinion hermeneutically useful; see Ustinova 2018: 115.

defined as ersatz-death.[38] In the Trophonium, the supplicant first symbolically died and obliterated his personality by drinking from the water of Lethe, thus completing his entrance into the netherworld. Then with a gulp of the water of memory he started preparations for the new life as a different person. The ritual of oracular consultation at the Trophonium therefore can be also interpreted as the suppliant's initiation.[39]

The interpretation of the journey in the Trophonium as an initiation is supported by other hints in Pausanias' account of the rite. Secrecy is the most conspicuous characteristic of initiations, and the privilege of beholding the statue attributed to Daedalus, the most illustrious mythic master of subterranean chambers, magician, and trickster, was bestowed only upon the initiates.[40] Furthermore, it is noteworthy that the supplicant wore special garments. The 'boots of the country' were not only another indication of a rupture with the regular way of life: special footwear was employed in several mystery rites, above all by the sacred officials at Eleusis.[41] As to the linen tunics, it was known to Herodotus that the Orphic and Bacchic initiates never buried their dead in woollen wrappings (woollen textiles being the default choice in Greece), and probably used for this purpose linen cloths.[42] The choice of a fabric that was unusual and associated with the funerary rites of some mystery initiates stresses the construal of the descent to Trophonius as an imitation of death and underscores the initiatory aspect of the ceremony. The suppliant's perception of the rite was undoubtedly affected by the fact that he was wearing initiate's shrouds and special 'initiation' boots.

We can observe a similarity between the ritual at the Trophonium and the texts of some Bacchic gold tablets, probably resulting from the prominent role of the two springs of magic water in the netherworld lore that was common knowledge in Greece and presumably appears in several distinct cults. However, the contrast between the two cults was quite notable. In the gold tablets, the initiate's soul arrives at the magic sources after the death and is instructed to drink only from the source of memory, while at the Trophonium the initiate had to drink from both sources, and his death was temporary and symbolic.

---

[38] Bernabé 2009: 107, 121 and 2016: 28, Turcan 1998: 121, Ustinova 2013. Segal 1990: 414 and Obbink 2011: 297 note the similarity between initiations and funeral rites.
[39] Bonnechere 1998a.
[40] Secrecy in Greek initiations: Burkert 1987: 9. For Daedalus and his magic abilities see Delcourt 1982: 156–170.
[41] Bonnechere 2003a: 240–245, Clinton 1974: 47.   [42] Hdt. 2. 81.

It is also noteworthy that in Greece water was considered the carrier of prophetic power, and prophetic figures in established sanctuaries such as Delphi and Claros drank water from sacred springs.[43] Drinking of magic water in the Trophonium served therefore not only as a transition rite, but also as a preparatory stage in an oracular ritual.

In summary, during the journey through the Trophonium the suppliant experienced ersatz-death and was driven to a state of trepidation and disorientation. At this stage of the ritual, initiatory elements were entwined with rites characteristic of other oracular cults.

In the Oracular Grotto

The grotto of Trophonius has not been discovered; therefore its layout can be only hypothetically reconstructed on the basis of Pausanias' account of the *katabasis*. The prophetic *adyton*, located on the hill, was most probably an artificial circular hole, several metres deep, connected to a small underground cavity.[44] The inquirer was conducted from the lowest part of the sanctuary, at the bank of the Hercyna, to its high part, on the hill above the grove. In the darkness of the night, this ascent to the prophetic location, following the descent to the river and the water sources, added further strain.

Pausanias' Account

The main stage of the ritual is described by Pausanias:

> They have made no way of descent to the bottom, but when a man comes to Trophonius, they bring him a narrow, light ladder. After going down he finds a hole between the floor and the structure. Its breadth appeared to be two spans, and its height one span. The descender lies with his back on the ground, holding barley-cakes kneaded with honey, thrusts his feet into the hole and himself follows, trying hard to get his knees into the hole. After his knees the rest of his body is at once swiftly drawn in, just as the largest and most rapid river will catch a man in its eddy (*dinê*) and carry him under. After this those who have entered the shrine learn the future, not in one and the same way in all cases, but by sight sometimes and at other times by hearing. The return upwards is by the same mouth, the feet darting out first.[45]

---

[43] On the prophetic qualities of water, see Ustinova 2009: 131–132, with further references; sanctuaries where water was instrumental in prophecy-giving: Friese 2010: 86–87.
[44] Paus. 9. 39. 11. On the shape of the prophetic cavern and the position of the inquirer see Bonnechere 2003a: 159–163. A different reconstruction: Rosenberger 2001: 37–38, fig. 2.
[45] Paus. 9.39.10–12, trans. W. H. S. Jones.

The inquirer descended into the terrifying well in the darkness using a ladder, having already been exposed to other frightening experiences. On the bottom of the grotto he expected to find Trophonius' snakes. Descending on a narrow ladder, he still had to hold the cakes for them, and probably had the wrong impression that the descent was longer, and the grotto much deeper than in reality. Snakes, who were believed to be crawling all over the netherworld, served as yet another powerful symbol of Hades.[46] The encounter with the snakes, whose number the inquirer perhaps misapprehended, given the limited space and the scare caused by feeling the touch of their cold silky skin against his own, completed the fearsome descent. The effect on the supplicant was achieved by a combination of kinaesthetic and tactile effects, while the visual and auditory input was minimal.

Having reached the bottom of the hole, the inquirer lay on the ground and then, according to Pausanias, was swiftly drawn into another hole, as if by an eddy (*dinê*). In fact, the image of the whirl probably derived from the vortex experienced by the inquirers at the beginning of their prophetic trance and could have been the result of an alteration of consciousness induced by the immersion into the dark coolness of the grotto, to be discussed shortly. The experience of a vortex is one of the most common in laboratory experiments investigating the effects of various hallucinogens, as well as stress factors,[47] and frequently appears in anthropological accounts of initial stages of altered states of consciousness experienced by shamans and other religious practitioners.[48] Tunnels are ubiquitous in hallucinations induced by various means, and even at the instant just before sleep.[49]

Pausanias detected the variance in the kind of hallucinations experienced in Trophonius' cave, observing that different inquirers visiting the prophetic chamber learned the future in different ways, either by sight or by hearing.[50] Much earlier, fifth- and fourth-century references to prophetic séances at the Trophonium include the opposition of memory and oblivion, independence of soul, and its levitation. It is therefore reasonable to assume that altered states of conscience were experienced in the Trophonium as early as the fifth century.[51] The duration of the inquirer's stay in the grotto and the manner of his return are obscure, since 'darting

---

[46] Ar. *Ran.* 142–143, Ogden 2015. [47] Siegel and Jarvik 1975: 116, 143.
[48] See Ustinova 2009: 29 and 2018: 332. [49] Blackmore 1993: 71. [50] Clark 1968: 70.
[51] Fifth-century mentions: Hdt. 1.36, 8.134 (referring to the sixth century), Ar. *Nub.* 508, Eur. *Ion* 300–302, 404–409, Pindar: Maehler 1984–1989, fr. 3. Cf. Babut 1984: 51, 72, Bonnechere 1998a: 452–453 and 2003a: 132–138, 192–196. On altered states of consciousness see also chapter 6, McGlashan and Patzelt, Chapter 5, in this volume.

out' with one's feet first, as described by Pausanias, is difficult to envisage.[52] It was, however, clearly a hint at funeral practices, because from Homer's time corpses were set with their feet facing the door, and were carried out feet first.[53] Although the inquirer emerging from the grotto was returning to the world of the living, rather than departing from it, the association with burial customs may be another sign of the perception of the visit to Trophonius as a brush with death.

Plutarch's Account

Pausanias describes the inquirer's experience, including the vortex, as an objective observer, but luckily the *katabasis* to the Trophonium is also reported in minor detail by Plutarch in *The Daimonion of Socrates*.[54] This is a fascinating account of the communication of a young man named Timarchus, who spent two nights and a day in the cave, in a world beyond normal experience. Either asleep or in a trance, Timarchus' soul flew above an ocean with shining isles, and in a state of mixed joyfulness and awe he heard voices that explained to him the mystery of metempsychosis and predicted his imminent death:

> He said that on descending into the oracular crypt his first experience was of profound darkness; next, after a prayer, he lay a long time not clearly aware whether he was awake or dreaming. It did seem to him, however, that at the same moment he heard a crash and was struck on the head, and that the sutures parted and released his soul. As it withdrew and mingled joyfully with air that was translucent and pure, it felt in the first place that now, after long being cramped, it had again found relief ...; and next it faintly caught the whirl of something revolving overhead with a pleasant sound ... He saw islands illuminated by one another with soft fire, taking on now one colour, now another, like a dye ... All this he viewed with enjoyment of the spectacle. But looking down he saw a great abyss ... most terrible and deep it was ... From it could be heard innumerable roars and groans of animals ... the mingled lamentations of men and women, and noise and uproar of every kind ... After an interval someone he did not see addressed him: "Timarchus, what would you have to explain?"

---

[52] The accounts of the emergence of inquirers far away from Lebadeia and even from Boeotia (Philostr. *V A* 8. 19, Lucian *Necyomantia* 9, 22) may have been exaggerated reflections of the actual blurred memories of leaving the prophetic grotto, if the almost unconscious suppliants were pulled out of the grotto and left to recover away from it. However, the evidence is clearly insufficient and untrustworthy, and this suggestion is no more than a guess. The notion of underground travelling of some inquirers in the Trophonium could be inspired by the labyrinthine nature of Hades (Ogden 2001: 204).

[53] Garland 1985: 24, 138.   [54] Plut. *Mor.* 590B–592F; Corlu 1970.

"Everything," he answered ...

"Nay,' the voice replied, 'in the higher regions we others have but little part, as they belong to gods; but you may, if you wish, inquire into the portion of Persephone [the Netherworld], administrated by ourselves ... Of these matters ... you will have better knowledge, young man, in the third month from now; for the present, depart."

... Once more [Timarchus] felt a sharp pain in his head, as though it had been violently compressed, and he lost all recognition and awareness of what was going on around him; but he presently recovered and saw that he was lying in the crypt of Trophonius near the entrance, at the very spot he had first laid himself down ... When he had come back to Athens and died in the third month, as the voice had foretold, we were amazed ...[55]

For the purposes of the present discussion, Timarchus' historicity as a person is insignificant.[56] The details of the conversation between the suppliant and the divine voice were probably elaborated by Plutarch, but the gist of this narration, focused on a personal encounter between the suppliant and a supernatural being, are congruent to the accounts of prophecy-giving at the Trophonium by other ancient authors. The most substantial inference from Plutarch's description is that a suppliant in the sanctuary of Trophonius lived through an alteration of consciousness, in a semi-hallucinatory state between wakefulness and dreaming, experienced in profound darkness. Lying on the floor of the grotto for a long time is not mentioned by Pausanias, who passes directly from the descent into the cave to the vortex sensation. Plutarch gives a particularly detailed account of auditory experiences in the Trophonium, from a sweet 'whirling' noise at the beginning of Timarchus' sojourn, to bellowing and terrible noises during his flight, and the prophetic conversation with the supernatural voice.[57] Plutarch's testimony adds therefore an important detail, a prolonged sojourn in the total darkness and silence of the deep grotto, which can be defined in modern terms as a state of sensory deprivation.

Sensory deprivation is one of the common techniques of inducing altered states of consciousness; elimination of external stimuli forces the human mind to concentrate within itself and brings about an intensive discharge of inner imagery.[58] Visions appearing in a dream-like state are

---

[55] Plut. *Mor.* 590B–592F, trans. Ph. D. De Lacy and B. Einarson.
[56] Cf. Bonnechere 1998a: 449.
[57] See Bonnechere 2018, esp. 219–221 on the sounds of *katabasis*, and the *topos* of 'terrible noise during the contact between worlds'.
[58] For the neurophysiological mechanism of hallucination in the state of sensory deprivation see Lex 1979: 132–147, Bentall 2000: 97–98, Andersen et al. 2014: 224, Schjødt and Jensen 2018: 326–327, cf. Andresen 2001: 260–261.

often perceived as more real than everyday experience. In contemporary traditional societies and in the past, sensory deprivation was attained in caves and artificial grottoes, and prolonged sojourns in monastic cells and other retreats are known to produce the same effect.[59] Even restricted environmental stimulation in controlled experiments results in visual anomalies, uncanny emotions, and other altered state-like experiences in many subjects.[60] Partial sensory deprivation, restricting incoming information, leaves unchecked the expectations and beliefs formed before the experience, and thus facilitates adoption of suggested interpretations and narratives.[61] When combined with all the preparatory rites, sensory deprivation is a very plausible explanation for alteration of consciousness of the suppliants at the Trophonium.

Timarchus' lack of awareness evolved into an out-of-body experience that included a passage through darkness to translucent and pure light, flight over a magnificent country, visual and auditory hallucinations, and a mixture of joyfulness and awe. Most significantly, Timarchus' soul was 'released', which implies an out-of-body experience.[62] It is noteworthy that Plutarch's account does not refer to Trophonius' epiphany, but instead reports a conversation between the suppliant and an anonymous voice. This voice explained to Timarchus the mystery of metempsychosis, and endowed him with the gift of clairvoyance, which allowed the prediction of his imminent death. Unsurprisingly, Timarchus' altered state of consciousness was accompanied by culturally patterned visions, reflecting Greek religious and philosophical ideas, such as the mythical geography of the netherworld, as well as the notions of the soul, its liberty, and need for purification.

The vortex, a journey through a dark void to awe-inspiring light, is clearly indicated in both Plutarch's and Pausanias' accounts. In modern accounts of similar experiences, the main feature of the vortex experience is a tunnel-like perspective, which often terminates in a bright light appearing in the centre of the field of vision, the light sometimes described as warm or kindly, or as brightly lit human forms. All the senses are involved in the experience of the vortex: people hear voices and sounds, feel breathless and weightless (therefore floating or flying), their vision may blur, and they may gain the impression of being in a different world. These

---

[59] Ustinova 2009: 32–41. [60] Farthing 1992: 191, Andersen et al. 2014.
[61] Schjødt and Jensen 2018: 321–322.
[62] Plut. *Mor.* 590B: *methienai tēn psuchēn*. On out-of-body experiences see Gabbard and Twemlow 1984, Metzinger 2005.

sensations, which are universal, result from the neurological processes in the human brain.⁶³ In the extant ancient testimonies about the Trophonium, Pausanias underscores the physical sensation of the vortex, reporting the sensation of being caught in an eddy (*dinê*) and carried by its flow; as to the revelations, he only indicates that they can be 'by sight sometimes and at other times by hearing'. Plutarch describes the feeling of the soul's flight in the darkness over shining spots to luminous light, and various sounds and voices perceived during this journey. Thus, his narrative is focused on the contents of multi-sensory hallucinations in Trophonius' grotto, kinaesthetic, visual, and auditory at the same time.

Plutarch's account of the descent into the subterranean grotto in the Trophonium is reminiscent of his description in a famous passage of the initiate's experience during mystery rites. This comprises a long movement through the darkness, with a marvellous light at its end, visions, happiness, and meetings with kindly people, as well as the soul's reunification with the body, which implies that they were conceived as temporarily separated during the experience.⁶⁴ Other Greek and Latin texts alluding to mystery experiences probably hint at the vortex sensation.⁶⁵ At the end of mystery rites, a great secret was revealed to the initiates, focusing on the enigma of death and life.⁶⁶ According to Plutarch, a suppliant at the Trophonium could inquire into the knowledge confined to the netherworld. Thus, the most conspicuous elements of the experience at the Trophonium and during mystery initiations – alteration of consciousness, a vortex sensation accompanied by joyful visions, and revelation of secret knowledge – were compatible.

The Return from the Grotto

Immediately after his stay in the underground cave, the suppliant remained under the supervision of the experts, as reported by Pausanias:

> After his ascent from Trophonius the inquirer is again taken in hand by the priests, who set him upon a chair called the chair of Memory, which stands not far from the shrine, and they ask of him, when seated there, all he has seen

---

⁶³ Siegel 1980: 923, Drab 1981: 145–146, Blanke et al. 2002.
⁶⁴ Sandbach 1967: fr. 178, Stob. *Flor.* 4. 52. 49; Ustinova 2018: 129–132.
⁶⁵ For instance, Apul. *Met.* 11. 23: 'I approached the boundary of death, and treating on Proserpina's threshold, I was carried through all the elements, after which I returned. At dead of night I saw the sun flushing with bright effulgence. I approached close to the gods above and the gods below and worshipped them face to face' (trans. I. G. Griffiths); Ustinova 2009: 249–250 and 2018: 141–142.
⁶⁶ Burkert 1987: 91–101, Bremmer 2014: 11–16, Ustinova 2018: 116, 127–129.

or learned. After gaining this information they then entrust him to his relatives. These lift him, paralyzed with terror and unconscious both of himself and of his surroundings, and carry him to the building where he lodged before with Good Fortune and the Good Spirit. Afterwards, however, he will recover all his faculties, and the power to laugh will return to him.[67]

The inquirer returned to the realm of Mnemosyne, from whose water he drank before the *katabasis*, taking a seat on the chair of memory, and recounted his experience to the temple officials. The questioning by the priests closely followed the ascent from the grotto. The supplicant was still semi-conscious and paralyzed with terror, and his state of mind easily malleable. Talking to him directly after the ascent from the grotto and putting open-ended questions, the priests could get exhaustive non-edited reports of his experience.

As recent research on cognitive resources in religious interaction demonstrates, depletion of cognitive resources during rituals impairs the individual's ability to realize their experience, making the impact of prior expectations and post-ritual influences more significant than the person's own muted, actual perceptions.[68] Furthermore, believers are prone to invest fewer cognitive resources in error monitoring when the source of information is a religious authority, whose instructions may subordinate the believer's own subjective experience.[69] Finally, highly hypnotizable individuals are able to suppress models that are based on their own experience, when it conflicts with suggestions by religious experts.[70] The descent into the grotto, involving anxiety, fear, and apprehension, depleted the cognitive resources of the inquirer, who therefore easily adopted the hinted suggestions of authoritative priests, as well as the information he received prior to the *katabasis*, as his own memories.

During questioning the practised temple officials could shape the inquirer's memories, and by means of carefully formulated questions suggest images and ideas that the inquirer would accept as his own. While the visions of the subterranean world were felt as powerful but ineffable, articulation rendered them more real and significant not only for the inquirer, but also for other people. If the prophetic experience was dim and dreamlike, prompts and suggestions could add colour and confidence.[71] The questioning was therefore of ultimate importance, providing

---

[67] Paus. 9.39.12–13, trans. W. H. S. Jones. [68] Schjoedt et al. 2013, Schjødt 2019: 367.
[69] Schjødt 2019: 365. [70] Schjødt 2019: 370.
[71] Ineffability of altered states of consciousness: Ahlberg 1982: 68–72, Farthing 1992: 210; on the importance of cultural environment for verbalization of seemingly ineffable experiences of alteration of consciousness see Geels 1982: 52. Ineffability of mystical experiences in Greece: Ustinova 2018: 142–144, 323–331, 339–341.

the feedback from the inquirers to the temple authorities, conditioning the message taken by the suppliants to the world, and sustaining the reputation of the sanctuary.

Only after the procedure of questioning was the exhausted suppliant allowed to be taken away from the grotto, to rest in the building where he stayed at the preparatory stage.[72] The underground experiences of the inquirers were so awe-inspiring that they lost the ability to laugh, which prompted the proverb 'He consulted the Trophonium.'[73] Only after some time did the inquirer return to normality. In many cultures, laughter was regarded as 'a sign of life', and the loss of laughter as equivalent to death,[74] therefore this proverb accentuates the similarity between the *katabasis* to Trophonius and a brush with death.

The descent to Trophonius was dreadful, but Pausanias reports that it killed only one person, who did not perform the preliminary rites and went to the grotto with unholy thoughts.[75] This remark of Pausanias invites comparisons with the Pythia who died when compelled to prophesy (i.e. contrary to the traditional practice) and multiple references of ancient authors to the importance of minute adherence to the custom in mystery initiations.[76] All in all, established ritual ensured, firstly, the desired results and, second, the safety of the inquirers. Neglect of the ritual could be fatal.

Conclusions

In the subterranean chamber of the Trophonium, the inquirer experienced alteration of consciousness induced by sensory deprivation and comprising vortex and out-of-body experiences, as well as hallucinations and the sensation of unmediated communication with supernatural beings. The core experience was preceded by a series of preparatory rites, each involving a different cognitive and/or physiological mechanism. The preliminary stages of the suppliant's experience, beginning from his journey to the sanctuary of Trophonius, enhanced his ability to attain alteration of consciousness and were therefore of major importance. Obviously, not all the pilgrims could be influenced in the same manner by the ritual enacted in the Trophonium, and only those whose personality was found suitable were admitted, due to preliminary selection.

---

[72] Bonnechere 2003a: 249–271.   [73] Ath. 614B.   [74] Bremmer 1983: 86–88.
[75] Paus. 9. 39. 12.
[76] Irregular prophetic séances at Delphi: Plut. *Mor.* 438AB, Luc. 5. 147–196; Ustinova 2009: 140–141. Mystery initiations: Pl. *Phdr.* 244E, Eur. *Bacch.* 79, Synesius *Dio* 8, Porph. *Abst.* 4. 5; Ustinova 2018: 132–133.

At the Trophonium,[77] the achievement of oracular visions was associated with an initiatory ritual. Initiatory aspects of the *katabasis* to Trophonius were noticed in antiquity.[78] An analysis of the inquirer's experiences during the night of the *katabasis* suggests that initiatory features were fundamental for attaining inspired visions at the Trophonium, and therefore belonged to the very essence of the cult.[79] The ritual at the Trophonium was based on a combination of cognitive and neuropsychological mechanisms also found in other initiatory and oracular cults, which could not be disentangled. The cult of Trophonius therefore defies one-dimensional definition as either an oracular or an initiatory ritual.

The procedure at the Trophonium comprised an enhanced (i.e. tougher) version of the complex of ritual requirements, environment, and triggers that incited 'engodedness' in oracular priests in established prophetic centres.[80] Elaborate preparations and allusions to a journey to the netherworld, in addition to a long solitary sojourn in an underground space, were the 'heavy artillery' that was employed in order to enable inexperienced laymen to achieve altered states of consciousness. In contrast, practised cult officials needed gentler mechanisms to attain similar results. The reason for this disparity ensues from the fact that an experienced and trained person can manipulate his or her consciousness in a more efficient fashion:[81] professional mediums from Delphi, Claros, Didyma, and other sanctuaries needed much less in terms of environment, duration of the session, and driving factors in order to reach divine inspiration (i.e. alteration of consciousness). In addition, exposure to the strain of the oracular trance was sufficient to strip the inquirer of the ability

---

[77] And at the Acharaca cave, where sick people were initiated into mysteries and then brought into a cave in order to receive instructions on their healing in visions sent by the gods. The place was forbidden and deadly to everybody but the initiated patients and the priests (Strabo 14.1.44). Thus, in Acharaca participating in initiations involved receiving revelations by means of *katabasis* into a cave (Ustinova 2009: 86–87).

[78] Aristophanes in the *Clouds* incorporates elements of the cult at Lebadeia, such as the opposition of memory and oblivion, *katabasis*, and honey cakes in a travesty of an initiation rite, and the scholiasts to Aristophanes used the words *teletai* (mystery rites) and *muêsis* (mystery cult) in their references to the Trophonium: Ar. *Nub.* 483–485, 505–508, Schol. in Ar. *Nub.* 508, Tzetzes on Ar. *Plut.* 842. For a detailed discussion of these and other passages see Bonnechere 1998a and 2003a.

[79] As Bonnechere 2003b argues, and contrary to the opinion that mystery overtones were a later addition to the oracular ritual.

[80] The word used by Hoffmann 1997: 30. G. Rouget called this state 'endieué' (Rouget 1990: 346). For the term *entheos* see Briand 2003, Ustinova 2018: 2–3.

[81] Rouget 1990: 89, Shanon 2002: 302–303, Ustinova 2018: 26, 58–67.

to laugh, that is, almost to kill him; such an awe-inspiring experience could be afforded once in a lifetime or very rarely. Thus, the extreme conditions of the Trophonium were effective in manipulating the consciousness of suppliants but could not be imposed upon people who had to attain prophetic visions on a regular basis.

BIBLIOGRAPHY

Ahlberg, N. 1982. 'Some Psycho-physiological Aspects of Ecstasy in Recent Research', in N. G. Holm, ed. *Religious Ecstasy*, 63–73. Stockholm.

Andersen, M., U. Schjødt, K. L. Nielbo, and J. Sørensen 2014. 'Mystical Experience in the Lab', *Method & Theory in the Study of Religion* 26(3): 217–245.

Andresen, J. 2001. 'Conclusion: Religion in the Flesh: Forging New Methodologies for the Study of Religion', in J. Andresen, ed. *Religion in Mind: Cognitive Perspectives on Religious Belief, Ritual, and Experience*, 257–287. Cambridge.

Babut, D. 1984. 'Le dialogue de Plutarque "Sur le démon de Socrate". Essai d'interprétation', *Bulletin de l'Association Guillaume Budé*: 51–76.

Benedetti, F. 2009. *Placebo Effects:. Understanding the Mechanisms in Health and Disease*. Oxford.

Bentall, R. P. 2000. 'Hallucinatory Experiences', in E. Cardeña, S. J. Lynn, and S. Kripper, eds. *Varieties of Anomalous Experience: Examining the Scientific Evidence*, 85–120. Washington, DC.

Bernabé, A. 2009. 'Imago Inferorum Orphica', in G. Casadio and P. A. Johnston, eds. *Mystic Cults in Magna Graecia*, 95–130. Austin, TX.

2015. 'What Is a Katábasis? The Descent into the Netherworld in Greece and in the Ancient Near East', *Les Études Classiques* 83: 15–34.

2016. 'Aristotle and the Mysteries', in M. J. Martín-Velasco and M. J. García Blanco, eds. *Greek Philosophy and Mystery Cults*, 27–42. Newcastle upon Tyne.

Bernabé, A. and A. I. Jiménez San Cristóbal 2008. *Instructions for the Netherworld. The Orphic Gold Tablets*. Leiden.

Blackmore, S. 1993. *Dying to Live: Near-Death Experiences*. Buffalo, NY.

Blanke, O., S. Ortigue, T. Landis, and M. Seeck 2002. 'Stimulating Illusory Own-body Perceptions', *Nature* 419(6904): 269–270.

Bonnechere, P. 1998a. 'La scène d'initiation des *Nuées* d'Aristophane et Trophonios: nouvelles lumières sur le culte lébadéen', *Revue des Études Grecques* 111(2): 436–480.

1998b. 'Les dieux du Trophonion lébadéen: panthéon ou amalgame?', in V. Pirenne-Delforge, ed. *Les Panthéons des cités des origines à la Périégèse de Pausanias. Actes du Colloque organisé à l'Université de Liège du 15 au 17 mai 1997. Kernos Suppl.* 8, 91–108. Liège.

1999. 'La personalité mythologique de Trophonios', *Revue de l'Histoire des Religions* 216(3): 259–297.

2003a. *Trophonios de Lébadée*. Leiden.

2003b. 'Trophonios of Lebadea. Mystery Aspects of an Oracular Cult in Boeotia', in M. B. Cosmopoulos, ed. *Greek Mysteries. The Archaeology and Ritual of Ancient Greek Secret Cults*, 169–192. London and New York, NY.

2007. 'The Place of the Sacred Grove (*alsos*) in the Mantic Rituals of Greece: The Example of the Oracle of Trophonios at Lebadeia (Boeotia)', in M. Conan, ed. *Sacred Gardens and Landscapes: Ritual and Agency*, 17–41. Washington, DC.

2010. 'Notes trophoniaques, iv: avancées, retours, mises au point', *Les Études Classiques* 78: 57–72.

2018. 'The Sounds of Katabasis: Bellowing, Roaring, and Hissing at the Crossing of Impervious Boundaries', in E. G. and I. Nilsson, eds. *Round Trip to Hades in the Eastern Mediterranean Tradition. Visits to the Underworld from Antiquity to Byzantium*, 214–229. Leiden.

Bonnechere, P. and M. Bonnechere. 1989. 'Trophonios à Lebadée. Histoire d'un oracle', *Les Études Classiques* 67(4): 289–302.

Bonnechere, P. and G. Cursaru, eds. 2015–2016. *Katábasis dans la tradition littéraire et religieuse de la grèce ancienne*. Vol. 1: *Les Études Classiques* 83 (2015); vol. 2: *Cahiers des Études Anciennes* 53 (2016).

Bremmer, J. N. 1983. *The Early Greek Concept of the Soul*. Princeton, NJ.

2014. *Initiation into the Mysteries of the Ancient World*. Berlin and Boston, MA.

Briand, M. 2003. 'Inspiration, enthousiasme et polyphonies: *entheos* et la performance poétique', *Noesis* 4: 97–154.

Burkert, W. 1987. *Ancient Mystery Cults*. Cambridge, MA.

Calame, C. 1999. 'Indigenous and Modern Perspectives on Tribal Initiation Rites: Education according to Plato' in M. W. Padilla, ed. *Rites of Passage in Ancient Greece: Literature, Religion, Society*, 278–312. London and Toronto.

Cardeña, E. and S. Krippner. 2010. 'The Cultural Context of Hypnosis', in S. J. Lynn, J. W. Rhue, and I. Kirsch, eds. *Handbook of Clinical Hypnosis*, 743–771. Washington, DC.

Clark, R. J. 1968. 'Trophonios: The Manner of His Revelation', *Transactions of the American Philological Association* 99: 63–75.

1979. *Catabasis: Vergil and the Wisdom-Tradition*. Amsterdam.

Clinton, K. 1974. *The Sacred Officials of the Eleusinian Mysteries*. Philadelphia, PA.

Corlu, A. 1970. *Plutarque, le démon de Socrate. Texte et traduction avec une introduction et des notes*. Paris.

Delcourt, M. 1982. *Héphaistos, ou la légende du magicien*. Paris.

Dillon, M. 1997. *Pilgrims and Pilgrimage in Ancient Greece*. London.

Dodd, D. B. and C. A. Faraone, eds. 2003. *Initiation in Ancient Greek Rituals and Narratives*. London and New York, NY.

Drab, K. 1981. 'The Tunnel Experience: Reality or Hallucination?', *Anabiosis: The Journal of Near-Death Studies* 1: 126–152.
Edelstein, L. and E. J. Edelstein. 1948. *Asclepius*. Baltimore, MD.
Ekroth, G. and I. Nilsson, eds. 2018. *Round Trip to Hades in the Eastern Mediterranean Tradition. Visits to the Underworld from Antiquity to Byzantium*. Leiden.
Farthing, G. W. 1992. *The Psychology of Consciousness*. Englewood Cliffs, NJ.
Friese, W. 2010. *Den Göttern so nah. Architektur und Topographie griechischer Orakelheiligtümer*. Stuttgart.
Gabbard, G. O. and S. W. Twemlow. 1984. *With the Eyes of the Mind: An Empirical Analysis of Out-of-Body States*. New York, NY.
Garland, R. 1985. *The Greek Way of Death*. London.
Geels, A. 1982. 'Mystical Experience and the Emergence of Creativity', in N. G. Holm, ed. *Religious Ecstasy*, 27–62. Stockholm.
Graf, F. and S. I. Johnston. 2013. *Ritual Texts for the Afterlife: Orpheus and the Bacchic Gold Tablets*. London and New York, NY.
Hoffmann, H. 1997. *Sotades. Symbols of Immortality on Greek Vases*. Oxford.
Kaptchuk, T. J. 2002. 'The Placebo Effect in Alternative Medicine: Can the Performance of a Healing Ritual Have Clinical Significance?', *Annals of Internal Medicine* 136(11): 817–825.
Leclerc, Y. 2015. 'Les chemins de la catabase. Paysages des dieux, paysages des hommes', *Les Études Classiques* 83: 155–174.
Lex, B. W. 1979. 'The Neurobiology of Ritual Trance', in E. D'Aquili, C. D. Laughlin, and J. McManus, eds. *The Spectrum of Ritual*, 117–151. New York, NY.
Macías Otero, S. N. 2015. 'On the Threshold of Hades: Necromancy and *Nékyia* in Some Passages of Greek Tragedy', *Les Études Classiques* 83: 137–153.
Maehler, H. 1984–1989. *Pindari Carmina cum Fragmentis*. Leipzig.
Metzinger, T. 2005. 'Out-of-Body Experiences As the Origin of the Concept of a "Soul"', *Mind and Matter* 3(1): 57–84.
Obbink, D. 2011. 'Poetry and Performance in the Orphic Gold Leaves', in R. E. Edmonds, ed. *The "Orphic" Gold Tablets and the Greek Religion*, 291–309. Cambridge.
Ogden, D. 2001. *Greek and Roman Necromancy*. Princeton, NJ.
    2015. 'Katábasis and the Serpent', *Les Études Classiques* 83: 193–210.
Panagiotidou, O. 2014. 'The Asklepios Cult: Where Brains, Minds and Bodies Interact with the World Creating New Realities', *Journal of Cognitive Historiography* 1(1): 14–23.
Quaglia, R. 2000. 'Il Trophonios di Cratino', *Maia* 52(3): 455–466.
Raz, A. 2007. 'Hypnobo: Perspectives on Hypnosis and Placebo', *American Journal of Clinical Hypnosis* 50(1): 29–R36.
Rosenberger, V. 2001. *Griechische Orakel. Eine Kulturgeschichte*. Darmstadt.
Rouget, G. 1990. *La Musique et la Trance*. Paris.

Rutherford, I. 2013. *State Pilgrims and Sacred Observers in Ancient Greece*. Cambridge.
Sandbach, F. H. 1967. *Moralia* Vol. 7. Leipzig.
Schachter, A. 1967. 'A Boeotian Cult Type', *Bulletin of the Institute of Classical Studies* 14: 1–16.
1981–1994. *Cults of Boeotia*. London.
1984. 'A Consultation of Trophonios (*IG* 7.4136)', *American Journal of Philology* 105: 258–270.
Schjødt, J. P. 1986. 'Initiation and the Classification of Rituals', *Temenos* 22: 93–108.
Schjødt, U. 2019. 'Predictive Coding in the Study of Religion: A Believer's Testimony', in A. Klostergaard Petersen, I. S. Gilhus, L. H. Martin, J. S. Jensen, and J. Sørensen, eds. *Evolution, Cognition, and the History of Religion: A New Synthesis*, 364–379. Leiden.
Schjødt, U. and J. S. Jensen. 2018. 'Depletion and Deprivation: Social Functional Pathways to a Shared Metacognition', in J. Proust and M. Fortier, eds. *Metacognitive Diversity: An Interdisciplinary Approach*, 319–342. Oxford.
Schjoedt, U., J. Sørensen, K. L. Nielbo, D. Xygalatas, P. Mitkidis, and J. Bulbulia. 2013. 'Cognitive Resource Depletion in Religious Interactions', *Religion, Brain & Behavior* 3(1): 39–55.
Segal, C. 1990. 'Dionysus and the Gold Tablets from Pelinna', *Greek, Roman and Byzantine Studies* 31(4): 411–419.
Shanon, B. 2002. *The Antipodes of the Mind. Charting the Phenomenology of the Ayahuasca Experience*. Oxford.
Shariff, A. F., A. K. Willard, T. Andersen, and A. Norenzayan, 2016. 'Religious Priming: A Meta-analysis with a Focus on Prosociality', *Personality and Social Psychology Review* 20(1): 27–48.
Shiv, B., Z. Carmon, and D. Arieli 2005. 'Placebo Effects of Marketing Actions: Consumers May Get What They Pay For', *Journal of Marketing Research* 42: 383–393.
Siegel, R. K. 1980. 'The Psychology of Life after Death', *American Psychologist* 35 (10): 911–931.
Siegel, R. K. and M. E. Jarvik. 1975. 'Drug-induced Hallucinations in Animals and Man', in R. K. Siegel and L. J. West, eds. *Hallucinations: Behaviour, Experience, and Theory*, 81–161. New York, NY.
Sliwinski, J. and G. R. Elkins 2013. 'Enhancing Placebo Effects: Insights from Social Psychology', *American Journal of Clinical Hypnosis* 55(3): 236–248.
Turcan, R. 1998. 'Initiation', in E. Dassmann, ed. *Reallexikon für Antike und Christentum 18*: 87–159. Stuttgart.
Ustinova, Y. 2002. '"Either a Daimon, or A Hero, or Perhaps a God": Mythical Residents of Subterranean Chambers', *Kernos* 15: 267–288.
2009. *Caves and the Ancient Greek Mind. Descending Underground in the Search for Ultimate Truth*. Oxford.

2012. 'Madness into Memory: *Mania* and *Mnêmê* in Greek Culture', *Scripta Classica Israelica* 31: 109–132.
2013. 'To Live in Joy and Die with Hope: Experiential Aspects of Ancient Greek Mystery Rites', *Bulletin of the Institute of Classical Studies* 56(2): 105–123.
2018. *Divine Mania. Alteration of Consciousness in Ancient Greece*. London.

Wehrli, F. 1944–1969. *Die Schule des Aristoteles*. Basel.

PART II

Representation

CHAPTER 3

Ancient Greek Smellscapes and Divine Fragrances
Anthropomorphizing the Gods in Ancient Greek Culture

Esther Eidinow

Introduction: Sensing Divinity

Both classicists and researchers in the cognitive science of religion have commented on the distinctively anthropomorphic nature of Greek gods; from Martin Nilsson, who observed (in 1925) how 'Anthropomorphism is the distinguishing mark of Homer and all later Greek religion', to Pascal Boyer, who more recently noted that 'the Greek gods were extraordinarily anthropomorphic, and Greek mythology really is like modern soap-opera, much more so than other religious systems'.[1] But while this may be their distinctive characterization – scholarship has asserted that across the extant corpus of ancient Greek divine representations, those that are other than human are remarkably rare, especially in comparison with representations of gods in other cultures[2] – in fact, as this chapter sets out, the picture is more complex. Greek gods were represented and worshipped both in, and moving between, a multitude of forms. Indeed, it has been suggested by Richard Gordon that this variability was one reason why the Greeks anthropomorphized their divinities in their artistic representations of them, in order to create, like a dictionary, an illusion of coherence, some 'settled significations' for entities that were otherwise constantly in flux.[3]

This chapter sets out to explore this complexity, examining the ways that Greek gods were perceived as anthropomorphic (in the next section, 'Divine Appearances') and positing why and how these perceptions may have developed in relation to specific cultural forms such as narrative ('Forming God Concepts'). By drawing on the theory of situated conceptualization, within the framework of grounded cognition (as developed by Lawrence Barsalou), it aims to explore how the mind, body, and physical and social environments were inextricably linked in shaping god concepts

---

[1] Nilsson 1925: 142, Boyer 2002: 162.   [2] Buxton 2009: 189.   [3] Gordon 1979: 13.

in ancient Greek culture ('Grounding the Greek Gods').[4] Examining both narrative as a cultural form, and narratives that described or alluded to other cultural forms, including ritual activities, it will investigate how descriptions of smell and smelling could evoke, and in turn shape, experiences of a divine presence for their audience (in the sections, 'The Smell of the Divine', 'Divine Smellscapes', and 'Divinities Smelling'). Such an approach, it argues, allows for cultural, group, and individual variation within the constraints of shared cultural forms, illuminating how ancient Greek conceptions of the gods became embedded, while at the same time allowing for the variety of a polytheistic culture, and, in addition, the personal response of individuals ('Divine Smells and Embodied Religion'). As such, I hope that this discussion may also contribute to explorations of belief in ancient Greek cultures, by offering some suggestions for the ways in which concepts of the divine may have been formed, shared, personalized, embodied, and embedded within, across, and between communities.

Divine Appearances

In his account of the 'remaking' of the statue of the Black Demeter of Phigalia, Pausanias reports that the commissioned artist, Onatas, who was to 'remake' the horse-headed *agalma* or 'statue' after the original was destroyed by fire, took as his model a picture of a copy of that original: the goddess would be represented in an image that was already familiar, at least to the local community.[5] But this story also introduces a thread of ambiguity: Pausanias notes that 'it is said' that Onatas' most important inspiration was the sight of the goddess in dreams. This addition introduces the possibility that the appearance of the goddess was distinct from her previous artistic representations. Whether this is intended to be a confirmation of the original artwork's veracity or not is unclear, nor is it certain whether what Onatas saw was understood as being a subjective view or an objective image.[6] While acknowledging the role of tradition in the creation of a divine image, Pausanias' narrative draws attention to the

---

[4] This chapter follows Barsalou et al. 2005 in arguing that (at least some) religious knowledge, like mundane knowledge, is 'embodied' knowledge, where (p. 24) 'embodiment refers generally to the entire physical context of cognition, including not just bodily states, but also modality-specific systems and environmental situations'. In later publications (Barsalou 2016) he draws a distinction between embodied and grounded cognition. The approach of this essay thus differs from some current ancient historical research, which has tended to privilege mind *or* body as its focus, for example, by distinguishing sensory from cognitive approaches.

[5] Paus. 8.42.7.   [6] Cf. Platt (2011: 272).

fluidity of divine appearance, and keeps open the possibility of there being, under all this, a separate, 'real' divine appearance.

This idea of several possible appearances – and some kind of underlying reality – is a common topos of ancient literature, expressed as early as Homeric epic, where gods are described as appearing 'in the form of' various mortal shapes: for example, the goddess Athena may look like a familiar friend (the old man Mentor) or take on the appearance of a 'tall, handsome and accomplished woman'.[7] Indeed, a difficulty that mortal characters frequently face in the Homeric epics is knowing to whom exactly they are talking. As a suitor says to Antinous, reproving him for his assault on the visitor that, ironically, through divine intervention, no one has yet recognized as Odysseus: ' ... you did wrong to strike this unfortunate beggar – to your cost, if he turns out to be a god from heaven. Yes, the gods do take the form of strangers from other lands, any shape they wish, and they go about the world to observe both men's violence and their fair dealing.'[8]

In such cases, outward forms may at first sight appear familiar, but, at the same time, there are clues that all is not as it seems: these figures are taller, more radiant, more beautiful, and they smell extraordinarily fragrant (an aspect on which this chapter will focus). Moreover, these human forms may only be a brief stop in a kaleidoscope of divine shape-shifting: for example, the *Homeric Hymn to Apollo* demonstrates serial metamorphoses by the god Apollo, who is described as taking on the form of a dolphin and a star, as well as a youth.[9]

Evidence demonstrates that this shape-shifting nature was not simply a literary confection. Some gods were worshipped in animal form: for example, Zeus Meilichius, and perhaps Zeus Ctesius, could be anguipedes; Black Demeter at Phigalia was horse-headed (the head accompanied by other beasts); at Elis, Sosipolis was worshipped because of his transformation into a snake.[10] Aniconic representations add a further layer of convolution: examples include the famous cultic rock that represented the goddess Aphrodite in Paphos, Cyprus.[11] Whether or not an object was

---

[7] E.g. *Od.* 13.288, and 16.157; the key Greek term is *eïkto*, 'had the appearance of, looked like'. Mentor: Hom. *Od.* 2.268; a woman: Hom. *Od.* 16.157–160 and 20.30–31. See also discussion Buxton 2009: 29–47.
[8] Hom. *Od.* 17.483–487 (trans. Hammond 2000).
[9] *Hom. Hymn Apollo* 3.400 (dolphin), 440 (star), 450 (man).
[10] Zeus Ctesius: Nilsson 1908. Meilichius: Picard 1943. Demeter: Paus. 8.42.4; Sosipolis: Paus. 6.20.2 and 6.25.4.
[11] This rock – a meteorite – is in the Cyprus museum, Nicosia.

considered itself to be a manifestation of a god or simply represented the possibility of divine power remains unclear, for both figural and non-figural examples.[12]

This already indistinct line is further blurred if we remember that there were also objects that required reverence, such as the spear in Chaeronea, Boeotia, which received sacrifices every day, according to Pausanias.[13] The problem of the question of a divine presence is thus multiplied: how are we to regard Theophrastus' *Superstitious Man*, anointing the stones at the crossroads with oil, and falling on his knees in reverence before them?[14] This vignette may mock worshipful behaviours taken to ridiculous conclusions; nevertheless, it also illustrates the potentially pervasive – and malleable – presence of the divine, occurring as objects that seem to assert 'the limits of anthropomorphism'.[15]

Further limits emerge if we delve deeper into epiphanies of the gods: as Françoise Frontisi-Ducroux has argued, in discussion of Homeric epiphanies, not only the appearance of the god, but also his or her disappearance may become a signal of divinity – and similar patterns occur in accounts of 'historical' epiphanies.[16] Often arising in moments of crisis, such epiphanies are frequently straightforward appearances of the gods in human form as discussed above.[17] As an example, a common context of crisis was battle, in which, as illustrated by the stories of epiphanies during the battles of the Persian wars, gods and heroes were said to appear in human fighting form.[18] Such figures, stories relate, appeared suddenly – and, often, just as suddenly disappeared – as Pausanias describes of Echetleus at the battle of Marathon.[19] Herodotus provides a distinctive version of one of these stories: in his account, the supernatural figure is fighting on the non-Greek side, and it is not the figure that disappears, but the soldier (Epizelus) who has seen him who goes blind.[20]

But other battle descriptions are less specific: for example, Pausanias is silent about what it was that the Mantineans saw that made them think

---

[12] Gaifman 2012 compellingly demonstrates. [13] Paus. 9.40.11–12.
[14] Theophr. *Char.* 16. 5–6. [15] See Gaifman 2012: 169–175; 308.
[16] Frontisi-Ducroux 2003: 90–91: she argues that disappearance is about the inability of humans to see the gods. On epiphany, see also Budelmann, Chapter 4, and McGlashan, Chapter 6, in this volume.
[17] Petridou 2015: 18 describes the 'epiphanic schema' in which epiphanies are prompted by a crisis, which they then help to resolve.
[18] E.g. Hdt. 8.38–39 and 84.2; Paus. 1.15.3 and 1.32.4, Plut. *Thes.* 36.8. [19] Paus. 1.32.5.
[20] Hdt. 6.117. Described as a case of post-traumatic stress disorder by Tritle 2000: 64; discussed alongside other examples of battle epiphany adduced by Herodotus in Hornblower and Pelling 2017: 260–261 (ad 117).

Poseidon was present.[21] It is possible that he felt no need to give details because the narrative pattern was so common that the god's human form was implied. Further examples, however, suggest that a god need not have been present at all: in addition to appearance and disappearance, we can also add non-appearance as a signal of divinity.[22] In one illustrative episode, Herodotus describes how, after an attack on Delphi by the Persians, the presence of the divine was seen in the sacred arms outside the shrine, thunderbolts, a very noisy rockfall, and, finally, a shout and cry of triumph from within the temple of Athena.[23] More generally, an attack of plague or some other environmental danger was often taken to signal divine anger: a manifestation of the divine, if not a direct epiphanic event.[24]

A divine presence could also be traced through phenomena even less tangible, for example, by means of an individual's affective response to the presence of the divine. This might include awe or reverence;[25] but evidence for such an experience could also be traced through other changes in individual affect. These could be observed in oneself: for example, in Plato's *Phaedrus*, we note Socrates' sense that there is something 'supernatural' happening to him; he invokes the nymphs as he observes his enjoyment of his rustic surrounding by the river Ilissus.[26] Alternatively, or in addition, it could be observed by others: as Xenophon says in the *Symposium*, in discussion of those who are in love, 'all who are under the influence of any of the gods seem well worth gazing at'.[27] The idea that one could feel the presence of a divinity is adduced for the foundation of shrines to the nymphs – Odysseus' cave on Ithaca provides, perhaps, the earliest example.[28] In turn, a negative impression of a landscape as gloomy or threatening may explain why some particular locations seemed appropriate for the establishment of necromantic shrines.[29]

In consideration of these examples, we have moved from physical representations of the divine, through environmental phenomena, to a simple 'awareness', *a sense*, of the divine. Should the variability of the representation of the gods in the ancient world concern us? Henk Versnel suggests not. He notes how the powers of the gods appear or disappear according to the literary context: 'The only thing [the gods] need to do is

---

[21] Paus. 8.10.8–10. [22] Buxton 2009: 32–33, 35–37.
[23] Attack on Delphi: Hdt 8.37.1–8.38.1; whether this was the same in Pausanias' report of the destruction of the Gauls at Delphi by a god and demons is left unclear (8.10.9).
[24] Examples are too numerous to mention, but there is an illustrative example of a question on the subject from Dodona: see Eidinow 2013: 351 (appendix 1, no. 12).
[25] *Hom. Hymn Dem.* (188–190) or that to Aphrodite (82–91).
[26] Pl. *Phdr.* 229A-B and 238C. This sense of a presence may be one explanation for the inclusion of the names of gods among those inscribed on rocks at Thera; cf. Gaifman 2012: 136–157.
[27] Xen. *Symp.* 1.10. [28] Hom. *Od.* 13.347–348. [29] Paus. 1.17.5.

cross over to a different kind of discourse, a different representation or a different perspective.'[30] Any inconsistencies were taken care of by what he calls that 'elegant winking process' that enabled the Greek mind to keep conflicting perceptions 'deftly apart'.

As we will see, certain research on modern approaches to god concepts provides some useful parallels to this analysis and may support further understanding of the ways in which the human mind processes such inconsistencies. But I would also argue that the presence of conflicting perceptions is informative in and of itself. The range of examples considered up to this point indicates that while the physical form of the god is certainly of significance, so is its variability and the fluidity of its representation, which Greek art and literature continually evokes. These phenomena offer a rich polysemous discourse of insights into the perceived ontology of the gods, pointing to a profound, essential ambiguity not only about the form and nature of the gods themselves, but also of their perceived relationship with mortals. In this context, and relevant to the topic of this chapter, the range of examples considered above has also broadened the theme of anthropomorphism, taking us beyond representation in a human form to the depiction of other key characteristics of the human; I turn to this aspect next.

Forming God Concepts

Cognitive approaches to anthropomorphism have explored the question of the use of the human form: Stewart Guthrie argued that anthropomorphism is an 'involuntary, perceptual strategy' of human beings.[31] More recent research suggests that the tendency to give imagined agents (not only gods, but also aliens) physical bodies could be attributable to the fact that people's own bodies 'are so central in their own cognition'.[32] The addition of extraordinary, non-human powers – the ability to shift shape or to walk through walls – may then make religious concepts more memorable and more easily transmissible.[33] As we have seen, however, the

---

[30] Here and below, Versnel 2011: 438.
[31] Guthrie 1995; criticized for lack of empirical evidence in Johnson et al. 2013. Van Leeuwen and van Elk (2019) discuss the lack of connection between Guthrie's account of perceptual experiences and longer standing supernatural beliefs.
[32] Barsalou et al. 2005: 42–43, citing for the aliens Finke, Ward, and Smith 1992.
[33] These are 'minimally counterintuitive' (MCI) features; see also Sandwell, Chapter 11, in this volume. MCI theory has not been clearly formulated and has been variously criticized, see Purzycki and Willard 2016. Recent research indicates that other forms of cultural learning may be required to reinforce the valence of MCI features; for them to become memorable, they may need to change or be updated in response to specific expectations and experiences.

representations of the Greek gods took a variety of forms: significantly, even those representations of the gods in other than human shape still gave them human processes of cognition. This is not uncommon across time or place: as cognitive theorists have observed, it is not simply that humans attribute human features in general to gods and spirits; it is that we attribute minds to them. As Pascal Boyer has argued, 'the only feature of humans that is always projected onto supernatural beings is the mind'.[34]

The capacity to attribute mental states to others (theory of mind) may account for the widespread tendency to assume supernatural entities have minds, and to attribute intentionality and agency to them, whatever form they take.[35] In what follows, however, I want to suggest that, perhaps, as part of that attribution of mind, other sensory features of human behaviour may be a significant part of this projection. While theologies may depict supernatural agents as superhuman, studies suggest that people attribute simpler and more human-like behaviours to them. For example, in a classic study by Barrett and Keil on anthropomorphism of god concepts, study subjects who professed (in a questionnaire) to a theologically accurate description of god, nevertheless imagined religious deities as exhibiting a range of human qualities. These included the need to use sensory information (without always being able to differentiate between competing sensory information), having a limited focus of attention, performing tasks serially, and existing in one location at a time.[36]

The study used processes of telling and listening to stories in order to 'tap into the God concepts that subjects use in their daily lives to make judgements in real time, rather than into their theological knowledge'.[37] The researchers suggested 'that people have at least two parallel God concepts that are used in different contexts, and these concepts may be fundamentally incompatible'.[38] They argued that it was the story context that prompted subjects to use their anthropomorphic, rather than theological, concepts of God. Barrett went on to argue elsewhere that this occurred because, under cognitive pressure, people find it easier to process a more basic concept.[39]

---

[34] Boyer, 2001: 163. In support of this, Barrett 2000, citing Avis and Harris 1991, Sperber 1996, and Walker 1992a and 1992b. Here I move my focus from what has been called imaginative anthropomorphism, the representation of imaginary and fictional characters as human-like, to interpretative anthropomorphism, which is when we attribute intentions, beliefs, and emotions to non-human agents, in particular animals; see Urquiza-Haas and Kotrschal 2015.

[35] Barrett and Keil (1996: 238–242, esp. 239–240); cf. McCauley and Lawson 2002: 24. See also Sandwell, Chapter 11, in this volume.

[36] Barrett and Keil 1996.   [37] Barrett and Keil 1996: quotation 223.

[38] Barrett and Keil 1996: quotation 240.

[39] Barrett and Keil 1996: 230. Barrett 1999: 338 for concepts under pressure.

Other theorists have placed more emphasis on the importance played in this experiment by narrative: for example, Peter Westh argues that humans are 'hyperactive storytellers'.[40] Rather than reverting to a simpler set of symbols, he suggests, people are in fact responding to the language of stories with whatever god concept best fits the textual and contextual cues, 'as a kind of abductive reasoning'.[41] Thus, certain cultural forms 'may act as cognitive and interactional frames facilitating specific conceptual structures over others' and, specifically, that narrative may be strongly linked to anthropomorphism.[42] In what follows I want to explore these ideas, investigating how certain ancient Greek cultural forms may have prompted specific god concepts, including not only narrative as a cultural form, but also narratives that describe or allude to other cultural forms, including ritual activities. To do this, I will build on and extend Westh's suggestions by drawing on a theory of situated conceptualization, within the framework of grounded cognition, as developed by Lawrence Barsalou.

Grounding the Greek Gods

Grounded cognition is a form of embodied cognition, but, it can be argued, it places greater emphasis on the role of the sensory-motor systems, and the physical and social environments.[43] This sets cognition as emerging in the context of these other domains; Barsalou argues that in this context it 'operates as a mediator between perception and action' rather than being 'an end in itself'.[44] While acknowledging that his approach is theoretical, Barsalou has suggested a framework for how this may work

---

[40] Westh 2014: 410.
[41] Westh 2014: 409. See Sandwell, Chapter 11 in this volume, for the work of Ilkka Pyysiäinen on this question.
[42] Westh 2014: 410, citing McCauley 2000: 78 and Fludernik 2003.
[43] Barsalou 2016: 14; also Barsalou et al. 2005: 21–24 and Barsalou 2008: 618. Grounded cognition may also be called '4e cognition' (see Barsalou 2020: 2). As summarized by Newen, Gallagher, and De Bruin 2018: 1–16, who recognize that (p. 4) 'there are continuing disagreements about a variety of issues within and among these embodied approaches', 4e cognition argues that cognition is i) embodied, that is, supported by all bodily states and systems; ii) embedded in its surroundings; iii) extended, so as to include both physical and immaterial tools; and, finally, iv) enactive – so that cognition is concerned not only with thinking, but with action and interactions. A useful summary of the crucial role of embodiment in the study of cognition can also be found in the introduction to Gibbs 2005. Its significance for the study of ritual in Kundtová Klocová and Geertz 2019.
[44] Barsalou 2020: 3–4. In explaining how that process works, Barsalou has recently posited the 'Situated Action Cycle', in which perception, cognition, action, environment, affect, and outcomes interact to form what he calls situational memories, underlying a series of memory patterns that can be used in similar future situations. As Barsalou notes (p. 5), this approach expands the perspective even of research on grounded cognition, which often does not take sufficient account of the larger context of affect, action, and outcomes.

that turns on what he calls pattern completion inferences with situated conceptualizations. This approach builds on widely researched, but still controversial, theories about the role of multimodal simulation in the processing of conceptual and semantic information.[45] It argues that when people experience a situation and process information, their sensory-motor processes and brain areas become active across different modalities (e.g. visual, auditory, motor, touch, affective, motivational states). Barsalou has argued that representations not only occur in actual experience, they are also partially captured during that experience and used later for conceptual representations, simulating entities and events in their absence.[46] Thus, when we encounter a particular element from a previous situation on another occasion, it may activate a situated conceptualization held in memory, producing inferences about what is likely to happen; this is part of our brain's reasoning process, which enables us to anticipate our response.[47] These so-called pattern completion inferences are expressed as simulations that re-enact brain-states from a previous experience, which may be affective or perceptual, for example; they also help to create and retrieve memories.

This is important not only for our responses to situations, but also for the way we form concepts. Situated conceptualizations mean that we do not just have isolated knowledge about, say, a pizza or a bicycle; instead, we aggregate information from situated conceptualizations associated with the categories of, on the one hand, pizza, and on the other hand, bicycles – and our knowledge grows continually as we experience new situations.[48] In this sense, a concept is 'a dynamical distributed system in the brain that represents a category in the environment or experience and that controls interactions with the category's instances'.[49] Importantly, for the purpose of this chapter, this process may support both representations of entities and events that a person has actually experienced, and, by combining them, also create novel entities.[50]

If we replace pizza above with the concept of god or of particular gods, this process may help to explain how god concepts are developed: each

---

[45] See Barsalou 2020: 7 for further references. [46] Barsalou et al. 2005: 22–23.
[47] Barsalou 2016: 19–20.
[48] Barsalou 2020: 5: going back to the broader cognitive environment outlined by the theory of grounded cognition, Barsalou has recently drawn attention to the need to frame these representations within the larger context of affect, action, and outcomes.
[49] Barsalou 2016: 11. See Barsalou 1999, and constraints on development of concepts, Simmons and Barsalou 2003, and Barsalou 2016: 12.
[50] Barsalou et al. 2005: 17.

individual accumulates information about a god (from across relevant interactions and experiences) to form a concept of that god, which becomes the basis of their interactions with gods in specific situations. Shared concepts of gods would arise from shared experiences, novel concepts of gods would then emerge from situations that provide new learning.[51] In each situation, embedded in its particular background setting, alongside other entities and actions, an experience of god would produce all kinds of inferences stored from previous experiences. Alongside autobiographical memories, these inferences could include tacit embodied knowledge about that god, expectations of the god's characteristics and how to interact with the god, and affective and perceptual responses.

As Barsalou emphasizes, any element of a situated conceptualization can activate it, and in what follows I want to focus in particular on the role of smell in activating situated conceptualizations and creating powerful simulated inferences, including emotional responses.[52] Modern western humans are surprisingly bad at describing smells, and our descriptive language in this area is remarkably limited.[53] Nevertheless, smell is a powerful modality: if we consider the semiotics of smell, we can see how smell is understood as demarcating a separate entity; it evokes an ambiguous quality – an allusion to an absent presence, evidence of a present absence – that eludes the other senses.[54] Odour can influence mood, cognition, and behaviour, often, it seems, by evoking memories that are experienced as highly emotional.[55]

A variety of analyses in this area highlight different types of perceptions of odour. Paul Rodaway, for example, distinguishes between 'generalized olfaction' and 'specialized olfaction'. The first is a perception that we tend passively to accept: it gives an imprecise sense of location but detailed qualitative information. We can relate this to Maria Larsson's discussion of olfactory memory, and the role of procedural memory, which underlies 'the acquisition of skills and other aspects of knowledge that are not directly accessible to consciousness'; this type of memory produces odour and taste aversions.[56] Rodaway's other type of smell, specialized olfaction, comprises 'discrete "episodes" or "events" of olfactory encounter' and

---

[51] To what extent that god became a shared cult would depend on the cultural context: see Eidinow, in press.
[52] Smell is briefly mentioned by Barsalou 2016: 23.   [53] Chastrette 2002, Yeshrun and Sobel 2010.
[54] Martin and Ringham 2006: 180.
[55] Herz 2002: 16 and 168. As research suggests, there seems to exist a strong link between smell, memories, and emotions, see Saive et al. 2014 and Herz 2016; see also Bowden, Chapter 1 in this volume.
[56] Larsson 2002: 232–233.

tends to lead us to 'exploratory behaviour ... excited by certain odours, intensities, associations or memories'.[57] In Larsson's typology, it relates to the process of recalling smells through episodic memory, which allows one to recollect 'personally experienced events'.[58] These analyses may relate not only to smells themselves, but also to odour-related words and metaphors, which may stimulate parts of the brain that not only extend into language processing areas but also reach the olfactory system.[59]

Building on these ideas, I want to suggest that smell as a modality may have been particularly powerful for evoking gods – not only smell as an experience, but also descriptions of smells. As a signal of a present absence, an absent presence, smell could signal the arrival of an entity whose actual form was unseen and unknown. It was also a crucial part of physical and social environments in which individuals encountered the divine in ancient Greek culture, and which individuals stored in memory. When it was re-encountered on different occasions – in reality or through narrative – it became a powerful cue for activating situated conceptualizations of the divine. In what follows, I start with narratives that describe the smell of a divinity. I then turn to some that depict the gods' own sense of smell.

The Smell of the Divine

I start with some smells that are emotionally powerful, but, or perhaps in part because, they lack descriptive detail. In the *Prometheus Vinctus*, Prometheus, bound to a rock, has no idea what creature may be approaching when he asks:[60]

> Hey, what is that?
> What sound, what scent (*odma*) has been wafted to me, unseen,
> from gods, from mortals, or from both together?
> Has someone come to this rock at the end of the world
> to be a spectator of my sufferings – or what do they want?

Prometheus' 'visitor' turns out to be the daughters of Ocean, who are, as the chorus, reassuringly humanoid and sympathetic; but the emotional

---

[57] Rodaway 1994: 115.   [58] Larsson 2002: 238–239, quotation 239.
[59] On the interaction between odour sensation and language see Rindisbacher 2015 and Schab and Crowder 1995. González et al. 2006, esp. p. 910 on how 'reading odour-related words elicits activation of olfactory brain regions'. Lee and Schwarz 2012: 745 note how 'metaphorically associated knowledge ... has behavioral, cognitive, and perceptual consequences', with a particular focus on smell.
[60] Aesch. *PV* 114–118.

relief is temporary, as the Oceanids describe the terrifying activities of Zeus, followed by Prometheus' account of the events that led to his punishment. In introducing the scene, Prometheus' attention to his own senses underlines for the audience his physical helplessness as 'the prisoner, the god in misery'.[61] The sounds and smells he describes with such terror evoke a threatening presence that looms over the scene that follows: Prometheus' enemy, Zeus. All the more menacing for its initial formlessness, this presence is slowly brought into focus – given a name and context – in the conversation that follows.

In contrast, in Euripides' *Hippolytus*, the dying Hippolytus immediately identifies the odour that announces the presence of Artemis, and responds with joy:[62]

> Hippolytus:
>   But what is this?
>   O breath of divine fragrance (*odmês*)! Though I am in misfortune
>   I feel your presence and my body's pain is lightened.
>   The goddess Artemis is in this place!
> Artemis:
>   Poor one, she is, dearest of gods to you.
> Hippolytus:
>   Do you see me, lady, see my wretched state?
> Artemis:
>   Yes, but the law forbids my shedding tears.
> Hippolytus:
>   No more do you have your huntsman and your servant!
> Artemis:
>   No, but though you die, I love you still.

Like Prometheus, Hippolytus is incapacitated and reduced to snuffing the air. In both cases, the performance of sensing smell is important in terms of the depiction of emotions and development of suspense. Here, the role of smell is evocative of the relationship between Hippolytus and his god, drawing him emotionally closer (it lightens his pain), while underlining the distance between mortal and god, a distance that is both physical and metaphysical. This divinity is present – at least as a voice, as well as a smell – but her form remains ambiguous. Hippolytus' body lies before us broken and dying, the goddess floats somewhere above him; she is forbidden to perform the human acts of shedding tears or comforting the dead. Her final words underline this distance:[63]

---

[61] Aesch. *PV* 119. [62] See Eur. *Hipp.* 1391–1398 (trans. here and below, Kovacs 1995).
[63] Eur. *Hipp.* 1435–1439.

> As for you, Hippolytus, I urge you not to hate your father. For the manner of your death has been fated. Farewell: it is not lawful for me to look upon the dead or to defile my sight with the last breath of the dying. And I see that you are already near that misfortune.

In these two examples, it is smell that initially and primarily evokes the powerful presence of a divinity. These smells are not described in any objective detail nor is a special term used: the unremarkable *odmê* is employed in both cases without additional description.[64] Instead, the emotional responses of the mortals who smell them provide the audience with the information needed to construct their understanding of the nature of the god. In both examples, smell is a marker of a physical presence that is never realized in human form; its absence alludes to both a physical and metaphysical distance between the mortal and divine worlds.

References to smell achieve something of the same effect in the *Homeric Hymn to Demeter*. When the goddess first appears in a mortal space, she is noticeably, visually different, although still difficult to distinguish from a well-born mortal (for Metaneira at least):

> Demeter stepped onto the
> threshold: her head reached to the rafter, and she filled the
> doorway with divine radiance.[65]

As she moves further into the mortal realm, and as she begins to be more physically active (e.g. her care of the baby Demophon), Demeter's smell begins to be described. It brings her physical presence closer to the audience of this poem, but at the same time it draws attention to what distinguishes her from mortals.

> With these words she took him into her fragrant (*thuôdei*) bosom and immortal arms, and his mother was delighted.[66]
> ... Demeter would anoint him with ambrosia, as if
> he were the son of a god, breathing her sweet breath over him as
> she held him in her bosom.[67]

As readers, we note how carefully the poem constructs what Vernant has called the 'superbody' of the gods; it is as if Demeter's divinity cannot be

---

[64] In Hippolytus' greeting to Artemis, the Greek for 'breath of divine fragrance' is, in Greek, literally, 'divine breath of smell'.
[65] Hom. *Hymn Dem.* 188–189 (trans. here and below West 2003).
[66] Hom. *Hymn Dem.* 231–232.   [67] Hom. *Hymn Dem.* 236–238.

contained.[68] Her fragrance, her breath, exhaled over Demophon, betrays her. Here, unlike the two previous examples, the description of her smell is perhaps more appropriate to, or evocative of, a divinity: her bosom is *thuôdes*, that is, it is redolent of incense. And, in her final revelation, that fragrant smell, like her physical attributes, is fully unleashed; her *odmê* is *imeroessa*, that is, it excites desire, and the association with incense is preserved in the description of her dress as *thuêentôn*.

> With these words the goddess changed her form and stature,
> thrusting old age away; beauty wafted all about her, a lovely
> fragrance (*odmê d'imeroessa*) spread from her scented (*thuêentôn*) dress, and a radiance shone afar
> from her immortal body; flaxen locks bestrewed her shoulders, and
> the sturdy house was filled with a brilliance as of lightning as she
> went out through the hall.[69]

This is not to say that mortals are not fragrant – in fact, Metaneira is also associated with a similar fragrance[70] – but this juxtaposition emphasizes the gap between mortal and divine bodies. Demeter's fragrance is powerful and somehow active, it signals her transformation, and it also has powers to transform others, even while she is disguised.

The implications of smell in god concepts in these three narratives are manifold: these divine figures are like us – they smell – and yet they are not like us. To smell is mundane, but the gods' smells are beyond ordinary, as are the emotions they provoke. In the first two examples, smell is a powerful modality that announces the presence of a god who is absent; the odours are sufficiently potent to prompt strong emotions – of very different kinds – in the mortals who sense them. In each case, this aspect of these gods alludes to a humanoid form: in the first instance, this expectation is met, since it precedes the appearance of the daughters of Ocean, who are also the chorus of the play; but in the second example, the expectation of a human form is generated, only to be denied by the goddess herself. Finally, in the *Homeric Hymn to Demeter*, the goddess's new and powerful smell is just one sign of her divine reality as she shifts from the form of an old woman to an anthropomorphic superbody that is far more than human.

---

[68] Vernant 1989.   [69] *Hom. Hymn Dem.* 275–281.
[70] For example, *Hom. Hymn Dem.* 242–251: 'Indeed she would have made him ageless and deathless, if in her folly fair-girt Metaneira had not waited for the night-time and spied from her fragrant (*thuôdeos*) chamber . . .'

In creating this description, it is also possible that another allusion is being brought to mind: the description of Demeter, in terms of a beautiful, majestic, and gleaming body could have recalled for its audience a statue of the goddess. If that is the case, then it may be that this description would have cued situated conceptualizations of experiences of ritual that involved such statuary; while the reference to fragrance may have recalled and cued experiences in which incense was burned. This possible allusion to a ritual setting introduces my next set of examples.

Divine Smellscapes

So far, the evocations of divine fragrance have given little information about what kind of smell it was. Hesiod provides a rare description of the smell of a god in his account of the rape of Europa:

> Zeus saw Phoenix's daughter Europa plucking flowers together with maidens in a meadow, and he was seized by desire for her. He came down and changed himself into a bull whose breath was saffron scented. Deceiving Europa in this way he let her mount him, and carrying her across the sea to Crete he mingled with her.[71]

Saffron is a mundane smell with a leathery, bitter aspect, but it may have had potentially powerful implications for the experience of the audience. To begin with, it was used as a perfume: in Aristophanes' *Clouds*, Strepsiades lists it as one of the sensuous, sophisticated characteristics of his wife.[72] There is clear evidence that it was also used as a dye, with specifically female associations: female divinities and nymphs are described as 'saffron-robed',[73] and literary evidence suggests that young women would dress in saffron robes for particular ritual events, including the famous ritual, the Brauronia, at the temple of Artemis in Brauron, in which young girls dressed as 'little bears'.[74] More specifically, the veils of young women at marriage may also have been saffron-dyed.[75] Research suggests that colour and odour can become related, according to their culturally specific meanings: the description of saffron in the abduction of Europa by Zeus could therefore have brought to mind such ritual

---

[71] Hes. fr. 140 (Most 2018).   [72] Ar. *Nub.* 51.   [73] Hom. *Od.* 15.250, Hes. *Theog.* 381.
[74] Ar. *Lys.* 645.
[75] Day 2011: 365 citing Llewellyn-Jones 2003: 224–225. Barber 1994: 162 suggests that it was used as a medicine for menstrual ills and its use as a dye may have been apotropaic, intended to turn these away ahead of time.

contexts – and the account of the divine could therefore have become both more vivid and more personally meaningful for some of its audience.[76]

Hesiod's allusion to saffron is an initial example of what I want to describe here as the evocation of a smellscape in a narrative, that is the foregrounding, through smell, of the physical and social environments in which individuals encountered the divine in ancient Greek culture, which may have evoked an experience of the divine. A vivid example of what I mean by this is the well-known description by Trygaeus of the smells of the goddess Peace in Aristophanes' play of that name:[77]

> Trygaeus:
> My Lady, Bestower of Grapes, how shall I express my greeting?
> Where can I get a ten-thousand-litre word to greet you with? I've
> got nothing that large of my own. Greetings, Holiday, and you too,
> Cornucopia. What a
> countenance you've got, dear goddess! And what an aroma (*hoion pneis*),
> how
> delightful to my heart, utterly luscious, with its hints of
> demobilization and perfume!
> Hermes:
> Not the same as you get from a soldier's knapsack, I take it?
> Trygaeus:
> I spit away an odious man's most odious bag![78] It smells of oniony
> vinegar belches [*krommuoxuregmias*], while she smells of harvest time,
> parties, festivals
> for Dionysus, pipes, tragedians, songs by Sophocles, thrush meat,
> Euripides' *bons mots* –
> Hermes:
> You'll regret telling that lie about her: she doesn't enjoy a composer
> of forensic phraselets.
> Trygaeus:
> – ivy, a wine strainer, bleating flocks, the bosoms of women
> scampering to the fields, a drunken slave girl, an upturned jug, and
> a host of other fine things!

This episode focuses clearly on the senses: it emphasizes both very specific odours (with Michael Silk we can note the 'carnival compound' of the initial smell of the soldier's knapsack, *krommuoxuregmias*, which he translates as 'indigeonionestion' – a combination of the English words onion and indigestion);[79] and settings evocative of smells. The 'characteristic discontinuities' (as Silk describes them) of the list of the smells of Peace

---

[76] Levitan et al. 2014.   [77] Ar. *Peace* 520–538 (trans. Henderson 1998).
[78] Eur. *Telephus* fr. 727, substituting 'bag' for 'child' as Henderson 1998, ad loc.
[79] Silk 2000: 301. The Greek is κρομμυοξυρεγμίας.

move the audience between different sensory experiences, between the concrete and the abstract, the mundane and the sacred.[80] Contrary to some analyses, I want to stress how these smells are not evocative of the goddess – or not simply so.[81] Rather, Trygaeus is describing, and in the process evoking, specific social and religious contexts: the smellscape of a Dionysian festival,[82] or, to borrow the term of Paul Rodaway, the 'sensuous geography' of such an event.[83]

Rodaway's exploration of odour is useful for this passage: the description of the soldier's knapsack evokes a rather generalized disgusting smell and has the additional quality (thanks to the compound construction of the term) of providing a physical and taste sensation as well. It stands in contrast to the mysterious sweet fragrance of the goddess, which, I would argue, is an example of a specialized olfaction. But it is not one particular smell. Indeed, it is particularly intriguing that in this initial description of the goddess's aroma, despite the English translation, in Greek no noun for smell is used. Trygaeus' perception of the goddess is rather phrased as a question (*hoion pneis* 'what kind of thing breathes/smells') in concert with a kaleidoscope of sensation words pertaining to the 'sensuous geography' of a community festival. For the audience of his play, the fragrance of the goddess, which Aristophanes' words conjured, was not a single mysterious odour but a familiar smellscape, likely to have cued situated conceptualizations of similar ritual experiences, and to have prompted relevant autobiographical memories and emotions.[84]

Divinities Smelling

So far, I have discussed the fragrances that gods diffuse, and we have seen how these odours may cue situated conceptualizations of previous ritual experiences. Much less frequently we find descriptions of the gods themselves performing the act of smelling. Again, I would argue that these scenes prompt the recollection of previous memories and cue situated conceptualizations of previous ritual experiences; but while we might expect the addition of such details to make a god seem more 'like us', the effect may be, I would argue, more complex. The first example is Herodotus' account of the response by Apollo to Croesus' so-called test of the oracles:[85]

---

[80] Silk 2000: 301.   [81] Thus, my analysis differs from that of Clements 2015: 57–59.
[82] For the term 'smellscape', see Porteous 1985.   [83] Rodaway 1994.
[84] These can perhaps be related to what Massumi has called microperceptions: each microperception is a bodily 're-cueing' that is usually unconscious and that creates a new affective response (see Massumi and McKim 2009): Trygaeus provides us with a list of these small shocks.
[85] Hdt. 1.47.3 (trans. Godley 1920). On its description as a test, see Eidinow 2019.

> I know the number of the grains of sand and the extent of the sea,
> And understand the mute and hear the voiceless.
> The smell (*odmê*) has come to my senses of a strong-shelled tortoise
> Boiling in a cauldron together with a lamb's flesh,
> Under which is bronze and over which is bronze.

This passage explores the divine omniscience of Apollo, revealing its sensory composition. The verb *oida*, translated here as 'I know', is the perfect form of *eidein*, 'to see'. The god proclaims his capacity to know detail (sand) and distance (the sea's measures); he boasts that he can hear the voiceless and understand what is senseless.[86] This description of his senses draws attention to the key characteristic of this god: his extraordinary perceptive powers. Paradoxically, this is achieved by some very human details, a paradox that is embodied in the person of the Pythia, a human possessed by a god. The focus of the oracle is the smell of Croesus' offering: the active noun is the smell itself, described as a substantive that reaches the senses (in Greek, the *phrenes*, the seat of the mental capacities). The audience is left unclear, presumably deliberately, as to whether these refer to the Pythia's senses or those of an anthropomorphized Apollo.

Turning to the description of the smells involved, it is possible that these would have prompted in the audience certain autobiographical memories, alongside other inferences, associated with similar religious experiences. The odour of boiling lamb was one that many in an ancient audience would recognize from sacrificial settings. The question of the significance of the tortoise meat, however, is more complex. It may be that it would be hard to distinguish the smell of tortoise flesh from the odour of boiling lamb, and the point of this passage was that Apollo's capacity to distinguish this smell demonstrated the extent to which his sense of smell (like all his senses) exceeded mortal faculties. But would Herodotus' audience consider the smell of tortoise flesh to have been an unusual smell? This detail is often assumed to be an addition to the passage that would have marked this sacrifice as 'other' in Greek eyes, indicating Croesus' 'barbarian' character.[87] It is possible, however, that the smell of boiling tortoise was familiar to some of Herodotus' audience: archaeological evidence suggests that tortoise may have been an ancient foodstuff,

---

[86] The imagery may have been proverbial: e.g. Pind. *Ol.* 2.95–100, 13.43–46. *Pyth.* 9.43–49.
[87] See Nagy 2013. https://chs.harvard.edu/read/nagy-gregory-the-ancient-greek-hero-in-24-hours/ Hour 15, n. 72.

while later literary sources indicate that boiled tortoise meat was considered to be medicinal.[88]

The choice of a tortoise – a *chelônê* – may also have had a further smell-related connotation: in the *Homeric Hymn to Hermes*, Hermes uses a *chelônê* to construct the first lyre, which he gives as a gift to Apollo with whom it then becomes identified.[89] In the poem, Hermes scrapes out the tortoise shell with an iron scoop,[90] but it is a more effective process to boil a tortoise, allowing the meat of the body to separate cleanly from the shell. In Herodotus' time, the boiling of a tortoise may well have been part of the process of creating Apollo's own instrument.[91] If so, and these associations were available for Herodotus' audience, then this particular sensory detail may have been both evocative of a divine smellscape and indicative of the Lydian king's close relationship with Apollo.[92]

My second example of gods doing the smelling returns to the *Homeric Hymn to Hermes*, in which the youthful eponymous god steals the cattle of Apollo, slaughters two, and cooks them. He proceeds to divide the meat up into twelve portions, and we are told how the smell of the meat tempts him – but he manages to resist.[93]

> Whereupon glorious Hermes craved his own
> due of meat, for the sweet smell tormented him, immortal though
> he was. Nevertheless his stout heart did not give way to his longing
> to let it pass down his holy throat.

At one level, the episode likely serves an aitiological purpose. Perhaps most persuasive is the idea that this may be related to images of Hermes in his role as *keryx* performing sacrifice to other divinities; the twelve portions suggest to Nicholas Richardson a likely *aition* for the cult of the Twelve Gods at Olympia.[94] But why include the detail about Hermes' response to the smell of the roasting meat? This question is especially apposite, since

---

[88] E.g. Plin. *HN* 32.14 and (citing Apollodorus) 32.15. Mikrakis 2013: 226 discusses evidence for the remains of tortoise shells that may be sacrificial or from ritual meals (Kalapodi, Bronze Age). Evidence for tortoise as a possible food source is either much earlier than the Classical period or from Roman sites: Heurtley and Hutchinson 1925: 45 note tortoise among the remains of animals in the settlement at Vardaroftsa in Mycenean and sub-Mycenean Macedonia and see also Archibald et al. 2013: 13 (Palaeolithic-Mesolithic, Kalamakia Cave, Laconia). Mackinnon 2007: 477 reports that Fiorelli (1873; *non vidi*) lists animals identified from excavations at Pompeii, including tortoise, deer, and wild boar, and complete skeletons of dogs, chickens, and horses; this does not mean that the animals were eaten as food, but the evidence of Pliny does suggest that they were kept for specialized use at least.
[89] *Hom. Hymn to Hermes* 475–477.   [90] *Hom. Hymn to Hermes* 41–42.
[91] West 1992: 56 and see Roberts 1981: 304.
[92] See discussion of these approaches in Eidinow 2019.
[93] *Hom. Hymn to Hermes* 130–133 (trans. West 2003).   [94] Richardson 2010: 23.

the sacrifice that Hermes prepares is in many, if not most ways, quite abnormal, perhaps particularly with regard to his choice to roast the meat (the gods' portion at a sacrifice is burnt, not roasted).[95]

One answer may be that Hermes' response was deliberately included here because it conveyed an experience of an extremely human response to sensory experience. The terminology is also used in Homer's *Odyssey* to describe oppressive smells or hunger[96] and it is probable that the audience of the poem would themselves have experienced something similar. That Hermes is tempted but does not partake may be a humorous reference to the idea that he has sacrificed to the twelve gods – of whom he is one – or, as Versnel has argued, it may be an allusion to Hermes' 'thoroughly human nature'.[97] Alternatively, it could also be meant to bring to mind the story of Prometheus' deception of the gods, looking back to a time when men and gods feasted with each other.[98] Whether any of these interpretations is correct, for an ancient audience, the description of the smell of roasting meat, and Hermes' physical response to it may have evoked a strong olfactory memory of their own, similar experiences as discussed above.

But what kind of god concept does this prompt? For all his anthropomorphic characteristics, Hermes refuses to succumb to simple human appetites. This description of the god in the act of smelling, while it may have suggested a being that was sympathetically humanoid in both his faculties and his temptations, also drew attention to the boundary between human and divine.[99]

Divine Smells and Embodied Religion

Theories of grounded cognition emphasize the importance of not only minds and bodies in human cognition, but also the physical and social environments in which humans perceive, cognize, and act. The theory of

---

[95] *Hom. Hymn to Hermes* 121–123. Versnel (2011: 309–373, esp. 372) argues that the apparent confusion created by Hermes' behaviour 'is a perfect mythical metaphor of the god's cultic status in everyday life'; cf. Jaillard (2007) who argues (pp. 114–118) that this sacrifice recalls later *trapezomata* and *theoxenia* (see Ekroth 2011: 21).

[96] Hom. *Od.* 4.441–442 (smell) and 12.332 and 369 (hunger), cf. Richardson ad loc.

[97] Allen and Sikes 1904 ad loc., Versnel 2011: 318; but see Peels 2016: 249, n. 284.

[98] As Peels (2016: 249) argues: 'we may interpret the sacrificial proceedings as a poetic play of the author who is looking back at the mythical events in the *Theogony*', specifically the time before 'Prometheus' deceitful "sacrifice", when humans and gods feasted together'.

[99] Deliberately problematized in Aristophanes' comedy the *Birds* (ll. 1515–1524) as a way of 'feeding' the gods. This can be taken as an example of a minimally counterintuitive feature (see above, n. 33).

situated conceptualization emphasizes this link with the environment, illuminating how our experiences of previous situations, held in memory as situated conceptualizations, can be cued by an element in our current situation and become active in shaping our understanding and response to it. I have used this idea to explore some possible responses to literary depictions of Greek gods, focusing on the element of smell – both divine fragrances and gods in the act of smelling – and argued that these may have activated for their audience a situated conceptualization with similar perceptual and conceptual content.

Looking at these texts in that light draws attention to the potential role of these descriptions of odours and the sense of smell in the development of ancient Greek conceptions of the gods. Some mention the extraordinary nature of a divine fragrance, giving little sensory detail, but marking in this way the power of the divine, and the affect it affords. Others give further information about the smell of a god, evoking the social/religious events associated with that divinity. Fewer narratives provide descriptions of the gods themselves in the process of smelling odours, but, as we have seen, these too offer information about the nature of the gods and their perceived relations with mortals. Because of their effect on the individual, I want to suggest, each of these literary descriptions could have helped to shape god concepts in ancient Greek culture, not only prompting memories of previous conceptualizations, but also helping to establish new conceptualizations.

Such a process may help to illuminate how ancient Greek 'belief' in the gods became embedded, while at the same time allowing for the variety of a polytheistic culture, and the personal response of individuals. As Barsalou has emphasized, situated conceptualizations vary from culture to culture, community to community, and person to person. Within the constraints of shared cultural forms, different experiences even of the same situations would result in individuals accumulating different sets of situated conceptualizations. Within a polytheistic culture, there was room for many of these to be expressed, for example, in personalized rituals (perhaps to be sold to others as offering distinct insights about the gods).[100] This depiction of an individualized, dynamic, and emergent cognitive process may provide a way of explaining the ongoing construction, including the variety, of ancient Greek concepts of divinity: imagining the gods comprised an elegant process of conceptualization that was both individual and shared, encompassing sensory, embodied, and mental domains, and inextricable from wider social and cultural contexts.

[100] Cf. Eidinow 2022.

BIBLIOGRAPHY

Allen, T. W. and E. E. Sikes. 1904. *The Homeric Hymns, Edited, with Preface, Apparatus Criticus, Notes, and Appendices*. London.

Archibald, Z., C. Morgan, D. M. Smith, H. Murphy-Smith, R. Pitt, C. Papadopoulou, F. Marchand, M. Haysom, A. Livarda, and D. Stewart. 2013. 'Archaeology in Greece 2013–2014', *Archaeological Reports* 60: 1–135.

Avis, J. and P. L. Harris. 1991. 'Belief–desire Reasoning among Baka Children: Evidence for a Universal Conception of Mind', *Child Development* 62: 460–467.

Barber, E. 1994. *Women's Work, The First 20,000 Years: Women, Cloth, and Society in Early Times*. New York, NY.

Barrett, J. L. 1999. 'Theological Correctness: Cognitive Constraint and the Study of Religion', *Method & Theory in the Study of Religion* 11: 325–339.

Barrett, J. L. 2000. 'Exploring the Natural Foundations of Religion', *Trends in Cognitive Sciences* 4: 29–34.

Barrett, J. L. and F. C. Keil. 1996. 'Conceptualizing a Nonnatural Entity: Anthropomorphism in God Concepts', *Cognitive Psychology* 31: 219–247.

Barsalou, L. W. 1999. 'Perceptual Symbol Systems', *Behavioral and Brain Sciences* 22: 577–660.

2003. 'Situated Simulation in the Human Conceptual System', *Language and Cognitive Processes* 18: 5–6, 513–562.

Barsalou, L. W., A. K. Barbey, W. K. Simmons, and A. Santos. 2005. 'Embodiment in Religious Knowledge', *Journal of Cognition and Culture* 5 (1–2): 14–57.

2008. 'Grounded Cognition', *Annual Review of Psychology* 59: 617–645.

2016. 'Situated Conceptualization: Theory and Applications', in Y. Coello and M. H. Fischer, eds. *Foundations of Embodied Cognition: Perceptual and Emotional Embodiment*, 11–37. London.

2020. 'Challenges and Opportunities for Grounding Cognition', *Journal of Cognition* 3(1): 31, 1–24.

Boyer, P. 2002. *Religion Explained: The Human Instincts That Fashion Gods, Spirits and Ancestors*. London.

2001. *Explaining Religion: The Evolutionary Origins of Religious Thought*. New York.

Buxton, R. 2009. *Forms of Astonishment: Greek Myths of Metamorphosis*. Oxford.

Campenni, C. E., E. J. Crawley, and M. E. Meier. 2004. 'Role of Suggestion in Odor-induced Mood Change', *Psychological Reports* 94: 1127–1136.

Caporael, L. R. and C. Heyes. 1997. 'Why Anthropomorphize? Folk Psychology and Other Stories', in R. W. Mitchell, N. S. Thompson, and H. L. Miles, eds. *Anthropomorphism, Anecdotes, and Animals*, 59–73. Albany, NY.

Carr, E., Kever, A., and Winkielman, P. 2018. Embodiment of Emotion and its Situated Nature', in A. Newen, L. De Bruin, and S. Gallagher, eds. *The Oxford Handbook of 4E Cognition*. Oxford. Retrieved 5 January 2020, from www.oxfordhandbooks.com/view/10.1093/oxfordhb/9780198735410.001.0001/oxfordhb-9780198735410-e-30.

Chastrette, M. 2002. 'Classification of Odors and Structure-Odor Relationships', in C. Rouby, B. Schaal, D. Dubois, R. Gervais, and A. Holley, eds. *Olfaction, Taste and Cognition*, 100–113. Cambridge.
Chen, D. and P. Dalton. 2005. 'The Effect of Emotion and Personality on Olfactory Perception', *Chemical Senses*, 30(4): 345–351.
Classen, C., D. Howes, and A. Synott. 1995. *Aroma – the Cultural History of Smell*. New York, NY.
Clements, A. 2015. 'Divine Scents and Presence', in M. Bradley, ed. *Smell and the Ancient Senses*, 46–59. London.
Day, J. 2011 'Crocuses in Context. A Diachronic Survey of the Crocus Motif in the Aegean Bronze Age', *Hesperia* 80: 337–379.
Dunbar R. I. M. 2003. 'The Social Brain: Mind, Language, and Society in Evolutionary Perspective', *Annual Review of Anthropology* 32(1): 163–181.
Eidinow, E. 2013. *Oracles, Curses, and Risk among the Ancient Greeks*. Oxford.
  2019. 'Testing the Oracle? On the Experience of (Multiple) Oracular Consultations', in L. G. Driediger-Murphy and E. Eidinow, eds. *Ancient Divination and Experience*, 44–67. Oxford.
  2022. 'The Problem of Relating to the Gods', in S. Deacy and E. Eidinow, eds. *Bulletin of Classical Studies*, special issue 'Problems with Greek Gods', 66(1).
Ekroth, G. 2011. 'Meat for the Gods', in V. Pirenne-Delforge and F. Prescendi, eds. *'Nourrir les dieux?': sacrifice et représentation du divin. Actes de la VIe rencontre du Groupe de recherche européen "Figura, représentation du divin dans les sociétés grecque et romaine" (Université de Liège, 23–24 octobre 2009)*. Kernos Suppl. 17, 15–41. Liège.
Finke, R. A., T. B. Ward, and S. M. Smith. 1992. *Creative Cognition: Theory, Research and Application*. Cambridge, MA.
Fiorelli, G. 1873. *Gli Scavi di Pompei dal 1861–1872*. Naples.
Fludernik, M. 2003. 'Natural Narratology and Cognitive Parameters', in D. Herman, ed. *Narrative Theory and the Cognitive Sciences*, 243–267, Stanford, CA.
Frontisi-Ducroux, F. 2003. L'Homme-cerf et la femme-araignée. *Figures grecques de la métamorphose*. Paris.
Gaifman, M. 2012. *Aniconism in Greek Antiquity. Oxford Studies in Ancient Culture and Representation*. Oxford.
Gervais, W. M., A. K. Willard, A. Norenzayan, and J. Henrich. 2011. 'The Cultural Transmission of Faith: Why Natural Intuitions and Memory Biases Are Necessary, but Insufficient, to Explain Religious Belief', *Religion* 41(1): 389–400.
Gibbs, R. ed. 2005. *'Introduction', in* Embodiment and Cognitive Science, 1–13. Cambridge.
Godley, A. G. 1920. *Herodotus: The Histories*. Cambridge, MA.
González, J., A. Barros-Loscertales, F. Pulvermüller, V. Meseguer, A. Sanjuán, V. Belloch, and C. Ávila. 2006. 'Reading Cinnamon Activates Olfactory Brain Regions', *NeuroImage* 32: 906–912.

Gordon, R. 1979. 'The Real and the Imaginary: Production and Religion in the Graeco-Roman World', *Art History* 2: 5–34.
Guthrie, S. E. 1995. *Faces in the Clouds: A New Theory of Religion*. Oxford.
Hammond, M. 2000. *Homer. The Odyssey*. London.
Henderson, J. 1998. *Aristophanes Volume II. Clouds. Wasps. Peace*. Cambridge, MA.
Herz, R. 2002. 'Influences of Odors on Mood and Affective Cognition', in C. Rouby, B. Schaal, D. Dubois, R. Gervais, and A. Holley, eds. *Olfaction, Taste and Cognition*, 160–177. Cambridge.
— 2016. 'The Role of Odor-Evoked Memory in Psychological and Physiological Health', *Brain Sciences* 6(3), 22: 1–13.
Heurtley, W. A., and R. W. Hutchinson. 1925. 'Report on Excavations at the Toumba and Tables of Vardaróftsa, Macedonia, 1925, 1926: Part I. The Toumba', *The Annual of the British School at Athens* 27: 1–66.
Hornblower, S. and C. Pelling, eds. 2017. *Herodotus. Histories Book 6*. Cambridge.
Jaillard, D. 2007. *Configurations d'Hermès. Une 'théogonie hermaïque'*, Kernos Suppl. 17. Liège.
Johnson, D. D. P., D. T. Blumstein, J. H. Fowler, and M. G. Haselton, 2013. 'The Evolution of Error: Error Management, Cognitive Constraints, and Adaptive Decision-Making Biases', *Trends in Ecology & Evolution* 28(8): 474–481.
Jones, W. H. S. and H. A. Ormerod. 1918. *Pausanias. Pausanias Description of Greece*. Cambridge, MA.
Kovacs, D. 1995. *Euripides. Children of Heracles. Hippolytus. Andromache. Hecuba*. Cambridge, MA.
Krusemark, E. A., L. R. Novak, D. R. Gitelman, and W. Li. 2013. 'When the Sense of Smell Meets Emotion: Anxiety-State-Dependent Olfactory Processing and Neural Circuitry Adaptation', *Journal of Neuroscience* 33(39): 15324–15332.
Kundtová Klocová, E. and A. W. Geertz. 2019. 'Ritual and Embodied Cognition', in R. Uro, J. J. Day, R. E. Demaris. and R. Roitto, eds. *The Oxford Handbook of Early Christian Ritual*, 74–94. Oxford.
Larsson, M. 2002. 'Odor Memory: A Memory Systems Approach', in C. Rouby, B. Schaal, D. Dubois, R. Gervais, and A. Holley, eds. *Olfaction, Taste, and Cognition*, 231–245. Cambridge.
Lee, S. W. and N. Schwarz. 2012. 'Bidirectionality, Mediation, and Moderation of Metaphorical Effects: The Embodiment of Social Suspicion and Fishy Smells', *Journal of Personality and Social Psychology* 103: 737–749.
Levitan C. A., J. Ren, A. T. Woods, S. Boesveldt, J. S. Chan, K J. McKenzie, M. Dodson, J. A. Levin, C. X. R. Leong, and J. J. F. van den Bosch. 2014. 'Cross-Cultural Color-Odor Associations', *PLOS ONE* 9(7): e101651.
Llewellyn-Jones, L. 2003. *Aphrodite's Tortoise: The Veiled Woman of Ancient Greece*. Swansea.
Mackinnon, M. 2007. 'Osteological Research in Classical Archaeology', *American Journal of Archaeology* 111(3): 473–504.

Martin, B. and F. Ringham. 2006. *Key Terms in Semiotics*. London.
Massumi, B. and J. McKim. 2009. 'Of Microperception and Micropolitics An Interview with Brian Massumi, 15 August 2008', *INFLeXions No. 3 – Micropolitics: Exploring Ethico-Aesthetics* (October 2009). www.inflexions.org/n3_massumihtml.html.
McCauley, R. 2000. 'The Naturalness of Religion and the Unnaturalness of Science', in R. Wilson and F. C. Keil, eds. *Explanation and Cognition*, 61–86. Cambridge.
McCauley, R. and T. Lawson. 2002. *Bringing Ritual to Mind: Psychological Foundations of Cultural Forms*. Cambridge.
Mikrakis, M. 2013. 'The Destruction of the Mycenaean Palaces and the Construction of the Epic World: Performative Perspectives', in J. Driessen, ed. *Destruction: Archaeological, Philological and Historical Perspectives [International Workshop, Centre d'Étude des Mondes Antiques, Louvain-la-Neuve, Belgium, 24-26 November 2011]*, 221–242. Louvain-la-Neuve.
Mithen, S. and P. Boyer. 1996. 'Anthropomorphism and the Evolution of Cognition', *Journal of the Royal Anthropological Institute* 2(4): 717–721.
Most, G. 2018. *Hesiod Volume II. The Shield. Catalogue of Women. Other Fragments*. Cambridge, MA.
Nagy, G. 2013. *The Ancient Greek Hero in 24 Hours*. Cambridge, MA. http://nrs.harvard.edu/urn-3:hul.ebook:CHS_NagyG.The_Ancient_Greek_Hero_in_24_Hours.2013.
Newen, A., S. Gallagher, and L. De Bruin. 2018. 'Introduction: 4E Cognition: Historical Roots, Key Concepts, and Central Issues', in A. Newen, L. De Bruin, and S. Gallagher, eds. *The Oxford Handbook of 4E Cognition*, 3–15. Oxford.
Nilsson, M. P. 1908. 'Schlangesnstele des Zeus Ktesios' *Athenische Mitteilungen* 33: 279–88 [repr. 1951]. *Opuscula selecta linguis Anglica, Francogallica, Germania conscripta vol. 1*, 25–34. Lund.
(trans. F. J. Fielden). 1925. *A History of Greek Religion*. Oxford.
Oosterwijk, S., S. Mackey, C. Wilson-Mendenhall, P. Winkielman, and M. P. Paulus. 2015. 'Concepts in Context: Processing Mental State Concepts with Internal or External Focus Involves Different Neural Systems', *Social Neuroscience* 10: 294–307.
Peels, S. 2016. *Hosios: A Semantic Study of Greek Piety*. Mnemosyne Suppl. 387. Leiden.
Petridou, G. 2015. *Divine Epiphany in Greek Literature and Culture*. Oxford.
Picard, C. 1943. 'Sanctuaires et representations et symboles de Zeus Meilichios', *Revue de l'Histoire de Religions* 126: 97–127.
Platt, V. 2011. *Facing the Gods: Epiphany and Representation in Graeco-Roman Art, Literature and Religion*. Cambridge.
Pollatos, O., R. Kopietz, J. Linn, J. Albrecht, V. Sakar, A. Anzinger, R. Schandry, and M. Wiesmann. 2007. 'Emotional Stimulation Alters Olfactory Sensitivity and Odor Judgment', *Chemical Senses* 32(6): 583–589.
Porteous, J. D. 1985. 'Smellscape', *Progress in Human Geography* 9(3): 356–378.

Purzycki, B. G. and A. K. Willard. 2016. 'MCI Theory: A Critical Discussion', *Religion, Brain & Behavior* 6(3): 207–248.

Richardson, N. J. 2010. *Three Homeric Hymns: To Apollo, Hermes, and Aphrodite*, Cambridge.

Rindisbacher, H. J. 2015. 'What's This Smell? Shifting Worlds of Olfactory Perception', *KulturPoetik* 15(1): 70–104.

Roberts, H. 1981. 'Reconstructing the Greek Tortoise-shell Lyre', *World Archaeology* 12: 3: 303–312.

Rodaway, P. 1994. *Sensuous Geographies: Body, Sense and Place*. New York, NY.

Russell, Y. I., and F. Gobet. 2013. 'What Is Counterintuitive? Religious Cognition and Natural Expectation', *Review of Philosophy and Psychology* 4 (4): 715–749.

Saive, A. L., J. P. Royet, and J. Plailly. 2014. 'A Review on the Neural Bases of Episodic Odor Memory: From Laboratory-based to Autobiographical Approaches', *Frontiers in Behavioral Neuroscience* 8, 240.

Schab, F. R. and R. G. Crowder, eds. 1995. *Memory for Odors*. Hillsdale, NJ.

Shapiro, L. 2011. *Embodied Cognition*. New York, NY.

Silk, M. S. 2000. 'Aristophanes versus the Rest: Comic Poetry in Old Comedy', in D. Harvey and J. Wilkins, eds. *The Rivals of Aristophanes: Studies in Athenian Old Comedy*, 299–315. London.

Simmons, W. K. and L. W. Barsalou. 2003. 'The Similarity-in-Topography Principle: Reconciling Theories of Conceptual Deficits', *Cognitive Neuropsychology* 20: 451–486.

Sperber, D. 1994. 'The Modularity of Thought and the Epidemiology of Representations', in L. A. Hirschfeld and S. A. Gelman, eds. *Mapping the Mind: Domain Specificity in Cognition and Culture*, 39–67. New York, NY.

———. 1996. *Explaining Culture: A Naturalistic Approach*. Oxford.

Tritle, L. A. 2000. *From Melos to My Lai: War and Survival*. London and New York, NY.

Urquiza-Haas, E. G. and K. Kotrschal. 2015. 'The Mind behind Anthropomorphic Thinking: Attribution of Mental States to Other Species', *Animal Behaviour* 109: 167–176.

Van Leeuwen, N. and M. van Elk. 2019. 'Seeking the Supernatural: The Interactive Religious Experience Model', *Religion, Brain & Behavior* 9(3): 221–251.

Vernant, J.-P. 1989. 'Dim Body, Dazzling Body', in M. Feher, ed. *Fragments for a History of the Human Body, Part One (Zone3)*, 18–47. New York, NY.

Versnel, H. 1987. 'Some Reflections on Greco-Roman Epiphany', in D. van der Plas, ed. *Effigies Dei: Chapters on the History of Religions*, 42–55. Leiden.

———. 2011. *Coping with the Gods: Wayward Readings in Greek Theology*. Leiden.

Walker, S. 1992a. 'Developmental Changes in the Representation of Word-Meaning: Cross-Cultural Findings', *British Journal of Developmental Psychology* 10: 285–299.

———. 1992b. 'Supernatural Beliefs, Natural Kinds and Conceptual Structure', *Memory and Cognition* 20: 655–662.

West, M. 1992. *Ancient Greek Music*. Oxford.
    2003. *Homeric Hymns. Homeric Apocrypha. Lives of Homer.* Cambridge, MA.
Westh, P. 2014. 'Anthropomorphism in God Concepts: The Role of Narrative', in A. W. Geertz, ed. *Origins of Religion, Cognition and Culture*, 396–413. Abingdon.
Willard, A. K., J. Henrich, and A. Norenzayan. 2016. 'Memory and Belief in the Transmission of Counterintuitive Content', *Human Nature* 27 (3): 221–243.
Wilson, A. and S. Golonka. 2013. 'Embodied Cognition Is Not What You Think It Is', *Frontiers in Psychology* 4: 58. https://doi.org/10.3389/fpsyg.2013.00058
Yeshrun, Y. and N. Sobel. 2010. 'An Odor Is Not Worth a Thousand Words: From Multidimensional Odors to Unidimensional Odor Objects', *Annual Review of Psychology* 61: 219–241.

CHAPTER 4

Belief, Make-Believe, and the Religious Imagination
The Case of the Deus Ex Machina *in Greek Tragedy*

Felix Budelmann

The foundational move of the cognitive science of religion is the adoption of a naturalist stance. Religion is examined as a psychological phenomenon, and religious beliefs and practices explained as a by-product of human mental predispositions. It is our cognitive make-up that leads us to detect agents, divine and otherwise, even where there are none, and makes us create, remember, and pass on 'minimally counterintuitive concepts' like that of the supernatural hero.[1] Hypotheses such as these have considerable explanatory force. At a transhistorical and transcultural level, they open our eyes to patterns that link different forms of religion and provide psychologically grounded explanations for these patterns. At the level of the particular religion in its particular time and place, they account for seemingly inexplicable or strange beliefs, encourage properly founded consideration of the intuitive and emotional appeal of religious practice, and enhance our understanding of synchronic phenomena by placing them against the backdrop of long, often evolutionary, timescales. Even though classicists have started to explore this approach only recently, its potential for the study of ancient religions is already beginning to become clear, and the field is likely to develop apace in the coming years.[2]

The challenge, however, when looking for cognitive models of religious *experience*, as this volume sets out to do, is to go beyond origins, causes, and biases, and to try to construct the broadest possible account of the religious imagination. The term 'imagination' appears frequently in the cognitive science of religion, but it usually describes a mental function that

---

I am grateful to Evert van Emde Boas, the participants in the *Cognitive Approaches to Ancient Religious Experience* workshop in London, the editors of this volume, and the anonymous readers for the Press, for helpful comments on earlier versions.

[1] For discussion of agency detection, see also McGlashan, Chapter 6, in this volume; for discussion of minimally counterintuitive concepts, see also Eidinow Chapter 3, and Sandwell, Chapter 11, in this volume.
[2] This volume itself is of course part of this development. Probably the most high-profile publication to date is Larson 2016; cf. Panagiotidou and Beck 2017, which is comparable in its methodology.

misleads us into (e.g.) imagining faces in the clouds rather than, as we require here, one that engages in imaginative visualization, productive counterfactual thinking, or artistic creativity. It is the desirability (as I see it) of developing a thicker account of the religious imagination that prompts two methodological choices made in this chapter.[3]

The first is to move beyond the well-rehearsed canon of psychological mechanisms that dominate research in the cognitive science of religion. Psychologists outside this field have long-standing and wide-ranging interests in the imagination, and many of those interests have the potential to expand our understanding of the religious imagination, not least so for a culture such as ancient Greece where religion suffused all aspects of life, mental and otherwise. The particular psychological capacity that I shall focus on in this chapter is the human propensity for make-believe – for consciously constructing and entering temporary imaginary worlds, be it as children by engaging in pretend-play or as adults by reading novels and going to the cinema or theatre.[4]

The second methodological choice is to put culture in the driver's seat: cultural and religious practices will be looked at not as driven by mental mechanisms but as exploiting those mental mechanisms to generate particular forms of experience.[5] The issue is in part rhetorical – everybody agrees that nature and culture operate in concert – but it seems to me that as interpreters of a particular culture we gain a fuller picture of that culture if we study individuals and communities as religious actors who in a meaningful way understand and shape what they think and do than if we treat them as wholly at the mercy of physiological mechanisms of which they are unaware. In so far as this position may seem to echo the concerns of historians and literary critics who are altogether wary of cognitive approaches (which at least in principle I am not), the point to emphasize is that we should certainly view those religious actors as drawing on, and indeed constrained by, mental capacities and predispositions when they individually and collectively shape religious practices, beliefs, and environments. However, this research agenda is most likely to have a broad impact, I believe, and most likely to be capable of productive interaction with 'traditional' work in classics, if it adopts a maximally capacious and

---

[3] Neither, it should be emphasized, is it unprecedented in the study of ancient religion. See in particular the work of Esther Eidinow (e.g. Eidinow 2015, 2016) and Peter T. Struck (Struck 2016).

[4] Pretend-play features as a part of an evolutionary account of the religious imagination in Lieberoth 2013.

[5] See also the Introduction to this volume.

generous account of the ancient Greek (and Roman) religious imagination, and one that looks to the whole range of disciplines interested in human cognition, rather than exclusively the cognitive science of religion with its diachronic and evolutionary priorities.

My particular subject in this chapter, the *deus ex machina* of Attic tragedy, is chosen as a case in point. Created by individual poets, the epiphanic stage deities of Euripides and his peers are very obviously the products of self-conscious artistry and thus call for a different set of approaches than, say, questions about the cross-cultural ubiquity of anthropomorphic gods.[6] At the same time, they are also a form of religious practice, and it is in order to do them justice as such that I will discuss them alongside enactments of divinity in more narrowly ritual contexts.

The first section ('Belief and Make-believe') draws on work in psychology and anthropology to set out a persistent characteristic of make-believe: from cinema-going and children's pretend-play to evangelical practices of conversing with God, most forms of make-believe intertwine self-conscious awareness of fictionality with emotional commitment. I suggest that a similarly complex experience, combining an understanding that the actors are human with a sense of divine presence, characterized divine performances in Greek antiquity. Because of the nature of our sources such an argument is inevitably speculative – for the *deus ex machina* specifically we have no testimony of audience response – but I hope that it is nevertheless suggestive and worthwhile. The second section ('Variation: *Deus Ex Machina* and Ritual Impersonation of the Divine Compared') asks how the *deus ex machina* compares in this respect to other, non-dramatic, practices of enacting divinity. The differences, it is suggested, are ones of degree rather than kind, and among the continuities, going back to the first section, is the importance of the worshippers' 'willing suspension of disbelief'. The third and final section ('Faith, Obedience, Trust') analyzes the text of the *deus* scenes and especially the human characters' responses. What is at stake in the dialogues between the *deus* and the characters is not just what the gods are like (their justice, authority, power, understanding, and so on), but also what relationships humans can form with them and what attitudes they should adopt towards them: in response to the *deus*' speech, the characters articulate their faith, compliance, and trust, and even undergo emotional transformation, despite all that is unsatisfactory in the deity's words and behaviour. Both externally, then, as a form of make-believe, and internally through their

---

[6] On these questions, see Eidinow, Chapter 3 in this volume.

dialogue, *deus ex machina* scenes pull systematically in two directions. The religious experience they enable is one in which there is room for belief as well as disbelief, faith as well as distrust, acceptance as well as distance.

Belief and Make-believe

Divine impersonation, like epiphany in general, is very obviously grounded in an anthropomorphic conception of the divine, and would therefore lend itself to analysis in terms of theory of mind, agency detection, and minimally counterintuitive concepts.[7] This chapter nevertheless takes a different approach and focuses, more specifically, on the feature that sets divine performances apart from other forms of anthropomorphic representation, such as myths and statues: the impersonation of a god by a human. The actor playing the *deus ex machina*, the priestesses involved in the 'sacred drama' of Kore and Persephone at Eleusis,[8] and (in a later period) the all-male Athenian *Iobakchoi*, who used sortition to distribute among themselves the roles of Dionysus, Kore, Palaemon, Aphrodite, and Proteurhythmos, all pretended to be something that they were not – deities.[9] Comparable practices, while by no means a routine feature of Greek rituals and festivals, are documented for various Greek cities.[10]

Discussion of the cognitive dimension of such divine enactments goes back to, and still often centres on, Herodotus' account of Pisistratus and Phye. When relaying how Pisistratus fitted out the human Phye as Athena for his processional entry into Athens, Herodotus famously complains that the allegedly clever Athenians should not have been taken in by what was blatant play-acting (Hdt.1.60). In view of the reasonably well-attested tactical use of staged battlefield epiphanies in later periods,[11] the possibility that Pisistratus did indeed aim to deceive cannot be dismissed out of hand, but the majority view now, going back to an influential 1987 article by W. R. Connor, is that Herodotus (in error or out of mischief) misrepresents what was going on.[12] Comparing Xenophon of Ephesus' description of a

---

[7] See Larson 2016: 67–73.
[8] If 'drama' is the right word: the evidence is uncertain. See Clinton 2004 and Petridou 2015: 265–266, with further references.
[9] *Iobakchoi*: *IG* II², 1368.121–127 (second century CE).
[10] The evidence for rituals enacting epiphanies (in many cases relatively late) is collected and discussed by Petridou 2015: 43–49. Many of them involve a single figure enacted by the deity's priest. See also below, p. 108.
[11] See Platt 2011: 14–20, Petridou 2015: 142–168.
[12] Connor 1987, quotations from pp. 44 and 46.

divine impersonation in a procession in honour of Artemis, Connor argued that the Athenians knowingly went along with Pisistratus' make-believe Athena: 'The crowds might have chosen to express coolness, disinterest or downright hostility. Instead, it appears that they delighted in the shared drama and let their enthusiasm be known.'

The suggestion that the Athenians played along rather than being outwitted has much going for it and must be at least part of the explanation. More difficult to decide, however, and arguably more important for the *deus ex machina* (whose nature as a pretend rather than real god was obvious to all), is how we should conceptualize the belief or disbelief involved in this playing along. Can we, in some way, say that the Athenians felt that they were worshipping Athena? Did they, in some way, feel that they were in the presence of a deity even though they knew that they were watching a costumed woman? Connor himself does not explicitly address such questions, but the language he uses is certainly not religious: to understand the Phye episode, he suggests, we need to 'enter into the playful and mimetic mentality of what Gerald Else has called "the histrionic period" of Greek history'. For a rather different view one might compare Rebecca Sinos, who, again on the basis of Xenophon's novel, argues that the play-acting will not always have been transparent and posits a rather less ludic mind-set: 'When they see this girl in costume they honor her as a goddess, as if the ritual transcends reality by the symbolic power of the procession. This must be the ideal and expected reaction to the ritual representation of a god. It suggests a blurring of the boundaries between actor and god, thus uniting mortals and gods, a goal of many rituals of worship.'[13]

This is hardly an area in which certainty is attainable, and in any case Jennifer Larson must be right to emphasize individual variation – differing 'degrees of openness to the symbolic statement', as she puts it[14] – but there is a general observation to be made, and one that opens out from Phye to other forms of divine enactment, including the *deus ex machina*: engagement with pretence can, at the same time, be characterized by both clear-headed awareness of the pretence and emotional investment. To understand better how this is so, I shall in the remainder of this section briefly compare work in other fields (child psychology, the study of narrative fiction, and the psychology and anthropology of religion); such

---

[13] Sinos 1993: 84. Recent treatments that broadly follow Connor include Petridou 2015: 147–170 and Larson 2016: 89–91; see also Koch Piettre 2018.
[14] Larson 2016: 90.

comparison cannot recover ancient Greek religious experience, but it helps us to set out parameters and possible patterns. My aims are generalizing in the first instance: this section will discuss the dynamic of emotional-commitment-cum-conscious-complicity in its relevance to all divine performance in Classical Greece; differences and similarities between 'ritual' and 'literary' performances will be the subject of the next section.

Pretend-play is the subject of an established research programme in developmental psychology. The first point that stands out with reference to the interests of this chapter is that – even where children are concerned – there is nothing naive about make-believe, and that pretend-play involves no loss of reality: a number of studies have shown that even young children take their knowledge of the real world with them into the make-believe world, and do not on the whole confuse the two. This view has been developed in particular by Paul L. Harris, who argues that make-believe is not an isolated capacity but enables essential functions such as counterfactual reasoning and the mental engagement with persons and things that are not currently seen.[15] In an argument that for classicists recalls the debate over whether Greeks of the Archaic period entertained concepts of fiction and myth, Harris positions himself against older assumptions, associated with Jean Piaget, according to which children retreat into fantasy worlds and lose their grasp of the fantasy/reality distinction when they engage in pretend-play. Any attempt to map modern child psychology neatly onto ancient make-believe in religious contexts is bound to go astray, but what we may usefully take away is a reminder that make-believe involves complicity and self-consciousness, and with this reminder a warning against assuming too readily naivety, confusion, or loss of reality.

Next, and coming as it were from the other end, there is the observation, familiar to every reader of novels and every cinema- or theatre-goer, that fiction has the power to move even if its status as fiction is well understood (as it usually is). Philosophers call this the 'paradox of fiction' and continue to debate its solution.[16] Is it that the emotions elicited by fiction are not real? Or is it possible to have real emotions in response to something that is not real? Or do we, in some relevant sense, get ourselves to believe that the fictional world is real? Whatever is the most promising way of tackling the paradox, the essential observation for our purposes here is simply that the experience of engagement with fiction supports the notion that it is perfectly possible for divine impersonators of all sorts to

---

[15] See most conveniently his monograph *The Work of the Imagination* (Harris 2000).
[16] For a recent overview with references see Friend 2016.

involve their audiences without deceiving them. Or, to put it differently, onlookers at Pisistratus' procession, participants in ritual divine enactments, and spectators watching a *deus ex machina* scene do not need to forget that they are watching a costumed human in order to find the display affecting.[17] The nature and strength of their response will depend on their individually and culturally varied attitudes, the particular context, and the nature of the performance (more on this in the next section) but the basic principle seems beyond doubt.

Crucially, the two modalities often operate in concert. Even though we are always conscious, at one level, that we are reading a book or watching a play, this awareness will only rarely interfere with our immersion in the fictional world. In fact, it is not just that, on the whole, we fail to perceive a tension between immersion and awareness, but it is this very 'double vision' that affords the kind of engagement that is characteristic of fictional narratives, not least so those of Greek tragedy. Spectators can allow themselves to be moved by Philoctetes' pain or be gripped by the lead-up to the murder of Agamemnon without having to run on stage to alleviate or prevent the suffering. Self-conscious make-believe and emotional involvement can form a package.[18]

In its own way, the same integrated dual response comes into its own in (modern) religious practice. In *When God Talks Back*, psychological anthropologist T. M. Luhrmann explores how evangelical Christians relate to God. A recurring theme in her study, which is the product of a sustained period as a participant-observer in a US church, is the value of pretence.[19] For evangelical Christians, maintaining belief is not a given but takes effort, and one dimension of this effort is a form of pretence. Members of the church teach themselves, alone and in groups, to talk to God like with a good friend, asking him about things large and small, and even laying a place for him at their dinner table. At the same time, they are perfectly aware that despite this practice of familiarity God does not have the same status as a real friend. (Luhrmann compares the attitude of young children who have an 'imaginary companion' that they talk to in their heads.)

This is itself suggestive, but Luhrmann goes further and observes that knowing pretence is not just a necessary staging-post on the road to belief

---

[17] For Phye a similar suggestion is made by Larson 2016: 90–91.
[18] The psychological dimension of this observation is expanded by Polvinen 2017.
[19] Luhrmann 2012, esp. 72–100, 320–322. Comparison with children's imaginary companions is made on pp. 79–80.

but becomes part of the experience of belief and of what God means to evangelical Christians. Here is an extract:[20]

> There was a sense of in-betweenness in these experiences of God. These congregants were clear that God was real, but they were not always clear that God was present in specific playlike practices the way they were pretending that he was. When I asked Stacy whether she believed that God was truly present when she imagined him in front of her, she said, "I can sit here and have a conversation with God as if he's in that chair. I know that I experience God. I know that I hear him. But how do I know that it's different than, you know, my imaginary friend Harold? I don't." The ambiguity simply became part of the nature of God.

The practice of imagining God as present and talking to me, which in the first instance is the effort necessary to form a relationship with him, ends up shaping the nature of religious experience. God inhabits a place in the imagination that is consciously created by the believer, yet, in a very specific way, real nevertheless.

Inward and often repeated, the routines of evangelical Christians can only ever provide a loose comparandum for the annual or occasional, but in any case infrequent, staged epiphanies of Classical Greece, be it the *deus ex machina*, the *Iobakchoi*, or the 'sacred drama' at Eleusis. In their different ways, divine impersonation in ancient Greece and faith practices in the United States in the early twenty-first century both intertwine self-conscious recourse to the imagination with emotional and cognitive arousal so as to create divine encounters. Both give the divine a presence that is consciously fictional but in its conscious fictionality has the potential to acquire a particular sense of reality.

For the divine performances of ancient Greece, two contextual considerations add flesh to the bone. The first is Verity Platt's observation that Graeco-Roman visual and textual representations of epiphanies tend to combine the manifestation of the god's presence with high levels of artificiality. For example, she writes as follows about votive reliefs:[21]

> First, they illustrate the mutually reinforcing relationship between deities and their visual representations.... Images ... can simultaneously symbolise and *constitute* divine presence.... Second, however, these votive reliefs demonstrate how a ready engagement with the phenomenological verities

---

[20] Luhrmann 2012: 95.
[21] Platt 2011: 47–49, similarly Platt 2015 and 2018. On epiphany in general see, apart from Platt's work: Versnel 1987, Koch Piettre 2001, Petridou 2015, and the articles in Marinatos and Shanzer 2004 and Petridou and Platt 2018. See also McGlashan, Chapter 6, and Eidinow, Chapter 3, in this volume.

of the divine in Greek culture existed side by side – and in constant dialogue – with an experimental, conceptualising approach to the possibilities offered by different strategies of representation, so generating a rich tradition of cultural commentary, both visual and literary, upon ritual and artistic means of apprehending the gods.

All epiphany, Platt and others have shown, is epistemologically challenging. To believe in the existence of the gods is one thing; to be confident that the figure before one is (or is not) a god is quite another (cf. Phye and the Athenians).[22] In this context, the properties of divine enactment that I have been discussing are a heightened version of what is true for epiphany in general. The suffusion of divine presence and mediated representation that Platt draws out is particularly pronounced here: enacted gods are manifested in the flesh, yet this manifestation is overtly manufactured by human pretence.

The second relevant context, broader and potentially more significant, concerns make-believe in Greek religion more widely. In a substantive chapter of *Coping with the Gods*, H. S. Versnel argues that what he variously calls 'honest pretence', 'suspension of disbelief', and 'as if' is the cognitive mechanism that forms the basis of Hellenistic ruler cult: when Greeks worshipped human rulers as gods, he suggests, they adopted a form of sincere make-believe. The evidence Versnel amasses is strong, but what is most important for our purposes here is his less systematically developed suggestion that similar cognitive modes are at work much more widely: '*As if*, as we will note in several chapters of this book, is perhaps the most productive and promising strategy in religion.'[23] Along similar lines, albeit more briefly, Thomas Harrison suggests that 'a kind of "suspension of disbelief" is in operation' in Greek attitudes to the mythical past.[24]

This is not the place to evaluate just how prevalent such make-believe stances were in Greek religion, but it certainly stands to reason that the enacted gods that are my topic are an embodied variant not just of representations of divine epiphany in general but also of a broader mode of belief. There is of course a nagging question here as to whether the suspension of disbelief about, say, the reality of a mythical story involves

---

[22] Cf. Versnel 1987: 46 'The result [of the divine habit of appearing in human guise] was that ancient man could never be sure whether the person he was talking to was not actually a god in disguise.'
[23] Versnel 2011; he discusses ruler cult in ch. 6, and the quotation is from p. 279 (his italics). One of Versnel's most explicit pieces of evidence is Philemon fr. 118.3–4 Kock (considered spurious by Kassel/Austin): 'Don't try to learn whether god exists or not, worship him as if he exists and is present forever' (εἴτ' ἔστιν εἴτ' οὐκ ἔστι μὴ βούλου μαθεῖν, | ὡς ὄντα τοῦτον καὶ παρόντ' ἀεὶ σέβου).
[24] Harrison 2017: 33.

the same cognitive process as the suspension of disbelief about the reality of the Apollo figure that appears on top of the stage building at the end of *Orestes*, but a significant connection is hard to deny – much the same connection, in fact, as obtains between the make-believe involved in reading novels and watching plays, two forms that are routinely discussed side by side by psychologists. An advantage of treating all these phenomena as related is that Luhrmann's telling analysis of how the pretence of conversing with (an unembodied) God becomes part of the experience of God is brought firmly within remit.

My general suggestion, then, is as follows. Enactments of divinity draw on make-believe capacities that are practised since childhood and that in a less embodied form were probably a regular aspect of Greek religious experience. They involve conscious investment – Coleridge's 'willing suspension of disbelief', or more accurately the willing maintenance of belief – rather than confusion or magical thinking. There is no reason to believe that the Greeks who watched divine impersonation doubted that they were seeing priests or actors. It is this knowing type of investment, as Luhrmann shows so well, that is central to certain forms of religious belief and experience. Anthropomorphic gods may be a cognitive by-product of the human mentalizing apparatus as the cognitive science of religion argues, but cultural tools and practices are required to maintain and shape the belief in these gods and to make them part of a person's life. Divine enactment is one of many such tools, in that it allows participants and onlookers to negotiate, knowingly and with varying degrees of hope, certainty, ambivalence, and distance, encounters with the divine.

Variation: *Deus Ex Machina* and Ritual Impersonation of the Divine Compared

The nature of these encounters varies greatly, not just from individual to individual, but also from enactment to enactment. To introduce some vital specificity, this section asks how the tragic *deus ex machina* and self-standing ritual impersonation of the divine (both versatile forms in their own right) overlap and differ in the way they employ make-believe. The case for such a comparative treatment is evident; the reason it is not often made is no doubt the peculiarity of the *deus ex machina* when viewed as a religious practice. Speaking at length and saying many questionable things, as well as integrated into an intricately crafted dramatic plot that is set in a place and time other than the here and now, the *deus ex machina* has long been the domain primarily of literary scholarship, where it is discussed with a view to issues such as closure, meta-theatre, artificiality, irony, morality, and authority.[25] Non-dramatic rituals, by contrast, are typically studied by historians of religion and have their place in treatments of epiphany.[26] My aim in looking at both types in conjunction is to highlight both similarities and differences.

First, then, the *deus ex machina*. No recent scholar goes further in situating the *deus* within the context of mythological and ritual epiphany than Christiane Sourvinou-Inwood, who argues strongly for continuities with lived religion in general and ritual epiphany in particular, and concludes that 'far from diluting, or subverting, the religious content of tragedy, Euripidean tragedies with a deity *ex machina* gave it a new and powerful injection of religious significance and resonance'.[27] This is surely right. Despite everything that is problematic about the *deus*, it is still a type of divine enactment and as such cannot be cleanly divorced from other forms of reflective and pre-reflective engagement with the divine. The more difficult question, as ever, is exactly how we should think of this 'religious significance and resonance' in the context of what is not simply the human enactment of a god with all the artifice that any such enactment entails but, what is more, is an enactment in the context of a dramatic competition, and one that gives the god-character words that raise profound questions about divine action, causation, and motivation.

The answer, I suggest, or at least part of it, is that the *deus ex machina* confronts its audience with a maximally heightened version of the 'as if'. Compared to other representations of epiphany, including ritual enactment, *deus* scenes *both* do more to coax spectators into the world of the fiction *and* give them greater cause to maintain a self-conscious distance. On the one hand, the *deus* is multiply framed as human rather than divine. The deity is embodied by an actor who earlier in the tragedy played a human character and who competes for the prize as best actor. A frequent theme of the dialogue, explicitly or implicitly, is the all-too-human behaviour of the gods. In performance as well as text, therefore, the *deus ex machina* self-consciously highlights the contradictions inherent in

---

[25] On the *deus ex machina* see in particular Spira 1960, Mikalson 1991: 64–68, Easterling 1993, Dunn 1996, Mastronarde 2010: 181–195. The discussion that goes furthest in analyzing the connection to ritual enactments is Sourvinou-Inwood 2003 ch. III.4.1; see next paragraph. I limit my remit here to gods appearing at the end of tragedies (irrespective of whether they use the *mêchanê*). Divine appearances at the beginning of tragedies, or in comedy, raise related but different issues.

[26] See esp. Petridou 2015: 43–49. For a discussion of epiphany that includes the *deus ex machina* see Koch Piettre 2018. For brief references to the *deus* in discussions of epiphany see e.g. Platt 2011: 17, Petridou 2015: 47.

[27] Sourvinou-Inwood 2003: 492.

anthropomorphism. On the other hand, the tragedians marshal all means at their disposal to endow the divine performances with the power to persuade and impress. The deity typically appears on top of the stage building, visibly out of human reach. Often, moreover, he or she flies through the air by means of the crane.[28] The artificiality of that contraption is evident – a further dose of in-your-face make-believe – but artificial though it is, the crane is doubtless the most exciting piece of stage-machinery that the Theatre of Dionysus had to offer, and it is surely significant that this stage-machinery was invented and primarily used for gods. (One might compare the automata, among them machines conjuring mechanical epiphanies, which came to be employed in cult in the Hellenistic period.[29]) In short, the dramatists pulled out all the stops for their divine performances at the same time as marking them as exactly that – performances.

The *deus ex machina*, then, encourages spectators to suspend disbelief while giving them every reason not to. One consequence may well be a greater variation of response from one spectator to the next: what Larson argues with relation to the responses to Pisistratus' Phye holds also for the contradictory incentives created by the *deus ex machina* scenes.[30] Even so, we should not overestimate the likelihood that spectators refused to go along altogether. Drama relies on the audience's willingness to entertain the fiction, and while the *deus ex machina*, as a god, will not prompt quite the same response as the Oedipuses, Medeas, and Agamemnons, to posit a complete rupture in the final scene of the play would be to throw out the baby with the bathwater.[31]

So much for the *deus ex machina*. What, in turn, about ritual enactments of epiphanies outside plays, at Eleusis for example? One thing to note is that, so far as we can tell, they were not overwhelmingly frequent.[32] Whereas staged gods remained a common feature of Greek and Roman drama, passed on from tragedy to Greek and subsequently Roman New Comedy (after making appearances already in Old Comedy), non-dramatic impersonation of the divine, while firmly attested in various

---

[28] The use of the crane (assumed in the conventional term *deus ex machina*) is certain for some plays and debated for others; see Mastronarde 1990.
[29] Mechanical epiphanies: Fragaki 2012: 57–59.   [30] Cf. p. 100, above.
[31] One difference may well be that audiences are more willing to construct mind-states for human than divine characters: in so far as the *deus* cannot be fully understood in human terms, there is presumably a limit to any 'mentalizing' that the *deus* solicits. This distinction deserves proper exploration but is of limited significance for the sense of divine presence under discussion here.
[32] See Petridou's work cited in n. 10 for full documentation.

cities, does not seem to have been a standard feature of Greek festivals, and it is worth contemplating potential reasons.[33] Is it possible that embodiment has drawbacks as a representational strategy for the divine? Compared to evangelical Christians who listen out for God's voice, to epiphanic dreams at Epidaurus, to Harrison's suggestion that acceptance of the mythical past was a matter of suspension of disbelief, and even to cult statues, divine impersonation leaves rather little to the imagination. Human enactment creates vividness, no doubt, but perhaps this vividness comes at the expense of credibility. Agency too may be a factor. Epiphany is a spontaneous divine act: you can pray for it, but you will never be certain that the god will indeed appear, and the other way round many epiphanies are spontaneous and unexpected. Perhaps enacting divine presence in what is an evidently human-controlled performance risks striking a jarring note. It can be no accident that such rituals usually are enacted by a priest, who acts as the deity's agent, but there is still considerable human control. Maybe we need to reckon with a variant of the 'uncanny valley'. Creators of humanoid robots, animations, and such like have learned that we often respond better to machines and other representations that are *either* very persuasively human-like *or* fairly evidently artificial, but can be repulsed or have an eerie sensation when confronting those that resemble humans nearly but imperfectly (the 'valley' in between).[34] In a similar way, one might tentatively conjecture, representations of epiphany were perhaps most effective *either* if, as in deceptive battlefield epiphanies, it was impossible to exclude the possibility that the human-looking figure is a god, *or* if the fictionality was clearly marked, be it through the frame of a drama or through the lifeless materiality of a statue, whereas the space in between, human enactments that are less overtly fictional, may have been more problematic.

That said, non-dramatic practices of divine enactment did exist, and we should ask what there is to be learned from comparing them to the *deus ex machina*. If comparison with non-dramatic divine impersonation prevents us from denying *deus ex machina* scenes *all* sense of divine presence, the *deus*, vice versa, can serve as a reminder that for its part the experience afforded by ritual divine impersonation will have been characterized by at least *some* complicity and knowing suspension of disbelief. This specific

---

[33] Both McGlashan and Patzelt in this volume consider this topic in terms of mimicry.
[34] The 'uncanny valley' goes back to a short, and in various ways now dated, 1970 article by Masahiro Mori, translated into English as Mori 2012. The concept has been much discussed and is more difficult than my one-sentence summary can convey.

point about complicity in ritual divine impersonation leads to a more general consideration. One significant benefit of the *deus ex machina* for thinking about religious experience more widely is that it serves as a reminder to pay due attention to volition, consent, and even effort as integral components of belief as well as practice. The *deus* points up a path that goes some way, perhaps, towards taking us beyond the unsatisfactory binary of intuition and reflection with which both religious and literary scholars struggle. The suggestion would be that we should add as a third element volition and attitudinal stance, which straddle the division between intuition and reflection and thus allow us to construct a more organic model. This suggestion will be developed in the next section.

Faith, Obedience, Trust

The discussion so far has been concerned with the spectators' and worshippers' relationship to divine enactment. In this final part of the argument, I shall turn to the relationships between humans and gods on stage to ask how the dramatists present the characters' response to the *deus ex machina*. My focus will be on modes of belief.

After several decades in which historians of Greek religion have treated the notion of belief with suspicion, relegating it to a rather distant second place behind practice, recent years have seen a comeback.[35] Not least because of its Judeo-Christian associations, the term continues to prove challenging, and will remain so, but there is an increasing willingness to confront those challenges. One thing that has become clear in the course of this welcome development is that belief is best understood as a manifold phenomenon: rather than just asking *whether* the Greeks believed in their gods or their stories we should also explore *how* they believed. The contribution the *deus ex machina* can make to these discussions is that it presents, on stage, one particular mode of belief – a form of compliance and trust that foreshadows the notion of faith, which comes to prominence in later periods and above all in Christianity, but which, in a rather different guise and with less prominence, may have existed already in the fifth century BCE.

One of the most stable patterns in the varied corpus of *deus ex machina* scenes is the characters' ready acquiescence to the divine commands, an

---

[35] See esp. Versnel 2011: 539–559, Kindt 2012: 30–32, Harrison 2015, Petrovic and Petrovic 2016, Ambasciano and Pachis 2017: 11–13, Davies 2018, Eidinow 2019, Bremmer 2020. Along with this interest in belief goes renewed engagement with scepticism and 'atheism', e.g. Whitmarsh 2016 and Edelmann-Singer et al. 2020.

acquiescence moreover that often constitutes a 180-degree turn. In *Helen* Theoclymenus releases Helen, in *Iphigenia in Tauris* Thoas gives up his pursuit of Iphigenia and Orestes, in *Philoctetes* Philoctetes goes to Troy, in *Hippolytus* Hippolytus makes peace with Theseus, as does Orestes with Menelaus (marrying Hermione into the bargain) in *Orestes*, and so on. Some plays introduce complications – in *Bacchae* either Cadmus or Agave remonstrates with Dionysus, in *Hippolytus* the title character complains about the gods, in Euripides' *Electra*, Electra and Orestes ask difficult questions about divine behaviour – but the characters' acceptance of the *deus*' ordinances is never in doubt.[36]

In several plays this obedience is thematized by the word *peithesthai*. Both Orestes in *Orestes* and Theseus in Euripides' *Supplices* affirm that 'I shall obey/trust (*peisomai*) your words', and Philoctetes similarly declares that 'I shall not fail to obey/trust (*ouk apithêsô*) your words'. Connecting current and former behaviour, Hippolytus states 'for in the past too I obeyed/trusted (*epeithomên*) your words', while Menelaus, expressing himself more generally, pronounces in the *Orestes* that 'it is necessary to obey/trust (*peithesthai*)'.[37] It is difficult to be certain whether such expressions retain the notion of persuasion that is at the root of the verb ('I shall have myself persuaded', 'I shall trust') or whether they convey obedient compliance without any indication of attitude, but in any case a willingness to trust the *deus* certainly enters the scene in other ways.

Most explicitly so, Ion uses three expressions of belief and trust in as many lines:[38]

> Pallas, daughter of the greatest Zeus, it is not with distrust (*ouk apisitiai*) that I received your words. I believe you (*peithomai*) that I am the son of Apollo and this woman. Even previously this was not unbelievable (*ouk apiston*).

Apistos appears also in *Iphigenia in Tauris*, where Thoas responds to Athena's speech by pronouncing that 'whoever is *apistos* upon hearing the gods' words is not in their right mind'.[39] The majority of translators and commentators opt for a translation such as 'disobedient', and indeed this is an established meaning where *apistos* as here has an active sense, but the more frequent active meaning is 'mistrustful, incredulous' and the

---

[36] Eur. *Ba.* 1344–1349 (speaker uncertain), *Hipp.* 1415, *El.* 1298–1304.
[37] Eur. *Or.* 1670, *Suppl.* 1227, Soph. *Phil.* 1447 (cf. nn. 44 and 49 below), Eur. *Hipp.* 1443, *Or.* 1679.
[38] Eur. *Ion* 1606–1608: ὦ Διὸς Παλλὰς μεγίστου θύγατερ, οὐκ ἀπιστίαι | σοὺς λόγους ἐδεξάμεσθα· πείθομαι δ' εἶναι πατρὸς | Λοξίου καὶ τῆσδε· καὶ πρὶν τοῦτο δ' οὐκ ἄπιστον ἦν.
[39] Eur. *IT* 1475–1476 τοῖσι τῶν θεῶν λόγοις | ὅστις κλυὼν ἄπιστος, οὐκ ὀρθῶς φρονεῖ.

notion of distrust and incredulity will at the very least remain present in the background. In other plays, where characters just use the thinner *peisomai* ('I shall obey/trust') or the other similarly thin phrases cited in the previous paragraph, the context is usually more forthcoming. Hippolytus' declaration of obedience follows on from a statement about his 'long-standing companionship' with Artemis, and Philoctetes' comes straight after he has expressed his delight at hearing Heracles' voice: 'oh you who have appeared at long last and is sending me the voice that I have longed for'. Orestes has just pronounced that Apollo is a truthful prophet after all, while Theseus goes on to say to Athena that 'you put me right so that I do not make mistakes'.[40]

A further factor that militates against a bleak interpretation of coerced obedience straight and simple is the emotional transformation effected by some of the divine epiphanies. In *Andromache* Peleus stops grieving for Neoptolemus, in *Iphigenia in Tauris* Thoas is no longer angry with Iphigenia and Orestes, in *Hippolytus* and *Helen* Hippolytus and Theoclymenus bury their respective grudges, in *Orestes* Orestes 'makes his peace with what has happened' in response to Menelaus' starker 'one must obey', in *Ion* Creusa now looks upon Apollo's temple with joy, a change that draws approving comment from Athena.[41] The suddenness of these transformations can seem suspect (more on this shortly), but for now the thing to note is that the change brought about by the *deus ex machina* is often an emotional and attitudinal as much as a behavioural one.

Finally, it is important that the *deus ex machina* is in many plays a deity with whom the characters have a prior connection.[42] Thetis is Peleus' former wife (*Andromache*), Dionysus is Cadmus' grandson (*Bacchae*), Castor and Polydeuces are not just the epiphanic deities *par excellence* but also Helen's brothers (*Helen*), Electra's and Orestes' uncles (*Electra*) and Electra's former suitors (*Electra* again). Artemis is the goddess Hippolytus favours above all others (*Hippolytus*) and Apollo the god who led Orestes to kill his mother (*Orestes*), while Heracles was Philoctetes' great friend when alive (*Philoctetes*). In the overwhelming majority of cases the *deus* holds a particular meaning for the characters. In so far as many *deus ex machina* scenes raise doubts about divine behaviour, sometimes explicitly so through the characters' own statements, we should note that the particular god who in fact appears tends to be on the characters' side,

---

[40] Eur. *Hipp.* 1441, Soph. *Phil.* 1445–1446, Eur. *Or.* 1667, Eur. *Suppl.* 1228.
[41] Eur. *Andr.* 1276, *IT* 1477–1478, *Hipp.* 1442, *Hel.* 1680–1681, *Or.* 1679–1680, *Ion* 1611–1614.
[42] Cf. Mastronarde 2010: 188.

and that it is often the absent gods who are criticized.⁴³ In trying to establish what *deus ex machina* scenes say about the gods in general we risk missing the nature of the interaction with the humans of the epiphanic *deus* in particular.

Taking all this together, I suggest that the great majority of *deus ex machina* scenes present us not simply with examples of human submission to the divine, rendered inevitable by the enormous gulf in power and knowledge (though divine power is certainly on display). Often, they also enact human relationships with particular gods and a willingness of humans to have themselves affected by deities they trust and to act on their requests. Such relationships of course go back to epic,⁴⁴ and in that sense *deus ex machina* scenes, like the plays as a whole, stage a mythical past in which humans and gods interacted more easily, but at the same time, again like the plays as a whole, they are firmly rooted in the late fifth century. By way of *mise-en-abyme* of this contemporary significance it is worth returning briefly to the appearance of the root *peith-/pist-* in so many of the *deus* scenes. The modern debate about belief has typically homed in on the term *nomizein*: does it denote 'believe in' or 'worship' or something in between?⁴⁵ The *deus* scenes suggest that the root *peith-/pist-* deserves similar attention. Language of credence, trust, obedience, and faith, arguably, is no less important to the phenomenology of Greek belief, complementing as it does belief in the sense of conviction that a god exists with belief as a relationship with, and attitude towards, a god. The huge religious significance of the term *pistis* – 'faith' – in both Christian and pagan religions of antiquity developed considerably later,⁴⁶ but it has antecedents in the Classical period as Dennis R. Lindsay has pointed out.⁴⁷ Already in the fifth century, *pistis*, *pisteuein*, and other cognates are used for faith in oracles, sometimes with the gods themselves as the

---

⁴³ Particularly pronounced examples are Euripides' *Electra* (Castor and Pollux rather than Apollo), *Hippolytus* (Artemis rather than Aphrodite), and *Ion* (Athena rather than Apollo). The most notable exception is *Bacchae* (where the unforgiving Dionysus appears himself).

⁴⁴ The reprise of epic is certainly not without changes. Philoctetes' 'I shall not fail to obey/trust your words' (*Phil.* 1447 οὐκ ἀπιθήσω τοῖς σοῖς μύθοις) looks back to the epic formula οὐδ' ἀπίθησε(ν), which however is normally used for interactions among just gods or just humans (see *LfgrE* s.v. ἀπιθήσω, where the formula is glossed as 'willig, gerne bereit sein'). Sophocles transfers it to a relation between a god and a human.

⁴⁵ The most thorough treatment is Fahr 1969, the best recent discussion, with references to other accounts, Versnel 2011: 542–545, 554–558.

⁴⁶ See the large-scale treatment of Morgan 2015 and the collection Frey, Schliesser, and Ueberschaer 2017.

⁴⁷ Lindsay 1993: 7–15; he does not discuss the *deus ex machina*. On the use of *pistis* and *peithô* in early philosophy (esp. political philosophy), see Bontempi 2013.

dative object, for example Creon's 'now you will believe (*pistin pherois*) the god' in *Oedipus Tyrannus*, alluding to Oedipus' difficult relationship with Apollo,[48] or Neoptolemus' 'trusting (*pisteusanta*) the gods and my words', addressed to Philoctetes and subsequently resonating in Philoctetes' own words to Heracles that I quoted earlier on.[49] A fourth-century inscription from Epidaurus reports the case of a man who was at first unbelieving (*apistei*) when he read of Asclepius' past cures only soon to be cured himself,[50] and Thucydides' Pagondas asks the Boeotians to 'trust (*pisteusantas*) god that he will be on our side'.[51] Perhaps the single most interesting phrase is one Xenophon uses when arguing that Socrates, contrary to the charge on which he was convicted, did believe in the existence of the gods. Xenophon interprets Socrates' habit of saying that he received signs from the *daimonion* as a form of 'trusting the gods' and asks rhetorically: 'if he trusted (*pisteuôn*) the gods, how could it be that he didn't believe (*enomize*) they existed?'[52] Trust in the gods and belief in their existence are here explicitly linked as well as distinguished.

The *pist*-lexicon is drawn on only in two *deus ex machina* scenes, those of *Ion* and *Iphigenia in Tauris* (quoted in notes 38 and 39), and the precise nuance of *peithesthai*, which characterizes the response to so many other *dei*, is difficult to establish,[53] but even so, the *deus* scenes are surely part of the same broad trend. They explore a willingness to put one's faith in the gods and to let oneself be affected by them, to listen out for their messages, and to maintain individual relationships with them.

Conclusion

From the audience's perspective of course, certainly so far as modern critics are concerned, many Euripidean gods are rather problematic figures. Their accounts of what has happened, and equally their stipulations for the future, can be worryingly incomplete. Their benign attitude, such as it is, is often out of keeping with what the rest of the play suggests. While their power is rarely in dispute (though Zeus to whom several *dei* appeal as

---

[48] Soph. *OT* 1445, καὶ γὰρ σὺ νῦν γ' ἂν τῶι θεῶι πίστιν φέροις, possibly an interpolation.
[49] Soph. *Phil.* 1373–1374 θεοῖς τε πιστεύσαντα τοῖς τ' ἐμοῖς λόγοις, (Neoptolemus) echoed at 1447 (Philoctetes, cited in n. 44 above).
[50] *IG* IV², 1 212 [= RO 102], l. 24, ἀπίστει τοῖς ἰάμασιν, 'he did not believe the cures'.
[51] Thuc. 4.92.7, πιστεύσαντας ... τῶι θεῶι πρὸς ἡμῶν ἔσεσθαι.
[52] Xen. *Mem.* 1.1.5, πιστεύων δὲ θεοῖς πῶς οὐκ εἶναι θεοὺς ἐνόμιζεν.
[53] The (later) material discussed by Morgan 2015 shows that *pist*- and *peith*- expressions are not strongly connected but co-occur in some passages; see esp. pp. 250–251, 511.

the ultimate authority remains off stage, just as he stayed away from Homer's battlefields), the justice of what they say and do is often doubtful, sometimes severely so.[54] There is a discrepancy, in other words, between on the one hand the emotional transformation and ready compliance demonstrated by the characters, and on the other the more churlish questions that audiences may find themselves asking as they watch the proceedings. As a result, the spectators' stance towards the *deus ex machina* will frequently be a complex one (as of course is that of modern critics). Will they refuse to join in the characters' acceptance of, and in several plays joy at, the resolution brought about by the god? Or will they knowingly allow themselves to go along with the characters' faith in the divine arrangement of their affairs, even though they would have good reason not to? Ultimately, attitudinal questions of trust and emotional investment are not confined to the stage, but at one remove affect the spectators.[55]

Here the play-external and play-internal perspectives, the dynamics of make-believe (the first two sections) and the on-stage interactions (the third section), finally come together. Both through the combination of artifice and immersive force in the staged impersonation and through the characters' accepting encounters with problematic gods, the *deus ex machina* adumbrates the promise and fragility of divine presence in the lives of individuals and communities.[56] At more than one level and in more than one way, the audience has to negotiate a pull both towards and away from acceptance. Such a combination of trust, doubt, confidence, hesitation, and knowing going-along is, in one permutation or other, bound to have been a recurring quality of interactions with the divine in Classical Athens and beyond, and is what, more than anything else, makes the *deus ex machina* a tool for exploring and indeed generating (a specific kind of) religious experience.

I began this chapter by stating the case for a maximally capacious and generous account of the religious imagination, one in which the imagination is enabling as much as constraining and controlling.[57] In their different ways, the different disciplines studying the human imagination

---

[54] Cf. n. 25.
[55] I have explored related issues with a focus on one whole play (*Iphigenia in Tauris*) rather than one feature in multiple plays (the *deus ex machina*) in Budelmann 2019.
[56] It is worth noting that *peithesthai* is also the verb that Herodotus uses when complaining about the Athenians' gullibility in relation to Phye: 'believing (*peithomenoi*) that the woman was the goddess herself, they prayed to this human woman and welcomed Pisistratus' (1.60.5).
[57] Cf. the broad conception of the *literary* imagination from a cognitive perspective in Richardson 2015.

all confront the apparent paradox that the imagination conjures unreal worlds, yet by conjuring such worlds achieves something important for the way we navigate reality. Philosophers ask how the imagination is capable of yielding knowledge, child psychologists ponder the contribution pretend-play, imaginary companions, and role-playing make to a child's development, evolutionary psychologists and evolutionary literary theorists form hypotheses about the adaptive benefits of story-telling for human communities.[58] We do not need to follow them in adopting a similarly functionalist perspective to find it productive to consider what the imagination allows us to do across all aspects of life. The *deus ex machina*, drawing as it does on the imagination's capacity for make-believe to create a particular kind of encounter with the divine, has provided material, I hope, for thinking about one such aspect.

BIBLIOGRAPHY

Ambasciano, L. and P. Pachis. 2017. 'Strangers in a Strange Land No More: Introducing the Book Review Symposium Section and Jennifer Larson's Understanding Greek Religion (2016)', *Journal of Cognitive Historiography* 4: 10–23.

Bontempi, M. 2013. *La fiducia secondo gli antichi: 'pistis' in Gorgia tra Parmenide e Platone*. Naples.

Boyd, B. 2009. *On the Origin of Stories: Evolution, Cognition, and Fiction*. Cambridge, MA.

Bremmer, J. N. 2020. 'Youth, Atheism, and (Un)Belief in Late Fifth-Century Athens', in B. Edelmann-Singer, T. Nicklas, and J. E. Spittler, eds. *Sceptic and Believer in Ancient Mediterranean Religions*, 53–68. Tübingen.

Budelmann, F. 2019. 'Dare to Believe: Wonder, Trust and the Limitations of Cognition in Euripides' *Iphigenia in Tauris*', in D. Braund, E. Hall, and R. Wyles, eds. *Ancient Theatre and Performance Culture around the Black Sea*, 289–303. Cambridge.

Clinton, K. 2004. 'Epiphany in the Eleusinian Mysteries', *Illinois Classical Studies* 29: 85–109.

Connor, W. R. 1987. 'Tribes, Festivals and Processions: Civic Ceremonial and Political Manipulation in Archaic Greece', *Journal of Hellenic Studies* 107: 40–50.

Davies, J. P. 2018. 'The Value(s) of Belief: Ancient Religion, Cognitive Scence, and Interdisciplinarity', in N. P. Roubekas, ed. *Theorizing 'Religion' in Antiquity*, 32–58. Sheffield.

---

[58] One example each: for the puzzle of knowledge through imagination see Kind and Kung 2016, for developmental psychology (again) Harris 2000: esp. ch. 9, for storytelling Boyd 2009.

Dunn, F. M. 1996. *Tragedy's End: Closure and Innovation in Euripidean Drama.* New York, NY, and Oxford.

Easterling, P. E. 1993. 'Gods on Stage in Greek Tragedy', in J. Dalfen, G. Petersmann, and F. F. Schwarz, eds. *Religio Graeco-Romana: Festschrift für Walter Pötscher*, 77–86. Graz.

Edelmann-Singer, B., T. Nicklas, J. Spittler and L. Walt, eds. 2020. *Sceptic and Believer in Ancient Mediterranean Religions.* Tübingen.

Eidinow, E. 2015. 'Φανερὰν ποιήσει τὴν αὑτοῦ διάνοιαν τοῖς θεοῖς: Some Ancient Greek Theories of (Divine and Mortal) Mind', in C. Ando and J. Rüpke, eds. *Public and Private in Ancient Mediterranean Law and Religion*, 53–73. Berlin.

2016. *Envy, Poison, and Death: Women on Trial in Classical Athens.* Oxford.

2019. 'The (Ancient Greek) Subject Supposed to Believe', *Numen* 66: 56–88.

Fahr, W. 1969. Θεοὺς νομίζειν: *Zum Problem der Anfänge des Atheismus bei den Griechen.* Hildesheim.

Fragaki, H. 2012. 'Automates et statues merveilleuses dans l'Alexandrie antique', *Journal des Savants*: 29–67.

Frey, J., B. Schliesser, and N. Ueberschaer. 2017. *Das Verständnis des Glaubens im frühen Christentum und in seiner jüdischen und hellenistisch-römischen Umwelt.* Tübingen.

Friend, S. 2016. 'Fiction and Emotion', in A. Kind, ed. *The Routledge Handbook of Philosophy of Imagination.* London.

Harris, P. L. 2000. *The Work of the Imagination.* Oxford.

Harrison, T. 2015. 'Belief vs. Practice', in E. Eidinow and J. Kindt, eds. *The Oxford Handbook of Ancient Greek Religion*, 21–28. Oxford.

2017. 'Cognitive Science of Religion As Challenge to Prevailing Models of Greek Religion?', *Journal of Cognitive Historiography* 4: 30–35.

Kind, A. and Kung, P. eds. 2016. *Knowledge through Imagination.* Oxford.

Kindt, J. 2012. *Rethinking Greek Religion.* Cambridge.

Koch Piettre, R. 2001. 'Images et perceptions de la présence divine en Grèce ancienne', *Mélanges de l'École française de Rome – Antiquité* 113: 211–224.

2018. 'Anthropomorphism, Theatre, Epiphany: From Herodotus to Hellenistic Historians', *Archiv für Religionsgeschichte* 20: 189–209.

Larson, J. 2016. *Understanding Greek Religion: A Cognitive Approach.* London.

Lieberoth, A. 2013. 'Religion and the Emergence of Human Imagination', in A. W. Geertz, ed. *Origins of Religion, Cognition and Culture*, 160–177. Durham.

Lindsay, D. R. 1993. *Josephus and Faith: Πίστις and Πιστεύειν as Faith Terminology in the Writings of Flavius Josephus and in the New Testament.* Leiden.

Luhrmann, T. M. 2012. *When God Talks Back: Understanding the American Evangelical Relationship with God.* New York, NY.

Marinatos, N. and D. Shanzer, eds. 2004. *Divine Epiphanies in the Ancient World* [Special issue]. *Illinois Classical Studies* 29.

Mastronarde, D. J. 1990. 'Actors on High: The Skene Roof, the Crane, and the Gods in Attic Drama', *Classical Antiquity* 9: 247–294.

2010. *The Art of Euripides: Dramatic Technique and Social Context*. Cambridge.
Mikalson, J. D. 1991. *Honor Thy Gods: Popular Religion in Greek Tragedy*. Chapel Hill, NC, and London.
Morgan, T. 2015. *Roman Faith and Christian Faith: Pistis and Fides in the Early Roman Empire and Early Churches*. Oxford.
Mori, M. 2012. 'The Uncanny Valley', trans. K. F. MacDorman and N. Kageki, *IEEE Robotics and Automation Magazine* 19(2): 98–100.
Panagiotidou, O. and R. Beck. 2017. *The Roman Mithras Cult: A Cognitive Approach*. London.
Petridou, G. 2015. *Divine Epiphany in Greek Literature and Culture*. Oxford.
Petridou, G. and V. Platt, eds. 2018. 'Making Contact with the Divine Other. Means and Meanings' [Special issue], *Archiv für Religionsgeschichte* 20(1): 185–274.
Petrovic, A. and I. Petrovic. 2016. *Inner Purity and Pollution in Greek Religion. Volume 1: Early Greek Religion*. Oxford.
Platt, V. 2011. *Facing the Gods: Epiphany and Representation in Graeco-Roman Art, Literature and Religion*. Cambridge.
  2015. 'Epiphany', in E. Eidinow and J. Kindt, eds. *The Oxford Handbook of Ancient Greek Religion*, 491–504. Oxford.
Platt, V. J. 2018. "Double Vision: Epiphanies of the Dioscuri in Classical Antiquity", *Archiv für Religionsgeschichte* 20: 229–256.
Polvinen, M. 2017. 'Cognitive Science and the Double Vision of Fiction', in M. Burke and E. T. Troscianko, eds. *Cognitive Literary Science: Dialogues between Literature and Cognition*, 135–150. Oxford.
Richardson, A. 2015. 'Imagination: Literary and Cognitive Intersections', in L. Zunshine, ed. *The Oxford Handbook of Cognitive Literary Studies*, 225–245. New York, NY.
Sinos, R. H. 1993. 'Divine Selection: Epiphany and Politics in Archaic Greece', in C. Doughery and L. Kurke, eds. *Cultural Poetics in Archaic Greece*, 73–91. Cambridge.
Sourvinou-Inwood, C. 2003. *Tragedy and Athenian Religion*. Lanham, MD.
Spira, A. 1960. *Untersuchungen zum deus ex machina bei Sophokles und Euripides*. Kallmünz.
Struck, P. T. 2016. *Divination and Human Culture: A Cognitive History of Intuition in Classical Antiquity*. Princeton, NJ.
Versnel, H. S. 1987. 'What Did Ancient Man See When He Saw a God? Some Reflections on Greco-Roman Epiphany', in D. van der Plas, ed. *Effigies Dei: Essays on the History of Religions*, 42–55. Leiden.
  2011. *Coping with the Gods: Wayward Readings in Greek Theology*. Leiden.
Whitmarsh, T. 2016. *Battling the Gods: Atheism in the Ancient World*. London.

CHAPTER 5

Chanting and Dancing into Dissociation
The Case of the Salian Priests at Rome

Maik Patzelt

The ritual song of the Salian priesthood – the *carmen Saliare* – has remained a well-hidden secret right up to the present day. The fragmentary character of this cult song,[1] and, in particular, its inscrutable Latin, have challenged a legion of philologists to attempt to (re)compose and decode this religious enigma.[2] Already in antiquity, outstanding scholars such as L. Aelius Stilo made efforts to extract some degree of sense from the obscure language of the song,[3] which was entirely cryptic to him and to other scholars working as early as the first century BCE.[4] The archaic character of the song – or songs[5] – has even encouraged modern philologists to compare the *carmen Saliare* with the similarly inscrutable *carmen Arvale*.[6] Due to the high interest in the ritual language of the Salians, only a few modern studies have concentrated on the whole ritual performance within which the song was embedded, which did not merely include odd

---

I would like to take the opportunity to thank Paul Scade for once again proofreading my contribution.

[1] Composed fragments and single words are found in, among others, Varro *Ling.* 5.110, 7.26–27 and 9.61, Ter. *De Orth.* 8.6, Festus 222L and 230L or Serv. *Aen.* 2.166. The most comprehensive linguistic study of each fragment is found in Sarullo's recent study (2014: 143–312; itemized on 305–307).

[2] Maurenbrecher 1894, Guittard 2007: 79–92, Sarullo and Taylor 2013. An impressive account of research into this question is provided by Sarullo 2014: 91–142.

[3] Festus 230, 12L, Varro *Ling.* 7.2.

[4] Quint. *Inst.* 1.6.40, Cf. Hor. *Epist.* 2.1.86, Varro *Ling.* 7.2, Symm. *Ep.* 3.44, Sidon. Apoll. *Epist.* 8.164, Macrob. *Sat.* 1.9.14, Isid. *Orig.* 9.1.6. They all, with different key words of course, refer to these 'most ancient' (*vetustissimi*) or just 'first' (*prima*) songs.

[5] Scholars debate whether there was only one *carmen Saliare* or several *carmina*, as for instance mentioned by Quint. *Inst.* 1.6.40 (Sarullo 2014: 267–271, Guittard 2007: 74–76). Historians and philologists normally adopt this ancient view, although this approach is rather problematic. If these songs were as stable and fixed as Quintilian (*Inst.* 1.6.41) implies, Germanicus could not have been added to the Salian hymn, as Tacitus (*Ann.* 2.83.1) reports. Festus 3L even makes the contemporary priests responsible for these songs. It is, thus, quite likely that the Salian priests, still being literate aristocrats, joined in professional religious discourse, as Gordon suggests for the *pontifices* (1990: 188–191) and argues for the Greek hymns (2020).

[6] Reichardt 1916, Cirilli 1913: 104.

words but also the physical movements of dance (*tripudia*), special accoutrements (a fake war robe), and music.

Those studies that have examined the performance as a whole have, for the most part, been carried out by antiquarians and historians of ancient religions who were interested in reconstructing the ritual procedures: the ritual setting, the procession route, and the sequences of activities involving gestures, words, and objects as well as the symbolic meanings of these gestures, words, and objects.[7] Recent research on choruses and priestly dancing groups in Greek antiquity has stimulated scholars of Roman ritual dance to think about the social function of ritual choruses within and beyond the ritual community. Starting from concepts of performance, performativity, and Victor Turner's application of Arnold van Gennep's notion of *rites of passage*, these studies present ritualized dance performances as strategies that evoke sociality and thereby maintain social order, power relations, and (collective) political identities.[8] These approaches have been applied to the Salian dances by, for example, Thomas Habinek,[9] who treats the Salian dances as initiation rites[10] that play an important role in the 'foundation and maintenance of social order and on song's power to transform the everyday into the eternal [past]'.[11]

Prevailing approaches to the transformative power of the Salian ritual dances have, thus, concentrated on the role of performance in world construction and in the creation and maintenance of coherent social systems. However, the roles of experience and excitement in this ritual dance have remained untouched, despite the fact that a number of studies have foregrounded precisely this aspect when examining the ritual dances and chants of the Galloi and the Bacchants, or the so-called Greek rituals in general.[12] One reason for these different scholarly foci might be that the ritualized practices of the Salii are only recorded in very fragmentary sources.[13] However, the most important reason lies at a more fundamental level. Scholars working on Roman religions, and on Roman rituals in particular, have reproduced the ancient hegemonic literary discourse that

---

[7] Guittard 2007: 61–97 and 2013, Habinek 2005, Heinzel 1996, Cirilli 1913, Helbig 1905, Borgna 1993.
[8] Turner 1974, Calame [1977] 2001, Kowalzig 2007. [9] Habinek 2005: 8–57.
[10] Habinek 2005: 17–19. The idea of initiation through these and similar performances in antiquity was already raised by Ceccarelli 1998: 150–157, Graf 1995, Torelli 1984 and 1990.
[11] Habinek 2005: 6–10, cit. 9.
[12] E.g. Bremmer 2017 and 2019, Šterbenc Erker 2013. On the emotional character of Greek rituals in Greece see, for instance, Chaniotis 2013.
[13] Liv. 1.20.4, Hor. *Epist.* 2.1.86, Cic. *De or.* 3.197, Ov. *Fast.* 3.387–388, Quint. *Inst.* 1.10.20, Lydus *Mens.* 4.2, Plut. *Vit. Num.* 13.4–5, Dion. Hal. *Ant. Rom.* 2.70.

draws a clear line between the 'Roman' proper and the 'foreign', most particularly in its manifestation as the 'oriental'. In so doing they articulate a distinction based on gender stereotypes and ethnic clichés. The aspect of the lived experience of those who partake in rituals, commonly discussed and presented in terms of excessive emotionality and lunacy, is particularly vulnerable to being cast in terms of these stereotypes. And it is from views such as these that the ideal of a formalized, severe, and emotionless, indeed dispassionate, 'Roman' ritual practice emanates and is projected onto the performances of the Salian priests.[14]

Other scholars have already deconstructed the hegemonic Roman discourse in this respect.[15] The present contribution now seeks to unveil the essential aspect of (religious) experience that is encoded in the ritualized practices of the Salii. The fragmentary evidence for these practices reflects little of the experiential quality of the ritualized dance and chant due to the fact that the ancient authors who preserve the fragments invariably do so while pursuing other interests (e.g. aetiology). Taking account of this source base, this chapter joins in a recent debate that foregrounds a *cognitive approach* to religious practice as *embodied* practice.[16] This is to say that this approach concentrates on the 'interplay between sensory, cognitive and socio-cultural aspects of world-construction'[17] – an interplay that will be reconstructed in the following pages. To this end, the cognitive approach to religion offers an analytical model that supports a comparative approach to our fragmentary sources based on our knowledge about cognitive processes. The approach I take thus consists of three steps. Starting from a comparison with other priestly groups, I (a) unveil the ritualized patterns of practice deployed in the Salian performances, (b) explain the cognitive effects that these patterns elicit, and (c) identify the symbolic, indeed *embodied*, cognition of these effects. With very few exceptions (e.g. Nonius Marcellus, third to fourth century CE) the bulk of our sources are from the period between the first century BCE and the first century CE.

---

[14] See recently Scheid 2015, 113–118.   [15] Šterbenc Erker 2013.
[16] Concepts of cognitive embodiment applied to ancient religion: Ustinova 2009, 2018, and 2021, Panagiotidou 2014 and 2017, Czachesz 2015 and 2016, Harkins and Popović 2015, Chalupa 2014. As for the applications of the complementary debate on embodiment from the point of view of religious aesthetics and mediality (Grieser and Johnston 2017, Meyer 2010, Münster 2001): Alvar 2021, Feldt 2017, Harvey 2006 and 2014, Pentcheva 2014.
[17] Grieser and Johnston 2017: 2. Cf. Czachesz 2016: 8–23, Geertz 2010, Hick 2010, Schjødt 2009, Taves 2009, McNamara 2009, Azari et al. 2005.

Embodied Techniques of Experience: The Dissociative Mind

A cognitive approach starts from the assumption that cultural and biological processes are intertwined. It emphasizes a non-Cartesian dialectical interaction between the body, the brain, and the cultural and social environments in which body and brain are embedded or, better, in which cognition is 'embodied' and 'embrained'.[18] The symbolic construction of the world, which is instantiated through rituals, is thus intrinsically tied to the human nervous system.[19] From this perspective, rituals are not merely performative or transformative in a symbolic or social respect. Rather, there is also another, psychosomatic, dimension to this transformation – a range of sensorial, emotional, and cognitive responses that are intrinsically tied to the symbolic transformation.

Given this dialectical connection between body and brain 'through an intricate nervous system',[20] scholars and scientists have discussed ritual performances in terms of *techniques* that are able to 'manipulate' the nervous system and, thus, the performer's cognition.[21] As cross-cultural comparisons in anthropology and psychology illustrate, these techniques range from rehearsed postures, such as standing with raised arms or kneeling, to a commitment to rhythmic movements, such as dancing and leaping. The consumption of drugs and the castigation of the body can serve the same ends.[22] These psychosomatic and culturally embodied techniques can be described as 'body techniques', following the language used by the French sociologist Marcel Mauss in the context of the magical (and thus symbolic) effectiveness of culturally embodied actions.[23]

Vocal techniques complement these body techniques. Just like body techniques, vocal techniques manipulate the nervous system through rhythms and melodies. A smooth, regular pace elicits a different response than a fast or quickening pace.[24] Further vocal techniques range from the use of archaisms, foreign words, repetitions, alliterations, and echo pairs to the use of extraordinary sounds (those of animals for instance), grunts,

---

[18] Geertz 2010: 306–308, Kundtová Klocová and Geertz 2019: 76–80.
[19] Andersen and Schjødt 2017.   [20] Geertz 2010: 306.
[21] Kundtová Klocová and Geertz 2019: 85–88, Andersen and Schjødt 2017: 321, Geertz 2010, Atran 2002: 149–173.
[22] Geertz 2010: 306–308, cf. Ustinova 2021, Konvalinka et al. 2011.
[23] Mauss [1936] 1979: 103–105 and 115–116. Others refer to them as ritualized 'patterns' or 'schemes' (Panagiotidou 2014, Habinek 2005: 55–57). On the relation between ritual action/manipulation and socially constructed meaning/doctrine also see Kundtová Klocová and Geertz 2019, 85–88.
[24] Laderman 1996, Atran 2002: 166–167.

growls, and obscenities of all kind. Probably the best-known technique in ancient religions is glossolalia –speaking in tongues.[25]

The psychosomatic reactions that result from these manipulations go far beyond mere states of arousal or emotionality. Rhythmic and energetic practices tend to result in 'altered mental states'[26] and sometimes even in a loss of volitional control, a 'feeling of being absent or disconnected from one's surroundings', or a feeling of 'absorption' and 'depersonalisation'.[27] Patrick McNamara conceives of this effect as a 'decentering process', which other scholars identify as 'hypnotic induction' or as a 'dissociation process'.[28] *Dissociation* is, however, not to be understood in too clinical a sense. It does not refer to a split brain, a mental disorder, or any such similar division. Rather, it indicates a process in which 'the Self is inflated and the sense of agency enhanced via hypnosis, suggestion, placebo treatment, drug ingestion, and so forth [so that] the old identity is temporarily bracketed'.[29] Against this background, it seems appropriate to consider body and vocal techniques as *dissociative techniques*.

However, experiences are neither reducible to a body-brain dualism, nor are they necessarily religious. Experiences are culturally learned, recognized, and embodied. Humans appropriate, cultivate, and enhance an (un)conscious mental reference system – sometimes thought of as a 'mental map' or 'modality-specific system'[30] – that is linked to the technique and the social and ritual context in which it occurs.[31] Whilst body techniques can elicit a dissociative mind, a self-induced hypnotic state, this altered state of 'standing next to one's actions' in turn invites the individual's mental maps to *suggest* plausible meanings to the mind when it is in this state.[32]

---

[25] Forbes 1995, Pattison 1968.
[26] Geertz 2010: 307, McNamara 2009: 56, Taves 2009: 58–62. For the context of ancient religions, see Ustinova 2018.
[27] Jegindø et al. 2013: 173.   [28] McNamara 2009: 5–6, 44–58, and see e.g. Deeley et al. 2014.
[29] McNamara 2009: 56 and 171.
[30] Barsalou et al. 2005: 23–24, Damasio 2010: 62–64, cf. Geertz 2010, Atran 2002: 159–164; see Eidinow, Chapter 3 in this volume.
[31] Kundtová Klocová and Geertz 2019: 77–80.
[32] Recent research speaks about 'predictive processing', 'predictive coding', or the 'predictive mind' in general; see also the Introduction, Ustinova, Chapter 2, McGlashan, Chapter 6, and Scott, Chapter 8, in this volume. A recent and encompassing study in respect of divine agency detection is provided by Andersen 2019. An exemplary experiment is provided by Andersen et al. 2019. The guiding research is provided in the monograph by Hohwy 2013. The basic idea is that 'predictive processing explains how the brain, through a single neuronal mechanism, approximates Bayesian inference to represent the world in a fairly accurate manner, while only spending a minimum of resources doing so' (Andersen et al. 2019: 54). Coming from this point of view, those people who were raised religiously or who attended regularly at rituals or, as for Rome, were raised within a world of present gods, would tend to *interpret* the ritually deployed techniques and signals as resulting from 'divine' agency, because their social and cultural background *suggested*, indeed *predicted*, this interpretation

Dissociation, in other words, initiates a 'suggestive process' that is influenced by the imageries and expectancies of the performer's mind, as well as by the social gathering in which the performance is embedded.[33] In cultures in which religious ideas and narratives determine the collective and individual imagination, the dissociative mind is most commonly ascribed to an external superhuman agency that restores, indeed replaces, this control.[34] The ritual setting supports the prior expectations of a divine agency that in turn guides and predicts the individual perception of the body's state and its corresponding dissociative mind.[35] Strictly speaking, the practitioner replaces his or her identity with their model of the deity's identity. This *dissociative identity* is not, then, random, but is, rather, culturally 'patterned' as a superhuman identity.[36]

Reconstructing the Body Techniques: The Salii Going Wild?

The hallmark of the Salii is their dance, which is commonly referred to as *tripudium*.[37] According to the poet Horace, who mentions this dance in one of his odes, this dance takes its name from the fact that the Salii 'stomp' (*quatient*) their feet three (*tri-*) times.[38] Even though Horace directly connects the *tripudium* to the Salii, we also find the term used in other contexts. In his philosophical elaboration on the nature of things (*Natural Questions*), Seneca the Younger, for instance, describes it as a popular dance that requires professional training by famous dancers, *saltatores*.[39] Moreover, *tripudiare* is what the supposedly wild, indeed lunatic, Galloi, Bacchants, matrons, and, particularly, the prophesying women do as well, while singing their prayers and hymns.[40] Likewise, the Arval Brethren and the augurs – two supposedly archaic Roman institutions – *tripodaverunt* in ritual.[41] One might suggest, then, that '*tripudium*' was merely a general term used to describe all sorts of dances.[42] However, since Horace connects a precisely detailed depiction of a

---

as the most likely choice. The error ratio is quite limited with this collectively shared knowledge about gods. As Andersen and Schjødt (2017: 320) formulate it in their summary, 'Guided and repeated attempts to interpret reliable but situation-specific body states and external cues as supernatural manifestations (e.g., trembling, dizziness, auditory and visual events) may gradually allow believers to minimize prediction error by inferring supernatural presence.'

[33] Deeley et al. 2014: 118.   [34] Deeley et al. 2014, Caillois [1958] 2001: 87–97.
[35] Andersen and Schjødt 2017.   [36] Chalupa 2014.
[37] Liv. 1.20.4, Hor. *Carm.* 4.1.28. See Habinek 2005: 22–30.   [38] Hor. *Carm.* 4.1.28.
[39] Sen. *QNat.* 7.32.3   [40] Catull. 63,26, Liv. 39.15.9, Accius *Bacchae* fr. 4, Varro *Ling.* 7.8.
[41] Arvals: ILS 5039=CIL VI 2104a=CFA 100a, 31–38. Augurs: Guittard 2007: 70–71 (based on the venerable reconstruction offered by Maurenbrecher 1894: 345–346).
[42] I thank Harriett Flower for this suggestion.

tripudium to the Salii, Seneca mentions a particular training program for the dance, and other authors use the term for the wild performances of Bacchants and prophesying women, it is reasonable to suspect that it was a specific body technique used to manipulate the nervous system for the sake of creating altered states or dissociative minds.[43]

It is our Greek sources that provide the best insight into the nature of this technique. In his attempt to provide a biography of the mythical Roman king Numa, the Greek author Plutarch, presumably dependent on the Roman Varro, writes:[44]

> Now the Salii were so named, not, as some tell the tale, from a man of Samothrace or Mantinea, named Salius,[45] who first taught the dance in armour; but rather from the leaping (*haltikos*) which characterized the dance itself. ... [They carry] small daggers with which they strike the shields. But the dance is chiefly a matter of step; for they move gracefully, and execute with vigour and agility certain shifting convolutions, in quick and oft-recurring rhythm.

The Greek historian Dionysius of Halicarnassus, who may have had the chance to see the Salii in action, draws a similar picture in his historiographical work *Roman Antiquities*:[46]

> The Romans call them Salii from their lively motions. For to leap (*exallomai*) and skip is by them called *salire*; and for the same reason they call all other dancers *saltatores*, deriving their name from the Salii, because their dancing also is attended by much leaping (*halma*) and capering (*skirtêma*). ... For they execute their movements in arms, keeping time to a flute, sometimes all together, sometimes by turns, and while dancing sing certain traditional hymns.

Since both authors are interested in providing an aetiology of the Salii accompanied by a description of the essential characteristics of the

---

[43] See Bremmer 2008: 296 and 2019, Pachis 1996, and particularly for Rome, Bremmer 2017.
[44] Plut. *Vit. Num.* 13.4–5 (trans. Perrin 1914): σάλιοι δὲ ἐκλήθησαν, οὐχ, ὡς ἔνιοι μυθολογοῦσι, Σαμόθρακος ἀνδρὸς ἢ Μαντινέως, ὄνομα Σαλίου, πρώτου τὴν ἐνόπλιον ἐκδιδάξαντος ὄρχησιν, ἀλλὰ μᾶλλον ἀπὸ τῆς ὀρχήσεως αὐτῆς, ἁλτικῆς οὔσης, ... ἐγχειριδίοις δὲ μικροῖς τὰ ὅπλα κρούοντες. ἡ δὲ ἄλλη τῆς ὀρχήσεως ποδῶν ἔργον ἐστί: κινοῦνται γὰρ ἐπιτερπῶς, ἑλιγμούς τινας καὶ μεταβολὰς ἐν ῥυθμῷ τάχος ἔχοντι καὶ πυκνότητα μετὰ ῥώμης καὶ κουφότητος ἀποδιδόντες. cf. Habinek 2005: 11–19, 28–30.
[45] Cf. Serv. *Aen.* 8.285, 663, Festus 329L.
[46] Dion. Hal. *Ant. Rom.* 2.70 (trans. Cary 1937): ὑπὸ δὲ Ῥωμαίων ἐπὶ τῆς συντόνου κινήσεως. τὸ γὰρ ἐξάλλεσθαί τε καὶ πηδᾶν σαλίρε ὑπ' αὐτῶν λέγεται. ἀπὸ δὲ τῆς αὐτῆς αἰτίας καὶ τοὺς ἄλλους ἅπαντας ὀρχηστάς, ἐπεὶ κἂν τούτοις πολὺ τὸ ἅλμα καὶ σκίρτημα ἔνεστι, παράγοντες ἀπὸ τῶν σαλίων τοὔνομα σαλτάτωρας καλοῦσιν. ... κινοῦνται γὰρ πρὸς αὐλὸν ἐν ῥυθμῷ τὰς ἐνοπλίους κινήσεις τοτὲ μὲν ὁμοῦ, τοτὲ δὲ παραλλὰξ καὶ πατρίους τινὰς ὕμνους ᾄδουσιν ἅμα ταῖς χορείαις. cf. Ov. *Fast.* 3.87–3.88.

performance, most of all the miraculous buckles and the military dress, they do not go into detail concerning any dissociative effects. There may also be another reason. As I have explained above and elsewhere,[47] our sources on ritual dance engage in a discourse that articulates 'Romanness' and 'otherness' on the basis of gender stereotypes. Within this discourse, the dissociative techniques allow the signifying of their performers as effeminate. It is important to mention at this point that these priests were members of leading aristocratic families. In a discourse that renders Roman masculinity, therefore, there is no need to highlight any emotional or dissociative effect, regardless of how visible such effects may have been. It is, thus, not by chance that Plutarch defends the originally Roman character of this group and its rituals against any person who might argue for an origin from the immoderate East.[48] It may, thus, also not be by chance that most of our Roman sources offer little information about the technical details of this ritual.

However, even without naming the techniques and their effects, Plutarch and Dionysius provide perfect starting points for reconstructing these effects through the cognitive lens sketched above. Dionysius agrees with Plutarch that the dance is a matter of step, or rather a matter of leaping steps, as is illustrated by the etymological link between Salii and *salire* ('jumping', 'leaping'). That is to say, there is a particular quick pace according to which the Salii shift, convulse, and revolve as they move through their dance steps. The Salian performance is wild but simultaneously well-ordered, indeed well-rehearsed. They appear as a well-trained chorus, as Dionysius emphasizes. In case the etymology is not clear enough for his readers, Dionysius even marks off the Salian performance from the *tripudia* of the professional dancers, the previously mentioned *saltatores*. Dionysius formulates a hierarchy, which reveals the Salian leaping to be much wilder than that of the *saltatores*, who are themselves famous for their wild and excessive performances.[49]

In explaining quick physical exercises to his imagined penfriend Lucilius, Seneca does not even speak of dances but, rather, of Salian leaps (*saltus Saliaris*), which he associates with high and wide jumping. More precisely, he compares these leaps to a 'fulling jump' (*saltus fullonius*), presumably in order to stress the heavy and ramming character of these leaps.[50] In his didactic poem *On the Nature of Things*, the poet and philosopher Lucretius uses the *tripudium* of the Salii in this respect as a

---

[47] Patzelt 2018 and 2019. [48] Varro (*Ling.* 7.2) seems to do the same.
[49] Cf. the polemic of Val. Max. 2.4.4. [50] Sen. *Epist.* 15.4.

benchmark for the building of solid bridges.[51] Even though these and other Roman authors do not describe the leaping performance in any detail, as our Greek sources do, they clearly have some sort of wild and powerful performance in mind. As the Roman grammarian Sextus Pompeius Festus[52] points out, there is only one mechanism that ties together the movements of the leaping priests into a single choreographed performance.[53] This is the *praesul*, whom we have to consider as a sort of leading dancer.[54] To every step, Festus quotes, that the *praesul* takes (*amptruare*), the other Salii respond by the taking the same step (*redamptruare*) themselves.[55] As we are dealing with a well-rehearsed dance performed in public, it is extremely unlikely that the Salii patiently observed the *praesul* and did what he did. The *praesul* rather coordinates the pace of these steps and therefore the dance – the dance that is referred to as *exultationes Saliorum*, the exultations of the Salii.[56]

Describing the *tripudium* as *exultatio* moves our idea of a fast and rehearsed leaping performance into the semantic field of wild and outrageous capering. In a story about school boys given by the rhetorician Quintilian, this term expresses uncontrolled behaviour in which all the performer's power is required to leap upwards.[57] The term *exultare* also qualifies the (accompanying) mental states either as outrageous feelings or as mental distortions, such as *furor* (frenzy), in several instances.[58] *Furor* and *exultatio* appear either as synonymous expressions or as logical corollaries.[59] In Christian contexts, *exultatio* expresses extreme states, such as the unspeakable joy elicited by psalms or,[60] as in Tertullian's treaty against public games, the outrage of angels.[61] The fact that Roman sources

---

[51] Lucr. 17.5–7.
[52] Although Festus compiled his lexicon around the late second century, his work mainly consists of the encyclopaedia of Verrius Flaccus, who flourished under Augustus and Tiberius. There are, however, other quoted authors. In the present case he also quotes from Gaius Lucilius and a certain Pacuius (probably Pacurius of Iberia).
[53] Festus 334, 19–25L.　　[54] Guittard 2007: 63, cf. Cic. *Div.* 1.55 and 2.136.
[55] Festus quotes Lucilius in this respect: *quod est, motus edidit, ei referuntur invicem idem motus.*
[56] Festus writes *Redantruare dicitur in Saliorum exultationibus*, which may mean that the *Salii* deploy this word in their dances. This is quite unlikely, since *redantruare* is clearly used as a descriptive word in the writings about the Salian dances. Another translation of *in Saliorum exultationibus* may thus refer to a book that bears that title. Given the other appearances of *exultatio* and dance and given the fact that *exultare* indicates movements of dancing and jumping, it is quite likely that this work focuses on their dances.
[57] Quint. *Inst.* 2.2.9–12.
[58] Isid. *Diff.* 1.329, Cic. *Phil.* 2.65, *Milo* 56 and *Har. resp.* 39, Plin. *HN* 8.215, Quint. *Inst.* 2.2.9–12, Suet. *Nero* 24.1.
[59] For the first Cic. *Har. resp.* 39, *Sest.* 133. For the latter Cic. *Har. resp.* 1, *Sest.* 95, *Phil.* 13.20.
[60] Val. Cem. *hom.* 10,5, 724D, Cassiod. *in psalm. praef.* 10C.　　[61] Tert. *Spect.* 30.

frequently enhance or replace *tripudiare* with forms of *exultare*[62] provides an important insight into how they conceived of these dances – as outrageous leaping performances in which the performers are either delighted or completely out of their minds, yet somehow manage to keep to their choreographed roles. Our ancient authors always seem to connect this sort of dancing with the manipulation of the nervous system, as a comparison with the descriptions of the *tripudia* of the Galloi and Curetes, whose descriptions do not hesitate to report dissociative effects, will confirm.

In his version of the myth of Attis,[63] the poet Catullus describes a *chorus* performing a *tripudium* at a rapid yet still accelerating speed (*quo nos decet citatis celerare tripudiis*), measured out by the beat of a tambour (*tympana*). Attis sings:[64]

> Make glad our mistress speedily with your minds' mad wanderings. Let dull delay depart from your thoughts, together haste you ... where the ivy–clad Maenades furiously toss their heads, where they enact their sacred orgies with shrill–sounding ululations, where that wandering band of the Goddess flits about: there it is meet to hasten with hurried mystic dance (*tripudium*). ... [T]he chorus straightway shrills with trembling tongues (*linguis trepidantibus ululate*), the light tambour booms, the concave cymbals clang, and the troop swiftly hastes with rapid feet to verdurous Ida. Then raging wildly, breathless, wandering, with mind distraught, hurries Attis with her tambour.

Catullus emphasizes the hasty nature of the performance and directly correlates this with the performers' state of mind, as the description of Attis' breathless wandering implies (*furibunda simul anhelans vaga vadit animam agens*). The rushing rhythm of the voice, the matched rhythm of the dance and, not least, the choreographed actions of the performers explicitly refer to an ecstatic state of extreme dizziness, described by Catullus as frenzy (*furor*), which ultimately forces all the performers into sleep (*nimio e labore somnum capiunt*).

---

[62] Liv. 7.10.8, Plin. *HN.* 8.215, Verg. *Aen.* 8.663, Cic. *Sest.* 88, Lucr. 2.631, Stat. *Theb.* 4.790, Quint. *Inst.* 2.2.9–12.
[63] Catull. 63.12–38.
[64] Catull. 63.18–32 (trans. Burton 1897): *hilarate erae citatis erroribus animum./ mora tarda mente cedat; simul ite, .../ ubi capita maenades vi iaciunt hederigerae,/ ubi sacra sancta acutis ululatibus agitant,/ ubi suevit illa divae volitare vaga cohors,/ quo nos decet citatis celerare tripudiis/...thiasus repente linguis trepidantibus ululate,/ leve tympanum remugit, cava cymbala recrepant,/ viridem citus adit Idam properante pede chorus./ furibunda simul anhelans vaga vadit animam agens / comitata tympano Attis...*

The poet's conception of a *tripudium* might, when put into the analytical language of this approach, be described as employing a technique that manipulates the nervous system and leads to an altered state of mind. It is their hasty *tripudium* that shifts the performers' minds into their new inspired state. Catullus furthermore aligns the practice of a strenuously leaping *tripudium* with the tossing of heads, as if the rites are being performed by maenads. This movement of the head is itself a well-known technique for eliciting altered states.[65] The quickening rhythm, and thus the increased speed of the leaping, converts the simple *tripudium* into a wild but still synchronized and coordinated convolution of tossing heads. Catullus depicts a loss of the individual self in the practice – a loss of volitional control perhaps, described by some sources as *exultatio* and ascribed by others to the Salian rites.

In describing the very same patterns of performance that Plutarch and Dionysius identify in the Salian performance, Catullus draws a picture that we may identify as an altered state – a wild frenzy that follows the pattern of a dissociative process. Yet an interpretation of these states as a predictable divine presence or takeover is not to be detected here. In his epic poem *On the Civil War* (Pharsalia), when introducing the prophesying Sibyl, M. Annaeus Lucanus depicts the process of divine takeover by drawing on the reconstructed pattern of the *tripudium*:[66]

> As fully as ever in the past, he forced his way into her body, driving out her former thoughts, and bidding her human nature to come forth and leave her heart at his disposal. Frantic (*bacchatur demens*) she careers about the cave, with her neck under possession; the fillets and garlands of Apollo, dislodged by her bristling hair, she whirls with tossing head through the void spaces of the temple; she scatters the tripods that impede her random course; she boils over with fierce fire, while enduring the wrath of Phoebus.

From Lucan's account, we can identify a perfect example of a *dissociative identity* that is experienced as a superhuman takeover, a replacement of the human identity with a superhuman one, or, in short, a 'possession'. The Sibyl's dervish-like performance reflects the reconstructed picture of a leaping *tripudium*. She gives herself up to the spinning and whirling, and

---

[65] Bremmer 2008: 296 and 2019: 261–266; see also McGlashan, Chapter 6, in this volume; and, on examples of altered states in other ancient rituals, see Ustinova and Scott, this volume.

[66] Luc. 5.165–175 (trans. here and below Duff 1928): *tandemque potitus/ Pectore Cirrhaeo non umquam plenior artus/ Phoebados inrupit Paean mentemque priorem/Expulit atque hominem toto sibi cedere iussit/ Pectore. Bacchatur demens aliena per antrum/ Colla ferens, vittasque del Phoebeaque serta/ Erectis discussa comis per inania temple/ Ancipiti cervice rotat spargitque vaganti/ Obstantes tripodas magnoque exaestuat igne/ Iratum te, Phoebe, ferens.*

starts tossing her head. It is particularly noteworthy that Lucan labels as 'Bacchic' the tossing of the head in a circular manner, which, as we have seen above, matches the motions of the wild *tripudium*.[67] This tossing of the head elicits an altered state which the Sibyl and the spectators attribute to a takeover from an external agent. Lucan provides an exemplary description of the way in which the Sibyl's mind is replaced with that of Apollo as a consequence, or at least as a correlative effect, of her wild dance.

Even though the ingestion of a drug plays a key role in this particular scenario, the dissociative process and the wild *tripudium* are intrinsically linked: the one expresses the other. The characteristic symptoms of this process are noisy breathing, falling to the ground, trembling, crying, and foaming at the mouth.[68] Lucan's depiction thus complements the picture built up from other sources of a highly arousing and highly ecstatic, one might say, highly exultative *tripudia* by making manifest what Catullus implicitly indicates – the performance's potential to cause a dissociative mind that interprets this dissociation as divine takeover. Lucan presents the wild *tripudium* as a prophetic technique *par excellence*, one that not only reaches out to the divine but that brings it down into the world of immediate experience.

The comparative approach I have pursued so far has built up a picture of a leaping, outrageously capering, but still choreographed, performance. The movements are variously described in terms of *tripudiare, salire, exultare*, or even the tossing of heads. Since a range of ancient sources confirm that the *tripudia* is a dissociative body technique that manipulates the nervous systems of the performers, it appears quite likely that the Salii, who clearly make use of the same ritualized patterns of rhythmic and accelerating leaping as do the Galloi or the Sibyl, were similarly affected. In contrast to the case of the maenads, who are reported as becoming dizzy after a whole night of dancing,[69] both the comparisons and the way in which our brains work hint at the immediate impact of such manipulations. Of course, length of time must surely have increased the impact of these techniques, but the impact does not depend on it. Whether these manipulations gave the performers the power of divinely inspired prophecy or simply a feeling of joy will have depended on the embodied cognition and the expectations of the Salii –their mental maps.

---

[67] Cf. Liv. 39.15.9, Varro *Ling.* 7.87, Accius *Bacchae* fr. 4.
[68] Luc. 5.190–193: *spumea tum primum rabies vaesana per oral effluit et gemitus et anhelo clara meatu/ murmura.*
[69] Bremmer 2017; and see Chapter 6 by McGlashan, this volume.

As these performances were of a public nature, one might wonder how the observers, the Roman audience, reacted to them. Although we do not have any direct comments on this subject in our sources, we can at least make two points that allow us to assume that there **was** such an impact. First, we can argue in terms of our model. Ecstatic performances as introduced above were likely to have served as sensory stimuli for a human audience, who were thus invited to join the exultations of the Salii, just as Cicero complains in the context of *saltatores* during public festivals.[70] Second, we are well informed about the impact of *tripudium* dancing and capering women, who tended to the emotional needs of the ritual audience with such performances. Their excessive behaviour served as 'emotional work' on a semantic and, most importantly, a cathartic and thus sensory level.[71]

Reconstructing the Vocal Techniques: Chanting in Tongues?

In writing about the Latin language, Varro refers to the Salian chant – the *carmen Saliare* – as *prima verba poetica latina*.[72] Varro, just like Plutarch, seems to contribute to the discourse that sought to render a Roman identity through religious practices. Varro's argument, however, points to the aesthetic qualities of the Salian verses, as he explicitly aligns the Salian songs with those of the poets. As several poets, and Varro himself, attest, the act of composing and singing a *carmen* leads to an altered state of comprehension,[73] which many of these authors interpret as the Muses coming and replacing their identity.[74] These songs thus have an inherent dissociative potential.

Quintilian and Cicero both support this interpretation in the case of the Salian songs, since they reflect on the poetic, indeed the arousing, quality of the Salian *carmina*. Whilst Quintilian seeks to draw attention to the tradition of music at Rome, and in the Salian ritual in particular,[75] Cicero associates the Salian verses of his time with the most 'enflaming' outcomes of poetry.[76] From this we can see that the aesthetic qualities of the Salian verses were clear to these ancient observers. In order to reconstruct this 'enflaming', and presumably dissociative, sound, in what follows I focus on the rhythm of the Salian songs. Dionysius of Halicarnassus introduces this rhythm by reference to its metric marker. He writes:[77]

---

[70] Cic. *Leg.* 2.39. [71] Richlin 2014. [72] Varro *Ling.* 7.3. [73] Varro *Ling.* 6.52.
[74] Hardie 2005. [75] Quint. *Inst.* 1.10.20. [76] Cic. *De or.* 3.197.
[77] Dion. Hal. *Ant. Rom.* 2.70.5; see above for translation.

For they execute their movements in arms, keeping time to a flute (*pros aulon en ruthmôi*), sometimes all together, sometimes by turns, and while dancing sing certain traditional hymns.

Dionysius asserts that the Salii both sing and dance to the same rhythm, with the flutes setting the pace. In his treatise *On the Birthday*, the third-century author Censorinus, too, emphasizes the therapeutic and hypnotic potential of rhythmic flute-playing in ritual.[78] Plutarch, on the other hand, does not mention flutes at all. He merely points to the fact that the Salii dance and chant in quick rhythm (*en ruthmôi tachos*).[79] However, he aligns this observation with another peculiar detail. According to him, the Salii carry 'small daggers with which they strike the shields' – their miraculous *ancilia* – throughout the performance.[80] It seems obvious that Plutarch regards these shields as rhythmic devices.

A number of studies of these *ancilia* allow us to infer that the shields were used not just as rhythmic devices but as sonorous musical instruments as well. These studies emphasize the metallic material, presumably bronze, from which the shields were constructed.[81] The beating of daggers on the *ancilia* must have produced a grave, metallic, resonating sound that was beyond the normal auditory experience of the listeners, as cognitive studies suggest.[82] These unusual sounds will have had a significant impact on those who heard them. Ancient writers engaged in a wide-ranging discourse about the metallurgic craftsmanship needed for the creation of these loud and resonant shields, with some connecting the verse *mamuri veturi* to the mythical craftsman Mamurius Veturius.[83] We can conclude that the shields did not merely produce an enflaming rhythm. They also produced an enflaming sound.

Cicero and Quintilian focus on the arousing effects of the verses themselves rather than on the rhythms of musical instruments. If we build on Dionysius' observation that the pace of the instruments controls that of both the *carmen* and the dance, then the pace does not merely evoke an exultative and leaping dance but an exultative and leaping chant as well. Nonius Marcellus, another late antique grammarian, confirms this suspicion, referring *exsultare* to both the acting and the speaking.[84] Quintilian

---

[78] Censorinus *DN* 12, cf. Pl. *Resp.* 400b. [79] Plut. *Vit. Num.* 13.5. [80] Plut. *Vit. Num.* 13.4.
[81] Borgna 1993, Habinek 2005: 12–14, cf. Helbig 1905: 214–233.
[82] Atran 2002: 166–167. This effect is widely known as auditory driving. See, for instance, Trost and Vuilleumier 2013.
[83] Varro *Ling.* 6.49, Festus 117, 13–23L, Ov. *Fast.* 3.389–392. See Habinek 2005: 10–14, Guittard 2007: 77–79, Dumézil 1966: 216–217. For another interpretation that translates this verse into *memoriam veterem* see Plut. *Vit. Num.* 13.7.
[84] Nonius 300.31 L: *exsultare est gestu vel dictu iniuriam facere*.

and the Numidian writer Apuleius have it that a leaping performance (*exsultare*) causes a hoarse (*rauca*) and shuddering (*fracta*) voice that is indicative of a state of frenzy, which leads both authors to accuse the *exsultantes* performers of being effeminate (*vir mollior*).[85] Like the frenetic dances, the songs too build up to a leaping and whirling verbalization, which some authors refer to as *ululatio*, a term that is famous for its use in ecstatic contexts.[86]

The Roman poet P. Papinius Statius relates the *exultatio* of the Curetes to a sweet murmuring.[87] Lucan adds more detail. In his story about the Sibyl, a wild and trembling voice accompanies the wild and trembling *tripudium*:[88]

> When she found it, first the wild frenzy overflowed through her foaming lips; she groaned (*murmura*) and uttered loud inarticulate cries with panting breath; next, a dismal wailing (*ululatus*) filled the vast cave; and at last, when she was mastered, came the sound of articulate speech.

Fast rhythmic chanting influences the Sibyl's pronunciation, converting it into an incomprehensible hoarse and shuddering sound.[89] This is an example of the linguistic phenomenon best known as *glôssolalía* ('speaking in tongues'), which is a central device for 'magical' and 'prophetic' language.[90] Livy, when writing about the performances of Scipio Africanus, refers to prophetic performances as art (*ars*),[91] following on from Plato's description of prophetic prayers, and those of the Pythia (the 'original' Greek Sibyl) in particular, as the 'noblest art' (*kallistê technê*), which affords an inspired state of *mania*.[92] Whereas the performance of foreign words in a prophetic glossolalia may serve as a performative device that indicates the power and authority of the performance or performer within a particular setting,[93] the essential effect on the human mind is entirely dissociative. An occurrence of glossolalia manipulates the bodily and mental states of its performers.[94]

Lucan gives an insight into the patterns of this phonetic technique, indeed into the vocal art more broadly, when he introduces the wicked witch Erichtho.[95] Lucan's Erichtho, like Ovid's witch Circe, uses and even invents unknown, new (*incognita*), and strange (*obscura*) words, which she then puts into a *carmen* that is performed as *ululatio*,[96] again characterized

---

[85] Apul. *Met.* 8.26.2, Quint. *Inst.* 12.10.12. [86] Šterbenc Erker 2011.
[87] Stat. *Theb.* 4.786–792. [88] Luc. 5.190–193. [89] Crippa 1999: 95–101.
[90] For a comprehensive approach, see Dell'Isola 2019, Forbes 1995. [91] Liv. 26.19.4–9.
[92] Pl. *Phdr.* 244. [93] Corre 2013, Gordon 1987: 86–89, Samarin 1972: 123–125.
[94] McNamara 2009: 124–127. [95] Cf. Graf 1996: 193–198, Crippa 1999.
[96] The witch Erichtho ululates and mumbles '... *incognita verba temptabat cannemque novos fingebat in usus*' (Luc. 6.577–578). Ovid's Circe does something similar with '*obscura verba ... nova*' (Ov. *Met.* 14.57–58).

here as hoarse (*rauca*) and shuddering (*fracta*).[97] The conversion from a *carmen* consisting of these odd words to an *ululatio* is primarily a matter of pace. In Lucan's account,[98] the pace tightens to such a degree that Erichtho stops ululating and starts murmuring and barking. She supplements the now inscrutable *carmen* with further sounds that support an arousing soundscape of a type that, throughout Latin literature, signifies states of frenzy or even possession.

Lucan's representation of an *ululatio* as an exultative performance of new and foreign 'unknown' words is a perfect match for the *carmen Saliare*. As Quintilian emphasizes in the case of the Salian song, the Salii sing in languages that are *de facto* unknown to them, a point of no small irony given the efforts that have been expended in attempts to decode these songs. It is precisely this utterly strange vocabulary that led ancient authors to debate whether the songs were truly archaic or were actually imports from the East.[99] Quintilian's comment in this respect is noteworthy. While discussing the potentially archaic character of the Salian verses, he states that archaic words are consubstantial with new or foreign ones, since they are as odd and unknown to the ears of the contemporary listeners. Quintilian's comment fits perfectly with Pliny's typology of religious language – or 'sacred language', as the anthropologist Stanley Tambiah describes exactly the same linguistic phenomenon.[100] According to Pliny the Elder, who dedicated much space to the topic of sacred language in his *Natural History*, his contemporaries expect either 'foreign, unpronounceable words, or unexpected (i.e. supposedly archaic) Latin ones, which our mind forces us to consider absurd'.[101]

It is not possible to determine whether the *carmen Saliare* was considered archaic rather than magical by ancient performers or their audiences. We are, however, able to reconstruct the Salian chants as examples of dissociative vocal techniques that, again, impact both practitioners and observers. The Salii, the Galloi, and the prophetesses do not merely share the same body technique. Rather, they share the same vocal technique that is, as Dionysius and comparative sources on music and dance make clear,

---

[97] Ov. *Met.* 5.597–598, 13.565–569, 14.279–284, Luc. 6.685–693.   [98] Luc. 6.685–693.

[99] Plutarch's (*Num.* 13.4) arguing against the idea that the Salian dances were imported from Samothrace allows us to infer that there was a debate over this point. Further hints are found in Serv. *Aen.* 8.285, 663, Festus 329L, Varro *Ling.* 7.3, Macr. *Sat.* 1.9.14. See Heinzel 1996.

[100] Tambiah 1968. A recent, cognitive reflection on this language is delivered by Sørensen 2007: 19–24, which is followed (pp. 31–61) by a cognitive explanation of magic (magical language included).

[101] Plin. *HN* 28.20.

intrinsically tied up with the style of the body technique of leaping dance. Their chant 'leaps up' to the same degree as does the dance. That is to say the archaic words, which are themselves already hard to comprehend, speed up to match the pace that drives the *tripudium* to become an acrobatic exercise of high, fast, and repeating leaps. The vocal result is wailing and glossolalia. Whether this technique is called *ululatio*, magic murmuring, or archaic chant depends only on which ancient literate discourse is projected onto these scenes. The patterns of the underlying technique remain the same, regardless of the degree of the performer's commitment.

The Dissociative Identities of The Salii: The Mimicry of Mars

Prophetic practices exemplify the correlation between leaping dance, leaping chant, and an extreme form of the dissociative process. This is not to say that the Salii pursued prophetic ambitions or aimed at experiences of possession. They did, however, exercise a vocal technique that is known for its psychological impact at the same time as they used body techniques that produce corresponding results. The Salii, thus, enacted a performance that had significant potential for causing dissociative effects in the practitioners' minds. As outlined at the beginning of this chapter, it is the social and cultural background as well as the ritual setting that *suggests*, indeed *predicts*, an interpretation of these perceived body states. The current, socio-culturally specific ritual environment, strictly speaking, sets the expectation of what the participants will experience from the body and vocal techniques. Two examples from the ancient world may illustrate this idea. Whilst the setting of the Asclepian healing sanctuaries would tend to suggest the neurological manipulations as experiences of healing,[102] the sanctuary of Apollo would suggest a presence or even a takeover by the presiding god, as was the case for the Sibyl.[103] An important question, then, is which experiences might the Salii have embodied? Might the Salii relate their elicited bodily states to a superhuman agency or even takeover, as in the case of the Sibyl? Can we detect patterns of mimicry relating to any particular divinity?[104]

Plutarch, for instance, writes that, during their processions in honour of Mars, the Salii appeared 'clad in purple tunics, girt with broad belts of bronze, wearing bronze helmets on their heads, and carrying small daggers'

[102] Panagiotidou 2014. [103] Chalupa 2014.
[104] On mimicry, see both McGlashan and Budelmann in this volume.

while performing with their buckles.[105] According to a Roman source, the historian Livy, they also wore a brazen cuirass over the tunic.[106] Even though Dionysius refers to small hats (*apices*) instead of helmets,[107] the similarity between the costume of the performers and representations of Mars is striking and, perhaps, unsurprising given the objective of the processions.[108] In honouring Mars, the twelve Salii each seem to have appeared as a miniature of the god. This attempt at mimicry is also considered in Virgil's depiction of the Salian rite in honour of Hercules. Instead of armour, in his account the Salii wear pelts (*pelles*) and crowns made of poplar. They clothe themselves in accordance with their image of Hercules, as Virgil makes unmistakably clear.[109] Even though Virgil's account is surely imaginative, as it is embedded in the mythic epic about Aeneas, the great ancestor of the Romans, it is nevertheless striking that he emphasizes the act of mimicry – a mimicry that finds expression in Plutarch's and Dionysius' depictions of the Salian ritual dance. That Virgil, being a Roman author, stresses this point so heavily supports the possibility that Plutarch and Dionysius knowingly or unknowingly provide reports about this very strategy in regard to Mars.

Whether Virgil's story is pure fiction or not, it accords with the other two illustrations which draw on common strategies for the manipulation of the nervous system and then interweave these strategies with a mimicry of the deity being honoured. As illustrated in the preceding sections of this chapter, the use of body and vocal techniques elicits a hypnotic induction that results in a lack of voluntary control – a dissociative mind – that makes the agent vulnerable to suggestive processes. Since the current cultural, social, and most of all ritual environment provide the suggestive processes for the most part, the dissociative effect might be interpreted in accordance with the symbolic world created through ritual. As the deity is not merely addressed but imitated, the ritual environment most probably *suggests* that the performers should attribute the deity's identity to their state of mind. In the words of McNamara, 'donning a mask [of a deity] decenters the person's executive identity and makes it easier for the person to access alternative identities'.[110] The Salii achieve this result by donning

---

[105] Plut. *Vit. Num.* 13.4. Further gods that may be addressed are Ianus: Varro *Ling.* 7.26–27, Macrob. *Sat.* 1.9.11, 14; Jupiter: Dion. Hal. *Ant. Rom.* 2.70–71, Quint. *Inst.* 1.6.40–41, Lucian. *Salt.* 20; Hercules: Verg. *Aen.* 8.276–305.
[106] Liv. 1.20.4.   [107] Dion. Hal. *Ant. Rom.* 2.70.2.
[108] According to Helbig (1905: 236–240), these *apices* were also made of bronze.
[109] Verg. *Aen.* 8.276–305.
[110] McNamara 2009: 171. The sociologist Roger Caillois ([1958] 2001: 87–97) provides a similar, though less precise picture of this process of mimicry.

the garb of a deity. If the assumption is correct that the human observers were impacted by these performances as well, then the very same suggestive process might have made them believe that they had quasi-superhuman beings, or simply 'possessed' priests, before their eyes, just as the funerary attendants, according to Appian, believed in the 'possession' of Marc Anthony by the deceased Gaius Caesar during a similar dissociative performance.[111]

Taking the above together, the Salian performance was neither simple mimicry of nature nor a strategy to channel and 'organize' the human passion for anger and murder into a more peaceful 'world of harmony' physically constructed by the sound of flutes.[112] In contrast to the deeply rooted scholarly notion of affect control, an analysis based on cognitive principles is able to reconstruct these performances as highly arousing, dissociative techniques that most likely resulted in mimicry of the addressed and imitated gods.

BIBLIOGRAPHY

Alvar Nuño, A., J. Alvar Ezquerra and G. Woolf eds. 2021. *SENSORIVM: The Senses in Roman Polytheism*. Leiden.
Andersen, M. 2019. 'Predictive Coding in Agency Detection', *Religion, Brain, and Behavior* 9: 65–84.
Andersen, M. and U. Schjødt. 2017. 'How Does Religious Experience Work in Predictive Minds?' *Religion, Brain, and Behavior* 7: 320–323.
Andersen, M., T. Pfeiffer, S. Müller and U. Schjødt. 2019. 'Agency Detection in Predictive Minds: A Virtual Reality Study', *Religion, Brain, and Behavior* 9: 52–64.
Atran, S. 2002. *In Gods We Trust: The Evolutionary Landscape of Religion*. Oxford.
Azari, N. P., J. Missimer and R. J. Seitz. 2005. 'Religious Experience and Emotion. Evidence for Distinctive Cognitive Neural Patterns', *The International Journal for the Psychology of Religion* 75: 263–281.
Barsalou, L. W., A. K Barbey, W. K. Simmons and A. Santos. 2005. 'Embodiment in Religious Knowledge', *Journal of Cognition and Culture* 5: 14–57.
Borgna, E. 1993. 'Ancile e arma ancila: osservationi sullo scudo dei Salii', *Ostraka* 2: 9–42.
Bremmer, J. 2008. *Greek Religion and Culture: The Bible and the Ancient Near East*. Leiden.
   2017. 'Roman Maenads', in K. M. Coleman, ed. *Albert's Anthology*, 23–25. Cambridge, MA.

---

[111] App. *BC* 2.146.   [112] As suggested by Habinek 2005: 30–33.

2019. 'Greek Maenadism', in J. Bremmer, ed. *The World of Greek Religion and Mythology*. Wissenschaftliche Untersuchungen zum Neuen Testament 433, 251–271. Tübingen.
Burton, R. F. 1897. *Catullus. Carmina*. London.
Caillois, R. [1958] 2001. *Man, Play and Games*. Chicago, IL
Calame, C. [1977] 2001. *Choruses of Young Women in Ancient Greece: Their Morphology, Religious Role, and Social Functions*. Oxford.
Cary, E. 1937. *Dionysius of Halicarnassus. Roman Antiquities, Vols 1–7*. Cambridge, MA.
Ceccarelli, P. 1998. *La pirrica nell'antichità greco romana: studi sulla danza armata*. Pisa.
Chalupa, A. 2014. 'Pythiai and Inspired Divination in the Delphic Oracle: Can Cognitive Sciences Provide Us with an Access to "Dead Minds"? *Journal of Cognitive Historiography* 1: 24–51.
Chaniotis, A. 2013. 'Staging and Feeling the Presence of God: Emotion and Theatricality in Religious Celebrations in the Roman East', in L. Bricault and C. Bonnet, eds. *Panthée: Religious Transformations in the Graeco-Roman Empire*. Religions in the Graeco-Roman World 177, 169–189. Leiden.
Chiarini, S. 2016. 'Ἐγώ εἰμι Ἑρμῆς: Eine dramaturgische Facette der antiken Zaubersprache', *Tyche* 31: 78–101.
Cirilli, R. 1913. *Les prêtres danseurs de Rome: étude sur la corporation sacerdotale des Saliens*. Paris.
Corre, N. 2013. 'Noms barbares et "barbarisation" dans les formules efficacies latines', in M. Tardieu, A. van den Kerchove and M. Zago, eds. *Noms barbares, Vol.1 Formes et contextes d'une pratique magique*, 93–108. Turnhout.
Crippa, S. 1999. 'Entre vocalité et écriture: la voix de la sibylle et les rites vocaux des magiciens', in C. Batsch, U. Egelhaaf-Gaiser and R. Stepper, eds. *Zwischen Krise und Alltag: Antike Religionen im Mittelmeerraum*, 95–110. Stuttgart.
Czachesz, I. 2015. 'Religious Experience in Mediterranean Antiquity: Introduction to the Special Issue', *Journal of Cognitive Historiography* 2: 5–13.
  2016. *Cognitive Science and the New Testament: A New Approach to Early Christian Research*. Oxford.
Damasio, A. 2010. *The Self Comes to Mind: Constructing the Conscious Brain*. New York, NY.
Deeley, Q., D. A. Oakley, E. Walsh, V. Bell, M. A. Mehta and P. W. Halligan. 2014. 'Modelling Psychiatric and Cultural Possession Phenomena with Suggestion and fMRI', *Cortex* 53: 107–119.
Dell'Isola, M. 2019. '"They Are Not the Words of a Rational Man": Ecstatic Prophecy in Montanism', in V. Gasparini, M. Patzelt, R. Raja, A.-K. Rieger, J. Rüpke and E. Urciuoli, eds. *Lived Religion in the Ancient Mediterranean World: Approaching Religious Transformations from Archaeology, History and Classics*. Berlin.

Duff, J. D. 1928. *Lucan. The Civil War (Pharsalia)*. Cambridge, MA.
Dumézil, G. 1966. *La religion romaine archaïque*. Paris.
Feldt, L. 2017. 'The Literary Aesthetics of Religious Narratives: Probing Literary-Aesthetic Form, Emotion, and Sensory Effects in Exodus 7-11', in A. K. Grieser and J. Johnston, eds. *Aesthetics of Religion: A Connective Concept*, 121–143. Berlin.
Forbes, C. 1995. *Prophecy and Inspired Speech in Early Christianity and Its Hellenistic Environment*. Tübingen.
Geertz, A. W. 2010. 'Brain, Body and Culture: A Biocultural Theory of Religion', *Method and Theory in the Study of Religion* 22: 304–321.
Gill, C. 1985. 'Ancient Psychotherapy', *Journal of History of Ideas* 46: 307–325.
Gordon, R. 1987. 'Aelian's Peony: The Location of Magic in Graeco-Roman Tradition', *Comparative Criticism* 9: 59–95.
  1990. 'From Republic to Principate: Priesthood, Religion and Ideology', in M. Beard and J. North, eds. *Pagan Priests*, 179–198. London.
  2020. '(Re-)Modelling Religious Experience: Some Experiments with Hymnic Form in the Imperial Period', in V. Gasparini, M. Patzelt, R. Raja, A.-K. Rieger, J. Rüpke and E. Urciuoli, eds. *Lived Religion in the Ancient Mediterranean World: Approaching Religious Transformations from Archaeology, History and Classics*, 23–48. Berlin.
Gorea, M. 2013. 'Des noms imprononçables', in M. Tardieu, A. van den Kerchove and M. Zago, eds. *Noms Barbares, Vol.1 Formes et contexts d'une pratique magique*, 109–120. Turnhout.
Graf, F. 1995. 'Tanz und Initiation in der griechisch-römischen Antike', in M. Möckel and H. Volkmann, eds. *Spiel, Tanz und Märchen*, 83–96. Regensburg.
  1996. *Gottesnähe und Schadenszauber: Die Magie in der griechisch-römischen Antike*. Munich.
Grieser, A. and J. Johnston. 2017. 'What Is an Aesthetics of Religion? From the Senses to Meaning and Back Again', in A. K. Grieser and J. Johnston, eds. *Aesthetics of Religion: A Connective Concept*, 1–49. Berlin.
Guittard, C. 2007. *Carmen et prophéties à Rome*. Turnhout.
  2013. 'From the *Curia* on the Palatine Hill to the *Regia* on the Forum', in N. Cusumano, V. Gasparini, A. Mastrocinque and J. Rüpke, eds. *Memory and Religious Experience in the Greco-Roman World*, 177–184. Stuttgart.
Habinek, T. 2005. *The World of Roman Song: From Ritualized Speech to Social Order*. Baltimore, MD.
Hardie, A. 2005. 'The Ancient Etymology of *Carmen*', *Papers of the Langford Latin Seminar* 12: 71–94.
Harkins, A. K. and M. Popović, eds. 2015. Religious Experience and the Dead Sea Scrolls [Special issue]. *Dead Sea Discoveries* 22(3): 247–357.
Harvey, S. A. 2006. *Scenting Salvation: Ancient Christianity and the Olfactory Imagination*. Berkeley.
  2014. 'The Senses in Religion: Piety, Critique, Competition', in J. Toner, ed. *A Cultural History of the Senses in Antiquity: 500 BC – 500 AD*, 91–114. London.

Heinzel, E. 1996. 'Über den Ursprung der Salier', in F. Blakolmer, ed. *Fremde Zeiten: Festschrift für Jürgen Borchhardt*, Vol. 2, 197–212. Wien.
Helbig, W. 1905. *Sur les attributs des Saliens*. Paris.
Hick, J. 2010. *The New Frontier of Religion and Science: Religious Experience, Neuroscience and the Transcendent*. Basingstoke.
Hohwy, J. 2013. *The Predictive Mind*. Oxford.
Jegindø, E.-M. E., L. Vase, J. Jegindø and A.W. Geertz. 2013. 'Pain and Sacrifice: Experience and Modulation of Pain in a Religious Piercing Ritual', *International Journal for the Psychology of Religion* 23: 171–187.
Konvalinka, I., D. Xygalatas, J. Bulbulia, U. Schjødt, E.-M. Jegindø, S. Wallot, G. Van Orden and A. Roepstorff. 2011. 'Synchronized Arousal between Performers and Related Spectators in a Fire-Walking Ritual', *Proceedings of the National Academy of Sciences* 108: 8514–8519.
Kowalzig, B. 2007. *Singing for the Gods: Performances of Myth and Ritual in Archaic and Classical Greece*. Oxford.
Kundtová Klocová, E. and A. W. Geertz. 2019. 'Ritual and Embodied Cognition', in R. Uro, J. J. Day, R. E. DeMaris and R. Roitto, eds. *The Oxford Handbook of Early Christian Ritual*, 74–94. Oxford.
Laderman, C. 1996. 'The Poetics of Healing in Malay Shamanistic Performances', in C. Laderman and M. Roseman, eds. *The Performance of Healing*, 115–142. London.
Linforth, I. M. 1946. 'The Corybantic Rites in Plato', *University of California Publications in Classical Philology* 13: 121–162.
Maurenbrecher, B. 1894. *Carminum Saliarium Reliquiae*. Leipzig.
Mauss, M. [1936] 1979. 'Techniques of the Body', in *Sociology and Psychology: Essays*, 97–123. London.
McNamara, P. 2009. *The Neuroscience of Religious Experience*. Cambridge.
Meyer, B. ed. 2010. *Aesthetic Formations: Media, Religion, and the Senses*. Basingstoke.
Münster, D. 2001. *Religionsästhetik und Anthropologie der Sinne: Vorarbeiten zu einer Religionsethnologie der Produktion und Rezeption ritueller Medien*. Munich.
Newberg, A., N. A. Wintering, D. Morgan and M. R. Waldman. 2006. 'The Measurement of Regional Blood Flow during Glossolalia: A Preliminary SPECT Study', *Psychiatry Research: Neuroimaging* 148: 67–71.
Pachis, P. 1996. 'Γαλλαῖον Κυβέλης ὀλόλυγμα (Anthol. Palat. VI, 173): l'élément orgiastique dans le culte de Cybèle', in E. N. Lane, ed. *Cybele, Attis and Related Cults: Essays in Memory of M. J. Vermaseren*. Religions in the Graeco-Roman World 131, 193–222. Leiden.
Panagiotidou, O. 2014. 'The Asklepios Cult: Where Brains, Minds, and Bodies Interact with the World', *Journal of Cognitive Historiography* 1: 14–23.
2017. *The Roman Mithras Cult: A Cognitive Approach*. London.
Pattison, E. M. 1968. 'Behavioral Science Research on the Nature of Glossolalia', *Journal of the American Scientific Affiliation* 20: 73–86.

Patzelt, M. 2018. *Über das Beten der Römer: Gebete im spätrepublikanischen und frühkaiserzeitlichen Rom als Ausdruck gelebter Religion*. Berlin.

2019. 'Praying As a "Woman among Men": Reconsidering Clodius' Failed Prayer in Cicero's Speech On his House', *Religion in the Roman Empire* 5(2): 271–291.

Pentcheva, B. 2014. 'The Power of Glittering Materiality: Mirror Reflections between Poetry and Architecture in Greek and Arabic Medieval Culture', *Ancient Near Eastern Studies. Supplementa* 47: 223–268.

Perrin, B. (trans.) 1914. *Plutarch. Lives, Volume I. Theseus and Romulus. Lycurgus and Numa. Solon and Publicola*. Cambridge, MA.

Reichardt, A. 1916. *Die Lieder der Salier und das Lied der Arvalbrüder*. Leipzig.

Richlin, A. 2014. *Arguments with Silence: Writing the History of Roman Women*. Ann Arbor, MI.

Rouget, G. 1985. *Music and Trance: A Theory of the Relations between Music and Possession*. Chicago, IL.

Samarin, W. 1972. 'Variation and Variables in Religious Glossolalia', *Language in Society* 1: 121–130.

Sarullo, G. 2014. *Il 'Carmen Saliare': indagini filologiche e riflessioni linguistiche*. Berlin.

Sarullo, G. and D. J. Taylor. 2013. 'Two Fragments of the Carmen Saliare and the Manuscript Tradition of Varro's De Lingua Latina', *Zeitschrift für Buchgeschichte* 91/92: 1–10.

Scheid, J. 2015. *The Gods, the State, and the Individual: Reflections on Civic Religion in Rome*. Philadelphia, PA.

Schjødt, U. 2009. 'The Religious Brain: A General Introduction to the Experimental Neuroscience of Religion', *Method and Theory in the Study of Religion* 21: 310–339.

Sørensen, J. 2007. *A Cognitive Theory of Magic*. Lanham, MD.

Šterbenc Erker, D. 2011. 'Stimme und Klang im Bacchuskult: Die *ululatio*', in E. Meyer-Dietrich, ed. *Laut und Leise: Der Gebrauch von Stimme und Klang in historischen Kulturen*, 173–194. Bielefeld.

2013. *Religiöse Rollen römischer Frauen in 'griechischen' Ritualen*. Stuttgart.

Tambiah, S. S. 1968. 'The Magical Power of Words', *Man* 3: 175–208.

Taves, A. 2009. *Religious Experience Reconsidered: A Building Block Approach to the Study of Religion and Other Special Things*. Princeton, NJ.

2016. *Revelatory Events: Three Case Studies of the Emergence of New Spiritual Paths*. Princeton, NJ.

Torelli, M. 1984. *Lavinio e Roma: riti iniziatici e matrimonio tra archeologia e storia*. Rome.

1990. 'Riti di passagio maschili di Roma arcaica', *Mélanges de l'École française de Rome – Antiquité* 102: 93–106.

Trost, W. and P. Vuilleumier. 2013. 'Rhythmic Entrainment As a Mechanism for Emotion Induction by Music: A Neurophysiological Perspective', in T. Cochrane, B. Fantini and K. R. Scherer, eds. *The Emotional Power of*

    Music: Multidisciplinary Perspectives on Musical Arousal, Expression, and Social Control, 213–225. Oxford.
Turner, V. 1974. *The Ritual Process*. Harmondsworth.
Ustinova, Y. 2009. *Caves and the Ancient Greek Mind: Descending Underground in the Search for Ultimate Truth*. Oxford.
    2018. *Divine Mania: Alteration of Consciousness in Ancient Greece*. London.
    2021. 'Hirpi Sorani and Modern Fire-Walkers: Rejoicing through Pain in Extreme Rituals', in A. Alvar Nuño, J. Alvar Ezquerra and G. Woolf, eds. *SENSORIVM: The Senses in Roman Polytheism*, 71–89. Leiden.

PART III

Gender

CHAPTER 6

The Bacchants Are Silent
Using Cognitive Science to Explore the Experience of the Oreibasia

Vivienne McGlashan

On account of this, in many cities of the Greeks in alternate years bacchic groups of women assemble, and it is lawful for *parthenoi* to carry the *thyrsos* [a ritual staff] and to come together in divine inspiration crying '*Euai*' and honouring the god, while the matrons, formed into groups, sacrifice to the god and perform bacchic ritual, and in general hymn the presence of Dionysus, acting the role of those, as history relates, who were in old times the companions of the god, the maenads.[1]

In the first century BCE, Diodorus Siculus described a ritual that, so far as we can tell, was performed for at least a thousand years, across many parts of Greece and the wider Mediterranean area.[2] Maenadic ritual was performed as part of civic cult, overseen by a high-ranking priestess, to bring Dionysus' favour to the city and avert his destructive wrath. Maenadic ritual practitioners were respectable women who honoured Dionysus by taking the role of his mythological entourage in a tightly regulated civic event. However, the women who carried out this valued public service had mythical counterparts who were portrayed in a very different way: the maenads who accompany Dionysus in myth, most famously depicted by the late fifth-century Athenian playwright Euripides in his play *Bacchae*. These mythical maenads are ecstatic devotees and companions of Dionysus, endowed with superhuman powers, but also raging, murderous avatars of the god's bloodthirsty vengeance.

This chapter is adapted from my doctoral thesis, in progress at the time of writing, under the supervision of Esther Eidinow and Emma Cole at the University of Bristol. I am immensely grateful for their advice and guidance, and for that of the faculty and postgraduate communities at the University of Nottingham, the CAARE project, Jan Bremmer, Richard Seaford, Ellie Mackin Roberts, Maria Haley, Devan Turner, Una Markham, and David Wilson. All errors and omissions in content and translation are mine.

[1] Diod. Sic. 4.3.3
[2] A full list of the scholarship on maenadic ritual is prohibitively extensive. For comprehensive and accessible overviews, the reader is referred to Dodds 1940, Henrichs 1978, Bremmer 1984, Henrichs 1984, Bowden 2010: 105–136, Ustinova 2018: 169–216.

The distinction between ritual performers and mythical maenads is frustratingly blurred in the surviving literature.[3] In our prose literary sources, the ritual performers are often simply called 'the women around Dionysus',[4] or by a collective group name particular to a centre of cult activity.[5] They may also be called *bakchai* (Romanized as 'bacchants'), a word whose etymology is uncertain but may relate to delirium or intoxication.[6] Or, more rarely, they are called *mainades*, 'madwomen', the same word that Diodorus uses for the mythical companions of Dionysus.[7] A female figure on a red-figured stamnos in Naples, apparently performing some sort of Dionysian ritual, is named MAINAS, 'madwoman'.[8] Any distinction that there may once have been seems to have disappeared entirely by the late antique period: the sixth-century CE grammarian Hesychius defines *mainades* simply as '*hai Bakchai*', and *Bakchê* as 'one of the *bakchai*, a woman of Dionysus'. If at some point in Greek history there was a precise difference in meaning, it is lost to us.

Lacking first-hand or eye-witness accounts of this mysterious ritual, historians have struggled to reconcile the 'madwomen' of myth with prestigious civic cult activity. This difficulty reflects the blurred boundary between performer and role: in Greek there is no distinction between an actor's face and the theatrical mask he wears, both are *prosôpon*. Plutarch mentions ritual performers undergoing some sort of change in mental state but does not elaborate on what he means or how common this was.[9] Were the ritual practitioners actually 'madwomen' in some way, and, if so, what would the ancient Greeks have understood by 'mad' in this context?

---

[3] Difficulties in using tragedy to draw conclusions about ritual: Seaford 1981, 1987 and 1996, Scullion 1999 and 2002. Interpreting maenadic ritual in art, see Lawler 1927, Edwards 1960, McNally 1978, Henrichs 1987, Hedreen 1994, Carpenter 1997: 52–69, 70–84, Moraw 1998, Peirce 1998, Heinemann 2016.

[4] Plut. *De mul. vir.* 13 (*Mor.* 249EF).

[5] Such as the Delphic Thyiades: Paus. 10.4.2–4, Plut. *De mul. vir.* 13 and 15 (*Mor.* 249EF and 251EF), *De primo frigido* 18 (*Mor.* 953D), also the 'Sixteen' in Elis: Paus. 6.26.1, Plut. *Mor.* 251E, 299B, Weniger 1883: 1–24, Brown 1982. Euiades: Posidippus AB44.2; also the Clodones and Mimallones: Plut. *Vit. Alex.* 2.5, Polyaenus, *Strat.* 4.1, Ath. 5.198E, Strabo 10.3.10.

[6] E.g. in Pl. *Ion* 534A. On the possible etymology of *bakchai*, see Santamaría 2013. Aesch. *Eum.* 25 uses *bakchai* to refer to mythical characters, and Euripides uses both terms throughout *Bacchae*.

[7] 'Maenads' as ritual groups: Eur. *Ion* 550–552, *IMagn.* 215.26, 32 in Kern 1900; the inscription is dated to the middle of the second century CE by letter forms (Henrichs 1978: 123–130), but the events described are dated to 278–250 BCE. 'Maenads' in line 26 is part of the oracular pronouncement, and may therefore be poetic, but line 32 refers to real women.

[8] Red-figured stamnos, late fifth century BCE: Naples Museo Archeologico Nazionale, Inv. H2419. On the Lenaea vases, which incorporate ritual elements, see Peirce 1998.

[9] Plut. *De mul. vir.* 13.

The question of whether ritual participants could have experienced anything like the ecstasy, violent rage, or epiphanic visions found in artistic depictions of mythical maenads has stimulated a long-running debate encompassing arguments about hysteria, belief, and the interplay between cult and myth. At one end of the spectrum are disturbing reconstructions in which Greek matrons tear apart living animals and devour the still-warm meat in a sacramental meal.[10] At the other extreme, the positivist approach privileges the 'hard' prosaic and epigraphic evidence, which rarely mentions personal experience.[11] These accounts neither manage satisfactorily to reconcile the civic context with the artistic depictions, nor do they adequately explain the enduring, elusive association of ritual practice with an alteration in participants' mental states. In this chapter I will try to integrate artistic and historical narratives by exploring the lived experience and religious identity of historical maenads. Inspired by Jan Bremmer's 1984 paper on the physiological effects of the *oreibasia*, I will revisit the ancient evidence with an interpretative framework drawn from cognitive sciences, looking at religious experience in the context of an embodied mind.[12]

Dancing for Dionysus: The Sources for Maenadic Ritual

The ritual is normally called simply the *oreibasia*, 'mountain-going', and was performed by groups of women on a trieteric basis (every two years) in honour of the god Dionysus.[13] Hellenistic inscriptions and an incomplete epigram for a ritual participant attest to the ritual's existence in Miletus and Magnesia-on-the-Meander in Asia Minor and in Macedonia.[14] Plutarch seems to have accepted the ritual's antiquity in Delphi, describing an occurrence during the Third Sacred War (around 356–346 BCE).[15] Although the ritual does not seem ever to have been celebrated in Attica it was familiar to the audiences of Classical drama: passing references

---

[10] E.g. Harrison 1903: 388–400, Dodds 1940 and 1960.
[11] E.g. Rapp 1872, Henrichs 1978, 1982, and 1984.
[12] Bremmer 1984, revised in Bremmer 2019.
[13] Mountain location: *IMilet.* 733.3 in Herrmann 1998, Posidippus *AB*44.4, Plut. *De primo frigido* 18 (*Mor.* 953D), *Vit. Alex.* 2. Biennial: Paus. 10.4.3, Diod. Sic. 4.3.3., *LSAM* 48.20 (= *CGRN* 138).
[14] Miletus: epitaph for a priestess of Dionysus, second century BCE, *IMilet.* 733; duties of the priestess, 276/5 BCE, *LSAM* 48. Magnesia-on-the-Meander: *IMagn.* 215. Macedonia: Posidippus *AB*44.
[15] Plut. *De mul. vir.* 13.

mention the Delphic ritual, maenadic activity in Thebes, and women's enthusiasm for Dionysian rites in general.[16]

On the evening of the ritual, groups called *thiasoi* would march through the city singing hymns and invoking Dionysus with cries of '*euai!*'[17] Participants would wear a *nebris*, a spotted fawnskin, and carry torches and a staff called a *thyrsos*, and perhaps even live snakes.[18] After a public procession and sacrifice, the *thiasoi* would then ascend a nearby mountain and dance through the night to the sound of drums.[19] A Hellenistic inscription from Miletus suggests that there might be several such *thiasoi*, all processing together; many of these might be mixed-sex and made up of private individuals, but at least one *thiasos* (perhaps as many as three in some cities) would be sanctioned by the city as taking primacy, and this group would be all-female and led by the local priestess of Dionysus.[20]

In poetic literature it is often difficult to tell whether the group referred to belongs to myth or ritual.[21] This is illustrated by the names of the groups or civic colleges that performed the ritual. At least two collegiate names, the famous Thyiades who danced on Parnassus and the Macedonian Mimallones, also seem to be used for mythical Dionysian women or nymphs, further blurring the boundaries between myth and reality.[22]

These mythical maenads are, according to Diodorus, the figures that the ritual maenads were thought to be imitating, but what did it mean in Greek religious thought to 'imitate' a maenad, and how far might such role play go? Eva Keuls claims that the Hellenistic *oreibasia* was a sham performance, that 'these latter-day raving madwomen were faking it'.[23] The important word in Diodorus' explanation is *mimoumenas*, which derives from *mimêsis*.[24] Plato, in his sustained attack on all art forms in

---

[16] Eur. *Cyc.* 63–72, *Ion* 550–554, *Phoen.* 1751–1757, Ar. *Lys.* 1–3, *Nub.* 603–606. Pausanias (10.4.3) tells us that Athenian women joined the Delphic group on Parnassus.

[17] 'Euai': Diod. Sic. 4.3.3, *SEG* 32.552, also suggested by Soph. *Ant.* 964, 1134, *OT* 211, *Trach.* 219, Eur. *Bacch.* 140, 1034, Callistratus, *Statuaram Descriptiones* 2.

[18] Fawnskin: Plut. *De Is. et Os.* 35. Torches: Alcm. fr. 56.1, in Campbell 1988: 433; Eur. *Ion* 550–554, 714–717; Plut. *De mul. vir.* 13. Thyrsos: Diod. Sic. 4.3.3. Snakes: Plut. *Vit. Alex.* 2.5, Ath. 5.196A–203B.

[19] Ritual reconstruction: Bremmer 1984: 274–282 (258–266 in Bremmer 2019).

[20] 'The *thiasos* of the populace' (*ton thiason … tou dēmosiou*) and its primacy above other *thiasoi*: *LSAM* 48.3–4; led by the priestess Alcmeonis: *IMilet.* 733.3, 'she led you ['city bacchants' *(poliêtides bakchai)*], to the mountain' *(hymas keis oros êge)* discussed Merkelbach 1972, Henrichs 1978: 148–149, Connelly 2007: 167–168, 255. In the first century CE, Klea was *archicla* of the Delphic Thyiades; this may be a cult title but is not attested elsewhere: Plut. *De Is. et Os.* 35=*Mor.* 364E.

[21] E.g. Soph. *Ant.* 1146–1152, Dioscorides' epigram for Aleximenes, Gow-Page, *GP* 25.

[22] Alcm. fr. 63, Strabo 10.3.10.   [23] Keuls 1985: 358.

[24] This is a notoriously difficult word to translate; see Halliwell 2009: 15–22.

The Republic,²⁵ described *mimêsis* as something to deceive children and fools, and this seems to be the interpretation that Keuls has adopted. But we should not assume that most Greeks would have agreed with Plato, or that Plato's focus on audience response means that there was no ancient conception of the effect of a performance on the performer.

'*Mimêsis*' is certainly used to denote what actors do on stage, but it does not always mean something that is consciously counterfeit or deceptive. *Mimêsis* is used of songs offered to the gods and other aspects of ritual performance: *mimêsis* was in fact highly enough regarded for the art to have its own Muse.²⁶ This suggests something that had a position in the ongoing dialogue between humanity and gods, that required the same sort of inspiration as the creation of poetry and music. If mimetic performance is, then, comparable to drama and music, we should also assume that it was understood to create an emotional effect in the same way. Plato himself acknowledges that music can affect the soul, and Aristotle is clear that he considered poetic *mimêsis* capable of producing an emotional effect.²⁷

The Greeks also knew perfectly well that mimetic performance affects the performer as well as the audience. Aristotle regarded the best kind of *mimêsis* as being that which is as close as possible to the original, with as little conscious interference from the performer as possible.²⁸ In the name of creative authenticity, Aristophanes' playwright Agathon adopts the costumes and mannerisms of the characters whose lines he is composing.²⁹ When Plato talks about the man who becomes corrupted through imitating his immoral master,³⁰ he clearly means that mimetic performance has changed the performer. We cannot assume that Diodorus means that the *mimêsis* of the bacchants is an empty performance.

Mythical Role Models: The Maenad in Greek Imagination

The mythical figures who were being imitated by the ritual participants are found in poetry from Homer onwards, and they feature frequently in vase-painting from at least the sixth century BCE.³¹ They were most vividly

---

²⁵ Pl. *Resp.* 10.598AD.
²⁶ Hom. *Hym. Apollo* 156–161, Aesch. fr. 57 in Sommerstein 2008. *Mimos* (*mimoi* in the fragment) is an early form of the noun *mimêsis*: Halliwell 2009: 17–18.
²⁷ Pl. *Resp.* 398C–400C, Arist. *Poet.* 1453B.   ²⁸ Arist. *Poet.* 1461B–1462A.
²⁹ Ar. *Thesm.* 146–152.   ³⁰ Pl. *Grg.* 510b–511A.
³¹ 'Like a maenad': Hom. *Hymn Dem.* 386, Hom. *Il.* 22.460, cf. 6.389. See Schlesier 1993. Lost or fragmentary plays by Aeschylus and Iophron, the titles of which suggest a chorus of maenads: Sommerstein 2008: 18–23, Suda s.v. Iophrôn. On *Bacchae* and maenadic ritual see footnote 2, particularly Dodds, Henrichs, and Bremmer.

brought to life in Euripides' play *Bacchae*, which depicts two groups of women worshipping Dionysus. One group, the Chorus, arrive with Dionysus from Asia, his companions and rapturous worshippers. The other group are the townswomen of Thebes, whom Dionysus has driven mad as punishment for the royal family's refusal to acknowledge his divinity. In their madness, the Theban matrons become passionate devotees of the new Dionysian cult, leaving home to dance for him on the mountain above the city.

There are certainly superficial points of comparison between *Bacchae* and the Hellenistic ritual, which may be due to imitation or archaizing. Both involve trieteric ritual dances on a mountain, fawnskins, *thyrsoi* and *tympana* (hand-held skin drums), and singing of Dionysus' presence.[32] Euripides knew about the *oreibasia*; in *Ion* he refers to a torchlit ritual at Delphi performed by 'the girls of Delphi, the maenads of Bacchus'.[33] There is no reason to believe that, when he dressed his mythical cult devotees in fawnskins, he deliberately chose to give them a different costume to that worn by the ritual maenads of his own day.

But mythical maenads are mythical, and there are elements of their behaviour which seem incongruous with civic ritual. The most shocking example of unlikely ritual behaviour, found in several maenadic myths and a small number of vase-paintings, is *sparagmos*, the act of tearing apart a living creature.[34] In *Bacchae*, the Theban women are attacked by a group of men who seek to abduct the king's mother and bring her back to Thebes.[35] The women come to her defence but, unable to catch their assailants, turn their fury instead on nearby cattle, which they tear into shreds.[36] Later, Pentheus' death is described in ghastly detail.[37] His mother Agaue, eyes rolling, wrenches his arm off, wedging her foot into his armpit to gain better leverage. His aunt Ino claws at his side, stripping the flesh from his ribs, while his other aunt, Autonoe, clamours to get close enough to join in. His pleas, and later his wordless groans, are lost in the shrill, triumphant calls of the women, who gleefully fling the shreds of his flesh into the air.

---

[32] Eur. *Bacch.* 132–167, 690–714, 723–727, also found in vase-painting: Moraw 1998: 29–66, 172–175.
[33] Eur. *Ion* 551–552.
[34] Eur. *Bacch.* 677–774, 1043–1147. Orpheus: Aesch. *Bassarids*: Sommerstein 2008: 18–19, Hyg. *Poet. astr.* 2.6, Eratosth. [*Cat.*] 24. *Sparagmos* in vase-painting: Moraw 1998: 58, 64–65, 142–162, Weaver 2009. The scholarship is best summarized in Bremmer 1984, Henrichs 1978.
[35] Eur. *Bacch.* 677–774.   [36] Eur. *Bacch.* 734–747.   [37] Eur. *Bacch.* 1043–1152.

Few scholars now accept the historicity of *sparagmos*, though some have interpreted it as representing fears about the suppressed rage of disenfranchised Greek women.[38] It seems highly unlikely that ritual maenads would actually carry out such a violent and polluting act. These are not marginalized women, or those whose activities were considered in some way peculiar or distasteful: in the *Cyclops*, Euripides lists female bacchic ritual as being among the great benefits of civilized life.[39] Two maenadic priestesses whose names we know, Alcmeonis and Clea, seem to have had no qualms about celebrating their participation in maenadic ritual; it was a sign of their status, not a comment on their mental health.[40] Likewise, the three Theban maenads who relocated to Magnesia were evidently important community members; they were buried at state expense and their burial places were still known centuries later.[41]

Sparagmos should probably be relegated to the world of myth. But there is another aspect of mythical maenadic behaviour that is more difficult to exclude. The women of *Bacchae* undergo an altered state of consciousness: they dance until exhausted then get up to dance again; they are insensible to pain; they cause springs of wine and milk to bubble from the ground; they experience visual hallucinations; and they nurse wild animals instead of babies.[42] They also have an intensely personal relationship with their god: the Chorus accompany Dionysus from Asia into Greece, singing of the joys of dancing with him and calling him 'the great light' of their celebrations.[43] Similarly, as maenadic iconography becomes established through the fifth century, in vase-painting we find Dionysus appearing surrounded by all-female groups; the satyr-nymph pairs of Archaic art disintegrate, leaving the maenads flanking their god and the satyrs more commonly relegated to supporting roles.[44]

---

[38] For example Keuls 1985: 357–379.   [39] Eur. *Cyc.* 64.
[40] Alcmeonis' epitaph ends by saying that she 'knew her allotted share of fine things': *IMilet.* 733.6. Clea's illustrious family and status are explored by Bowersock 1965: 267–268, Kapetanopoulos 1966: 128–130. On the role of the priestess as an agent of the *polis* during the ritual, see Goff 2004: 215–217.
[41] *IMagn.* 215.24–30.
[42] Eur. *Bacch.* 142–169, 677–768, 1168–1280. On altered states of consciousness in other religious rituals, see Ustinova and Patzelt, this volume.
[43] Eur. *Bacch.* 64–87, 608–609.
[44] Paired nymphs and satyrs flanking Dionysus: skyphos c. 520–500 BCE, Paris Cabinet des Médailles Inv. 343; three neck amphorae from around 510–490 BCE, one in the Berlin Antikensammlung Inv. F1845, another in the Mainz Universitat collection Inv. 73, a third in Munich's Staatliche Antikennsamlungen Inv. 1519. Single-sex groups: Belly amphora c. 500 BCE, Paris Musée du Louvre Inv. G46; hydria by the Kleophrades painter and cup, both c. 480 BCE and in Basel, Antikenmuseum und Sammlung Ludwig, hydria on loan, cup Inv. BS06.276. The changing relationships to Dionysus and satyrs: Moraw 1998: 66–99, 100–139.

Exploring Maenadic Madness: Difficulties and Controversies in Interpretation

In his story of the women of Amphissa, Plutarch describes a group of Dionysian ritual performers as being 'made mad', and, later, as 'not yet having returned to their right mind'.[45] In this state, he says, they wandered through hostile territory before collapsing in a town square thirty miles away. The point of the story is that as a result of their ritual performance the women are in an unusual mental state and unaware of their danger.[46] What Plutarch meant by 'mad' is unknown, but he was writing to a woman who had led the ritual herself, so was unlikely to suggest something she would find unrealistic. But Plutarch's testimony is not usually considered sufficient proof that the ritual could induce an altered state of consciousness. There are two chief schools of thought on whether this 'being out of one's mind' was simply a case of ritual performers simulating 'madness', or a real historical phenomenon.

Adolph Rapp, one of the most influential nineteenth-century writers on maenadic ritual, doubted that the strictly regulated Hellenistic ritual could induce any genuine 'ecstatic' effect, citing the absence of evidence for altered mental states in the prose evidence.[47] For Rapp, an experience of this kind would require a degree of personal faith and freedom of individual religious expression that he did not believe was found in the tightly controlled ancient civic cult, and he simply discards Plutarch's account.[48] In the second half of the twentieth century, Rapp's ideological successor Albert Henrichs produced a series of papers attempting to bridge the gap somewhat between the poetic and prose accounts, but also concluded that 'the peculiar religious identity of the maenads had more to do with sweat and physical exhaustion than with an abnormal state of mind'.[49]

The other main thread of scholarship, popular through the late nineteenth and early twentieth centuries, took the opposite extreme. Erwin Rohde and Jane Ellen Harrison drew on the new discipline of clinical psychology and anthropological research on trance rituals to argue that the ritual *could* induce such changes. Rohde proposed that an early Thracian form of the ritual had once been able to induce profound spiritual experiences, but that ritual regulation from Delphi had reduced classical

---

[45] Plut. *De mul. vir.* 13.
[46] Unlike perhaps the women interrupted while worshipping Demeter who fought back against the intruders using their ritual implements as weapons (Paus. 4.17.1).
[47] Rapp 1872.   [48] Ibid. at 22.   [49] Henrichs 1982: quote from pp. 146–147, 1978, and 1969.

maenadism to a faint afterimage of its original power.⁵⁰ Harrison embraced the intensity of Rohde's Thracian ritual but discarded his theory of its gradual erosion, claiming that the ritual form itself had the power to 'madden' participants.⁵¹ Harrison's work suffers from her desire to develop a unifying theory for all Dionysian cult activity, but her willingness to explore Greek religion using anthropological and psychological theories provided a foundation for Eric Dodds' work.

Dodds developed the use of these theories to build a stronger case for maenadic ritual's ability to induce an altered state of consciousness.⁵² His interpretation of maenadism contains some now discredited ideas,⁵³ but his work was the first serious attempt at addressing not only *whether* maenadic ritual could induce an altered state of consciousness, but also the more challenging question of *how* it might do so. However, like Rohde and Harrison, Dodds assumed that maenadic 'madness' was comparable to what the clinicians of his day would call madness, describing it as a 'mass hysteria' that was 'highly infectious'.⁵⁴

Both positions are problematic and ultimately unsatisfying. The scarcity of evidence for genuinely mind-altering ritual content is a serious problem for those attempting to bring the 'wild' maenad into the civic cult. Those adopting the sceptical approach, on the other hand, drive an unnatural wedge between the reality of the performed ritual and the way that contemporary artists and writers wanted to depict that ritual. One of the key problems is that neither group attempts to define what they mean by 'madness' or 'hysteria' or 'ecstasy'. Traditionally, scholars have tended to assume that any and all unusual behaviours or mental states were regarded in the same way by the ancient sources, and that everything from exhilaration to *sparagmos* would be equally possible once the 'elemental breaks through ... and civilization vanishes'.⁵⁵ Maenadic ritual must therefore either completely disinhibit participants or not induce any mental effects whatsoever. The first conclusion is clearly at odds with the extant evidence and civic context, but the second neglects the undeniable effects that ritual performance can have on the embodied mind.⁵⁶

---

⁵⁰ Rohde 1894 (2): 55. English translation: Rohde 1925: 288–289, with notes on 310–311.
⁵¹ Harrison 1903: 388–400, 478–571, quote from p. 382.
⁵² Dodds 1940; reprinted in Dodds 1951: 207–282.
⁵³ For example, problematic anthropological comparators for *sparagmos* and *omophagia* (eating of raw meat). Dodds 1940: 164–166, refuted by Henrichs 1978: 150–152. On Dodds' related interest in investigating spiritualism using scientific methods, see Lowe 2019.
⁵⁴ Dodds 1940: 157, 159. Against this view, see Bremmer 1984: 273–274 (=2019: 258).
⁵⁵ Dodds 1940: 159. ⁵⁶ Geertz 2010.

A third interpretative path, developed relatively recently, attempts to reconcile the two extremes and correct their faults. Jan Bremmer's essay, *Greek Maenadism Reconsidered*, assumed that the artistic maenadic motifs – including changes to mental state – developed and survived because they had some relevance to the historical ritual. He examined the established ritual elements, such as altitude, torchlight, and drumming, and argued that their physiological effects could induce euphoria and release from the weight of normal cares.[57] Bremmer's exploration does not closely examine the mechanisms by which these neurological changes would be effected,[58] but his work opened up two areas for discussion: first, how might the ritual form and environment affect the embodied mind, and, secondly, how might these changes be experienced and interpreted?

Cultural Knowledge in Predictive Processing

Bremmer's approach is particularly suitable for use with methods and theories from the cognitive science of religion (CSR). Although we have no accounts from ritual participants of what they thought or felt, we know broadly what they were doing and where they were doing it, and so we can make statements about what sensory information their brains would be receiving during the ritual. Furthermore, we have information about the sorts of associations and symbols that were present in Greek culture about the 'ideal' maenad as found in artistic depictions.

Cultural knowledge plays a role in how sensory information is processed by the brain, in a theory of cognition called predictive processing.[59] In order to exploit the environment, the brain needs to acquire and organize information about the environment. Information about the world is collected in the form of a constant stream of raw sensory data from around the body, which must be processed by the brain to understand or interpret what environmental cues have caused the sensory effects. To do this, the brain selects a model or 'schema', generated from knowledge about the world, drawn from the memory of experiences and learned and taught information. The brain generates many such schemata and selects the one

---

[57] Bremmer 1984: esp. 281–282, 285–286 (=2019: 265–266, 269).
[58] Based on neurophysiological research, it is unlikely that even Parnassus is high enough to impact on cognition: Gore et al. 1996, Shukitt-Hale and Lieberman 1996, Gore et al. 2008, Higgins et al. 2010.
[59] This is necessarily a simplified explanation: see Andersen 2019 for an overview, Clark 2013, Hohwy 2013 for more detail; see also the Introduction, and essays by Ustinova, Chapter 2, Scott, Chapter 8, and Patzelt, Chapter 5, in this volume.

that best matches the data, which is then used as the dominant working representation of what the environment is most likely to be like. These schemata form the 'top down' input that informs how the brain uses the 'bottom up' data to make predictions about the surroundings and prepare to deal with them. Cultural knowledge feeds into the creation of such schemata and therefore into how sensory data are interpreted.

The model of predictive processing provides a role for the artistic depictions of maenads in understanding the lived ritual experience; the artistic 'wild' maenad would have influenced interpretative schemata. If we accept, as seems to be indicated by the ancient usages, that the term 'maenad' represents both the cultural construct of the ideal companion of Dionysus and the historical ritual participants who imitated this ideal, then differentiating between mythical and historical maenads in art becomes immaterial.[60] Speculation on the historicity of artistic depictions is ultimately unnecessary if we are using the sources to establish the qualities of the 'ideal maenad' that the ritual practitioner might have been visualizing as she began her mimetic performance. References from Homer, religious hymns, quotable snatches of tragic verse, and elegant painted pottery would have informed the culturally defined model of the 'ideal maenad'.

Following Bremmer's proposal that recurring symbols in the poetic maenadic narrative represent physical effects of the ritual form, I propose to explore how participants' cultural knowledge interacted with sensory data, activating certain cognitive processes that appear as maenadic symbols. In the final section of this chapter, we will test this hypothesis by looking at epiphany, the symbolic representation of the maenad's closeness to or special relationship with Dionysus, and seeking ritual elements that might trigger such an experience.

Among the Greek pantheon, Dionysus is particularly predisposed to epiphany, to making eye contact with mortals. In vase-painting, the frontal mode – in which the subject is depicted not in profile but looking out of the visual space at the viewer – is rarely used of gods, but Dionysus appears frontally from the sixth century onwards.[61] Aside from two full-figure depictions, he also stares mask-like from drinking cups through the sixth

---

[60] Osborne 2010: esp. 379–381 with footnotes, contra Hedreen 1994, Carpenter 1997: 76–97, Isler-Kerényi 2001.
[61] Korshak 1987: 3, 18–20, 26–28 lists two examples in the Archaic period, but focuses on full figures, excluding images of mask-idols or free-floating faces.

and early fifth centuries BCE.⁶² The much-debated 'Lenaea vases' often show a mask of Dionysus mounted on a tree, either frontally, looking at the viewer, or in a position allowing the female figures to gaze upon his 'face'.⁶³ Whether these vessels depict particular or generic ritual scenes, they suggest that a female ritual event might involve interacting with a mask of Dionysus.⁶⁴ The event that prompted the Magnesians to summon maenadic practitioners from Thebes was the appearance of a likeness of Dionysus in a storm-hit tree:⁶⁵ this story may also hold echoes of the use of masks in maenadic ritual.

In poetry, Dionysus' gaze holds a peculiar power. When Pentheus interrogates the disguised Dionysus on how bacchic rites are passed on, Dionysus stresses that it is done face-to-face through eye contact: 'seeing him seeing me, he gave me the rites'.⁶⁶ Many gods were comfortable adopting human form, generally to aid a seduction or assist a favourite, but Dionysus' embodied exploits are more commonly associated with testing mortals on their ability to recognize him. Both Pentheus in *Bacchae* and the Tyrrhenian pirates in *Homeric Hymn 7* suffer for their failure to recognize him; the one pirate who is saved is the helmsman, who looks into his eyes and sees divinity. The helmsman becomes *panolbion*, 'all happy', 'blessed'.⁶⁷ When Dionysus finally appears before the Chorus of *Bacchae*, they greet him with delight: 'Oh greatest light of our joyful bacchic worship, how happy I am to see you, I, who was alone in the wilderness before!'⁶⁸ Could the ritual induce an experience that the participants might interpret as an epiphany? If epiphany can be shown to be induced through the ritual form, this would allow us to modify Rapp's position that the 'hard' evidence does not suggest a special emotional involvement. The type of experience generated will then help us modify the position taken by Harrison and Dodds by providing evidence for the ritual's ability to induce some unusual experience, but without the women involved having to be entirely transported or 'hysterical'.

---

[62] Full-figure: the François vase, volute krater c. 570–560 BCE, Florence, Museo Archaeologico Inv. 4209; black-figure eye cup in Boulogne-sur-Mer, Musée Communal, Inv. 559, both discussed by Korshak. Faces are usually found between enormous eyes, e.g. late sixth-century column krater (NY Met. Mus. Inv. 06.1021.101) and mid sixth-century cup (San Simeon Museum in California Inv. 9994). See Ferrari 1986, Bundrick 2015.

[63] See footnote 8.

[64] On the Dionysus mask: Vernant and Frontisi-Ducroux 1988: esp. 201–205, Frontisi-Ducroux 1989.

[65] *IMagn.* 215.3–9.   [66] Eur. *Bacch.* 470.   [67] Hom. *Hymn Dionysus* 54.

[68] Eur. *Bacch.* 608–609.

Epiphanic Experience in Maenadic Ritual

There is a cognitive function that seems to be heavily implicated in epiphanic or sensed presence experiences: 'agency detection', the name given to our ability to identify other sentient beings. Agency detection, simply put, is a human tendency to assume that unexpected phenomena are caused by an agent – a sentient being. It is what makes us see faces in clouds or ascribe malevolent characteristics to a drawer that stubbornly jams closed.[69] This model suggests that, when sensory data are unreliable, the brain relies more heavily on the 'top down' interpretative predictions drawn from experience and knowledge. If the subject expects an agent to be present, this is the schema that becomes dominant, and further incoming data are interpreted against this prior expectation.

There are several factors affecting whether or not an individual will experience the presence of a sentient agent when one is not present. Laboratory testing with virtual-reality (VR) environments has allowed researchers to test the conditions under which agency detection becomes more active. Based on the exacerbating factors suggested by agency detection theory, Marc Andersen's team at Aarhus University experimented using a VR forest environment with no cues present to suggest any presence.[70] Participants were shown either a dimly lit, misty forest or a brightly lit, sunny one (variable sensory reliability) and were told there was a 5% or 95% chance that a 'being' would be present (variable expectation). Low sensory reliability doubled the likelihood of subjects reporting a presence nearby; increased expectation raised the likelihood tenfold.

This evidence for exacerbation of agency detection through low sensory reliability and raised expectation allows us to explore these factors in maenadic ritual form. Sensory reliability would certainly be low: Plutarch describes the Thyiades as 'roaming around by night', and Euripides refers to the Delphic ritual as being 'in the torch-light of Bacchus'.[71] Lyric passages evoking the Dionysian environment describe the smoke writhing over the mountainside, flickering with torch-light.[72] From the second quarter of the fifth century,

---

[69] Guthrie 1993, Boyer 1994, Barrett 2000: esp. 30–31, Boyer 2001: 51–91, Atran and Norenzayan 2004, Barrett and Lanman 2008, summarized by van Leeuwen and van Elk 2018, Andersen 2019.
[70] Andersen et al. 2019. A third factor that the theory suggests should make agency detection more likely is fear or a sense of threat, but this has not yet been adequately tested in a VR environment with context-specific cues; Maij et al. 2019 used a 'creepy basement' VR environment but their test for agency detection was unrelated to environment cues, an issue recognized by Andersen et al. 2019: 60–61.
[71] Plut. *De mul. vir.* 13, Eur. *Ion* 550.
[72] Aesch. *Bassarids*: fr. 23b (Sommerstein 2008); Soph. *Ant.* 1126–1136, *OT* 209–215.

torches also regularly appear in the hands of Dionysian female figures in vase-paintings.[73] Other environmental factors will also have made for sensory confusion, including winds playing with the torch flames and shadows, and blowing through the trees.[74] The Bronze Age clearances had driven wildlife to just the type of wild landscapes where we also find maenads.[75] These uncultivated, heavily wooded areas, well away from cities, would have been the home of wild animals, such as bears, wild boar, and wolves, whose passage through the undergrowth would certainly have been audible.[76]

Secondly, in addition to visual and auditory sensory confusion from environmental factors and shouting, singing, and banging drums or cymbals, the distinctive pose found in vase-painting and poetry, with the head flung backwards or forwards, seems to be a movement particularly associated with maenadic dancing.[77] The act of shaking one's head back and forth would also impact on participants' ability to process sensory data. The brain is constantly modelling what sensory input it expects, and neurological research suggests that vestibular malfunctions can inhibit this modelling.[78] The vestibular system interacts with somatosensory processing, the brain function that interprets the individual's position in space, and the effects of vestibular disruption are particularly relevant when the subject is attempting to navigate with limited visual input to help calibrate the signals from the vestibular system.[79] By disrupting their vestibular systems through repeated head-shaking, in conditions that at best provided uncertain and unreliable sensory input, the maenadic dancers were actively interfering with their brains' ability to make sense of their surroundings and increasing the likelihood of the brain having difficulty processing inbound signals.

---

[73] Becoming frequent enough attributes as to identify a woman as being Dionysian even without the more common *thyrsos*: Moraw 1998: 60.
[74] The relatively new field of auditory archaeology may add insights into the aural effects of the landscape: e.g. Mills 2016: 60–65.
[75] Hughes 1994: 76–77, MacKinnon 2014b: 204–207.
[76] Hdt. 7.125–126, Soph. *Phil.* 936–937, 954–956, Arr. *Cyn.* 34.1–36.4: MacKinnon 2014a: 163–169.
[77] Dodds 1951: 273–274. Carpenter 1997: 83–84 suggested that it represents singing, but this does not adequately explain the corresponding forward extension of the neck found in many of these images, nor its prevalence in artistic descriptions of maenads: lecythos c. 470/460 BCE in the Museo Archaeologico Nazionale in Syracuse, Inv. 24554, or cups by Douris (Naples Museo Archeologico Nazionale, Inv. 128333), the Brygos Painter (Fort Worth, Kimbell Art Museum, Inv. AP2000.02, Paris, Cabinet des Medailles, Inv. 576), and the Briseis Painter (London, British Museum 1843.11-3.54). Cf. *Bacchae* 184–185 and 930–931, and a Hellenistic epigram calling on the Thyiades to 'whirl your long flowing curls' (περιδινήσασθε μακρῆς ἀνελίγματα χαίτης): Dioscorides, Gow-Page, *GP* 25.
[78] Tian and Poeppel 2010, Mast and Ellis 2017.
[79] Lopez and Blanke 2011, Seemungal 2017: 25–26, 37–40.

Under such circumstances of low sensory reliability, our brains tend to rely much more heavily on existing predictive assumptions about the world. This is where context-specific priming becomes important: it informs how any 'sensed presence' will be interpreted. Participants in the VR forest experiment generally identified the 'presence' as a woodland animal, suggesting that context defines how a presence is interpreted. We are told that, as well as consciously performing *mimêsis*, the ritual maenads prepared for ritual by singing hymns that celebrated 'the presence of Dionysus'.[80] This would provide active priming to influence interpretation of the confusing sensory data.

Experimental research also suggests that a prior acceptance of the existence of the supernatural increases the likelihood of agency detection.[81] This raises the question of whether these Hellenistic women believed in epiphanic gods. One strand of classical scholarship argues that 'belief' refers only to a personal faith or spiritual commitment of the sort found in modern religions, which does not easily translate to ancient Greek religion.[82] The functionalist view of religion as a social tool has been applied to civic cult, interpreting the emphasis on shared public ritual to mean that there is no room in this structure for personal belief.[83]

Recent scholarship, however, has moved away from a strict dichotomy of belief/non-belief, to a more nuanced approach in which intensity or focus of belief may change depending on situational context.[84] Practices such as oracular consultation, curse tablets, and votive dedications, for example, can all be understood to illustrate a personal engagement with religion – a belief that these practices accessed a power normally beyond human reach.[85] Assumptions about such powers and how to negotiate with them also lie behind ritual practices such as purification and initiation.[86] These fundamental assumptions are termed 'low intensity' beliefs, dependent on context and activity, and should not be thought of as the result of deep theological reflection.[87]

---

[80] Diod. Sic. 4.3.3: τὴν παρουσίαν ὑμνεῖν τοῦ Διονύσου.   [81] Riekki et al. 2013, van Elk 2013.
[82] Parker 2011: 31–34, Versnel 2011: 539–559, Harrison 2016.
[83] Versnel 2011: 554–555. *Polis* religion in its original formation makes the undeniable case for integration of religious structures into the state, but does not claim that engaging in public religion requires no personal commitment: Sourvinou-Inwood 1990.
[84] For the development of contextual subtleties of belief, see Versnel 2011: 539–559, Parker 2011: 1–39, Kindt 2012, Harrison 2015 and 2016, Eidinow 2019.
[85] Eidinow 2007, Kindt 2012: 64–69, 90–123, Ustinova 2018.
[86] E.g. Martin 2006, Petrovic and Petrovic 2016.
[87] Versnel 2011: 548–551, Harrison 2016, Eidinow 2019.

Epiphanic experiences also come under this category. The variety of ways in which Greek gods were thought to make their presence known to mortals includes dreams, omens, oracles, and auditory phenomena, as well as direct face-to-face contacts.[88] The diversity of epiphanic experiences indicates general 'low-level' acceptance of the power of gods to infiltrate the mortal plane, more a matter of interpretation than of revelation. Not everyone might have a vision of Athena in full wargear, but they could comfort themselves with the knowledge that even her favourite Odysseus sometimes had to make do with recognizing her voice in a heron's cry.[89]

Finally, it is worth returning to the red-figure paintings. Robin Osborne proposes that the red-figure iconography of the years 520–480 BCE shows a growing interest in images that show the inner life of characters: instead of action being the most important element, the emphasis changes gradually to prompt viewers to create a narrative and imagine what the figures might be feeling.[90] If this theory is correct, it might explain the iconographic changes we see in maenadic figures during this period. By comparison with orderly black-figure dancers, as the maenads move closer to their god their dance poses become more exuberant. Each dancer in a red-figure maenad group twists her body into a different attitude, neck extended, arms raised. Head-tossing and drumming have long been associated by anthropologists with trance-inducing techniques in dancing rituals,[91] and both are found with maenads. The Chorus of *Bacchae* sing in praise of the *tympanon*,[92] used by several ecstatic cults in the Classical period, and these instruments are found in vase-paintings that also show ritual elements such as altars and cult statues.[93] The apparent inclusion of trance-inducing elements may mean that the painters are attempting to depict an altered state of consciousness, comparable to that found in poetry. Regardless of whether the painted maenads are mythical or historical, they now show a consistent, specifically 'maenadic' identity that includes such altered mental states.

---

[88] See Herman 2011, Platt 2011, Petridou 2016: esp. 8–9, Platt 2016.   [89] Hom. *Il.* 10.274–277.
[90] Osborne 2018.
[91] Trance rituals, see I. M. Lewis 1971. Interpretation in a maenadic context, Bremmer 1984, Kefalidou 2009: 92–94.
[92] Eur. *Bacch.* 120–134.
[93] On the so-called 'Lenaea vases' see footnotes 7 and 51 above. Drumming for Dionysus: Ar. *Lys.* 1–3, Dioscorides Gow-Page, *GP* 25, Eur. *Cyc.* 63–72, Ath. 5.28. Music and drumming as an aid to trance: Lewis 1971: 39, 42–43, Rouget 1985: esp. 73–93.

Conclusion

Adopting an interpretative framework from CSR has allowed us to demonstrate that the maenadic ritual form was characterized by the sort of environment and activity that made it more likely that susceptible participants would have sensed a presence near them. Under the influence of cultural and context-specific priming, predictive schemata would make it more likely that those who experienced an 'agent' being present would interpret this as a Dionysian epiphany. This is not to say that every member of a maenadic *thiasos* would have had the same experience, or that every member who experienced agency detection would have interpreted the experience in the same way, but the ritual environment and activity greatly increased the chance that at least some ritual maenads would feel that they had encountered divinity on the mountainside. Such an event would not be the result of Dodds' 'hysteria', but a natural human response to sensory data and cultural priming. The prosaic evidence for the Hellenistic ritual contains all the necessary factors to induce a powerful, even alarming, experience that contradicts Rapp's conclusion that participants were simply going through the motions without any emotional effect. Simply through ritual performance, ancient maenads could have an experience which, for them, was the presence of god. And, after all the adrenaline, anxiety, and exercise, this experience was a joyful one; perhaps, once again, the poetic vision of *Bacchae* is not that far from the reality of the lived ritual experience.

BIBLIOGRAPHY

Andersen, M. 2019. 'Predictive Coding in Agency Detection', *Religion, Brain & Behavior* 9(1): 1–20.

Andersen, M., T. Pfeiffer, S. Müller, and U. Schjoedt. 2019. 'Agency Detection in Predictive Minds: A Virtual Reality Study', *Religion, Brain & Behavior* 9 (1): 52–64.

Atran, S. and A. Norenzayan. 2004. 'Religion's Evolutionary Landscape: Counterintuition, Commitment, Compassion, Communion', *Behavioral and Brain Sciences* 27(6): 713–730.

Barrett, J. L. 2000. 'Exploring the Natural Foundations of Religion', *Trends in Cognitive Sciences* 4(1): 29–34.

Barrett, J. L., and J. A. Lanman. 2008. 'The Science of Religious Beliefs', *Religion* 38(2): 109–124.

Bowden, H. 2010. *Mystery Cults in the Ancient World*. London.

Bowersock, G. W. 1965. 'Some Persons in Plutarch's Moralia', *Classical Quarterly* 15(2): 267–270.

Boyer, P. 1994. *The Naturalness of Religious Ideas: A Cognitive Theory of Religion.* Berkeley and Los Angeles, CA and London.
    2001. *Religion Explained: The Evolutionary Origins of Religious Thought.* New York, NY.
Bremmer, J. N. 1984. 'Greek Maenadism Reconsidered', *Zeitschrift für Papyrologie und Epigraphik* 55: 267–286.
    2019. 'Greek Maenadism', in J. N. Bremmer, ed. *The World of Greek Religion and Mythology: Collected Essays II*, 251–278. Tübingen.
Brown, C. 1982. 'Dionysus and the Women of Elis: *PMG* 871', *Greek, Roman, and Byzantine Studies* 23(4): 305–314.
Bundrick, S. D. 2015. 'Athenian Eye Cups in Context', *American Journal of Archaeology* 119(3): 295–341.
Campbell, D. A. 1988. *Greek Lyric, Volume II: Anacreon, Anacreontea, Choral Lyric from Olympus to Alcman.* Cambridge, MA.
Carpenter, T. H. 1997. *Dionysian Imagery in Fifth-Century Athens.* Oxford.
Clark, A. 2013. 'Whatever Next? Predictive Brains, Situated Agents, and the Future of Cognitive Science', *Behavioral and Brain Sciences* 36(3): 181–204.
Connelly, J. B. 2007. *Portrait of a Priestess: Women and Ritual in Ancient Greece.* Princeton, NJ.
Dodds, E. R. 1940. 'Maenadism in the Bacchae', *The Harvard Theological Review* 33(3): 155–176.
    1951. *Greeks and the Irrational.* Berkeley and Los Angeles, CA and London.
    1960. *Euripides' Bacchae.* Oxford.
Edwards, M. W. 1960. 'Representations of Maenads on Archaic Red-Figure Vases', *Journal of Hellenic Studies* 80: 78–87.
Eidinow, E. 2013 [2007]. *Oracles, Curses, and Risk among the Ancient Greeks.* Oxford.
    2019. 'The (Ancient Greek) Subject Supposed to Believe', *Numen* 66(1): 56–88.
Ferrari, G. 1986. 'EYE-CUP', *Revue Archéologique* 1: 5–20.
Frontisi-Ducroux, F. 1989. 'In the Mirror of the Mask', in C. Berard, ed. *A City of Images*, 151–167. Princeton, NJ.
Geertz, A. W. 2010. 'Too Much Mind and Not Enough Brain, Body and Culture. On What Needs to be Done in the Cognitive Science of Religion', *Historia Religionum* 2: 21–38.
Goff, B. 2004. *Citizen Bacchae: Women's Ritual Practice in Ancient Greece.* Oakland, CA.
Gore, C. J., A. G. Hahn, G. C. Scroop, D. B. Watson, K. I. Norton, R. J. Wood, D. P. Campbell, and D. L. Emonson. 1996. 'Increased Arterial Desaturation in Trained Cyclists during Maximal Exercise at 580 m Altitude', *Journal of Applied Physiology* 80(6): 2204–2210.
Gore, C. J., P. E. McSharry, A. J. Hewitt, and P. U. Saunders. 2008. 'Preparation for Football Competition at Moderate to High Altitude', *Scandinavian Journal of Medicine & Science in Sports* 18(s1): 85–95.
Guthrie, S. 1993. *Faces in the Clouds: A New Theory of Religion.* New York, NY and Oxford.

Halliwell, S. 2009. *The Aesthetics of Mimesis: Ancient Texts and Modern Problems.* Princeton, NJ.
Harrison, J. E. 1903. *Prolegomena to the Study of Greek Religion.* Cambridge.
Harrison, T. 2015. 'Beyond the Polis? New Approaches to Greek Religion', *Journal of Hellenic Studies* 135: 165–180.
  2016. 'Belief vs. Practice', in E. Eidinow and J. Kindt, eds. *The Oxford Handbook of Ancient Greek Religion*, 21–28. Oxford.
Hedreen, G. 1994. 'Silens, Nymphs, and Maenads', *Journal of Hellenic Studies* 114: 47–69.
Heinemann, A. 2016. *Der Gott des Gelages: Dionysos, Satyrn und Mänaden auf attischem Trinkgeschirr des 5. Jahrhunderts v. Chr.* Berlin and Boston, MA.
Henrichs, A. 1969. 'Die Maenaden von Milet', *Zeitschrift für Papyrologie und Epigraphik* 4: 223–241.
  1978. 'Greek Maenadism from Olympias to Messalina', *Harvard Studies in Classical Philology* 82: 121–160.
  1982. 'Changing Dionysiac Identities', in B. F. Meyer and E. P. Sanders, eds. *Jewish and Christian Self-Definition*, vol. 3, 137–160. London.
  1984. 'Loss of Self, Suffering, Violence: The Modern View of Dionysus from Nietzsche to Girard', *Harvard Studies in Classical Philology* 88: 205–240.
  1987. 'Myth Visualized: Dionysos and His Circle in Sixth-Century Attic Vase-Painting', in *Papers on the Amasis Painter and His World*, 94–124. Malibu, CA.
Herman, G. 2011. 'Greek Epiphanies and the Sensed Presence', *História: Zeitschrift für Alte Geschichte* 60(2): 127–157.
Herrmann, P. 1998. *Inschriften von Milet, Teil 2: Inschriften n.407-1019.* Berlin and New York, NY.
Higgins, J. P., T. Tuttle, and J. A. Higgins. 2010. 'Altitude and the Heart: Is Going High Safe for Your Cardiac Patient?', *American Heart Journal* 159(1): 25–32.
Hohwy, J. 2013. *The Predictive Mind.* Oxford.
Hughes, J. D. 1994. *Environmental Problems of the Greeks and Romans: Ecology in the Ancient Mediterranean.* Baltimore, MD.
Isler-Kerényi, C. 2001. 'Review: Susanne Moraw, Die Mänade in der attischen Vasenmalerei des 6. und 5. Jahrhunderts v. Chr.', *Gnomon* 73(4): 336–342.
Kapetanopoulos, E. 1966. 'Klea and Leontis: Two Ladies from Delphi', *Bulletin de Correspondance Hellénique* 90: 119–130.
Kefalidou, E. 2009. 'The Iconography of Madness in Attic Vase-Painting', in J. H. Oakley and O. Palagia, eds. *Athenian Potters and Painters Volume II*, 90–99. Oxford.
Kern, O. 1900. *Die Inschriften von Magnesia am Maenader.* Berlin.
Keuls, E. C. 1985. *The Reign of the Phallus: Sexual Politics in Ancient Athens.* Berkeley and Los Angeles, CA.
Kindt, J. 2012. *Rethinking Greek Religion.* Cambridge.
Korshak, Y. 1987. *Frontal Faces in Attic Vase Painting of the Archaic Period.* Chicago, IL.

Lawler, L. B. 1927. 'The Maenads: A Contribution to the Study of the Dance in Ancient Greece', *Memoirs of the American Academy in Rome* 6: 69–112.

Lewis, I. M. 1971. *Ecstatic Religion: A Study of Shamanism and Spirit Possession*. New York, NY.

Lopez, C. and O. Blanke. 2011. 'The Thalamocortical Vestibular System in Animals and Humans', *Brain Research Reviews* 67(1): 119–146.

Lowe, N. J. 2019. 'The Rational Irrationalist: Dodds and the Paranormal', in *Rediscovering E. R. Dodds: Scholarship, Education, Poetry, and the Paranormal*. Oxford.

MacKinnon, M. 2014a. 'Fauna of the Ancient Mediterranean World', in G. L. Campbell, ed. *The Oxford Handbook of Animals in Classical Thought and Life*, 156–179. Oxford.

— 2014b. 'Hunting', in G. L. Campbell, ed. *The Oxford Handbook of Animals in Classical Thought and Life*, 203–215. Oxford.

Maij, D. L. R., H. T. van Schie, and M. van Elk. 2019. 'The Boundary Conditions of the Hypersensitive Agency Detection Device: An Empirical Investigation of Agency Detection in Threatening Situations', *Religion, Brain & Behavior* 9(1): 23–51.

Martin, L. H. 2006. 'Cognitive Science, Ritual, and the Hellenistic Mystery Religions', *Religion and Theology* 13(3–4): 383–395.

Mast, F. W. and A. W. Ellis. 2017. 'Internal Models, Vestibular Cognition, and Mental Imagery: Conceptual Considerations', in E. R. Ferrè and L. R. Harris, eds. *Vestibular Cognition*, 89–106. Leiden and Boston, MA.

McNally, S. 1978. 'The Maenad in Early Greek Art', *Arethusa* 11: 101–135.

Merkelbach, R. 1972. 'Milesische Bakchen', *Zeitschrift für Papyrologie und Epigraphik* 9: 77–83.

Mills, S. 2016. *Auditory Archaeology: Understanding Sound and Hearing in the Past*. New York, NY.

Moraw, S. 1998. *Die Mänade in der attischen Vasenmalerei des 6. und 5. Jahrhunderts v. Chr*. Mainz.

Osborne, R. 2010. 'The Ecstasy and the Tragedy: Varieties of Religious Experience in Art, Drama and Society', in R. Osborne, ed. *Athens and Athenian Democracy*, 368–404. Cambridge.

— 2018. *The Transformation of Athens: Painted Pottery and the Creation of Classical Greece*. Oxford and Princeton, NJ.

Parker, R. 2011. *On Greek Religion*. Ithaca, NY and London.

Peirce, S. 1998. 'Visual Language and Concepts of Cult on the "Lenaia Vases"', *Classical Antiquity* 17(1): 59–95.

Petridou, G. 2016. *Divine Epiphany in Greek Literature and Culture*. Oxford.

Petrovic, A. and I. Petrovic. 2016. *Inner Purity and Pollution in Greek Religion: Volume I: Early Greek Religion*. Oxford.

Platt, V. J. 2011. *Facing the Gods: Epiphany and Representation in Graeco-Roman Art, Literature and Religion*. Cambridge.

— 2016. 'Epiphany', in E. Eidinow and J. Kindt, eds. *The Oxford Handbook of Ancient Greek Religion*, 493–504. Oxford.

Rapp, A. 1872. 'Die Mänade im griechischen Cultus, in der Kunst und Poesie', *Rheinisches Museum für Philologie* 27: 1–22, 563–611.
Riekki, T., M. Lindeman, M. Aleneff, A. Halme, and A. Nuortimo. 2013. 'Paranormal and Religious Believers are More Prone to Illusory Face Perception than Skeptics and Non-believers', *Applied Cognitive Psychology* 27(2): 150–155.
Rohde, E. 1894. Psyche: Seelencult und Unsterblichkeitsglaube der Griechen, vol. 2. Tübingen.
  1925. *Psyche: The Cult of Souls and Belief in Immortality among the Greeks*. London and New York, NY.
Rouget, G. 1985. *Music and Trance: A Theory of the Relations Between Music and Possession*. Chicago, IL and London.
Santamaría, M. A. 2013. 'The Term βάκχος and Dionysos Βάκχιος', in A. Bernabé, M. Herrero de Jáuregui, A. I. Jiménez San Cristóbal, and R. Martín Hernández, eds. *Redefining Dionysos*, 38–57. Berlin and Boston, MA.
Schlesier, R. 1993. 'Mixtures of Masks: Maenads as Tragic Models', in T. H. Carpenter and C. A. Faraone, eds. *Masks of Dionysus*, 89–114. Ithaca, NY.
Scullion, S. 1999. 'Tradition and Invention in Euripidean Aitiology', *Illinois Classical Studies* 24/25: 217–233.
  2002. '"Nothing to Do with Dionysus": Tragedy Misconceived As Ritual', *Classical Quarterly* 52(1): 102–137.
Seaford, R. 1981. 'Dionysiac Drama and the Dionysian Mysteries', *Classical Quarterly* 31(2): 24.
  1987. 'Pentheus' Vision: Bacchae 918-22', *Classical Quarterly* 37(1): 3.
  1996. *The Plays of Euripides: Bacchae*. Oxford.
Seemungal, B. M. 2017. 'The Components of Vestibular Cognition – Motion versus Spatial Perception', in E. R. Ferrè and L. R. Harris, eds. *Vestibular Cognition*, 25–42. Leiden and Boston, MA.
Shukitt-Hale, B., and H. R. Lieberman. 1996. 'The Effect of Altitude on Cognitive Performance and Mood States', in B. M. Marriott and S. J. Carlson, eds. *Nutritional Needs and Cold and High-Altitude Environments: Applications for Military Personnel in Field Operations*, 435–451. Washington, DC.
Sokolowski, F. 1955. *Lois sacrées de l'Asie Mineure*. Paris.
Sommerstein, A. H. 2008. *Aeschylus III: Fragments*. Cambridge, MA.
Sourvinou-Inwood, C. 1990. 'What Is Polis Religion?', in O. Murray and S.R.F. Price, eds. *The Greek City: From Homer to Alexander*, 295–322. Oxford.
Tian, X. and D. Poeppel. 2010. 'Mental Imagery of Speech and Movement Implicates the Dynamics of Internal Forward Models', *Frontiers in Psychology* 1: Article 166.
Ustinova, Y. 2018. *Divine Mania: Alteration of Consciousness in Ancient Greece*. London.
van Elk, M. 2013. 'Paranormal Believers Are More Prone to Illusory Agency Detection than Skeptics', *Consciousness and Cognition* 22(3): 1041–1046.
van Leeuwen, N. and M. van Elk. 2018. 'Seeking the Supernatural: The Interactive Religious Experience Model', *Religion, Brain & Behavior*: 1–31.

Vernant, J. P. and F. Frontisi-Ducroux. 1988. 'Features of the Mask in Ancient Greece', in J. P. Vernant and P. Vidal-Naquet, eds. *Myth and Tragedy in Ancient Greece*, 189–206. Cambridge, MA and London.

Versnel, H. 2011. *Coping with the Gods: Wayward Readings in Greek Theology*. Leiden.

Weaver, B. 2009. 'Euripides' "Bacchae" and Classical Typologies of Pentheus' "Sparagmos" 510-406 BC', *Bulletin of the Institute of Classical Studies* 52: 15–43.

Weniger, L. 1883. *Das Kollegium der sechzehn Frauen und der Dionysosdienst in Elis*. Weimar.

CHAPTER 7

Who Is the Damiatrix?
Roman Women, the Political Negotiation of Psychotropic Experiences, and the Cults of Bona Dea

Leonardo Ambasciano

The Story of Rome between Sexual Violence and Cosmic Misogyny

In an interview published in *The Guardian* in 2016, Mary Beard said that 'if you're going to remove the sexual violence, you cannot tell the story of Rome.'[1] From the abduction of the Sabine women that took place soon after the foundation of the city to the rape and suicide of Lucretia that marked the birth of the Republic, landmark political episodes in the history of Rome were inextricably tied to episodes of sexual violence.[2] These were not disjointed anecdotes. Roman society was obsessed with the legal, social, and sexual control of women's behaviour. Law and religion were the pivots around which the '(continuous (re)creation of the objective and subjective structures of masculine domination' behind the patriarchal organization of the city revolved.[3] The life story of one mythic character in particular, Bona Dea, or the 'Good Goddess', exemplifies the toxic institutional loop between sexist categorizations, masculine expectations, and gender violence as they were conceptualized within the 'cosmic misogyny' of the Roman religious mindscape.[4]

In what follows, I will review the Bona Dea mythography and her cults, offering, first, a neurosociological interpretation of the mechanisms by which the Bona Dea worshippers were supposed to internalize the patriarchal codes regarding their own subordination as 'good' and 'natural' (and, thus, not subvertible)[5]; and, secondly, a socio-cognitive assessment

---

I am deeply indebted to Maria Dell'Isola, Luther H. Martin, Andrea Nicolotti, the editors, and two anonymous reviewers for their many helpful suggestions. Any remaining error is my sole responsibility.

[1] Williams 2016.   [2] Cantarella 2010, James and Dillon 2012, Holmes 2012.
[3] Bourdieu 2001: 82–83.   [4] Bloch 2009: 76, cf. Beard 2017.
[5] Lincoln 1981, Bourdieu 2001.

of the political negotiation behind the inclusion of two gendered cults within institutional Roman religion (*sacra publica*).[6]

Silence, Rape, and Homicide: The Good Goddess' Myths

According to the main literary variants, the origins of the Bona Dea cult were rooted in a homicide that took place in the royal settings of protohistorical *Latium*. When alive, the future Good Goddess was simply known as Fauna, that is, by the feminine form of her husband's name, the mythic Latin king Faunus. Her name reflected a complex series of interrelated patriarchal Roman laws, norms, and beliefs that deprived women of specific individual and family rights, and which culminated in the customary female lack of individual names (*praenomina*).[7] In the extant sources, Fauna is known as a silent and invisible, and thus perfect, symbol of virtuous matronal *pudicitia* ('sexual modesty'), to the point that no one even heard her name when she was alive.[8] Despite her rigorous code of conduct, she was the victim of her husband's violence, beaten and killed because – depending on the sources – she was either found drunk by Faunus himself[9] or slyly made drunk by her husband because he wanted to rape her.[10] In the latter scenario, Faunus, unsuccessful and frustrated despite having beaten Fauna, turns into a snake and finally succeeds in coercing an incestuous intercourse.[11] The cult would have been institutionalized soon after the queen's death by the remorseful king.[12]

The most striking social and legal aspect behind both mythographical variants is that the unregulated drinking of pure wine (*merum, temetum*) was formally forbidden to respectable *matronae*, that is married freeborn women. The penalty of death was sanctioned by the law, entrusted to husbands, and established in the most prestigious and ancient of times by Romulus himself because alcohol was thought of as a gender-altering, sexuality-enhancing substance biologically related to semen. Its

---

[6] Henry and James 2012. A Roman text defines *publica sacra* as follows: 'those (rites) performed at public expense on behalf of the people, on behalf of (the inhabitants) of mountains, villages, and consecrated meeting houses, and (groups centered around) sanctuaries' (Festus, 284L, translation from Ando and Rüpke 2006: 9, modified).

[7] Cantarella 1987: 125–126, Maganzani 2016. Other related onomastic variants are commented in Brouwer 1989: 324–326 (Lactantius' Fenta Fauna and Arnobius' Fenta Fatua).

[8] Lactant. *Div. inst.* 1.22.9 – 11, Macrob. *Sat.* 1.12.27.   [9] Plut. *Quaest. Rom.* 20.

[10] Macrob. *Sat.* 1.12.24–25.

[11] Macrob. *Sat.* 1.12.25. Macrobius reports Fauna as Faunus' daughter, while Lactantius describes her as his sister. On the socio-cognitive underpinnings of both Faunus' metamorphosis and incest see Ambasciano 2016a and 2016b.

[12] Arn. *Adv. nat.* 5.18, Lactant. *Div. inst.* 1.12.10–11; both accounts include the death of Fauna.

consumption would eventually lead to adultery which, in turn, would dramatically subvert the agnatic family relationships of the Roman aristocracy.[13]

Set and justified within a context dominated by the aggressive social and sexual competition between the male members of the Roman elite, the mythical plot of the first variant recalled above acted as a coercive mate-guarding strategy, that is, a patriarchal cautionary tale to dissuade women from engaging in unlawful behaviours, from drinking irresponsibly, and from defecting from mateship; the second variant may possibly reflect ancient, aristocratic, and endogamic customs while denouncing the royal excesses of the late Bronze Age local chiefdom.[14] In fact, Faunus, the mythical ancestor of the Latin people, is usually depicted as a wild, uncivilized, pre-urban boor (later conflated with Silvanus and the Greek Pan) whose personality traits strongly predict violence and sexual coercion.[15]

A third literary version written by Propertius channels the Augustan restoration of traditional mores and offers an aetiological explanation of the proximity of the temples of Bona Dea and Hercules in Rome. This variant reports the aggression enacted by a thirsty and cantankerous Hercules on the resolute but helpless priestess of the shrine that will become the temple of Bona Dea. The priestess, loyal to the religious duty that sanctioned the prohibition for all men to enter the sacred precincts of the temple, denies the demigod access to the temple fountain.[16] Hercules makes a plea in vain by recalling his past cross-dressing as a girl. Frustrated, he then retaliates by smashing through the door of the shrine and by establishing his own male-centred cult that mimics the Bona Dea female-centred devotion.[17]

One additional source, Trogus' epitome by Justin, closes the mythological circle by identifying Latinus, otherwise known as the son of king Faunus, as begotten by Hercules through his violence (*stuprum*) against Fauna herself, again intertwining the sexual violence embedded in the Bona Dea life story with the pseudohistorical foundation of the Latin chiefdom itself.[18]

How were all these disparate mythical elements reflected in the Bona Dea cult?

---

[13] Families tied by agnatic kinship trace their relation only through male individuals and ancestors. See Bettini 2009, Fitzgerald 2012.
[14] Ambasciano 2016b and 2016c; cf. Holland 2011: 223 and Scheidel 2014.
[15] See Dorcey 1992, Figueredo, Gladden, and Beck 2012: 82.
[16] Prop. 4.9.16–30; cf. Macrob. *Sat.* 1.12.28.   [17] Welch 2004, Ambasciano 2016c.
[18] Just. *Epit.* 43.1.9, Brelich 2010: 101, Ambasciano 2016c: 119. Mastrocinque (1993: 39–40) suggests that this variant narrates what happened after Hercules broke through the Bona Dea temple in Propertius' account, in which case the victim of Hercules' violence would be the priestess herself or one of the maidens. On the complicated genealogy of Latinus, cf. Moorton 1988.

Wine, Power, and Subordination: The December Festival

As far as we can say from the extant evidence, Bona Dea was the recipient of two main official occasions of devotion in the city of Rome.

An elite winter festival took place in the house of the Roman magistrate *cum imperio* (a consul or a pretor) on the night between 3 and 4 December as an integral component of the Roman *sacra publica*. On that occasion, the wife of the magistrate decked the mansion with flowers, bowers, and vine and brought inside the statue of the goddess herself from the temple. The Bona Dea *simulacrum* was then offered food and drink on a dedicated cushion. Then, assisted by the Vestal Virgins and the aristocratic *matronae* of Rome (here assisted by their female slaves), a sow was sacrificed and offered *pro populo* and *pro salute populi Romani*, that is, for the Roman people's wellbeing, and wine was liberally consumed. All the agents and the instruments of the mythical violence were either taboo (the myrtle with whose twigs Faunus beat his partner to death; men and all things related to the male sex) or disguised as something else (the wine and its container were subjected to onomastic magic and relabelled with innocuous names, respectively, 'milk' and 'honeypot'). For the rest of the night, and for that night only, the participants binged while dancing and making merry to the sound of music.[19]

Now, the scholarly consensus about the legal and religious capacity for Roman women to perform blood sacrifice and to engage in wine consumption has shifted from a rigorous prohibition with some strictly delimited institutional and religious exceptions to a more open-minded interpretation of the available sources, allowing a substantial degree of female agency.[20] However, there is no denying that a more or less misogynistic outlook and the undisputable coercive control exerted by a most powerful *pater familias* (the male head of the household) were the default cultural and legal settings of Roman society, especially insofar as the wives of the members of the Roman political elite were concerned.[21] In this sense, we might assume that the December festival of Bona Dea, with

---

[19] Plut. *Vit. Cic.* 19, Plut. *Vit. Caes.* 9–10, Plut. *Quaest. Rom.* 20, Macrob. *Sat.* 1.20.25; cf. Bettini 2009, Ambasciano 2016a. See also Cic. *Leg.* 2.9.21 on the prohibition for women to engage in night-time rituals except, presumably, those dedicated to Bona Dea. Additional bibliography in Brouwer 1989.

[20] Cf. for instance, Scheid 2002 with Flemming 2007. See also Beard 2015: 303–313. Among the most discussed ancient sources concerning these topics I can recall here the following: Dion. Hal. *Rom. Ant.* 2.25.6, Aul. Gell. *NA* 10.23.3, Val. Max. 6.3.9.

[21] Cantarella 1999, Beard 2017, Cantarella 2020.

its drinking party from which men were excluded, might have been judged as something abhorrent from the perspective of the male dominant elite.

However, the existence of the December festival exemplifies a typically Roman approach to class and gender conflicts.[22] In neurosociological terms, religious experiences are based on specific manipulations of the brain-body chemistry, and thus they impact on the regulation of behaviours and modulation of expectations while suggesting scripts and providing schemata.[23] As such, they can be exploited in inter-/intra-group competition and manoeuvred by dominant groups to exert normative control over subordinates.[24] This can be subtly achieved through cults or festivals intuitively designed to strengthen the 'civic cohesion of the community' by interrupting the daily routine and providing a neurophysiological 'diversion' in order to reaffirm the dominant rules.[25] The cult of *Fortuna Muliebris*, along with its sacrifice and female-only admittance, was conceded to Roman women by the Senate in the fifth century BCE as a reward for their successful diplomatic intervention against Coriolanus, the legendary exiled Roman general. In this case, civil rights were bargained for religious agency, insofar as access to socio-religious capital facilitated the acceptance of social subordination as natural.[26] Through the institutionalization of a 'ritualized transgression', the December festival of Bona Dea might have had a similar function, in this case via a sort of carnivalesque overturning of women's subordination. The festival acted as a stress-relief valve to decrease focus on everyday subordination and domestic violence while confirming the usual power networks that supplied that very stress in the first place.[27]

The management of social power need not be seen as exclusively repressive. In Foucauldian terms, power is a 'productive network which runs through the whole social body, much more than as a negative instance whose function is repression'.[28] Likewise, as Aldous Huxley described in his comparative musings on Orwell's *Nineteen Eighty-Four* and his own *Brave New World*, 'government through terror works on the whole less well than government through the non-violent manipulation [...] of the thoughts and feelings of individual men, women and children'.[29] According to the neurohistorical perspective heralded by Daniel L. Smail, in all past and present societies just as in all primate societies,

---

[22] C. Martin 2012: 45–69.
[23] See Geertz 2010 and 2013, Smail 2008, see also Martin, Chapter 9, in this volume.
[24] Cf. Turner et al. 2018.   [25] Bremmer 2004.   [26] Livy 2.40.1–2; cf. Scheid 2002: 389.
[27] Bloch and Sperber 2002: 733, Smail 2008: 174; see Ambasciano 2016a.
[28] Foucault 1980: 119; see also Foucault 1978 and Martin 2018: 113–123.   [29] Huxley 1984: 237.

'neurobiological states have political implications'.[30] In Rome, the male political elite controlled access to food, pleasure, and reward for subordinates (immortalized by Juvenal's *panem et circenses*, 'bread and circuses'), thus manipulating the nervous system of the subordinate classes via the alternation between ordinary socio-economic stressors and extraordinary neurophysiological reliefs through entertainment, religious rituals, and social events able to temporarily reduce that stress.

The benefits for the patriarchal status quo were clear. As far as the December cult of Bona Dea was concerned, the Foucauldian productive network served the male hegemonic class by allowing subordinates (in this case the wives and the mothers of the ruling elite) to access a psychotropic beverage that acted as a social lubricant and to experience pleasure and reward, so that those subordinates could accept and internalize their assigned gendered social roles as good wives (roles that, inscribed as they were in the 'urbigony' of the city itself, were considered 'natural' and thus inescapable).[31]

In conclusion, as Henk Versnel wrote, the festival was 'beneficial and necessary from a socio-biological point of view, but wrong and undesirable from a socio-cultural point of view'.[32] From such a socio-biological perspective, the rituals and the myths behind the December festival functioned at the same time as a neurophysiological ploy through frightening mythical storytelling to prevent wives' insubordination, adultery, or retaliation against their husband masters,[33] and as a symbiotic psychotropic mechanism (that is, a behaviour that can change moods and emotions through the reuptake of neurotransmitters in the brain and which benefits, albeit in different ways, all parties involved) able to stabilize temporarily the hierarchical social order of the urban aristocracy.[34]

Snakes, Medicines, and a Secret Sacrifice: The May Celebration

A second ritual took place on the Kalends of May in the Aventine temple (*aedes*) of Bona Dea Subsaxana. This location, the so-called 'Remoria' of the urban Regio XII, was one of the most prestigious spots in Rome, as Remus was thought to have taken the auspices before the founding of the city right there.[35] The ritual seemingly coincided with the anniversary of

---

[30] Smail 2010.
[31] Piccaluga 1964, Lincoln 1981, Bettini 2016: 13–34. Cf. Nencini 2009: 201, Dunbar 2013: 54.
[32] Versnel 1992: 48; cf. Versnel 1990.
[33] Culham 2004, Cantarella 2010: 67–75, Ambasciano 2016a.   [34] Smail 2008: 170–174.
[35] DiLuzio 2016: 95.

the foundation of the temple on the first day of May, reputedly by a Vestal.[36] Unfortunately, this ritual is almost completely unknown.

From the archaeological evidence available in Rome and its environs, as well as Aquileia, Tergeste (Trieste), and Glanum (St. Rémy-de-Provence), we know that the temples dedicated to Bona Dea were surrounded by a wall and were ideally characterized by the presence of some source of water and potentially a hearth or a fireplace, which could have become a kitchen in the largest structures.[37] In addition, the Aventine temple was said to have an *apotheca* (pharmacy) and freely wandering snakes were also present, possibly for therapeutic ritual biting.[38] Macrobius relates that a secret sacrifice of a pregnant sow akin to that which took place in December was performed by a priestess, and 'this is the only information we have about this feast'.[39] According to Hendrik H. J. Brouwer 'it is very likely that the two feasts in honour of the same goddess were quite similar'.[40] Other scholars have tried to identify the Aventine temple as a site for some unattested rites of passage tied to female fertility rituals with mixed results.[41] The key to understanding this enigmatic ritual could lie in the identity of the priestess behind the May ceremonial performance.[42] One final piece of information and a linguistic detour might provide some clues in this regard.

Who Is the *Damiatrix*?

In 1865, Domenico De' Guidobaldi claimed that the Bona Dea cult was an originally Italic and gynecocratic cult possibly imported into Rome by the Osci or the Sabines and then syncretistically fused with other Italic and Greek cults from Southern Italy, in particular the cult of Damia with its nuptial rites.[43] In the following decades, other scholars advanced the idea that the cult of Bona Dea was the result of the import of the Greek cult of Damia in Rome after the 272 BCE conquest of Tarentum, where a festival called *Dameia* was held in her honour.[44] In 1982, archaeological finds in

---

[36] Cic. *Dom.* 53.136, Ov. *Fast.* 5.155. See Brouwer 1989: 370, Chioffi 1993: 200–201; cf. Arnhold 2015.
[37] Chioffi 1993: 198, Ambasciano 2016c. A grove is also attested in both literary and epigraphic data; Brouwer 1989: 380, 429.
[38] Macrob. *Sat.* 1.12.26; see Ambasciano 2016b. Healing devotion is confirmed in the epigraphic record, see Ambasciano 2016d.
[39] Brouwer 1989: 370; cf. Macrob. *Sat.* 1.12.20–21. [40] Brouwer 1989: 370.
[41] Marcattili 2010 and 2012; cf. Mignone 2016. See also Piccaluga 1964. [42] Brouwer 1989: 371.
[43] De' Guidobaldi 1865. On protohistorical gynecocracy as patriarchal myth see Bamberger 1974 and Ustinova 2018.
[44] Giannelli 1913: 74, Brouwer 1989: 347, n.189, DiLuzio 2016: 92.

Paestum/Poseidonia reinforced the idea that the originally Greek cult of Damia was introduced in Rome via Magna Graecia.[45] One literary source – Sextus Pompeius Festus' second-century, twenty-volume epitome of Verrius Flaccus' Augustan *De Verborum Significatu* – supports the link with Damia:

> The *Damium* was a sacrifice [i.e. ritual] which took place in secrecy [*in operto*] in honour of Bona Dea; it was thus named because of its opposite meaning, as it was least of all δαμόσιον, i.e. public. Also, the goddess herself was called Damia, and her priestess *damiatrix*.[46]

Could this *damiatrix* be the priestess in charge of the May celebration? If so, a Greek origin of the cult would lend credit to the presence of orgiastic festivals and high-pageantry, mystery-like initiations.[47] But why the use of the past tense? According to Brouwer, this 'might indicate that [Festus] is referring to a tradition dating from the Augustan religious revival no longer applicable to his own time'.[48] However, the original manuscript by Festus is mutilated and for this entry we rely entirely on Paulus Diaconus' own late epitome of Festus' work (720–799 CE). Additionally, an entry about a secret female sacrifice offered to Bona Dea and called *damium* is available in Placidus' *Glossaria Latina* dating from the sixth century CE, in which the author uses the present tense.[49] Therefore, we cannot infer from Festus anything related to the longevity of the Bona Dea cult. Neither can we find any confirmation of the presence of the *damiatrix* in the other available sources. The priestesses of the goddess' temple were otherwise called *antistites* ('chief priestesses') by Macrobius (who also wrote of their phyto-pharmacological knowledge and role as dispensers of medicines);[50] Propertius' variant featured an *alma sacerdos* ('good priestess'), also called *anus* ('elder'), who was in charge of the local cult with some *puellae* ('maidens').[51] The epigraphic record reports the usual *sacerdos* as a widespread title for the Bona Dea priestesses,[52] along with a predominance of Greek or Graecophone freedwomen.[53]

Although we are still none the wiser about the identity, the role, and the social class of the *damiatrix*, if we want to give credence to Paulus

---

[45] Johannowsky, Griffiths Pedley, and Torelli 1983.
[46] Paulus-Festus, 60(L) = *Gloss. Lat.* 178 (trans. from Brouwer 1989: 209, modified).
[47] Frank 1927: 132, n. 2. Cf. Plut. *Vit. Caes.* 9–10 for an outsider (that is, Greek) and orgiastic interpretation of the Italic cult. See also Mastrocinque 2011a, 2011b, and 2014, Ambasciano 2015.
[48] Brouwer 1989: 237–238.
[49] However, Placidus does not mention the *damiatrix*; *Gloss. Lat.* 4.59–60. On the complicated philological history of Verrius Flaccus' work, see Zetzel 2018: 61–63, 96–98, 231.
[50] *Sat.* 1.12.26. On *antistites* as a probably exclusively female title, see Gaspar 2012: 48–49.
[51] Prop. 4.9.21–70. [52] Sources listed in Brouwer 1989: 36, 37, 40, 82, 47, cf. DiLuzio 2016: 94.
[53] Data collected and discussed in Ambasciano 2016c.

Who Is the Damiatrix?

Diaconus' epitome of Festus, the title could have been a Roman invention, on the grounds that Damia was the name under which the Greek goddess arrived in Italy, and that *-trix* was a normal Latin female suffix.[54] However, there are at least the following reasons to doubt the Greek roots of the cult:

1. The puzzling etymology of the 'not clearly Greek' and 'not clearly Latin' *damium* and *damiatrix* has also been suggested to be rooted in Oscan, an extinct Italic language related to Latin.[55] In Oscan, *damuse* and *dam(u)sennias* refer to some kind of offering or banquet.[56] Thus, *damium* would be a religious feast, and the *damiatrix* would be the priestess in charge of the sacrifice recalled by Festus and Macrobius.[57] Religious titles linguistically analogous to *damiatrix* are also well attested in Oscan. The Herentas epigraph, written in Paelignian – an Oscan offshoot – and dating to the first century BCE,[58] reports both the titles *sacaracirix* (**sacratrix*), or priestess, and *pristafalacirix*[59] which, as **prae-stibulatrix*, is understood to be the etymological equivalent of *antistita*, that is, 'she who stands above' in the priesthood hierarchy.[60]
2. The reading of the archaeological data from Paestum is inconclusive.[61] Moreover, Oscan was a major language in Paestum as a consistent part of its population was Oscan.[62] Should the identification of a Bona

---

[54] See Giannelli 1913: 75, n. 1 for a matronal use of the title during the December festival. Brouwer (1989: 371–372), instead, wrote that considering 'Festus' intention to describe the celebration of the mysteries in December, where certainly no priestess was in charge[,] we may assume that the reference to the *damiatrix* is attributable to the fact that Festus confused the two feasts'. Therefore, according to Brouwer, 'it is probable that the cult attached to the temple rather than the December rites will have been affected by outside influences [due to the presence of foreign freedwomen]. This might account for Festus' mention of a *damiatrix* and his identification of the foreign Damia with Roman Bona Dea' (Brouwer 1989: 372).

[55] Citations from Conway 1897: 49; cf. Baldi 2002: 28–29.

[56] See Buck 1904: 251, Whatmough 1931: 173; bibliography available in Untermann 2000: 155.

[57] *Damiatrix* might also have been subjected to the semiotic influence of *domitrix*, 'she who tames', possibly as a reference to the sacrificial role of the priestess (and not to hypothetical nuptial rites symbolizing marital subordination as speculated in De' Guidobaldi 1865: 58–59; on *domitrix* see Watmough 1995/1996). We also know from the epigraphic record that another phonologically similar divine epithet, the rare *dominatrix*, had been used to designate Bona Dea (AE 1964: 111, n. 270, Brouwer 1989: 127–128).

[58] The epigraph is dedicated to Angitia or Ceres. Incidentally, Macrobius assimilates the plebeian Ceres with Bona Dea (*Sat.* 1.12.23) and Bona Dea is called *Cereria* in an Augustan epigraph from an *aedes* in Aquileia (CIL 5.761 = ILS 3499). On this assimilation see Brouwer 1989: 116, 421. On the possible cult relationship between Ceres, Damia, Demeter, and Bona Dea see Whatmough 1931: 173.

[59] Crawford et al. 2011: 267–268; *ST* Pg 9 in Dionisio 2013: 231–232 (cf. *ST* MV 7).

[60] Alternatively, 'she who stands before the temple' (Dionisio 2013: 231). Cf. Martzloff and Machajdíková 2017: 153.

[61] Johannowsky, Griffiths Pedley, and Torelli 1983: 302, n. 29. [62] Cf. Wonder 2002: 42.

Dea inscription be confirmed, we should not discard the possibility of a Greek appropriation of a pre-existing Italic cult.
3. Greek names for freedmen and freedwomen cannot be used as a reliable proxy to infer someone's place of birth because slave names were subjected to ethnically unrelated onomastic fashions.[63]
4. A cultural geographical analysis based on literary, epigraphic, and archaeological artifacts indicates that the Bona Dea cult was mostly restricted to Central Italy and almost unattested in Graecophone Southern Italy. In particular, there seems to be a negligible presence in the Southern regions and, with the exception of the Roman colony of Aquileia and its environs, no documents at all from the Cisalpine area north of the Etruscan port of Pisae and Forum Cornelii, another Roman colony (both being themselves isolated cult outposts). Euromediterranean presence is even sparser, with a single civilian cluster of consistent archaeological finds located in the highly Romanized region of the Gallia Narbonensis (Southern France). Apparently, when and where the Bona Dea cult spread was mainly determined by settlers and veterans from Central Italy, presence of commercial seaways, and military deployments possibly interested in the ophthalmic and generally therapeutic qualities of the cult boosted by assimilation with other healing cults.[64]
5. It is doubtful that the Roman Senate would accept a blatantly orgiastic Bacchic cult as an official component of its state religion considering the repression of the Bacchanalia (186 BCE), and the sexual scandal that involved the politician Publius Clodius Pulcher committing sacrilege by entering the house where the Bona Dea December festival of 62 BCE was taking place.[65]

A couple of additional reflections might be of help insofar as the potential Italic origins of the cult are concerned. Although I have dismissed Brouwer's comment about the oblivion into which some of the cult's features fell by the time of Augustus, it should nonetheless be noted that Verrius' work was characterized by a distinct 'historical antiquarianism'.[66] It is important to note that antiquarian accounts 'of Roman institutions, specific rituals or bodies of norms [...] written by Romans about their

---

[63] Brouwer 1989: 259, n. 31, Scheidel 2011: 304.
[64] For an in-depth discussion see Ambasciano 2016c.
[65] See Tatum 1999. Admittedly, we ignore for how long such regulations were observed or maintained later on.
[66] Zetzel 2018: 63.

own past and present competed with accounts and interpretations of Roman history and culture by Greek authors'.[67] In this cultural competition, both parties had preconceived notions and false assumptions, and both produced intuitive origins for words and customs (especially religious ones), often resulting in questionable etymologies and aetiologies.[68] In this case, the banning of men from attending the rituals and the secrecy around everything that revolved around the cult of Bona Dea certainly contributed to obfuscating their origins, fuelling intellectual speculation.

Finally, since the cult had a geographically limited diffusion, it would not have been odd for the cult – at the very least until its Augustan restoration – to be alien or meaningless to the other ethnic communities present in the Italic peninsula.[69]

If we take into account all these factors, we might hypothesize a superimposition of the Greek Damia on the pre-existing central Italic Fauna. The assimilation of the two goddesses would be later justified through an erudite but pseudolinguistic interpretation that inverted a defining feature of the cult (that is, Festus' δαμόσιον) and fused together the December festivals and the May celebration.[70]

Two Orders, Two Cults, One Goddess

An Italic origin of the cult also lends itself to some interesting political considerations, which might explain its dual configuration. If the Bona Dea cult had been originally established in Central Italy to appease the family of the mythical ancestor queen after her homicide by King Faunus in order to contain a potential upheaval or a scandal among an emerging network of local oligarchic alliances,[71] then the institutionalization of the goddess' devotion could be thought of as the result of inter-class negotiation between the two main orders of Roman citizens, the aristocratic patricians who could claim to be the original ruling elite and the plebeian commoners. While the patricians had to reluctantly concede gradually increasing shares of political power to the plebeians over the course of the first centuries of the Republic

---

[67] Rüpke 2014: 260. [68] See Gabba 1981: 54, Ampolo 1999: 50.
[69] See Smith 1990 and Woolf 2014 on 'locative' cults. Cf. Farney and Bradley 2018: 188–190. On Empress Livia's role in the early imperial cult of Bona Dea see Ambasciano 2016c. On the localized survival of the Bona Dea cult until the fourth century CE see Ambasciano 2016d.
[70] Brouwer 1989: 257, Bettini 2016: 35–55. This does not rule out prior cult assimilations in the context of multi-ethnic Central Italy. Cf. Marcattili 2010: 17 and Mastrocinque 2014: 124–125 for potential points of contact between the two goddesses.
[71] Harders 2013, Maganzani 2016.

(c. 494–287 BCE), there always remained certain class prerogatives and distinctions insofar as religion was concerned.[72]

The existence of two official Bona Dea cults might have aimed on the one hand at incorporating or controlling a patrician euhemeristic commemoration into the Roman *sacra publica* while addressing, on the other hand, therapeutic and plebeian concerns in the Aventine temple and involving *libertae* (former slaves, or freedwomen) in some capacities.[73] Remarkably, this patrician/plebeian cult divide, featuring potentially diverse 'religiolects', was not unique.[74] The cult of *Pudicitia plebeia*, a gendered personification of female sexual and marital 'modesty', was established in the third century BCE by and for chaste *univirae* plebeian women (that is, married just once) excluded from the patrician worship of Pudicitia, granting them the right to perform (blood?) sacrifices.[75] Moreover, the gens Claudia, the Roman family institutionally most strictly tied to the Bona Dea cult, was reputedly of non-Latin, central Italic (Sabine) origins and divided into two branches, one patrician and one plebeian.[76] With all the necessary changes made, De' Guidobaldi's suggestion of a central Italic origin for the cult might not be too wide of the mark.

But what were the functions of the priestesses involved in those cults, and to what extent did the May celebration differ from the December festival, if at all? Without new and conclusive data many answers will remain speculative, but we can formulate a hypothetical explanation that could be confirmed or disconfirmed once such data are available. To do so, I will turn now to the overlapping fields of the cognitive and evolutionary sciences of religion.

A Socio-cognitive Reading of The Bona Dea Cults

There are currently many socio-cognitive approaches to human rituals.[77] In what follows, I will explore the usefulness of two seminal theories to make sense of the way the Bona Dea cults were organized and suggest a

---

[72] E.g. Beard 2015: 137, 146–153.
[73] Considering that religious beliefs and behaviours might be retroactively adjusted *ad hoc* to fit into the reinvention of archaic traditions (e.g. Stoczkowski 2002, Schelling and Rüpke 1987/2005), it is difficult to ascertain which of these two cults came first and in what form. However, the precedence of the patrician euhemeristic cult finds some support in the biocultural analysis of the deification of historical figures. This process leads to the extension of prosocial fictive kinship and is usually triggered by network pressures and ingroup instability as small communities mutate into larger groups (Dávid-Barrett and Carney 2016). On the *divus/diva* title for both human beings and older gods, including Bona Dea/Bona Diva, see Rüpke 2018: 276–277.
[74] Gilhus 2010: 107, n. 60.   [75] Livy 10.23. 3–10, Henry and James 2012: 92.
[76] C. J. Smith 2006: 52.   [77] For a preliminary overview see Legare and Watson-Jones 2016.

Table 7.1. *Ritual form hypothesis. Adapted from Larson 2016; see McCauley and Lawson 2002.*

	Special Agent Ritual	Special Patient/Instrument Ritual
Accountable agents	CPSA	People
CPSA involvement	Direct/active (ASC/surrogate)	Indirect or passive (instrument)
Performance frequency	Low	High
Consequences	Lasting	Temporary
Repetition	Unnecessary	Necessary
Ritual substitutions	Rare	Common
Sensory pageantry	High	Low
Memory	Episodic	Semantic/procedural

CPSA, culturally postulated superhuman agents (gods, ancestors, spirits, etc.); ASC, altered states of consciousness.

new understanding of the *damiatrix* and her role. According to the ritual form hypothesis, mnemonic capacity, neuroendocrine feedback, computational abilities as to the cognitive understanding of agentive cause and effect, and socio-behavioural responses constrain the list of all potential ritual combinations to a set of predictable outcomes (Table 7.1).[78]

Following this scheme, the December festival is understandable as a peculiar special agent ritual characterized by the presence of the goddess herself (through her simulacrum),[79] and by a highly arousing, once-a-year performance characterized by high sensory pageantry and euphoric stimulation. The goddess' presence guaranteed the successful transformation of the wine into an innocuous beverage,[80] and the sacrifice was performed by the Vestal Virgins and/or the magistrate's wife as surrogate agents of the Good Goddess herself. Even if rites of passage were absent, the psychotropic ritual itself was life-transforming per se, because the counterfactual celebration of the goddess' life led to the subversion of everyday behavioural expectations for women. The December festival also displayed key features of special patient rituals. In particular, the ritual came about thanks to a special instrument (i.e. the magically transformed wine), while the patients of the festival were both the whole populace of Rome (for whom the sacrifice

---

[78] McCauley and Lawson 2002; an overview is available in Ambasciano 2019. On the ritual form hypothesis, see also Bowden, Chapter 1, in this volume.
[79] Exceptional omens were also thought to be sent by the goddess on this occasion (cf. the prodigious flames of 63 BCE, Plut. *Vit. Cic.* 20, Cass. Dio 37.35.3-4).
[80] Ambasciano 2016b.

took place) and the participants themselves, transformed into the goddess' companions.[81] In time, habituation, tedium, and mutated social mores might have taken their toll on this festival: pleas to uphold the cult's purest, chaste form while lamenting its current excesses and sexual debauchery are a common trope of later imperial literary sources, although it is difficult to discern whether or not these pleas were genuine.[82]

Given that 'special agent rituals are non-repeatable' as their effects are deemed long-lasting[83] and that there was no actual reason to have a duplicate of a socio-politically undesirable gathering such as the December festival, the May celebration might have assumed the defining features of a special patient ritual that took place during the day. The celebration might have been characterized by the absence of explicitly *pro populo* aims and by the presence of freedwomen as both audience and *antistites*.[84] On that occasion, the likely non-patrician *damiatrix* could have performed a sober, low-engagement, repetitive, ritual commemoration, probably culminating in the sharing of a common meal after the sacrifice,[85] as suggested by the architectural structure of the temples and, as we have seen, by the title of the priestess herself. This one might be the institutional version of the cult that got copied and that was taken elsewhere by settlers, since this specific cult would not have encountered any socio-political or moral opposition from the institutional powers that be.[86] Additionally, as in other Graeco-Roman healing cults, another kind of special agent ritual called *incubatio* (which was designed to favour the goddess' direct therapeutic intervention through dreams experienced by ailing worshippers within or without the walls of the temples) might have been available to devotees (Table 7.2).[87]

The other competing, and slightly overlapping, model that I am going to tackle here is the theory of the modes of religiosity, which posits that memory

---

[81] Cf. McCauley and Lawson 2002: 193–194.
[82] See Juv. 1.2.82–90, 2.6.314–345 (Brouwer 1989: 202–205). Additional sources listed and commented on in Ambasciano 2016a.
[83] McCauley and Lawson 2002: 199. The ritual was interrupted in 62 BCE, but what had to be replicated afterwards was probably just the (repeatable) sacrificial procedure and not the psychotropic festival (Cic. *Att.* 1.13.3). See also McCauley and Lawson 2002: 181.
[84] Brouwer 1989: 372.
[85] On the possible sacrificial substitution with a black chicken see Plin. *HN* 10.56.77 (Brouwer 1989: 193). On ritual communal meals, see also Martin, Chapter 9 in this volume.
[86] The combination or coexistence of both ritual systems within a single religious cult was not unique; see Martin 2015.
[87] At least one epigraph seems to suggest the existence of such a ritual: CIL 14. 2251 = ILS 3503 (Brouwer 1989: 82–84); see Ambasciano 2016d.

Table 7.2. *Ritual form hypothesis applied to the Bona Dea cults. Text within square brackets indicates tentative reconstruction.*

	Magistrate house: December festival	Temple: May celebration	Temple: healing rituals
Accountable agents	(a) Bona Dea; (b) Vestals, magistrate's wife	[*damiatrix*]	Bona Dea and other goddesses
Goddess involvement	(a) Direct through her *simulacrum*; (b) ASC	[indirect]	Direct (through visions and dreams); indirect [through snakes, if ritual biting took place]
Performance frequency	Once a year	Once a year [but communal meals periodic?]	High
Consequences	[socially lasting; individually lasting?]	[temporary]	[lasting, only if successful]
Repetition	Necessary*	Unnecessary [necessary for communal meals?]	Unnecessary (only if successful)
Ritual substitutions	[possible]**	[possible]**	Possible (regarding both place and mode of experience)
Sensory pageantry	High	[low]	High
Memory	Episodic and procedural	[semantic/ procedural]	Episodic

* Cic. *Att.* 1.13.3. ** Plin. *HN* 10.56.77.
ASC, altered state of consciousness.

and social technologies constrain the origin and the development of rituals into two main groups: the imagistic mode, which triggers episodic memory through highly emotional and uncommon rituals, in turn supporting speculations, personal reflections, and a strong sense of ingroup belonging through vivid and shared imagery; and the doctrinal mode, which rests on monotonous, regular rituals supported by written texts and enforced by institutionalized religious hierarchy, with codified low-emotional sequential actions being impressed in semantic and procedural memory (Table 7.3).[88]

[88] The existence of two different socio-religious dynamics has long been recognized in both sociology and anthropology, although a comprehensive neurosociological explanation was lacking; see Whitehouse 2002. See also Bowden, Chapter 1 in this volume.

Table 7.3. *Theory of the modes of religiosity. Adapted from Whitehouse 2002: 309.*

	Doctrinal mode	Imagistic mode
Psychological features		
Transmissive frequency	High	Low
Level of arousal	Low	High
Memory system	Semantic/implicit	Episodic/flashbulb memory
Ritual meaning	Learned/acquired	Internally generated
Techniques of revelation	Rhetoric, narrative, logical integration	Iconicity, multivocality, multivalence
Socio-political features		
Social cohesion	Diffused	Intense
Leadership	Dynamic	Passive/absent
Inclusivity/exclusivity	Inclusive	Exclusive
Diffusion	Rapid, efficient	Slow, inefficient
Scale	Large	Small
Degree of uniformity	High	Low
Structure	Centralized	Noncentralized

Thus, the euphoric December festival would be classified as the first 'divergent imagistic modality [...] fully documented for Roman religion during the Republican era'.[89] Again, we cannot say much about the May celebration, except that, following the virtual reconstruction highlighted above, it might have been predominantly doctrinal with the addition of imagistic healing rituals, which would be in line with the Roman *sacra publica* sporting a peculiar mix of both modes (Table 7.4).[90]

Unfortunately, we have to acknowledge that we do not know how much the provincial cult differed from urban Roman worship, how much the urban cult(s) changed through time, whether the worshippers drank wine during the May celebration, if there were other occasions of special patient celebration, and how many times these might have taken place. Moreover, although Roman religion was largely characterized by the absence of written canons, we cannot discard the possibility of the existence of priestly scripts or personal accounts that might have contributed to clarify, justify, and explain the relation between these different cult experiences. As Venetian cardinal and humanist extraordinaire Pietro

---

[89] Martin 2009: 242.
[90] Whitehouse 2004, Chalupa 2009, Griffith 2009, Larson 2016: 196–198, Ambasciano 2019.

Table 7.4. *Organization and experiences of the Bona Dea cults and Roman state religion (sacra publica) according to the theory of the modes of religiosity (cf. Chalupa 2009, Griffith 2009). Text within square brackets indicates tentative reconstruction.*

	Magistrate house: December festival	Aventine temple: May celebration	All temples: healing rituals	Roman *sacra publica*
Psychological features				
Transmissive frequency	Low	[high]	[low]	High
Level of arousal	High	[low]	[high]	Low
Memory system	Semantic/procedural (sacrifice) and episodic (ASC)	[semantic]	[episodic]	Semantic
Ritual meaning	Learned and internally generated*	[learned]	[internally generated]	(variable)
Techniques of revelation**	Narrative, but multivocality	[narrative but multivalence]	[multivalence]	(variable)
Socio-political features				
Social cohesion	Intense	Intense	[diffused]	Diffused
Leadership	Dynamic + outsourced expertise (Vestals)	[priesthood hierarchy]	[passive]	Dynamic
Inclusivity/exclusivity	Exclusive (patrician)	Inclusive (mostly slaves and *libertae/-i*)	Inclusive	Inclusive
Diffusion	Highly inefficient	Highly inefficient	[relatively efficient]	Relatively inefficient
Scale	Small	Small	[relatively large]	Large
Degree of uniformity	Mythographically low, ritually high; stable iconography	Mythographically low, ritually high; stable iconography	[low]	(variable)
Structure	Potentially centralized	[potentially centralized]	Noncentralized	(variable)

* Plut. *Vit. Cic.* 20; Cass. Dio 37.35.3-4; ** normative and logical explanations as compulsory doctrinal basis.

Bembo (1470–1547) maintained in a posthumous essay, we may have at our disposal just one percent of all the Greek literature that ever existed.[91] I sincerely doubt that our knowledge of Latin literary sources fares much better.

Conclusion

We may never know who the *damiatrix* really was. However, admitting the extent of the limits of our current knowledge should not prevent us from providing a falsifiable hypothesis. At the end of this cross-disciplinary experiment, we can infer from linguistic, archaeological, literary, and socio-cognitive clues that the *damiatrix* might have been an original Italic title used to designate a plebeian or a freedwoman priestess at the top of an unattested religious hierarchy. The *damiatrix* might have overseen female-only special patient rituals in a mundane celebration that included also a sacrifice and a communal meal. In addition, healing rituals were available for external worshippers regardless of their social status or sex. The existence of a second, exclusively female, and well-attested patrician festival based on a special agent ritual with imagistic features raises interesting questions regarding the potential existence of an experiential class divide within the Bona Dea cult and devotion. It also points to the opportunistic, patriarchal, top-down exploitation of neurophysiological ploys through mythographic storytelling and rituals to control subordinates while securing sexual access and reproductive success.[92]

The beliefs and the rituals associated to the Bona Dea cults played a remarkable role in the modern reconstruction of how gender, religion, socio-political discourses concerning sexual mores, and power dynamics were understood and culturally transmitted in the late Roman Republic.[93] However, we still know too little. A bolder interdisciplinary push for a consilient, biocultural research programme is needed if we want to make sense of both the frustratingly fragmentary record and the elite and male documentary distortions regarding the religious experiences of subordinated and silenced social classes of the past.[94] Human societies are encultured neural networks that function on the basis of historically determined worldviews and imagined communities. No neurosociological study can clarify the socio-political coordinates of ancient Roman gender politics.

---

[91] Wilson 2003: 36–37.   [92] Cf. Gorelik and Shackelford 2012: 343.
[93] E.g. Marconi 1939: 244–253, Piccaluga 1964, Brouwer 1989, Kraemer 1992: 52–54, Versnel 1992.
[94] Scheid 2002, Culham 2004, Richlin 2009.

Likewise, no philological or historical analysis alone can contribute to illuminating the neurophysiological extent of religious experiences in ancient Rome. As a matter of fact, a cognitive historiography of sex and gender would require an unprecedented level of interdisciplinary collaboration and cross-disciplinary synthesis.[95] The epistemological promises of such an approach greatly outweigh any potential downside.[96]

BIBLIOGRAPHY

Ambasciano, L. 2015. 'Review of Mastrocinque, A. 2014. *Bona Dea and the Cults of Roman Women*. Stuttgart', *Culture and Religion: An Interdisciplinary Journal* (16)1: 110–112.

2016a. 'Wine, Brains, and Snakes: An Ancient Roman Cult between Gendered Contaminants, Sexuality, and Pollution Beliefs', *Journal for the Cognitive Science of Religion* 4(2): 123–164.

2016b. 'The Gendered Deep History of the Bona Dea Cult', *Journal of Cognitive Historiography* 3(1–2): 134–156.

2016c. 'The Goddess Who Failed? Competitive Networks (or the Lack Thereof), Gender Politics, and the Diffusion of the Roman Cult of Bona Dea', *Religio: Revue Pro Religionistiku* 24(2): 111–165.

2016d. 'The Fate of a Healing Goddess: Ocular Pathologies, the Antonine Plague, and the Ancient Roman Cult of Bona Dea', *Open Library of Humanities* 1(1): 1–34. p.e13. https://doi.org/10.16995/olh.42

2017. 'What Is Cognitive Historiography, Anyway? Method, Theory, and a Cross-Disciplinary Decalogue', *Journal of Cognitive Historiography* 4(2): 136–150.

2019. 'The Cognitive Study of (Ancient) Religions', in N. Roubekas, ed. *Theorizing Ancient Religion*, 327–360. Sheffield and Bristol.

Ampolo, C. 1999. 'La città riformata e l'organizzazione centuriata. Lo spazio, Il tempo, il sacro nella nuova realtà urbana', in A. Giardina and A. Schiavone, *Storia di Roma*, 49–85. Turin.

Ando, C. and J. Rüpke (eds, assisted by S. Blake and M. Holban). 2006. *Religion and Law in Classical and Christian Rome*. Stuttgart.

Arnhold, M. 2015. 'Male Worshippers and the Cult of Bona Dea', *Religion in the Roman Empire* 1(1): 51–70.

Baldi, P. 2002. *The Foundations of Latin*. Berlin and New York, NY.

Bamberger, J. 1974. 'The Myth of Matriarchy: Why Men Rule in Primitive Society', in L. Lamphere and M. Zimbalist Rosaldo, eds. *Women, Culture, Women, and Society*, 263–280. Stanford.

Beard, M. 2015. *SPQR: A History of Ancient Rome*. London.

2017. *Women and Power: A Manifesto*. London.

---

[95] See Ambasciano 2017.   [96] Scheidel 2014.

Bettini, M. 2009. *Affari di famiglia. La parentela romana nella letteratura e nella cultura antica*. Rome and Bari.
　2016. *Dèi e uomini nella città. Antropologia, religione e cultura nella Roma antica*. Rome.
Bloch, H. 2009. *Medieval Misogyny and the Invention of Western Romantic Love*. Chicago, IL and London.
Bloch, M. and D. Sperber. 2002. 'Kinship and Evolved Psychological Dispositions: The Mother's Brother Controversy Reconsidered', *Current Anthropology* 43(5): 723–748.
Bourdieu, P. (trans. R. Nice). 2001 [1998]. *Masculine Domination*. Stanford, CA.
Brelich, A. 2010 [1976]. *Tre variazioni romane sul tema delle origini. A cura di A. Alessandri*. Rome.
Bremmer, J. 2004. 'Review of Motte, A. and C. Ternes (eds). 2003. *Dieux, fêtes, sacré dans la Grèce et la Rome antiques*, Turnhout', *Bryn Mawr Classical Review* 2004.02.07. http://bmcr.brynmawr.edu/2004/2004-02-07
Brouwer, H. H. J. 1989. *Bona Dea: The Sources and a Description of the Cult*. Leiden and New York, NY.
Buck, C. D. 1904. *A Grammar of Oscan and Umbrian: With a Collection of Inscriptions and a Glossary*. Boston, MA.
Cantarella, E. (trans. M. B. Fant). 1987 [1981]. *Pandora's Daughters. The Role and Status of Women in Greek and Roman Antiquity*. Baltimore, MD.
Cantarella, E. 1999. 'La vita delle donne', in A. Giardina and A. Schiavone, eds. *Storia di Roma*, 867–894. Turin.
　2010 [1996]. *Passato prossimo. Donne romane da Tacita a Sulpicia*. Milan.
　2020 [2017]. *Come uccidere il padre. Genitori e figli da Roma a oggi*. Milan.
Chalupa, A. 2009. 'Religious Change in Roman Religion from the Perspective of Whitehouse's Theory of the Two Modes of Religiosity', in L. H. Martin and P. Pachis, eds. *Imagistic Traditions in the Graeco-Roman World: A Cognitive Modeling of History of Religious Research*, 113–135. Thessaloniki.
Chioffi, L. 1993. 'Bona Dea', 'Bona Dea Subsaxana', in E. M. Steinby, ed. *Lexicon Topographicum Urbis Romae I*, 197–198, 200–201. Rome.
Conway, R. S. 1897. *The Italic Dialects, Edited with a Grammar and Glossary*, vol. I. Cambridge.
Crawford, M., W. M. Broadhead, J. P. T. Clackson, F. Santangelo, S. Thompson and M. Watmough, eds. 2011. *Imagines Italicae: A Corpus of Italic Inscriptions*. London.
Culham, P. 2004. 'Women in the Roman Republic', in H. I. Flower, ed. *The Cambridge Companion to the Roman Republic*, 139–159. Cambridge.
Dávid-Barrett, T. and J. Carney. 2016. 'The Deification of Historical Figures and the Emergence of Priesthoods As a Solution to a Network Coordination Problem', *Religion, Brain & Behavior* 6(4): 307–317.
De' Guidobaldi, G. 1865. *Damia o Buona Dea. Ad occasione d'una iscrizione osca opistografa su di una terracotta campana del Museo Nazionale*. Naples.
DiLuzio, M. J. 2016. *A Place at the Altar: Priestesses in Republican Rome*. Princeton, NJ and Oxford.

Dionisio, A. 2016. 'Caratteri dei culti femminili a Corfinio', *Archeologia Classica* 64: 223–262.
Dorcey, P. J. 1992. *The Cult of Silvanus in the Roman World: A Study in Roman Folk Religion.* Leiden.
Dunbar, R. 2013. 'The Origin of Religion As a Small-Scale Phenomenon', in S. Clarke, R. Powell and J. Savulescu, eds. *Religion, Intolerance, and Conflict: A Scientific and Conceptual Investigation,* 48–66. Oxford and New York, NY.
Farney, G. D. and G. Bradley, eds. 2018. *The Peoples of Ancient Italy.* Berlin and Boston, MA.
Figueredo, A. J., P. R. Gladden and C. J. A. Beck. 2012. 'Intimate Partner Violence and Life History Strategy', in T. K. Shackelford and A. T. Goetz, eds. *The Oxford Handbook of Sexual Conflict in Humans,* 72–99. Oxford.
Fitzgerald, J. T. 2012. 'Egnatius, the Breathalyzer Kiss, and an Early Instance of Domestic Homicide at Rome', in A. C. Niang and C. Osiek, eds. *Text, Image, and Christians in the Graeco-Roman World,* 119–131. Eugene, OR.
Flemming, R. 2007. 'Festus and the Role of Women in Roman Religion', *Bulletin of the Institute of Classical Studies* 50(S93): 87–108.
Foucault, M. (trans. R. Hurley). 1978. *The History of Sexuality.* New York, NY.
  1980. *Power/Knowledge: Selected Interviews & Other Writings 1972–1977,* ed. C. Gordon. New York, NY.
Frank, T. 1927. 'The Bacchanalian Cult of 186 B.C.', *Classical Quarterly* 21(3/4): 128–132.
Gabba, E. 1981. 'True History and False History in Classical Antiquity', *Journal of Roman Studies* 71: 50–62.
Gaspar, V. M. 2012. *Sacerdotes piae: Priestesses and Other Female Cult Officials in the Western Part of the Roman Empire from the First Century B.C. until the Third Century A.D.* PhD Dissertation, University of Amsterdam.
Geertz, A. M. 2010. 'Brain, Body and Culture: A Biocultural Theory of Religion,' *Method and Theory in the Study of Religion* 22(4): 304–321.
  2013. 'Whence Religion? How the Brain Constructs the World and What This Might Tell Us about the Origins of Religion, Cognition and Culture', in A. W. Geertz, ed. *Origins of Religion, Cognition and Culture,* 17–70. London and New York, NY.
Giannelli, G. 1913. *Il sacerdozio delle Vestali romane.* Florence.
Gilhus, I. S. 2010. 'Contextualizing the Present, Manipulating the Past: Codex II from Nag Hammadi and the Challenge of Circumventing Canonicity', in E. Thomassen, ed. *Canon and Canonicity: The Formation and Use of Scripture,* 91–108. Copenhagen.
Gorelik, G. and T. K. Shackelford. 2012. 'Spheres of Sexual Conflict', in T. K. Shackelford and A. T. Goetz, eds. *The Oxford Handbook of Sexual Conflict in Humans,* 331–346. Oxford and New York, NY.
Griffith, A. B. 2009. 'The 'Modes Theory' and Roman Religion: National Catastrophe and Religious Response in the Second Punic War', in L. H. Martin and P. Pachis, eds. *Imagistic Traditions in the Graeco-Roman World: A Cognitive Modeling of History of Religious Research.* Thessaloniki.

Harders, A.-C. 2013. 'Agnatio, Cognatio, Consanguinitas: Kinship and Blood in Ancient Rome,' in C. H. Johnson, B. Jussen, D. W. Sabean and S. Teuscher, eds. *Blood and Kinship: Matter for Metaphor from Ancient Rome to the Present*, 18–39. New York, NY.

Henry, M. M. and S. L. James. 2012. 'Woman, City, State: Theories, Ideologies, and Concepts in the Archaic and Classical Periods,' in S. L. James and S. Dillon, eds. *A Companion to Women in the Ancient World*, 84–95. Malden, MA and Oxford.

Holland, L. 2011. 'Family Nomenclature and Same-Name Divinities in Roman Religion and Mythology', *Classical World* 104(2): 211–226.

Holmes, B. A. 2012. *Gender: Antiquity and Its Legacy*. London and New York, NY.

Huxley, A. 1984. *Brave New World and Brave New World Revisited*. London.

James, S. L. and S. Dillon, eds. 2012. *A Companion to Women in the Ancient World*. Malden, MA and Oxford.

Johannowsky, W., J. Griffiths Pedley and M. Torelli. 1983. 'Excavations at Paestum 1982', *American Journal of Archaeology* 87(3): 293–303.

Kraemer, R. S. 1992. *Her Share of the Blessings: Women's Religion among Pagans, Jews and Christians in the Greco-Roman World*. New York, NY and Oxford

Larson, J. 2016. *Understanding Greek Religion*. London and New York, NY.

Legare, C. and R. E. Watson-Jones. 2016. 'The Evolution and Ontogeny of Ritual', in D. Buss, ed. *The Handbook of Evolutionary Psychology. Volume 2: Integrations*, 829–847. Hoboken, NJ.

Lincoln, B. 1981. *Emerging from the Chrysalis: Studies in Rituals of Women's Initiation*. Cambridge, MA.

Maganzani, L. 2016. 'Per uno sguardo antropologico del giurista: il rapporto padre-figlio nel mondo romano', in A. McClintock, ed. *Giuristi nati. Antropologia e diritto romano*, 99–134. Bologna.

Marcattili, F. 2010. 'Bona Dea, ἡ θεὸς γυναικεία', *Archeologia Classica* 61: 7–40.

2012. 'Per un'archeologia dell'Aventino: i culti della media Repubblica', *Mélanges de l'École française de Rome – Antiquité* 124(1): 109–122.

Marconi, M. 1939. *Riflessi mediterranei nella più antica religione laziale*. Messina and Milan.

Martin, C. 2012. *A Critical Introduction to the Study of Religion*. London and New York, NY.

Martin, L. H. 2009. 'Conclusion: Imagistic Traditions in the Graeco-Roman World', in L. H. Martin and P. Pachis, eds. *Imagistic Traditions in the Graeco-Roman World: A Cognitive Modeling of History of Religious Research*, 238–247. Thessaloniki.

2014. *Deep History, Secular Theory: Historical and Scientific Studies of Religion*. Boston, MA and Berlin.

2015. *The Mind of Mithraists: Historical and Cognitive Studies in the Roman Cult of Mithras*. London and New York, NY.

2018. *Studies in Hellenistic Religions. Selected and Edited with an Introduction by P. Pachis*. Eugene, OR.

Martzloff, V. and B. Machajdíková. 2017. 'Structures strophiques dans la poésie épigraphique de l'Italie ancienne: inscription latine archaïque du *duenos* (CIL I2 4), épitaphe pélignienne de la *pristafalacirix* (ST Pg 9, Corfinium)', *Graeco-Latina Brunensia* 22(1): 147–163.

Mastrocinque, A. 1993. *Romolo. La fondazione di Roma tra storia e leggenda*. Este.

2011a. 'Orfismo nel culto romano di Bona Dea (OF 584)', in M. Herrero de Jáuregui, A. I. J. San Cristóbal, E. R. L. Martínez, R. M.Hernández, M. A. S. Álvarez and S. T. Tovar, eds. 2011. *Tracing Orpheus: Studies of Orphic Fragments in Honour of Alberto Bernabé*, 259–268. Berlin and New York, NY.

2011b. 'Religione e politica: Il caso di Bona Dea', in G. A. Cecconi and C. Gabrielli, eds. *Politiche religiose nel mondo antico e tardoantico: Poteri e indirizzi, forme del controllo, idee e prassi di tolleranza*, 165–172. Bari.

2014. *Bona Dea and the Cults of Roman Women*. Stuttgart.

McCauley, R. N. and E. T. Lawson, 2002. *Bringing Ritual to Mind: Psychological Foundations of Cultural Forms*. Cambridge.

Mignone, L. M. 2016. *The Republican Aventine and Rome's Social Order*. Ann Arbor, MI.

Moorton, R. 1988. 'The Genealogy of Latinus in Vergil's Aeneid', *Transactions of the American Philological Association* 118: 253–259.

Nencini, P. 2009. *Ubriachezza e sobrietà nel mondo antico. Alle radici del bere moderno*. Monte San Pietro (BO).

Piccaluga, G. 1964. 'Bona Dea. Due contributi all'interpretazione del suo culto', *Studi e materiali di storia delle religioni* 35: 195–237.

Richlin, A. 2009. 'Writing Women into History', in A. Erskine, ed. *A Companion to Ancient History*, 146–153. Malden, MA and Oxford.

Rüpke, J. 2014. 'Historicizing Religion: Varro's *Antiquitates* and History of Religion in the Late Roman Republic.' *History of Religions* 53(3): 246–268.

Rüpke, J. (trans. D. M. B. Richardson). 2018 [2016]. *Pantheon: A New History of Roman Religion*. Princeton, NJ and Oxford.

Scheid, J. 2002 [1992]. 'The Religious Role of Roman Women', in G. Duby, M. Perrot and P. Schmitt Pantel, eds. *A History of Women: From Ancient Goddesses to Christian Saints*, 377–408. Cambridge, MA and London.

Scheidel, W. 2011. 'The Roman Slave Supply', in K. Bradley and P. Cartledge, eds. *The Cambridge World History of Slavery, vol. I: The Ancient Mediterranean World*, 287–310. Cambridge.

2014. 'Evolutionary Psychology and the Historian', *American Historical Review* 119(5): 1563–1575.

Schelling, R. and J. Rüpke 1987/2005. 'Roman Religion: The Early Period', in L. Jones, ed. *Encyclopaedia of Religion* (2nd ed.), *vol. 12*, 7892–7911, Detroit, MI and New York, NY.

Smail, D. L. 2008. *On Deep History and the Brain*. Los Angeles and Berkeley, CA.

2010. 'An Essay on Neurohistory', in M. Bailar, *Emerging Disciplines: Shaping New Fields of Scholarly Inquiry in and beyond the Humanities*, 201–228. Houston, TX. https://cnx.org/contents/iqMKXpSE@1.4:tbT41NAE@4/An-Essay-on-Neurohistory

Smith, C. J. 2006. *The Roman Clan: The Gens from Ancient Ideology to Modern Anthropology*. Cambridge.
Smith, J. Z. 1990. *Drudgery Divine: On the Comparison of Early Christianities and the Religions of Late Antiquity*. Chicago, IL.
Stoczkowski, W. (trans. M. Turton). 2002 [1994]. *Explaining Human Origins: Myth, Imagination and Conjecture*. Cambridge.
Tatum, W. J. 1999. *The Patrician Tribune: Publius Clodius Pulcher*. Chapel Hill, NC and London.
Turner, J. H., A. Maryanski, A. K. Petersen and A. W. Geertz. 2018. *The Emergence and Evolution of Religion by Means of Natural Selection*. New York, NY and London.
Untermann, J. 2000. *Wörterbuch des Oskisch-Umbrischen*. Heidelberg.
Ustinova, Y. 2018. 'Amazons East and West: A Real-Life Experiment in Social Cognition', in A. K. Petersen, S. G. Ingvild, L. H. Martin, J. S. Jensen and J. Jesper Sørensen, eds. *Evolution, Cognition, and the History of Religion: A New Synthesis*, 461–474. Leiden and Boston, MA.
Versnel, H. S. 1990. 'What's Sauce for the Goose Is Sauce for the Gander: Myth and Ritual, Old and New,' in L. Edmunds, ed. *Approaches to Greek Myth*, 23–90. Baltimore, MD.
——— 1992. 'The Festival for Bona Dea and the Thesmophoria', *Greece & Rome, n.s.* 39(1): 31–55.
Watmough, M. M. T. 1995/1996. 'The Suffix -tor-: Agent-Noun Formation in Latin and the Other Italic Languages', *Glotta* 73 (1/4): 80–115.
Welch, T. S. 2004. 'Masculinity and Monuments in Propertius 4.9', *American Journal of Philology* 125(1): 61–90.
Whatmough, J. 1931. 'The Calendar in Ancient Italy Outside Rome', *Harvard Studies in Classical Philology* 42: 157–179.
Whitehouse, H. 2002. 'Modes of Religiosity: Towards a Cognitive Explanation of the Sociopolitical Dynamics of Religion', *Method & Theory in the Study of Religion* 14(3/4): 293–315.
——— 2004. 'Theorizing Religions Past', in H. Whitehouse and L. H. Martin, eds. *Theorizing Religions Past*, 215–232. Walnut Creek, CA.
Williams, Z. 2016. 'Interview with Mary Beard: 'The Role of the Academic is to Make Everything Less Simple', *The Guardian*, 23 April. www.theguardian.com/books/2016/apr/23/mary-beard-the-role-of-the-academic-is-to-make-everything-less-simple
Wilson, N. G. ed. 2003. *Pietro Bembo, Oratio pro litteris graecis*. Messina.
Wonder, J. W. 2002. 'What Happened to the Greeks in Lucanian-Occupied Paestum? Multiculturalism in Southern Italy', *Phoenix* 56(1/2): 40–55.
Woolf, G. 2014. 'Isis and the Evolution of Religion.' in L. Bricault and M. J. Versluys, eds. *Power, Politics and the Cults of Isis*, 62–92. Leiden.
Zetzel, J. E. G. 2018. *Critics, Compilers, and Commentators: An Introduction to Roman Philology, 200 BCE–800 CE*. Oxford.

PART IV
Materiality

CHAPTER 8

Walls and the Ancient Greek Ritual Experience
The Sanctuary of Demeter and Kore at Eleusis

Michael Scott

Introduction

Why Walls?

A key part of any Greek sanctuary was its *temenos:* the boundary marking the limits of the sacred space. The physical form of the *temenos* varied hugely across the ancient Greek world. It could have no, or very little, physical manifestation (for example, when Antigone in *Oedipus at Colonus* wandered into a sacred grove without realizing that she had done so; or at the sanctuary of Asclepius at Epidauros, where the boundary was marked only by a monumental gateway). It could, however, also be physically monumentalized in a variety of ways: with tightly packed banks of cypress trees (for example, at the sanctuary of Eurynome in Arcadia); with a low wall (for example, at the sanctuary of Olympia from the fourth century BCE onwards); or with high monumental walls (for example at the sanctuaries of Aphaia at Aegina, Poseidon at Sounion, and, perhaps most famously, Demeter and Kore at Eleusis).[1]

Despite this vast range of physical forms, what a *temenos* boundary looked like, and what effect it may subsequently have had on the ritual experience, is not a popular topic within scholarship.[2] Tomlinson, for example, did think about the varying nature of the boundary of the *temenos*, but concluded that 'while architecturally, in terms of visual

---

My deepest thanks to the editors for including me in this volume and their comments on this chapter as it developed. Sincerest thanks also to Dr Elizabeth Blagrove for her engaging guidance and comments on the cognitive aspects of this chapter.

[1] Soph. *OC* 16–18. Olympia: Mallwitz 1972: 121–122. Epidauros: Tomlinson 1976: 40. Eurynome in Arcadia: Paus. 8.41.4. Aegina: Goette 2001: 341–342. Sounion: Camp 2001: 307. Eleusis: Camp 2001: 283–289.

[2] Bergquist 1967: 116 examined the ways in which the *temenos*, the altar, and the temple worked together to create a particular volume for the sanctuary. But Bergquist was only interested in the form of a *temenos* boundary when it disrupted what she termed the 'unity' of a sanctuary ensemble.

appearance, the differences [were] considerable, religiously, [all types of boundary] had the same function'.³ The *temenos* as a topic receives good coverage in volume 4 of *ThesCRA* on cult places. Yet while, once again, the variety of forms a boundary could take is highlighted, *ThesCRA* does not dwell on the implications of these boundaries for the ritual experience.⁴

This absence of discussion about the impact of the physical form of the *temenos* is paralleled by a similar lack of discussion about the ritual impact of another – always monumental – set of walls within a sanctuary: the walls of the sanctuary's temple. Not every sanctuary had a temple, and, of course, the design of a Greek temple ensured that its outer colonnade was more visible than its inner walls. Yet, while temples have been well studied from the perspective of how the structure speaks to the particular values of its constructor and offers a particular message (often political) to its viewing public, the question of what impact temples (and in particular their monumental colonnades/walls) had on the *ritual* experience has been much more muted.⁵

Such absence of discussion about the ritual impact of the – potentially most monumental – physical structures around and inside sanctuaries, should, I think, strike us as surprising,⁶ especially given the ways in which, over the last forty years, monumental architecture, including walls, in spheres other than the religious (e.g. civic and governmental) has been re-characterized as an active and critical element in the construction of space, environment, human action, and experience; and given that, within the religious sphere, there have been an increasing number of spatial and architectural analyses of sacred landscapes, not to mention recent in-depth

---

³ Tomlinson 1976: 17. See a similar comment in Burkert 1985: 66.
⁴ '*Temenos*' in *ThesCRA* vol. 4: 5–12 (U. Sinn). Mylonopoulos 2008: 52, 78, however, has argued that the stronger presence of porticoes surrounding sanctuaries in the Hellenistic and Roman Imperial periods both reflected and helped construct an intensification of ritual performance. Most recently, see the interesting discussion on the ways in which the *temenos* constructs the sanctuary as divine property: Ekroth, in press.
⁵ Political message: Spawforth 2006: 28–30, 50–51: temple as 'assertion of community and temple's location as aspiring to have conspicuousness and loftiness. De Polignac 1995: temple as marker of territory. Snodgrass 1986: temples as examples of 'peer polity interaction' and rivalry. Scott 2010: 183–184: temples as symbols of victory in war. Ritual impact: Tomlinson 1976: 37: the sturdy solidarity of temple architecture reflecting strength and permanence appropriate to the cult of the gods. Spawforth 2006: 55: the colonnaded space around a temple as symbol of divine protection sought from the deity to whom the temple was dedicated. Spawforth 2006: 72: temple walls 'dramatised these ancient encounters with the sacred' (in reference to wider discussion of the ritual impact of cult statues within temples: Spawforth 2006: 72–81, 86–88).
⁶ Compare the discussion about the ritual impact of barriers within temples (often surrounding the cult statue): Hewitt 1909: 91, Mattern 2006, Mylonopoulos 2011: 287.

discussions of particular forms of sacred architecture (e.g. steps and doorways) and their impact on the ritual experience.[7]

Walls and the Ritual Experience

In this chapter, I situate a discussion of the active impact of *temenos* and temple walls within a cognitive approach to the ritual experience in order to examine how these architectural forms interacted with the ritual experience of the religious participants to create, reinforce, and augment their perceptions, experiences, conceptions, and memories of that ritual.[8] The model I am using for the cognitive experience of ritual is the predictive coding model, which understands cognition in the following way: the brain constantly makes models of the world around it, informed by prior expectations and experience (the top-down input).[9] The brain then constantly checks these models for error against the sensory information it receives at any given moment (the bottom-up input) and of course corrects the model accordingly. The application of this framework for the process of cognition in relation to religious experience has focused on how religious rituals and institutions impart particular top-down expectations to participants, but subsequently also hamper and constrain the ability of participants to check these expectations against bottom-up sensory information, in order to ensure maximum susceptibility to both pre-event expectations and/or post-ritual explanation as the basis for a person's 'understanding' of a religious event. In particular, studies have focused on the ways in which participants can find their attentional and executive cognitive resources (their ability to sense-check their expectation model) 'depleted', and/or on the ways in which participants can be 'deprived' of sensory information with which to check pre-installed expectations.[10]

---

[7] Analysis of non-religious architecture: e.g. Rapoport 1990, Pearson and Richards 1994, Maran 2006, Tilley 2004, Parker- Hamilakis 2013. Sacred landscapes: e.g. Cole 2004, Scott 2010, 2012, and 2015. In-depth analysis of the impact of particular architectural forms within sanctuaries: Jones 2000, Wescoat and Ousterhout 2012a, Hollinshead 2015.

[8] In this chapter I concentrate on the effects of *temenos*/temple wall construction, rather than the (potentially different) reasons for their construction (sometimes to do with the cult itself, sometimes to do with the need to demonstrate power and influence in the surrounding landscape by the sanctuary's controlling city, and sometimes even the need to defend the sanctuary from attack).

[9] See also the Introduction, Ustinova, Chapter 2, McGlashan, Chapter 6, and Patzelt, Chapter 5, in this volume.

[10] Schjoedt 2019: 364–365, Schjoedt and Jensen 2018: 321–322, Schjoedt et al. 2013a and 2013b, Friston 2010, Friston and Kiebel 2009, Frith 2007.

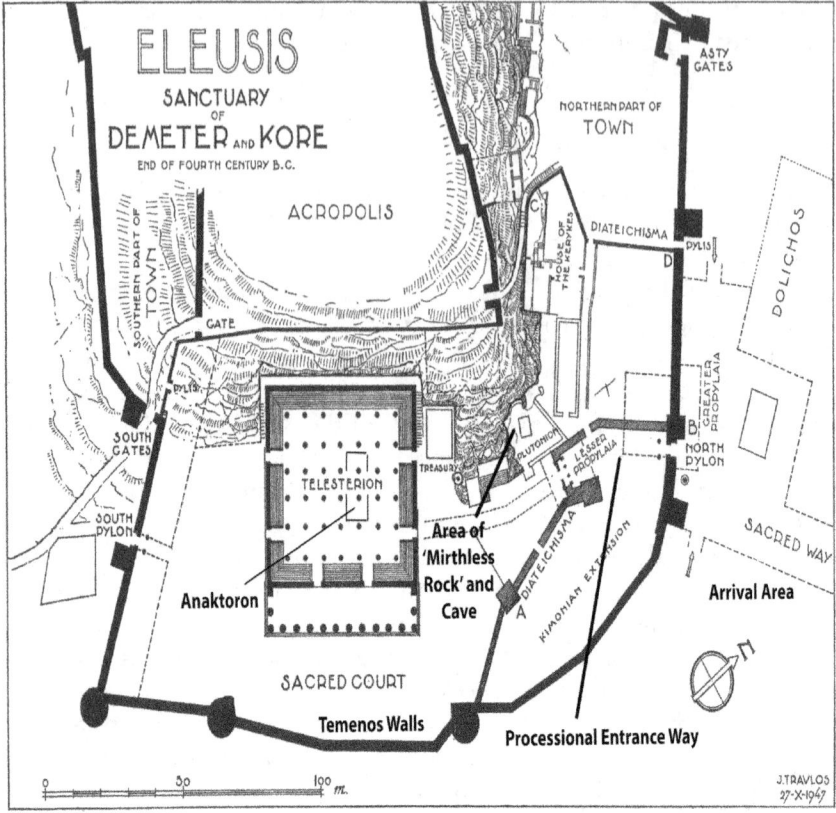

Figure 8.1 Plan of the sanctuary of Demeter and Kore at Eleusis by J. Travlos 'The Topography of Eleusis' *Hesperia* 1949 (18.1) pp. 138–147, adapted by M. Scott.

While this approach could (and should) be applied to a wide range of sanctuaries with (as outlined above) their wide range of types of *temenos* and temple wall in order to understand their varying impact on the religious experience, in this chapter I will apply the predictive coding model specifically to analyze the ritual impact of monumental *temenos* and temple walls at one particular sanctuary: the sanctuary of Demeter and Kore at Eleusis (Figure 8.1).

This sanctuary makes a particularly good case study for two reasons. First, because it was surrounded by high fortress-like *temenos* walls extending for some 580 m around the sanctuary from at least the sixth century BCE, and at its centre it had a very unusual square, non-colonnaded, temple structure (the *Telesterion*), designed to create a large internal space unviewable from the outside.[11] The second reason that Eleusis makes a good case study is the nature of the ritual conducted there: a mystery cult, which it was forbidden for non-initiates to witness.[12] Yet while the monumental *temenos* and *Telesterion* walls played an obvious, and well-studied, role in allowing the mystery cult to remain a mystery to outsiders, there has so far been very little scholarly investigation of the impact of the monumental *temenos* and *Telesterion* walls on those who *were* initiated into the cult.[13]

The Mystery Cult of Demeter and Kore at Eleusis

Initiates (*mystai*) had to complete a series of ritual acts at the Lesser Mysteries in Athens in early springtime. These acts seem to have focused on mentally preparing the initiate for the importance of what lay before them, ensuring their purification. The initiate completed them under the guidance of a *mystagogos* – an already initiated 'sponsor'.[14] The Greater Mysteries (held at Eleusis) happened in the month of Boedromion (September). In advance, Athens sent out special messengers around Greece announcing the Mysteries, asking for a holy truce from all states that used the sanctuary to allow people to attend, as well as dedications – a tithe of First Fruits – for Demeter.[15]

---

[11] For the height of the *temenos* walls (and for their successive rebuilds) cf. Pausanias 1.38, Eur. *Supp.* 980–989, Camp 2001: 283–289, Mylonas 1961, Lippolis 2006, Miles 2012, Evans 2002: 236–237, Clinton 1994: 162–163, Travlos 1988: 93–94. For discussion of the unusual architecture (and successive rebuilds) of the *Telesterion*: Evans 2002: 233, Camp 2001: 283, Clinton 1994: 163, Miles 2012: 123, Mylonas 1961: 114–138. For discussion of the internal landscape of the sanctuary: Clinton 1992: 96–97.

[12] Discussion of what happened inside the sanctuary with the on-initiated was forbidden on pain of death: Thuc. 6.27–29, Plut. *Vit. Alc.* 19–22, Andoc. 1, Lys. 6, Strabo 10.3.9; Camp 2001: 283. While a mystery cult, it was at the same time an official part of the public ritual calendar of the Athenian *polis*: Plut. *Vit. Per.* 12.1; Sourvinou-Inwood 2003: 26, Bowden 2010: 31, Clinton 1994: 162–163.

[13] The high, fortress-like nature of this sanctuary's *temenos* walls has also been explained by Eleusis' place as the westernmost Attic deme on the coast and thus something of an outpost facing the Peloponnese, with the need for substantial defensive fortifications (both of the sanctuary and of the Acropolis): Camp 2001: 283.

[14] Cf. Clem. Al. *Protr.* 2.21.2, *Strom.* 5.11.70.7–71.1; Bremmer 2014: 2, Mylonas 1961: 237, 240, Roussel 1930. This possibly included the discussion of 'secret information' required to be known to even enter the sanctuary at Eleusis: *IG* I³ 6.23–31; Larson 2016: 272. Initiation into the Lesser Mysteries was not an absolute pre-requisite for taking part in the Greater Mysteries: Larson 2016: 271–272, Parker 2005: 344 n.74.

[15] Text of sacred truce: *IG* I³ 6; Bowden 2010: 31, Mylonas 1961: 244.

Initiates first gathered on the fifteenth of the month of Boedromion in Athens. The initiates were an unusual group: the only requirements for being initiated were that you could speak Greek and that you had not committed murder.[16] The Mysteries were thus open to Athenians and other Greek speakers, to men and women, to slave and free.[17] Most likely, the initiate group each year ran to several thousand individuals.[18] In particular, *mystai* were joined at the Greater Mysteries not only by their *mystagogoi*, but also by the *epoptai* (*mystai* from a previous year who had seen the first part of the Mysteries and were now returning for a higher level of revelation).[19]

This mixed group gathered in the agora to hear the proclamation of the festival. The next day (16 Boedromion), the initiates went to the sea to purify themselves and the sacrificial animals (piglets) they would offer to Demeter.[20] On the morning of 19 Boedromion (after two days' rest, fasting, and other minor sacrifices in Athens), the group of *mystai, epoptai*, and *mystagogoi* assembled again in the agora and formed the procession that moved from Athens to the sanctuary of Demeter at Eleusis (some fifteen miles away).[21] This was headed by the Eleusinian dignitaries and accompanied by donkeys carrying provisions and torches required for the festival ahead.[22] They processed during the day over a fifteen-mile route, their progress interrupted by sacred dances, sacrifices, libation pouring, ritual washing, and the singing of hymns.[23] They arrived at Eleusis at nightfall on 19 Boedromion, and spent the night singing and dancing in honour of the goddesses in the outer court, outside the *temenos* walls of the sanctuary.[24] The initiation – when *mystai, mystagogoi and epoptai* went inside the *temenos* walls – happened the next night (20 Boedromion) and perhaps also on the night of 21 Boedromion.[25] Once the initiation was complete (after the

---

[16] Evans 2002: 240, Burkert 1985: 285.   [17] Cf. Bremmer 2014: 2.
[18] Hdt. 8.65 recounts, at the time of Persian invasion, the story of the sighting of a dust cloud arising as if from a crowd of 30,000 initiates (for discussion Miles 2012: 114–115); Ael. Ar. *Orat.* 1.257 'thousands of initiates'; Burkert 1985: 285 (most Athenians initiated); Bremmer 2014: 4 (c. 3000 initiates); Bowden 2010: 33–34 (several thousand); Clinton 1992: 85 (only a few hundred initiates). The initiation cost was about 15 drachmas (ten days' wage in the fourth century BCE): Bremmer 2014: 2, Foley 1994: 66.
[19] Clinton 1992: 85, Bremmer 2014: 5, Foley 1994: 66.
[20] Sea purification: Bremmer 2014: 4, Bowden 2010: 34, Robertson 1999: 1–10, Foley 1994: 66–68, Mylonas 1961: 244–245.
[21] Scholars differ on whether there was one procession (on 19 Boedromion) or two processions (one on the 19th and one on the 20th) cf. Robertson 1999: 19. One procession: Larson 2016: 272, Bremmer 2014: 5, Foley 1994: 66–68, Mylonas 1961: 256. Two processions: Bowden 2010: 36.
[22] Bremmer 2014: 5.   [23] Cf. Bremmer 2014: 6–7, Camp 2001: 283, Foley 1994: 66–68.
[24] Eur. *Ion* 1074.
[25] Two nights: Clinton 1992: 126. One night or perhaps two: Mylonas 1961: 258, 274.

20th/21st), the newly-initiated would re-engage with the wider community for a further day of celebrations and feasting on 22 Boedromion at Eleusis, followed by a return to Athens on the 23rd, and there was an Athenian assembly meeting on 24 Boedromion, marking the end of the festival.[26]

What went on inside the *temenos* enclosure during the night(s) of initiation? The general picture seems to have been as follows: having spent the day of the 20th fasting, resting, and purifying themselves, the initiate body drank a ritual drink (the *kykeon*), changed into new clothes they had brought with them for the occasion, and moved into the *temenos* enclosure.[27]

Once inside, initiation was composed of *dromena* ('things done'), *legomena* ('things said'), and *deiknymena* ('things shown').[28] The *dromena* were most probably a presentation of the story of Demeter wandering and wailing in search of her daughter, Kore, situated around the cave and 'mirthless rock' found inside the *temenos* enclosure, acted out by the chief priests at Eleusis (see Figure 8.1).[29] This night-time performance was perhaps accompanied by the initiates actively having to search for Kore. This aspect of the ritual was new for the *mystai*, but would have already been seen by *epoptai* and *mystagogoi*. The lead priest of the Mysteries – the *hierophant* – is thought to have sounded a gong to announce the summoning of Kore and reunification of Demeter and Kore.[30] This performance was most probably accompanied by the *legomena* – a series of invocations, which enabled initiates to understand what they were seeing.[31] Finally, for the *deiknymena*, the locus of action moved to the *Telesterion* structure. We are uncertain which of the following two scenarios occurred at this point.[32] In scenario one, both *mystai* and *epoptai* went inside and bore witness to a tremendous, brilliant light streaming from a smaller structure at the heart of the *Telesterion* (the *Anaktoron*), where the sacred objects were kept (see **Figure 8.1**). Subsequently the *epoptai* – in the only part of the initiation that was new to them – came forward to see the sacred objects as displayed by the *hierophant*, who once again spoke a series of *legomena* to aid comprehension of what was being seen.[33] In scenario two,

---

[26] Bremmer 2014: 16, Evans 2002: 240, Clinton 1992: 126, Mylonas 1961: 274.
[27] Mylonas 1961: 258–261. The *kykeon* as having a hallucinogenic effect: Ruck 2006.
[28] Cf. Evans 2002: 246, Richardson 1974: 302–308, Mylonas 1961: 261–274. Scholars who believe the initiation happened over two nights often place the *dromena* and *legomena* during the first night, and the *deiknymena* on the second night, cf. Bremmer 2014: 9–11.
[29] Clinton 1992: 85, 96, Mylonas 1961: 261.   [30] Apollod. *FGrH* 244F F 110b.
[31] Mylonas 1961: 272.
[32] In part this uncertainty relates to whether the *Telesterion* is the same structure as the *Anaktoron*, or whether the *Anaktoron* is the smaller structure within the *Telesterion*. For the ancient sources and discussion see: *IG* II² 3709, 3811, Philostr. *V S* 103 (Kayser), Plut. *Mor.* 81E; Clinton 1992: 126.
[33] Bremmer 2014: 11–13.

only the *epoptai* entered the *Telesterion*, with the *mystai* remaining outside.[34] All bore witness to the brilliant light (so brilliant it emanated out of the *Telesterion* via its doorways and hole in the roof), but once again only the *epoptai* saw (and heard about) the sacred objects themselves.[35]

Prior Expectations of Initiates at Eleusis

What kinds of prior expectations (the top-down input) might the initiate group about to participate in the mystery cult at Eleusis have had? This would depend of course on their ritual status. The *mystagogoi* – taking part again after having already experienced the full revelation of the Mysteries – would know precisely what to expect. The *epoptai* would have full knowledge of the first part of the ceremony (the *dromena* and the *legomena*, known collectively as the *telete*), but less knowledge of the revelations they were returning to receive for the first time (the *deiknymena* and further *legomena*, known collectively as the *epopteia*). And the *mystai* would be experiencing it all for the first time. In what follows, I will principally concentrate on the ritual experience of the *mystai*.

Mystai initiates came from very different backgrounds: Athenian and non-Athenian, men and women, slave and free. Each would have had different experiences of Athenian religious ritual up to this point. Yet all would have been united by the fact that this ritual was outside the realm of their normative experience: both in terms of the company the initiates found themselves in (nowhere else in Athenian society did such a wide social group come together), and in the unusual and secret nature of the ceremony itself.[36] As such, despite their different backgrounds and levels of normative ritual knowledge, we might imagine them all having a fairly similar set of limited prior expectations about this particular ceremony. Crucially, what they did expect would have depended almost exclusively on what was revealed to them during their process of preparation by their trusted *mystagogoi*.

---

[34] Clinton 1992: 88–90.
[35] Discussion of brilliant light: *IG* II² 3811, Plut. *Mor.* 81E. For a possible fire on top of the smaller interior structure (with smoke/light emitted through 'roof light' in larger '*Telesterion*' structure): Foley 1994: 68, Burkert 1985: 288. Nature of sacred objects revealed to *epoptai* by the *hierophant* (the chief priest): *Hom. Hymn Dem.* 473–482; Bremmer 2014: 11–13, Clinton 1992: 89 and 1974: 46.
[36] The ceremony was also unusual in that it contained no animal sacrifice (there were no altars inside the sanctuary). The piglets that initiates had to purify in the sea were sacrificed prior to the initiates' entry into the sanctuary at Eleusis; cf. Evans 2002.

The nature of the preparation is likely reflected in the various surviving literary sources that describe the Mysteries. The *Homeric Hymn to Demeter* is one of a collection of thirty-three hymns praising different Greek gods composed in the seventh or sixth centuries BCE, and still well-known and respected in the fifth century BCE, contemporary with the practice of the Mysteries. In this text, it is made clear that he who is initiated at Eleusis is blessed, and that the initiated and uninitiated do not share the same lot in death.[37] In the fourth century BCE, Isocrates, an Athenian political and philosophical commentator, also claimed, as part of one of his political speeches calling for greater unity across Greece, that the initiates have 'sweeter hopes concerning the end of life and all eternity'.[38] According to the fourth-century CE rhetorician and philosopher Sopatros, initiation seemingly changed one's status with the gods and altered one's journey after death.[39] Equally, the experience of going through initiation was marked as a highly emotional one.[40] Plutarch comments on how 'terror, anxiety and bewilderment turned to wonder and clarification'.[41] He compares the experience of initiation to death itself: in which panic, shivering, sweat gives way to being 'set free and loose from all bondage'.[42] This emotional impact of initiation is perhaps best underlined by Aristotle's summary of initiation as not being a process of learning (*mathein*), but an experience of suffering (*pathein*) leading to a change in state of mind.[43]

The Eleusis *Temenos* Walls and the Ritual Experience

As we have seen, the initiate group would have approached the high, fortified *temenos* walls of the sanctuary tired, in near darkness, accompanied by torchlight, at the end of a fifteen-mile, day-long procession filled with individual ritual events.[44] Having spent that night singing and

---

[37] Hom. *Hymn Dem.* 473–482.
[38] Isoc. *Paneg.* 28. See also Ar. *Ran.* 154-8, 448–455, Pl. *Leg.* 7.334b7; Mikalson 1983: 81.
[39] Cf. Sopatros *Rhetores Graeci* 8: 114–115 'I came out of the mystery hall feeling like a stranger to myself'; Larson 2016: 268–271. Cf. Foley 1994: 139. For this becoming a more important part of the initiation from the sixth century BCE onwards, as part of a wider set of shifting attitudes to death within Greek society: Sourvinou-Inwood 2003: 26–28.
[40] The crucial emotional nature of initiation: Larson 2016: 268, Foley 1994: 69, Evans 2002: 249, Sourvinou-Inwood 2003: 40, Bremmer 2014: 13.
[41] Plut. *Mor.* 47A, 943C, Ael. Ar. *Orat.* 19.2, Lactant. *Div. inst.* 23.
[42] Plut. fr. 168 in Stob. *Flor.* 4.52.49. For discussion of the important emotional shift from terror to wonder within the initiation: Clinton 1992: 87–89.
[43] Arist. fr. 15 (Synesius *Dion* 10 p.48a); Foley 1994: 69, Sourvinou-Inwood 2003: 40, Burkert 1985: 89–95.
[44] Cf. Bremmer 2014: 6–7.

dancing outside the sanctuary, as well as then recovering and fasting through to the following evening of 20 Boedromion, the initiates would by this point have spent a total of six days preparing/purifying/fasting/travelling/dancing in preparation for their initiation (not counting the Lesser Mysteries from the springtime). This is a significant amount of time in comparison to most other religious festivals with which they would have been acquainted. The investment of their time, the physical and mental journey they had been through, leading them to this moment, according to theories of embodied cognition and predictive processing, would have encouraged amongst the initiates conscious and unconscious forms of imagining of what lay ahead, amplifying the expectations they had already received.[45]

The initiates, arriving at the sanctuary over 19–20 Boedromion, would have been denied any sense of the sanctuary within by the high *temenos* walls (see **Figure 8.1**).[46] This denial of bottom-up sensory information with which to cross-check their amplified and heightened sense of expectation and imagination ensured their inability to challenge those mounting expectations. At the same time the continued denial of information about what the sanctuary was like even when they were now so close to it, may well have magnified even further their anticipation and excitement at what they were (finally) about to experience.

The Temenos *Walls and the Group's Sense of Self*

The initiates finally moved through the gateway in the sanctuary's high *temenos* walls on the night of 20 Boedromion. This act, and their resulting time together within the sanctuary, would have strengthened their sense of themselves as a group, and of their separation from the outside world, in four specific ways. First, their very ability to move through a monumental architectural demarcation like the high *temenos* walls (which non-initiates could not pass beyond) would have imbued them with a heightened sense of authority and importance.[47] Second, the darkness of the night environment, complemented by the high walls cutting off the world outside, would, according to theories of grounded cognition, have impacted upon the initiates' perception of themselves and

---

[45] Cf. Eidinow 2018 on the importance of embodied cognition for practices of divination. For studies of embodied cognition itself see: Decety and Grèzes 2016, Decety and Jackson 2004.

[46] In Eur. *Supp.* 980–989, the women remark that, while sitting at the altars of Demeter and Kore outside the sanctuary walls, they can see only the roof of the *Telesterion* above them.

[47] Pucci 2006: 171, Gerstel 2006: 3, Rapoport 1990, Eliade 1987: 25.

one another. Darkness increases people's tendency towards abstract processing, which will have encouraged the initiates to construe themselves as inter-dependent with other members of the group.[48] This interdependent construal of the self, promoted by darkness, in turn influences social behaviour, in particular towards acting more co-operatively.[49] Third, the high *temenos* walls impacted on initiates' visual perception to strengthen their sense of themselves as a group. The walls prevented the initiates from seeing the outside world and narrowed their visual field instead to looking at one another. As attention studies have shown since the nineteenth century, selective attention to a subset of a visual scene enhances the processing of information from the attended portion.[50] The walls thus cut the initiates off from the outside world and simultaneously encouraged them to focus on, and pay more attention to, one another. Fourth, the high *temenos* walls, combined with the darkness, also transformed the auditory environment. As demonstrated by attention and sense-deprivation studies, the loss of one sense leads to the brain placing greater emphasis on its input from others.[51] The darkness, combined with the smaller visual field, would thus not only have intensified initiates' attention on what they could see, but also encouraged them to rely more on their other senses, in particular what they could hear. At the same time, the high *temenos* walls would have altered and intensified the soundscape the initiates were listening to. The imposition of a high physical barrier around a group not only removes external ambient noise, increasing the sonic clarity and exclusivity of the noise made by those within the group, but also amplifies the sound coming from within, thus intensifying the auditory experience still further and giving it acoustic 'integrity' – the sense of the auditory experience as being qualitatively different from the normal hustle and bustle of everyday life.[52] As such, the high *temenos* walls and the darkness worked together to transform the auditory environment both in terms of its intensity and in terms of the sense it offered the group that they had moved into their own separate world.

---

[48] Lakoff and Johnson 1999, Trope and Liberman 2010, Bruce, Green, and Georgesen 2003, Forster, Liberman, and Kuschel 2008, Zhong, Bohns, and Gino 2010, Steidle, Werth, and Hanke 2011.
[49] Baumeister and Leary 1995, Zhong, Bohns, and Gino 2010, Steidle, Hanke, and Werth 2013.
[50] Purves et al. 2013: 169, Rosenblum 2010: 169, 194, Driver 2001, Lavie 1995, Treisman 1988.
[51] E.g. Rosenblum 2010: 33, 279.
[52] Cf. Helmer and Chichoine 2013, Hamilakis 2013: 170, Cross and Watson 2006, Yang and Kang 2005, Watson and Keating 1999.

The Temenos *Walls and the Initiates' Engagement with the Ritual*

The high *temenos* walls, along with the darkness, also would have increased the initiates' visual attention and focus on the *dromena* that was now enacted before them by the chief priests. Importantly, this was a ritual experience in which vision, the ability to see, was constantly underlined as a crucial part of the experience in several ways.[53] First, visual access was denied to those who were not to be initiated (thanks to the high *temenos* walls).[54] Second, the mythological explanations for the ritual at Eleusis emphasized how Demeter had originally 'revealed' her mysteries to the princes of Eleusis.[55] Third, vision was equated to initiation within the terminology used to describe those involved in the ritual itself. *Mystai*, for example, the term for those about to be initiated, translates as 'those who have been closed'; the *epoptai* as 'those who see'. The meaning of *hierophant* – the chief priest of the Mysteries – is 'he who shows the holy things' and the official name for the revelation of the sacred objects (the *deiknymena*) was the *epopteia* 'the viewing'.[56]

Furthermore, the architecture of the sanctuary, as we have seen above, transformed the auditory environment to create an environment with high acoustic integrity, in which initiates would have been encouraged to focus also on what they could hear. As such, the architecture of the sanctuary would also have encouraged initiates to focus more intently on the other important aspect of initiation – the *legomena* or 'the things said' – which helped initiates to understand what they saw.

However, the visual focus called for by the ritual and encouraged by the sanctuary architecture was also simultaneously frustrated. The *dromena* or 'the things done' were, ultimately, taking place in darkness, with the only light provided by flickering torches.[57] Clinton has argued that the performance may have taken place *inside* a cave within the already dark sanctuary (cf. Figure 8.1).[58] Initiates were thus simultaneously encouraged to focus

---

[53] Cf. Pind. fr. 137.1, Soph. fr 837 (Radt), Eur. *Her.* 613, Eur. *Hipp.* 25, Gregory Nazianzus *Orations* 39.4. Similarly in scholarship about Eleusis: Mylonas 1961: 261–274, Foley 1994: 62, 70, Evans 2002: 245, Bowden 2010: 37, Bremmer 2014: 11, Larson 2016: 268. Equally in ritual more generally: Smith 1987:103–104, Jameson 2014: 270, Mylonopoulos 2006: 93.

[54] Cf. Paus. 1.14.3, 1.38.7. Aelian recounts a story of an 'unholy man' who did not wish to become initiated but instead climbed up on the *temenos* walls at Eleusis to witness the festival. He apparently slipped, fell, and died: Ael. F43 (Hercher = 46ab Domingo-Forasté); cf. Dillon 1997: 178.

[55] *Hom. Hymn Dem.* 474–476; Sourvinou-Inwood 2003: 38.

[56] For discussion, cf. Clinton 2005: 50.

[57] The darkness of the experience (and the impact of the lit torches) e.g. Soph. *OC* 1049–1051, Plut. fr. 168. Cf. Clinton 1974: 68. The darkness of the first stages of the ritual contrasted with the brilliant light of the *epopteia* cf. Clinton 1992: 87.

[58] Clinton 1992: 96.

on what they could see and hear, but deprived of detailed visual information by the poor light conditions, which would have intensified their reliance still further on the *legomena* to help them interpret what was (only partially) visible in front of them. As a result, the sanctuary's architectural layout, combined with darkness, created an environment in which high expectations of visual attention, combined with an architectural focusing of visual and aural attention, met with unreliable visual sensory information and thus created additional reliance on aural explanation.[59]

The Walls and Emotional Contagion

The high *temenos* walls, combined with darkness, would also have affected the initiates' emotional experience by increasing significantly the potential for emotional contagion within the group.[60] Initiates had been primed via their top-down expectations, as well as their long physical preparations, for this to be an emotional experience.[61] They were confronted inside the sanctuary with the visual and aural performance (by the chief Eleusinian priests) of the sorrow of the goddess Demeter at the loss of her daughter, with the initiates perhaps even being asked to search for Kore themselves, thus imitating the Goddess and being encouraged to mimic her distress.[62] Studies of emotional contagion have shown that we subconsciously tend to mimic the body postures of those we engage with, and as a result 'catch' and 'feel' their emotions.[63] Crucially, studies have shown that we are more likely to 'catch' the emotion of someone if our attention has been focused on them, and that we are more likely to mimic the actions and catch the emotions of the most powerful person in any group.[64] In this instance, there was no-one more powerful, and no-one whose attention initiates would have been more focused on, than the figure of the Goddess herself, on display in front of the initiates, weeping and in sorrow for

---

[59] One of only two qualifications to be initiated was the ability to speak and understand Greek, underscoring the importance perhaps of being able to understand what was said during the initiation. Sopatros (*Rhetores Graeci* 8 p. 100 (Waltz)), relates the story of an individual's dream in which he saw the *dromena*, but did not hear the *legomena*, and as a result was not considered as initiated. Cf. Mylonas 1961: 272.
[60] Hatfield, Cacioppo, and Rapson 1994, 1993, and 1992.
[61] Those primed for an emotional experience are more vulnerable to emotional contagion: Hatfield, Cacioppo, and Rapson 1994: 155–160.
[62] Cf. Bremmer 2014: 9–10, Clinton 1992: 85.
[63] Hatfield, Cacioppo, and Rapson 1994: 5, 10–11, 16, 36–44 and 1992: 153–154.
[64] Catching the emotion of the person on whom attention is focused: Hatfield, Cacioppo, and Rapson 1994: 148. On catching the emotions of the most powerful person in the group: Hatfield, Cacioppo, and Rapson 1994: 175.

the loss of her daughter, a loss initiates were themselves asked to replicate, and thus empathize with, by 'searching' for Kore.

Those emotions of sorrow, picked up by the initiate group from Demeter, would also then have spread and intensified within the initiate group itself. We are also more likely to adopt others' emotions if we have been made to recognize our inter-relatedness to them.[65] The high *temenos* walls and the darkness explicitly worked together to encourage initiates to construe themselves as a connected group separated from the rest of the world. Moreover, emotional contagion is at its most powerful in environments in which there is both a high number, and most importantly, a high density, of people.[66] The large group of initiates, now contained within the high *temenos* walls in a denser environment, would thus have been even more susceptible to high emotional contagion. The sorrow, 'caught' from Demeter, would thus have been amplified and intensified as it was caught and re-caught amongst the large, dense, connected initiate group, almost as if in an 'echo-chamber' of emotions.

The visual, aural, and emotional impacts created by the high *temenos* walls and the darkness of the night-time initiation thus worked together to heighten and confirm a number of the initiates' top-down prior expectations (particularly in terms of their sense of themselves as a group having a highly emotional experience separated off from the rest of the world).[67] The walls and darkness also deprived initiates of the ability to cross-check their top-down expectations with particularly visual bottom-up sensory information, encouraging their susceptibility to both their top-down expectations and what they were told during the ceremony. At the same time, the high degree of emotional contagion amongst the initiates would have, in turn, depleted initiates' executive cognitive resources to effect individual critique of their top-down expectations with the bottom-up sensory information they did receive.[68]

The Presence of Religious Authority

This reduction of the initiates' ability to interrogate for themselves that which they saw and heard would have been further enhanced by the presence of religious authority. Studies have shown that participants reduce their own executive neural activity in front of trusted authorities.[69] Independent of the 'presence' of the Goddess during the initiation,

---

[65] Hatfield, Cacioppo, and Rapson 1994: 152, Freedman, Birsky, and Cavoukian 1980: 155.
[66] Freeman, Birsky, and Cavoukian 1980: 155–156, 160.   [67] Cf. Schjoedt and Jensen 2018: 328.
[68] Schjoedt and Jensen 2018: 323–324.   [69] Schjoedt and Jensen 2018: 327–328.

initiates were in fact never far from a number of trusted religious authorities throughout their initiation experience. These religious authorities came first in the form of the *mystagogoi*, who had been responsible for developing the initiates' sense of expectation in the first place, and who were with them (as were the *epoptai*) experiencing the ritual within the sanctuary. Indeed, the very name of the *mystagogoi* may have incited a degree of trust in them: they were 'the leaders of the *mystai*'. At the same time, the crucial *legomena*, which may have been especially relied on by initiates due to the poor visual conditions, were spoken by the ultimate religious authorities at Eleusis: the chief priests.[70] The initiates were thus constantly surrounded by, hearing from, and having to rely on, trusted religious authorities whose words and actions they were more likely to accept than question, depriving the initiates of the ability to cross-examine individually their top-down expectations with the bottom-up sensory information they were receiving.

These trusted authorities would also have contributed to the spread of emotion within the initiate group. In studies of emotional contagion, 'students' have been shown to be far more susceptible to mimicking the actions, and thus catching the emotions, of their 'teachers'.[71] The *mystagogoi*, as well as the chief priests, in terms of how they reacted to the things done and said by and about the Goddess, would thus have been powerful instigators of emotional response, which would subsequently have spread quickly through the group. Such additional intensification of the emotional experience of the event would thus have further depleted the initiates' cognitive resources to sense-check their top-down expectations.[72]

The *Telesterion* Walls and the Ritual Experience

The final key part of the Mysteries took place within the *Telesterion* – 'the hall of initiation': this was the *deiknymena* or 'the showing' of the sacred objects, preceded by the revealing of a great light (both undertaken by the chief priest, the *hierophant*). This moment, along with the sounding of the gong announcing the 'finding' of Kore, marked the emotional turning point of the ceremony from darkness to light, from terror to wonder.[73]

---

[70] One of the few requirements for the *hierophant*, the chief priest at Eleusis, was that he had a 'pleasing and melodious voice', indicating again the importance of what he said (and how he said it) as much as what he did: Clinton 1974: 46.
[71] Hatfield, Cacioppo, and Rapson 1994: 182.   [72] Schjoedt and Jensen 2018: 323–324.
[73] Cf. Clinton 1992: 87, 97.

From within the solid-walled *Telesterion*, aware that they were further insulated from the outside world by the solid *temenos* wall, those who entered would have felt distanced even further from the real world (see Figure 8.1). The walls of the *Telesterion*, combined now with a roof, would have created an even darker environment, especially as some scholars have claimed that all lit torches were extinguished when inside the *Telesterion*.[74] Such architectural and visual conditions would have worked to amplify all the same effects outlined above for the night-time ceremonies within the *temenos* walls: a further augmented sense of group cohesion (or rather, if only the *epoptai* entered, then a new sense of an even more exclusive group); a further narrowing down of visual fields and intensifying of visual focus on what could still be seen, accompanied by a further emphasis on what could be heard; an amplifying of sound and creation of further acoustic integrity; and an enhancement of emotional contagion due to the increased density of the crowd (and their increased sense of themselves as a group). At the same time, the darkness would have prevented (just as with the performance of Demeter inside her cave previously) *any kind of* close visual scrutiny by initiates of the *deiknymena* to come.

Some of these effects would have been enhanced still further by the interior architecture of the *Telesterion* space (see Figure 8.1). Eight rows of stone seats were set against each wall for participants to sit on. Hollinshead has argued, with regard to monumental steps in sanctuaries, which were often used for the gathering of a group to watch a ritual event, that the very act of gathering prompted by an architecture intensified further the awareness of a shared experience and conferred authority on the event.[75] Here in the *Telesterion*, that process of gathering on the stone benches, and thus the awareness of shared authoritative experience, was highly noticeable because the participants were forced by the architecture to perceive themselves gathering (either by dimly seeing participants gathering on all four sides of the structure, or at the very least, within the contained architectural environment, hearing them doing so). Furthermore the seats all prompted the initiates' (limited) visual focus in the same direction – towards the centre of the *Telesterion*, where a smaller internal structure housed the sacred objects, soon to be revealed by the *hierophant*. Initiates were once again confronted, at the apex of the initiation, with a trusted religious authority, whose very title was implicit in the act of knowledge revelation, and whose presence would have encouraged participants to

---

[74] Cf. 'the most mystic whiff of torches' within the *Telesterion*: Ar. *Ran.* 314; Bremmer 2014: 9.
[75] Hollinshead 2012: 27.

downgrade their neural activity and thus their critical scrutiny of what they were about to (just about) see.

Either to the *mystai* and *epoptai* gathered inside, or to *epoptai* inside and *mystai* outside, was first visible a great burst of light in the moments before the sacred objects were shown.[76] The sudden appearance of this light, given the context of the night-time ritual conducted within the even more dimly illuminated *Telesterion*, would have had huge sensory and emotional impact on both groups. It would also have impacted particularly on the *epoptai*'s ability to subsequently see in detail the sacred objects that were now revealed, as their eyes attempted to adjust to the shift from darkness to light.

Furthermore, the interior architecture of the *Telesterion* structure worked to deprive those same participants of a clear line of sight of the very thing they were being encouraged to focus on. The roof of the *Telesterion* was supported by a forest of forty-two columns, fragmenting visual access to the actions of the *hierophant* at the centre of the *Telesterion* as he displayed the sacred objects (see Figure 8.1).[77] The structure of the building, in combination with the sudden burst of light appearing in the darkness, thus both encouraged and frustrated greater visual interrogation of the sacred objects at the heart of the Mysteries, just as had happened outside with the performance of Demeter, with the result that participants were once again encouraged to rely more on what they heard.[78] In terms of what was heard, there may have been singing within the *Telesterion* structure, but we also know that the *hierophant* had to speak key phrases as part of the revelation of the sacred objects.[79]

The Post-ritual Understanding of the Mysteries at Eleusis

Initiation at Eleusis was a highly emotional experience. The participants' top-down expectations were heightened prior to entering the sanctuary through a long process of preparation combined with a frustration of visual

---

[76] Cf. Clinton 2005.
[77] The number of interior columns quoted here (forty-two) corresponds to the version designed by Koroibos and built in the fifth century BCE (we hear of a design by Iktinos that would have had only twenty columns, but this was not built) cf. Mylonas 1961: 113–116. Clinton has argued that participants were allowed to move around in order to have a better view of the sacred objects, or that the *hierophant* himself moved around the internal space with them (but there is no clear evidence for this): Clinton 1974: 46 and 1992: 90.
[78] Perhaps we should not be surprised that Plutarch described the participants sitting inside the *Telesterion* in 'awe and silence' since they needed to hear, in as much as they could not clearly see. Plut. *Mor.* 10F, 81E, 943C.
[79] Cf. Clinton 1992: 89, Bremmer 2014: 13.

access to the sanctuary until they began the initiation. The enclosed nature of the architectural environments creating high density amongst the large number of participants, and the ways in which the participants were encouraged to focus their attention on one another, as well as relate to one another because of the darkness, would have created an ever-increasing echo-chamber of emotional contagion. And the participants would have caught the emotions – of sorrow and terror changing to relief and happiness – from the multiple religious authorities (the Goddess, the chief priests, their *mystagogoi*, and *epoptai*) who were their constant companions in the experience, and on whom (especially the Goddess and the chief priest) they were encouraged by the sanctuary's architecture to focus.

The initiates emerged also with a sense of their altered place in the world. The sanctuary architecture encouraged and intensified a sense of the initiates as a group with their own special identity (and potentially a sub-group identity for the *epoptai*), that they had not had prior to initiation, by allowing them and only them access to a series of restricted spaces, and by controlling their visual and aural environments to make them feel physically separated off from the world. In addition, as we have seen, that same architecture, alongside the presence of the Goddess and trusted religious figures, had contributed to the swift, intense spread of emotion within the group through the initiation. High emotional contagion leads in turn to a greater sense of closeness and solidarity amongst the group who have, effectively, bonded through the emotions they have mimicked and 'caught' from one another.[80] As such, the sense of the initiated as a now special group, and its individuals as thus having been somehow changed by initiation, would, I argue, have been strongly felt in the aftermath of the event.

But what about their sense that their fate after death had changed? Here, I think, the predictive coding model shows us convincingly how initiates could have emerged with this top-down expectation (given to them in preparation by their trusted *mystagogoi*) intact. Through the process of initiation, we have seen multiple layers and forms of deprivation of sensory input and depletion of executive cognitive resources experienced by the initiates, in large part thanks to the architecture of the sanctuary, the darkness in which the initiation was undertaken, and the constant presence of various forms of trusted religious authority, which would have constrained the participants from challenging their top-down model of expectations at the time of the event. This inability to challenge the model

---

[80] Freedman, Birsky, and Cavoukian 1980: 155.

has been argued to create 'metacognitive gaps' in understanding that the brain is encouraged to fill in one of two ways: by the acceptance of the pre-established narratives as an accepted version of what happened, and/or the acceptance of post-narrative explanations provided by the group/society at large.[81]

Those pre-established narratives – in particular about initiation leading to a change in status after death – had been given to participants by those who had themselves been through the process (their trusted *mystagogoi*) and could not be challenged by anyone who had not experienced the initiation (thanks to the high *temenos* walls of the sanctuary and the enclosed *Telesterion* structure ensuring that no-one else could see it). Nor could they be discussed, on pain of death, in post-ritual discussions with anyone who had not taken part in the very same process. The rules of the mystery cult at Eleusis thus created a closed system for participants' understanding of what had happened. They formed a ritual echo-chamber, whose apex took place, as we have seen, within an architectural echo-chamber of senses and emotions, and which would, I argue, have strongly encouraged participants to accept the understanding given to them that this experience would change their fate after death.

Indeed, it was perhaps this combination of high emotion and forced reliance on a closed system of pre- and post-ritual understanding that made the Mysteries such a powerful transformative interaction with the divine. Recent studies of emotion have shown how much emotion impacts on memory within the individual brain, thanks to the ways in which the amygdala – the emotion centre in the brain – has high levels of connectivity to multiple areas of cognition processing.[82] In relation to memory, studies have shown that high emotion intensifies the process of memory encoding and retention, as well as the consolidation of memories in the hippocampus.[83] Yet, at the same time, those same studies have shown that high emotion, while making memories 'stronger', does not improve the accuracy of the memory; rather it increases the individual's sense of that memory's vividness and their own perception of its accuracy.[84] We remember more vividly – but not necessarily more accurately – experiences we have undergone in high emotional states.

---

[81] Schjoedt and Jensen 2018: 325–326.
[82] Phelps 2006: 28–32, Anderson and Phelps 2000, Whalen 1998.
[83] Phelps 2006: 33–34, Craik et al. 1996, Easterbrook 1959, Knowlton and Fanselow 1998, Squire and Zola-Morgan 1991.
[84] Phelps 2006: 35, Talarico and Rubin 2003, Neisser and Harsh 1992.

Our initiates would thus, in the morning after the night(s) before, within, and only within, their newly bonded group as the initiated, be filling metacognitive gaps with pre-event expectations and post-ritual explanations to form an understanding of an event, which, due to its highly emotional nature, was likely to have been encoded and retained in their brains as an incredibly vivid memory, which the individual at least thought they could remember with a high degree of accuracy. While there may well have been some spectrum of response among initiates – some more sceptical, some uncertain, as well as those who believed that their fates truly had changed – that spectrum would have been biased towards belief by the multiple predictive coding processes outlined above. It is, in fact, I think, little wonder that initiation into the Mysteries at Eleusis was felt to be such a life-changing moment in the life of an ancient Greek: 'as the most frightening and most resplendent of all that is divine for humankind.'[85]

BIBLIOGRAPHY

Anderson, A. K. and E. A. Phelps. 2000 'Perceiving Emotion: More than Meets the Eye', *Current Biology* 10: 551–554.
Baumeister, R. F. and M. R. Leary. 1995 'The Need to Belong: Desire for Interpersonal Attachments As a Fundamental Human Motivation', *Psychological Bulletin* 117 (3): 497–529.
Bergquist, B. 1967. *The Archaic Greek Temenos: A Study of Structure and Function.* Lund.
Bowden, H. 2010. *Mystery Cults of the Ancient World.* Princeton, NJ.
Bremmer, J. 2014. *Initiation in the Mysteries of the Ancient World.* Berlin.
Bruce, V., P. Green, and M. Georgesen. 2003. *Visual Perception: Physiology, Psychology and Ecology.* New York, NY.
Burkert, W. 1985. *Greek Religion: Archaic and Classical.* Oxford.
Camp, J. 2001. *The Archaeology of Athens.* Yale, CT.
Clinton, K. 1974. *The Sacred Officials of the Eleusinian Mysteries.* Philadelphia, PA.
 1992. *The Iconography of the Eleusinian Mysteries.* Stockholm.
 1993. 'The Sanctuary of Demeter and Kore at Eleusis', in N. Marinatos and R. Hägg, eds. *Greek Sanctuaries: New Approaches*, 110–124. London.
 1994. 'The Eleusinian Mysteries and Panhellenism in Democratic Athens', in W. Coulson, O. Palagia, T. L. Shear Jr, H. Shapiro, and F. Frost, eds. *The Archaeology of Athens and Attica under the Democracy*, 161–172. Oxford.
 2005. 'Stages of Initiation in the Eleusinian and Samothracian Mysteries', in M. Cosmopoulos, ed. *Greek Mysteries: The Archaeology and Ritual of Ancient Greek Secret Cults*, 50–78. Oxford.

---

[85] Ael. Ar. *Orat.* 19.2.

Cole, S. 2004. *Landscape, Gender and Ritual Space: The Ancient Greek Experience*. Berkeley, CA.
Craik, F., R. Giovanni, M. Naveh-Benjamin, and N. D. Anderson. 1996. 'The Effects of Divided Attention on Encoding and Retrieval Processes in Human Memory', *Journal of Experimental Psychology: General* 125: 159–180.
Cross, I. and A. Watson. 2006. 'Acoustics and the Human Experience of Socially-Organised Sound', in C. Scarre and G. Lawson, eds. *Archaeoacoustics* 107–116. Cambridge, UK.
de Polignac, F. 1995. *Cults, Territory and the Origins of the Greek City-State* (2nd ed.). Chicago, IL.
Decety, J. and J. Grèzes, 2016. 'The Power of Simulation: Imagining One's Own and Other's Behaviours', *Brain Research* 1079: 4–14.
Decety, J. and P. L. Jackson, 2004. 'The Functional Architecture of Human Empathy', *Behavioural and Cognitive Neuroscience Reviews* 3: 71–100.
Dillon, M. 1997. *Pilgrims and Pilgrimage in Ancient Greece*. London.
Driver, J. 2001. 'A Selective Review of Selective Attention Research from the Past Century', *British Journal of Psychology* 92: 53–78.
Easterbrook, J. A. 1959. 'The Effect of Emotion on Cue Utilisation and the Organisation of Behavior', *Psychological Review* 66 (3): 183–201.
Eidinow, E. 2018. 'A Feeling for the Future: Ancient Greek Divination and Embodied Cognition', in A. Klostergaard Petersen, I. S. Gilhus, L. H. Martin, J. Sinding Jensen, and J. Sørenson, eds. *Evolution, Cognition, and the History of Religion: New Synthesis. Festschrift in Honour of Armin W. Geertz*, 447–460. Leiden.
Ekroth, G. In press. 'A Room of One's Own?' Exploring the *Temenos* Concept As Divine Property', in J. Wallenstein, M. Haysom, and M. Mili, eds. *Stuff of the Gods: The Material Aspects of Religion in Ancient Greece*. Stockholm.
Eliade, M. 1987. *The Sacred and the Profane: The Nature of Religion*. New York, NY.
Evans, N. 2002. 'Sacrifices and the Eleusinian Mysteries' *Numen* 49 (3): 227–254.
Foley, H. ed. 1994. *The Homeric Hymn to Demeter*. Yale, CT.
Forster, J., N. Liberman, and S. Kuschel. 2008. 'The Effect of Global Versus Local Processing Styles on Assimilation versus Contrast in Social Judgement', *Journal of Personality and Social Psychology* 94 (4): 579–599.
Freedman, J., Birsky J., and A. Cavoukian. 1980. 'Environmental Determinants of Behavioural Contagion: Density and Number', *Basic and Applied Social Psychology* 1 (2): 155–161.
Friston, K. 2010. 'The Free-Energy Principle: A Unified Brain Theory?', *Nature Reviews Neuroscience* 11 (2): 127–138.
Friston, K. and S. Kiebel. 2009. 'Predictive Coding under the Free-Energy Principle', *Philosophical Transactions of the Royal Society of London B: Biological Sciences* 364 (1521): 1211–1221.
Frith, C. 2007. *Making Up the Mind: How the Brain Creates Our Mental World*. Oxford.

Gerstel, S. ed. 2006. *Thresholds of the Sacred: Architectural, Art Historical, Liturgical, and Theological Perspectives on Religious Screens.* Cambridge, MA.

Goette, H. 2001. *Athens, Attica and the Megarid: An Archaeological Guide.* Oxford.

Hamilakis, Y. 2013. *Archaeology of the Senses: Human Experience, Memory and Affect.* New York, NY.

Hatfield, E., J. Cacioppo, and R. Rapson. 1992. 'Primitive Emotional Contagion', in M. S. Clark, ed. *Review of Personality and Social Psychology, Vol. 14. Emotion and Social Behaviour,* 151–177. Thousand Oaks, CA.

1993. 'Emotional Contagion', *Current Directions in Psychological Science* 2 (3): 96–99.

1994. *Emotional Contagion.* Cambridge, UK.

Helmer, M. and D. Chicoine. 2013. 'Soundscapes and Community Organisation in Ancient Peru: Plaza Architecture at the Early Horizon Centre of Caylan', *Antiquity* 87: 92–107.

Hewitt, J. 1909. 'The Major Restrictions on Access to Greek Temples', *Transactions of the American Philological Association* 40: 83–91.

Hollinshead, M. 2012. 'Monumental Steps and the Shaping of Ceremony' in B. Wescoat and R. Ousterhout, eds. *Architecture of the Sacred: Space, Ritual and Experience from Classical Greece to Byzantium,* 27–65. New York, NY.

2015. *Shaping Ceremony: Monumental Steps and Greek Architecture.* Madison, WI.

Jameson, M. H. 2014. 'The Spectacular and the Obscure in Athenian Religion', in M. H. Jameson, *Cults and Rites in Ancient Greece: Essays on Religion and Society,* 270–290. Cambridge, UK.

Jones, L. 2000. *The Hermeneutics of Sacred Architecture* (vols. 1 & 2). Cambridge, MA.

Knowlton, B. J. and M. S. Fanselow. 1998. 'The Hippocampus, Consolidation and On-Line Memory', *Current Opinion in Neurobiology* 8 (2): 293–296.

Lakoff, G. and M. Johnson. 1999. *Philosophy in the Flesh: The Embodied Mind and Its Challenge to Western Thought.* New York, NY.

Larson, J. 2016. *Understanding Greek Religion: A Cognitive Approach.* London.

Lavie, N. 1995. 'Perceptual Load As a Necessary Condition for Selective Attention', *Journal of Experimental Psychology: Human Perception and Performance* 21: 451–468.

Lippolis, E. 2006. *Mysteria: Archeologia e culto del santuario di Demetra a Eleusi.* Milan.

Mallwitz, A. 1972. *Olympia und seine Bauten.* Munich.

Maran, J. 2006. 'Mycenaean Citadels As Performative Spaces', in J. Maran, C. Juwig, H. Schwengel, and U. Thaler, eds. *Constructing Power: Architecture, Ideology and Social Practice,* 75–92. Hamburg.

Mattern, T. 2006. 'Architektur und Ritual. Architektur also funktionaler Rahmen antiker Kultpraxis', in J. Mylonopoulos and H. Roder, eds. *Archäologie und Ritual auf der Suche nach der rituellen Handlung in den antiken Kulturen Aegyptens und Griechenlands,* 167–183. Vienna.

Mikalson, J. 1983. *Athenian Popular Religion*. Chapel Hill, NC.
Miles, M. 2012. 'Entering Demeter's Gateway: The Roman Propylon in the City Eleusinion', in B. Wescoat and R. Ousterhout, eds. *Architecture of the Sacred: Space, Ritual and Experience from Classical Greece to Byzantium*, 114–151. New York, NY.
Mylonas, G. 1961. *Eleusis and the Eleusinian Mysteries*. Princeton, NJ.
Mylonopoulos, J. 2006. 'Greek Sanctuaries As Places of Communication through Rituals: An Archaeological Perspective' in E. Stavrianopoulou, ed. *Ritual and Communication in the Graeco-Roman World*, 69–110. Liège.
　　2008. 'The Dynamics of Ritual Space in the Hellenistic and Roman East', *Kernos* 21: 49–79.
　　2011. 'Divine Images behind Bars: The Semantics of Barriers in Greek Temples', in M. Haysom and J. Wallensten, eds. *Current Approaches to Religion in Ancient Greece*, 269–292. Athens.
Neisser, U. and N. Harsch. 1992. 'Phantom Flashbulbs: False Recollections of Hearing News about the Challenger', in E. Winograd and U. Neisser, eds. *Affect and Accuracy in Recall: Studies of 'Flashbulb' Memories*, 9–31. London.
Parker, R. 2005. *Polytheism and Society at Athens*. Oxford.
Parker-Pearson, M. and C. Richards. eds. 1994. *Architecture and Order: Approaches to Social Space*. Oxford.
Phelps, E. 2006. 'Emotion and Cognition: Insights from Studies of the Human Amygdala', *Annual Review of Psychology* 57: 27–53.
Pucci, M. 2006. 'Enclosing Open Spaces: The Organisation of External Areas in Syro-Hittite Architecture', in J. Maran, C. Juwig, H. Schwengel, and U. Thaler, eds. *Constructing Power: Architecture, Ideology and Social Practice*, 169–175. Hamburg.
Purves, D., R. Cabeza, S. Huettel, K. LaBar, M. Platt, and M. Woldroff. 2013. *Principles of Cognitive Neuroscience*. New York, NY.
Rapoport, A. 1990. *The Meaning of the Built Environment. A Nonverbal Communication Approach*. Beverley Hills, CA.
Richardson, J. H. 1974. *The Homeric Hymn to Demeter*. Oxford.
Robertson, N. 1999. 'The Sequence of Days at the Thesmophoria and at the Eleusinian Mysteries', *Classical Views* 43 (18): 1–35.
Rosenblum, L. 2010. *See What I'm Saying: The Extraordinary Powers of our Five Senses*. New York, NY.
Roussel, P. 1930. 'L'initiation prélable et le symbole Éleusinien', *Bulletin de correspondance hellénique* 54: 51–74.
Ruck, C. 2006. *Sacred Mushrooms of the Goddess*. Berkeley, CA.
Schjoedt, U. 2019. 'Predictive Coding in the Study of Religion: A Believer's Testimony', in A. K. Petersen, I. Gilhus, L. Martin, J. Jensen, and J. Sørenson, eds. *Evolution, Cognition, and the History of Religion: A New Synthesis*, 364–379. Leiden.
Schjoedt, U. and J. S. Jensen. 2018. 'Depletion and Deprivation: Social Functional Pathways to a Shared Metacognition', in J. Proust and M. Fortier, eds. *Metacognitive Diversity: An Interdisciplinary Approach*, 319–342. Oxford.

Schjoedt, U., K. L. Nielbo, D. Xygalatas, P. Mitkidis, and J. Bulbulia. 2013a. 'Cognitive Resource Depletion in Religious Interactions', *Religion, Brain & Behavior* 3 (1): 39–55.
2013b. 'The Resource Model and the Principle of Predictive Coding: A Framework for Analyzing Proximate Effects of Ritual', *Religion, Brain & Behavior* 3 (1): 79–86.
Scott, M. 2010. *Delphi and Olympia: The Spatial Politics of Panhellenism in the Archaic and Classical Periods*. Cambridge, UK.
2012. *Space and Society in the Greek and Roman Worlds*. Cambridge, UK.
2015. 'Temples and Sanctuaries' in E. Eidinow and J. Kindt, eds. *Oxford Handbook to Ancient Greek Religion*, 227–240. Oxford.
Smith, J. Z. 1987. *To Take Place: Towards Theory in Ritual*. Chicago.
Snodgrass, A. M. 1986. 'Interaction by Design: The Greek City-State', in C. Renfrew and J. F. Cherry, eds. *Peer-Polity Interaction and Socio-Political Change*, 47–58. Cambridge, UK.
Sourvinou-Inwood, C. 2003. 'Mysteries: Aspects of the Eleusinian Cult', in M. Cosmopoulos, ed. *Greek Mysteries: The Archaeology and Ritual of Ancient Greek Secret Cults*, 25–49. Oxford.
Spawforth, A. 2006. *The Complete Greek Temples*. London.
Squire, L. R. and S. Zola-Morgan. 1991. 'The Medial Temporal Lobe Memory System', *Science* 253 (5026): 1380–1386.
Steidle, A, L. Werth, and E-V. Hanke. 2011. 'You Can't See Much in the Dark: Darkness Affects Construal Level and Psychological Distance', *Social Psychology* 42 (3): 174–184.
Steidle, A, E-V. Hanke, and L.Werth. 2013. 'In the Dark We Cooperate: The Situated Nature of Procedural Embodiment', *Social Cognition* 31 (2): 275–300.
Talarico, J. M. and D. C. Rubin. 2003. 'Confidence, Not Consistency, Characterises Flashbulb Memories', *Psychological Science* 14: 455–461.
Tilley, C. 2004. *The Materiality of Stone: Explorations in the Landscape Phenomenology*. Oxford.
Tomlinson, R. 1976. *Greek Sanctuaries*. London.
Travlos, J. 1988. *Bildlexicon zur Topographie des antiken Attika*. Tubingen.
Treisman, A. 1988. 'Features and Objects: The Fourteenth Bartlett Memorial Lecture', *Quarterly Journal of Experimental Psychology* 40A: 201–237.
Trope, Y. and N. Liberman. 2010. 'Construal-level Theory of Psychological Distance', *Psychological Review* 117 (2): 440–463.
Watson, A. and Keating, D. 1999. 'Architecture and Sound: An Acoustic Analysis of Megalithic Monuments in Prehistoric Britain', *Antiquity* 73: 325–336.
Wescoat, B. and R. Ousterhoust. eds. 2012a. *Architecture of the Sacred: Space, Ritual and Experience from Classical Greece to Byzantium*. New York, NY.
Wescoat, B. and R. Ousterhoust. 2012b. 'Preface' in B. Wescoat and R. Ousterhout, eds. *Architecture of the Sacred: Space, Ritual and Experience from Classical Greece to Byzantium*, xxi–xxiv. New York, NY.

Whalen, P. J. 1998. 'Fear, Vigilance and Ambiguity: Initial Neuroimaging Studies of the Human Amygdala', *Current Directions Psychological Science* 7: 177–188.
Yang, W. and J. Kang. 2005. 'Acoustic Comfort Evaluation in Urban Open Public Spaces', *Applied Acoustics* 66: 211–229.
Zhong, C-B., V. K. Bohns, and F. Gino. 2010. 'Good Lamps Are the Best Police: Darkness Increases Dishonesty and Self-Interested Behaviour', *Psychological Science* 21 (3): 311–314.

CHAPTER 9

Identifying Symptoms of Religious Experience from Ancient Material Culture
The Example of Cults of the Roman Mithras

Luther H. Martin

> If [the characters of my novels] had no body they would have no mind ... It's all one.
>
> *James Joyce*[1]

Introduction

What, exactly, is religious experience? How is to be identified? Described? Explained? Those who have addressed this issue are still largely influenced by William James' proposal, over 100 years ago, that the 'experiences of individual men in their solitude' are the basis of religion.[2] Apart from the Protestant bias of his proposition,[3] James does not attempt to clarify what he means by 'religious experience' until some 500 pages later, where, in the 'Conclusions' to his study, he offers his dubious characterization of religious experience as a 'consciousness' of 'union' with the 'More'.[4] If, however, such mystically tinged[5] and definitionally tenuous preconceptions about religious experience have proven problematic for modern research,[6] how much more might this be the case for identifying its symptoms for the religions of antiquity?

The personal experiences of any historical actor remain, of course, a subjective affect unavailable to dispassionate historical research. When

---

[1] Budgen 1972: 21.   [2] James 2008 [1902]: 31.
[3] James is affirming the Reformation principle that religion is justified by an individual's faith alone as confirmed by an experience of grace (Eph. 2: 8). Jonathan Edwards, for example, wrote in 1746 that '[t]rue religion consists so much in the Affections', – a Puritan expression for feelings or experiences – 'that there can be no true Religion without them' (Edwards 1960 [1746], 342). Interestingly, James' characterization of the basis of religion as the 'experiences of individual men in their solitude' corresponds to what some philosophers and psychologists now term 'qualia, popularly defined as 'individual instances of subjective, conscious experience' https://en.wikipedia.org/wiki/Qualia [accessed 20 August 2018]. A number of scholars have criticized this notion as a philosophical abstraction of no empirical consequence (e.g. Dennett 1991: 369–411).
[4] James 2008 [1902]: 508 and 511.   [5] James 2008 [1902]: 508.
[6] Taves 2009, Proudfoot 1985.

historians have attempted to infer religious experiences from among the remains of ancient religions, they have prioritized texts in which experiences allegedly are reported (or from which they are inferred), and, consequently, they have relied upon philological analyses and hermeneutical methodologies.[7] However, the (historical) accuracy of textual reports has long been contested, as have first-person accounts generally;[8] it is now recognized that both are the artefacts of constructed memory.[9] Further, ancient texts in particular have often been repeatedly redacted to maintain an idealized or orthodox position as such views shift over time. While textual sources should most certainly not be neglected, a textocentric proclivity by historians to 'read' even material evidence as 'textual' exhibits a cognitive predisposition for confabulating coherent narratives.[10] The cognitive predisposition for narrativizing is exemplified by the enduring propensity among *Homo sapiens* for storytelling, prompting some scholars even to suggest *Homo narrans* as a binomial name for the species.[11] This cognitive/cultural predisposition for storytelling prompts historians to seek linear causalities and explanations for their data where none may exist.[12] Such presumptions about the inexorable presence of narratives lead to a neglect of the non-narrative immediacy of material and imagistic evidence. Consequently, evidence for symptoms of religious experience from ancient material culture has been largely neglected by historians, especially by historians of religion, but that evidence also presents attractive historiographical challenges.

---

[7] E.g. Sanders and Johncock 2016. Because historians have conventionally understood 'history' to be a study of the past since the invention of writing, the study of history has focused primarily on textual evidence (Shryock and Smail 2011: 7). The study of the past based on the evidence of material culture has traditionally been relegated by historians to prehistorians, to palaeoanthropologists, or to archaeologists (Shryock and Smail 2011: x and 3). Recently, however, some historians have proposed a study of 'deep history', which they define as a 'broad-spectrum of hominins' and 'their immediate ancestors' that 'begins about 2.6 million years ago' (e.g. Shryock and Smail 2011: 14), or more (Ledoux 2019), with the shift in nature from 'passivity to agency' (Shryock and Smail 2011: 9) that had been so methodically argued in Darwin's historicizing of biology (Shryock and Smail 2011: x, 5, and 12). Consequently, the data for deep history are expanded from textual narratives to include those from material culture, such as 'genetic, bone, and behavioural evidence' (Shryock and Smail 2011: 14).
[8] Nisbett and Wilson 1977, Schooler and Schrieber 2004, Pronin 2009, Galen 2017: 228–229 and 249.
[9] For the distortions of memory in the production of historical texts and memoirs, see Fernández-Armesto 2015: 167–175.
[10] Boyd 2009, Harari 2014: 24–36, Rosenberg 2018, Zunshine 2006: 2010, Geertz and Jensen 2011.
[11] Ranke 1967, Fisher 1985. See also Eidinow, Chapter 3, in this volume, who explores the advantages of the human proclivity for narrativizing.
[12] Rosenberg 2018.

Two Historiographical Challenges

Before looking for evidence for symptoms of religious experience in material evidence, I should like, first of all, to stipulate an understanding of religious experience as itself material, that is, as neurophysiological.[13] This view is in contrast to dualistic presumptions about experience as a kind of 'ghost-in-the [material] machine',[14] on the one hand, or as a trendy kind of matter-mysticism on the other, in which material culture is itself taken to be an 'animate' and 'active' actor of an 'embodied, extended, and distributed' mind.[15] To paraphrase Joyce's literary portention from the epigraph of this chapter: 'If [historical agents] had no [physical] body they would have no [material] mind ... It's all one.'[16]

Secondly, I should like to explore the relevance of a material understanding of experience for identifying symptoms of religious experience from ancient material culture. While in no way negating traditional historiographical methods,[17] insights from the cognitive neurosciences promise to enhance this historiographical possibility. The cognitive neurosciences are concerned with (among other things) identifying pan-human experiential potentials. When expressed, by a religious practice for example, these potentials become understood in light of their context, are subject to material memorialization, whether in textual or material culture, and thereby afford the historical possibility for discerning symptoms of human experiences deemed to be religious.[18] I will explore examples of such material memorializations with reference to the cults of the Roman Mithras, the surviving evidence for which is almost entirely archaeological.

The Historiographical Challenge of Religious Experience

From the view of the cognitive neurosciences, '*an* experience' may be understood as the conscious awareness of neurophysiological states that

---

[13] For a similar argument for religious experiences as a consequence of material causal influences, see Galen 2017, Lewis-Williams 2002: 101–135.
[14] Ryle 1949: 15–16. [15] E.g. Malafouris 2013: 6, 12, and 15.
[16] For arguments – and evidence – for prescient understandings of the mental processes foreseen by artists, which neuroscientists are now confirming, see Lehrer 2007 and Kandel 2012, for Joyce, see Simone 2013.
[17] Shryock and Smail 2011: xi.
[18] For traces in material culture of emotions, the conscious apprehension of which may be understood as experiences, see the catalogue for 'A World of Emotions: Ancient Greece 700 BC – 22 AD' (Chaniotis et al. 2017), a museum exhibition organized by the Onassis Foundation at the Onassis Cultural Center, New York City, 9 March–24 June 2017, and at the New Acropolis Museum, Athens, 18 July–19 November 2017; see also Chaniotis 2012 and Chaniotis and Ducray 2013.

deviate from quotidian levels of sentience, that is, from 'normal' baseline processes. Whereas baseline measures of neurophysiological activity unquestionably vary from individual to individual, and from demographic context to context, they do not do so infinitely. Rather, a probabilistic model of phenotypic reaction norms for everyday neurophysiological activity might be calculated for defined populations – much as basal metabolism is calculated and graphed for various groups according to gender, age, and weight.[19] Conscious awareness of deviation from that phenotypic norm may incite an enhanced allocation of attention that is apprehended, and expressed existentially, as '*an* experience'.

Enhanced allocations of attention are especially incited by 'superstimuli', which visual neuroscientists Stephen Macknik and Susana Martinez-Conde describe as 'supersalient object[s] or event[s] that evoke ... a stronger neural and behavioural response than the normal stimulus for which the response evolved in the first place'.[20] While exaggerated deviations from normal neurophysiological processes may move in directions of pathology, they may also be fostered, modulated, or manipulated in controlled contexts, whether by neurophysiological excitement (e.g. high-sensory pageantry) or by inhibition (e.g. fasting, meditation).[21]

Responses to superstimuli are often emotion-laden, which enhances memorability.[22] The emotional salience of such experiences, and, hence, their memorability, depends, of course, on the focus and intensity of the technologies by which they are evoked, and their interpretation is determined by the contextually primed affordances of their performative environment.

Most simply, then, a '*religious*' experience can be understood as *any* deviation from a quotidian level of physiological or cognitive sentience, which is, however, contextually primed by, or under the influence of, institutionalized religious practices and, consequently, interpreted as 'religious' within that framework.[23] Apart from their interpretative

---

[19] McNab 1997. [20] Macknik and Martinez-Conde 2010, Dawkins 1999: 68–69.
[21] Techniques for psychologically manipulating others have long been a concern of the advertising and marketing industries (Packard 1957, esp. 3–4). To paraphrase one of social critic Vance Packard's conclusions, the manipulation of others often 'simply involves giving them recognition and individual attention or recognizing that status symbols can become enormously important to a person caught in a highly stratified' context – as in the Roman military organization or the Roman administrative bureaucracy (Packard 1957: 208–209). Such manipulations of the nervous systems of others are evolutionary adaptations widely documented, from lower forms of life to *H. sapiens* (Dawkins 1999: 55–80).
[22] Damasio 1994: 223–227, R. Whitehouse 2001.
[23] Galen 2017: 225, 227, 235, and 236–239. Other historiographical hypotheses for identifying 'symptoms of religious experience' can, of course, be proposed, but much research on experience often begs the question of what is to be considered 'experience', the 'symptoms' of which might be

elucidation, in other words, religious experiences, whether intense and dramatic or more measured and reflective, have no 'element or quality in them' which are 'literally and objectively true' and which can be met 'nowhere else'.[24] It was, for example, the realized neurophysiological potentials that were experienced in the rites and images of the cults of the Roman Mithras that demarcated these experiences as religious (i.e. as specifically Mithraic), and it was these Mithraic religious experiences that were memorialized in their material culture.

The Historiographical Challenge of 'Mithraism'

Cults of the Roman Mithras – in distinction from those of the Indian Mitra or the Persian Mithra[25] – are documented throughout the expanse of the Roman Empire from the end of the first until the end of the fourth centuries. Because material remains of the cults of the Roman Mithras are considerable, they offer a robust exemplar for the challenge of a neurocognitive historiography for identifying symptoms of religious experience in ancient material culture.

Manfred Clauss has recognized the discovery of some 420 Mithraic sites. Despite the existence of some 1000 Mithraic inscriptions,[26] seemingly no Mithraic texts survive, or were produced.[27] Consequently, these cults of the Roman Mithras offer a singular example for understanding an ancient religious tradition from the evidence of material culture, as well as for seeking to identify religious experience from this evidence.

Clauss considered the 'ancient world' to be characterized by the 'primacy of [its] images' and he considered the cults of the Roman Mithras to be a principal example.[28] Nevertheless, Clauss, epitomizing the cognitive/culture bias for narrative, endeavoured to uncover from that imagery the 'whole myth, the entire cult-legend' of a Mithraism.[29] Central to the problem of 'Mithraism' – a modern, essentializing term referring to cults

---

identified, while research proceeding from folk or intuitive assumptions about 'experience' is unproductive and generally exhibits confirmation bias.

[24] James 2008 [1902]: 515 and 45.   [25] Adrych et al. 2017.
[26] Clauss 2001: xxi. Of course, Mithraic remains have continued to be discovered since Clauss' inventory in 2001 and many more remain undiscovered. For example, archaeologist Filippo Coarelli has estimated that there may have been some 700 such sites within the Aurelian Wall of Rome alone (Coarelli 1979: 77).
[27] A papyrus fragment published in 1992 under the title 'A Mithraic Catechism from Egypt' (Brashear 1992) confirms the possibility of some Mithraic textual traditions. Its relevance, however, for the cults of the Roman Mithras during the Imperial period is questionable because of its late, fourth-century date (Brashear 1992: 16).
[28] Clauss 2001: 17.   [29] Clauss 2001: 101.

of the Roman Mithras collectively – is the absence of any centralized agency or regulatory body that might have stabilized the transmission and trans-generational survival of any commonly shared Mithraic myth or cult-legend or, apparently, even of the idea of such an authority.[30] This is noteworthy since Mithraists inhabited a literary culture,[31] and occasional Mithraic literacy is attested by their numerous dedicatory inscriptions.

Dedicatory inscriptions to Mithras as *Deus Sol Invictus* consistently indicate that Mithras was represented by his followers as a deity (*Deus*) and, therefore, that the Mithraic cults can be considered to be 'religions'.[32] However, Mithraic cults did not spread as a religious movement *per se*; they were spread among merchants who were Mithraic initiates during their mercantile transactions, by reassignments of Roman administrative functionaries who were Mithraic initiates, but, primarily, through the redeployments of the Roman legions or legionary units within which Mithraic cells were embedded.[33]

Although the contagious and contiguous diffusion of Mithraists and/or of Mithraic cells resulted in a fractal-like appearance of a Mithraic network, there seems to have been little, if any, reciprocal communication among the otherwise institutionally embedded Mithraic groups.[34] However, their incidental distribution likely accounts for some regional similarities among Mithraic images, and the often distant reassignments and redeployments

---

[30] Whereas the absence of a central legitimating authority was characteristic of pagan religious practice generally, the Mysteries of Demeter retained their centre at Eleusis under control of their dynastic priesthood throughout the Roman period, and the cults of Jupiter Dolichenus, which spread during the Roman Empire concurrently with the cults of Mithras and which exhibited many similarities with those cults, developed a priesthood centred in Doliche that came to exercise conceptual control over its adherents (Martin 2018b: 179–180, Collar 2013: 139–140). Also contemporaneous with the early cults of the Roman Mithras, those of the early Christians had begun by the second century to compile writings considered by their collectors to be authoritative (e.g. the compilation of the Synoptic Gospels by the growing Jesus tradition or the developing deutero-Pauline corpus).

[31] Stock 1983: 19–21.

[32] Many cognitive scientists of religion have adapted E. B. Tylor's 'minimum definition of religion' as a 'belief in Spiritual Beings' (Tylor 1958 [1871]: 8) as an anthropomorphic stipulation that their theoretical objects of study are those claims or practices that are legitimated by the authority of superhuman agents. And, while this stipulation is scarcely sufficient as a full definition of religion – as some critics of the cognitive science of religion have caricaturized it fallaciously (e.g. Strenski 2019: 383) – it is nevertheless useful as an initial proviso for identifying historical data as religious.

[33] For merchants, see the cluster of mithraea in Ostia, for the military, see Daniels 1975, Chalupa, et al. 2021. Reinhold Merkelbach has characterized Mithraism generally as a *'Religion der Loyalität zum römischen Kaiserreich'* (1984: 153–188).

[34] Martin 2018b, Adrych et al. 2017: 24.

of institutionally embedded initiates might explain comparable Mithraic representations from disparate geographical finds. Nevertheless, finds from the Mithraic cults, however comparable, were always subject to local interpretations.[35]

Ritualized Technologies of Mithraic Religious Experience

All religious (and many non-religious) groups employ ritualized techniques for establishing amity among new members and for reinforcing solidarity among continuing members by fostering, modulating, or manipulating neurocognitive deviations from phenotypic norms. Just the synchronic movement characteristic of ritualized behaviours may, for example, in itself alter quotidian neurocognitive processes by releasing such natural opioids as endorphins.[36] Daniel L. Smail has demonstrated how such technologies for neurocognitive inflections and their social corollaries may be tracked historically.[37] Two Mithraic ritualized practices for altering baseline neurocognitive processes and creating religious experiences are documented by archaeological evidence: their communal meals and their rites of initiation.

Communal Meals

The archaeological evidence documenting Mithraic meals is twofold: (1) dining couches along the side walls of every Mithraic gathering place, the mithraeum; (2) frescoes and reliefs from mithraea portraying members of the community sharing a meal and a number of iconographic representations portraying Mithras sharing a meal with Sol.[38]

The interior architecture of every mithraeum was characterized by dining benches along either side of a central aisle. The cult image of Mithras slaying a bull typically presided over the mithraeum from a virtual connecting third bench at the head of the central aisle. This third bench was the place of honour in the seating plans of domestic *triclinia*, the three dining couches that were characteristic of Roman dining rooms generally. It was this architectural allusion to a familiar domestic design that contributed to the fidelity of its transmission.

---

[35] Adrych et al. 2017: 167–168.   [36] Tarr et al. 2015, Cohen et al. 2010.   [37] Smail 2008.
[38] *CIMRM*, 'General Index', vols. 1 and 2: 'Mithras at the repast'. On ritual communal meals, see Ambasciano, Chapter 7 in this volume.

There is no doubt that Mithraists drank wine with their meal, as documented from depictions of Mithras (and/or of Sol) raising a *rhyton* or drinking horn.[39] Apart from wine, the Mithraists seem not to have ingested any other stimulants or sedatives.[40]

Loaves depicted on several reliefs indicate that Mithraists consumed bread with the wine.[41] Some have suggested that a Mithraic meal of bread and wine was in some sense a sacramental meal, as was developing in some contemporaneous Christian groups. In fact, some early Christian apologists (e.g. Justin and Tertullian) complained that the Mithraists had imitated the Christian sacramental meal.[42] Double-sided reversible reliefs in some mithraea feature a representation of Mithras slaying a bull on one side, and an image of participants dining together while seated on the hide of the slain bull on the obverse.[43] However, the Mithraic meal most certainly did not consist of the meat of a sacrificed steer, even as the earliest Christians did not feast on the flesh of the sacrificed Jesus, even symbolically.[44] The remains of numerous species – fowl, mammals, shellfish – that have been found in refuse-pits associated with some mithraea[45] suggest that the bread and wine consumed by Mithraists were not sacramental elements, but were simply staples of grape and grain that were consumed in virtually all ancient cultures.[46]

Sacrificial meal? Sacramental meal? Whatever its religious significance for various Mithraic groups, the sharing of meals is conducive to the release of the neurotransmitter oxytocin, which plays a significant role in social bonding,[47] and the convivial effects of wine (in moderation), which stimulate the release of the neurotransmitters serotonin and endorphins, are well known. While any single inference about the religious significance of the Mithraic meals cannot be generalized for all of the decentralized Mithraic cells over the some three centuries of their existence, the Mithraic meals were at least fellowship meals of the kind that characterized the *collegia* that proliferated during the

---

[39] *CIMRM*, 'General Index', vol. 1: 'rhyton' and vol. 2: 'drinking horn'.
[40] See the interesting if unconvincing argument by Ruck et al. (2011) for the use of drugs in the Mithraic cults.
[41] *CIMRM*, 'General Index' vols. 1 and 2: 'loaf'.
[42] Justin 1 *Apol.* 66 and Tert. *De praesc. haer.* 40.3–4
[43] *CIMRM*, 'General Index', vols. 1 and 2: 'Mithras at the repast'.
[44] Initially, that is (Martin 2014: 310–313).   [45] Lentacker et al. 2004, Clauss 2001: 115.
[46] Clauss 2001: 109. While ritualized behaviours by *H. sapiens* are common, not all such behaviours are religious (Boyer and Liénard 2006).
[47] Wittig et al. 2014, Kosfeld et al. 2005.

Hellenistic period and that promoted a social bond among those with shared interests[48] – including an experiential bond with a deity for those groups claiming the sponsorship of a divine patron.[49]

Initiation Rites

The archaeological exemplum for initiation into the cults of the Roman Mithras is the Mithraeum of Felicissimus in Ostia.[50] Mosaics down the central aisle of this mithraeum portray a seven-fold initiatory 'ladder', the rungs of which advance from the lowest rank of Mithraic membership, *corax* or raven, to the highest, *pater* – a sevenfold initiatory hierarchy represented in other mithraea (e.g. *CIMRM* vol. 1: 239, 288, also from Ostia), and referred to by Origen and, later, by Jerome.[51] The Felicissimus Mithraeum explicitly associates the sevenfold structure of initiation with the seven planets visible to the naked eye (which include the sun and moon), as does Origen.[52] Dedicatory inscriptions that note the initiatory grade of the dedicator also confirm this sevenfold initiatory hierarchy.[53]

---

[48] For the large population of Mithraists embedded in the military, communal meals would have reinforced a social bonding that would have occurred initially as a consequence of what Vegetius, the late fourth-century military historian, reports were four months of basic training for new recruits in the Roman military (Veg. *Mil.* 2.5; see also Martin 2015: 26), and, for those Mithraic brethren who had engaged together in battle, the bonding engendered by conflicts in the field (Veg. *Epit.* 2.23.). As Franz Cumont recognized in 1906 (in the original French edition), 'the fraternal spirit of the initiates calling themselves soldiers was doubtless more akin to the spirit of comradeship in a regiment that has *esprit de corps*' than to any characteristic of Mithraism that might distinguish it as distinctively religious (Cumont 1956 [1911]: 156). A modern analogy to a bonded exclusiveness of Mithraic initiates within the Roman military might be that of smaller, unofficial units within larger military organizations, admission to which involves hazing or its equivalent (e.g. Parks and Burgess 2019, Winslow 1999, H. Whitehouse 2021: 18 and Ch. 3). For example, a recent news article reported on a 'Hell Week' that, 'according to Naval Special Warfare Command ... is considered the pinnacle of training for Navy SEALS and consists of five days in which trainees are constantly cold, hungry, sleep deprived and wet' www.cnn.com/2022/02/05/politics/navy-seal-candidate-death/index.html. In the context of such concentrated commercial centres as the port of Ostia, the shared initiatory experiences of Mithraic merchants, presumably, would have afforded them a competitive edge of mutual trust and transparency not assumed of their non-fraternal competitors.

[49] Martin 2014: 94–106.

[50] *CIMRM* vol. 1: 299 and Fig. 83. Recent studies of initiation in the Graeco-Roman world include Bremmer 2014 and Bøgh 2014.

[51] Origen *C. Cels.* 6.2 and Jerome *Ep.* 107.2. The seven documented grades of Mithraic initiation are *corax*, *nymphus* (a peculiar word: *nymph* or 'bride' with a masculine ending *–us*, usually translated as 'bridegroom'), *miles* (soldier), *leo* (lion), *perses* (Persian), *heliodromus* (Runner of the Sun), and *pater* (Clauss 2001: 133–138).

[52] Origen *C. Cels.* 6.2. [53] *CIMRM* vol. 1: 353; vol. 2: 427.

Given the local autonomy of the Mithraic cults, however, this sevenfold initiatory regime was likely an astrologically patterned ideal that remained flexible in practice.[54] Nevertheless, hierarchical levels of initiation are clearly documented, whatever number of initiatory grades that were actually realized among the various Mithraic cells.

The initiatory experience that Mithraists initially underwent is suggested by five frescoed panels in the Capua Vetere Mithraeum.[55] The first of these frescos depicts an initiate as naked and smaller than the initiating official (the *pater*?), that is, as submissive and humbled, and as menaced by sword and by fire, a scene some interpret as a symbolic death.[56] Similarly, a scene on a cup discovered in a mithraeum in Mainz shows the initiating official aiming an arrow from his drawn bow directly at the head of the initiate who is portrayed, as in the Capua Vetere Mithraeum, as smaller and naked.[57] Stimuli resulting from such perceptions of danger, however tacit, can foster the release of epinephrine (adrenaline), no matter how secure the environment.[58] The release of this neurochemical, with its well-known fight-or-flight response, creates a surge of exhilarating energy.

The physiological and cognitive effects of initiatory stimuli could be further manipulated with lighting effects in the darkened environment of the mithraea.[59] Under darkened conditions, the human visual field is unstable and various illusions and entoptic phenomena can occur.[60] For example, some mithraea featured pierced reliefs, through which illumination from behind cast flickering rays from the Sun god's crown upon the shadowy gathering of initiates, suggesting the very presence of the deity.[61] Further, such visual displays could prime recipients for an experience of the deity by modulating blood oxygen level-dependent activity in the medial orbitofrontal cortex (mOFC), which, it is thought, encodes for pleasurable experiences.[62] In addition to visual effects, Mithraic initiations teased the aural senses with the disorienting effects of sounds, with bells,

---

[54] Chalupa 2008: 190–191. [55] Vermaseren 1971.
[56] Vermaseren 1963: 132, Clauss 2001: 103. [57] Horn 1994, Beck 2000, and Pl. XIII.
[58] This is the case, for example, with watching a scary horror film with friends in the safe confines of a neighbourhood theatre (Clasen 2017). Buddhist contemplation practices, which might be considered a type of sensory-deprivation exercise, can also evoke fear and anxiety effects (Lindahl et al. 2014 and 2017).
[59] Clauss 2001: 120–130. [60] Verplanck 1949, Green 2000.
[61] E.g. the Mithraeum of Santa Prisca (Vermaseren and van Essen 1965: 346.46 and Pl. LXXX).
[62] Plassmann et al. 2008: 1050.

for example,[63] and the olfactory senses with incense and fragrant scents[64] – all of which have also been correlated with neural modulations in the mOFC.[65]

Mithraic initiations seem to have been an intense theatre of non-ordinary experiences occasioned by adrenaline responses of heightened energy and alertness in response to perceived situations of threat-fear-vulnerability, together with mOFC-modulated experiences of pleasure, well-being, and safety, many illuminated by the enlightening presence of the deity, Mithras. Accordingly, the final panel of the frescoed scenes from the Capua Vetere Mithraeum shows the initiate with his blindfold removed,[66] that is, as having been 'reborn' from the darkness of his mortality into the redemptive light he can now see.[67]

As with the Mithraic meals, it is problematic whether any inference about Mithraic initiatory practices can be generalized for all distributed Mithraic cells over time. However, Mithraic groups are clearly defined by initiation rites, whatever their regimen, rather than by any instruction in and adherence to a common set of 'Mithraic beliefs'.[68]

Nothing is really documented for rites of initiation into the higher grades of the Mithraic brotherhood. However, higher-grade Mithraic brethren were present at the initial rites, just as families attend one-time Christian rites such as baptism and marriage (at least in theological principle). These higher-grade participants may have performed ceremonial duties, such as depicted in the 'procession of the seven grades' in the Santa Prisca Mithraeum.[69] More importantly, however, the presence of higher-grade initiates at lower-level rites of initiation would have reinforced and consolidated memories of their own experiences,[70] contributing to the locally confabulated interpretations of those experiences. Experimental evidence shows that such 'revelatory realities' have, for confabulating collaborators, the same neurocognitive underpinnings and

---

[63] Clauss 2001: 53.
[64] Clauss 2001: 127 and 136. Olfactory cues are especially implicated in engendering emotions and in triggering episodic memories because there are direct connections between the olfactory bulb and two brain areas that are strongly implicated in emotion and memory: the amygdala and the hippocampus, which do not process visual, auditory, and tactile stimuli (White 2015, Herz et al. 2004: 371–372 and 376–377). On the role of olfactory cues and emotions, see Bowden and Eidinow, Chapter 3 in this volume.
[65] Plassmann et al. 2008: 1052. [66] Vermaseren 1971, plate XXV.
[67] The third and fourth panels of the Capua Vetere scenes of initiation are damaged and the scenes portrayed there obliterated (Vermaseren 1971: 34, plate XXIII).
[68] Allen 1967: 5–6, Whitehouse 1995: 112 and 126, Turcan 1996: 309.
[69] Vermaseren and van Essen 1965: 155–160. [70] Greene 1987.

much of the same veridicality as actual events.[71] These 'realities' become shared by all grades of initiates within a particular Mithraic cell and support their social bonding.[72]

Iconographic Technologies of Mithraic Experience

According to archaeologist John Hoffecker, rituals, and especially initiatory rites, generally involve a sharing of complex externalized mental representations. These externalized representations, however, generally do not engage the material world through texts and narratives but with images,[73] which are memorialized and transmit more readily than ideas, beliefs, or doctrines.[74] Ever since William Playfair founded the field of statistical graphics in the late eighteenth century by inventing pie charts and bar graphs,[75] some historians have come to recognize that imagery is the best way by which complex information is presented and has been preserved, especially in antiquity.[76] This view of the historical preservation of information in images is especially significant with respect to the absence of any Mithraic texts but with the abundance of images that survive from Mithraic material culture.

Central to surviving Mithraic imagery is the tauroctony, a modern term for the image of Mithras slaying a bull,[77] over 700 depictions of which have been found,[78] whether in relief, fresco, or statuary. Scholars have rightly concluded that the tauroctony is key to any understanding of those

---

[71] Rubin 1995: 41–46, Schnider 2008: 194.   [72] Martin 2018a.   [73] Hoffecker 2011: 29–30.

[74] Dawkins 2006: 193–195. Daniel Dennett has argued that 'attentive observation followed by remembering' is 'the way most secrets get moved around' (Dennett 2017: 130). While human memory is fallible, imprecise, and subject to interference, recent memory research has shown that 'visual long-term memory' has a 'massive storage capacity' which is capable of storing the details of 'thousands of images' even 'after only a single viewing' (Brady et al. 2008: 14325, 14327–14328). A modern example of the robustness of visually encoded memories for the transmission of complex information is reported of the American businessman Francis Cabot Lowell (1775–1817). When Lowell was unsuccessful in purchasing the plans he desired for the steam power looms that had been invented in England by Edmund Cartwright in 1785 and, subsequently, developed and protected by the British textile industry, he surreptitiously viewed these looms in the mills of Lancashire and Scotland and, upon his return to Massachusetts in 1813, initiated an industrial revolution in the United States by replicating, from memory, the complex assemblage of the Cartwright looms (Ridley 2010: 263).

[75] Playfair 1786.

[76] This is the case, for example, with Manfred Clauss, one of the more important historians of the cults of the Roman Mithras (Clauss 2001: 17).

[77] 'Tauroctony' is an ancient Greek word (*tauroktonos* [Soph. *Phil.* 400, Aesch. *Sept.* 276]; *tauroktoneô* [Soph. *Trach.* 760]) that is, however, only used with reference to the Mithraic cult scene by modern scholars.

[78] Clauss 2001: xxi.

cults, as it is for those seeking symptoms of religious experience in ancient material culture.

The Visual Technology of the Tauroctony[79]

Most scholars of the Mithraic cults have interpreted the tauroctony as an event in a presumed mythic life of Mithras, and then support that interpretation by confabulating around that event a narrative assembled from various of the other less-documented and unevenly distributed Mithraic images, much as Christians construct a synoptic life of Jesus from the disparate early Christian traditions. Such a Mithraic narrative is suggested by a number of tauroctonies that are bracketed by panelled reliefs portraying various acts of Mithras in sequential scenes. However, Richard Gordon has shown that 'no two [of them] ... show the same selection of scenes, and ... no two reliefs present them in the same order'.[80] Rather, the serial episodes on these panels seem to have been local interpretations of and inferential embellishments upon the tauroctonous scene. For example, derivations from the tauroctonous image portray the bull being hunted, or captured, by Mithras, or carried on his shoulders to its sacrifice. Given the shared prime of the ubiquitous tauroctonous image for these inferential embellishments, it is unsurprising that many of them are similar, especially as they are from the same region.[81] In the most recent comprehensive study of 'images of Mithra', however, the authors argue that there is an inherent methodological danger in attempting to recreate a Roman cult of Mithras as 'a unified whole' by 'filling gaps' in one set of evidence from information gathered from very different contexts.[82]

What the panelled reliefs do document, however, is the cognitive default of *H. sapiens* for representing experiences through narrative, a cognitive presumption exemplified not only by the regional elucidations of the panelled reliefs, but by their modern interpreters as well.[83] If, however,

---

[79] The discussion in this section is an abbreviated version of the argument first developed by Martin 2021.
[80] Gordon 1996a: 211.
[81] The panelled reliefs are predominantly from the Rhine provinces. The differences in the inclusion and arrangement of scenes on these panels confirm local interpretations, even within a context of regional influence.
[82] Adrych et al. 2017: 22 and 103–104 and 158; see also Panagiotidou 2017: 12 and n.36.
[83] E.g. Clauss, who has emphasized the 'primacy of images in the ancient world' (Clauss 2001: 17), nevertheless proceeds to 'reconstruct' a Mithraic 'sacred narrative' that purportedly recounts the 'story of Mithras' saving action' (Clauss 2001: 62–101). Mastrocinque has constructed a coherent Mithraic scenario in which Mithras plays the 'role of Apollo in favouring Augustus' victory and the birth of the Roman Empire' (Mastrocinque 2017).

the tauroctony is not the portrayal of an event in a mythic life of Mithras, how, then, might it have been viewed by a Mithraic initiate? The experience of seeing visual representations – and the neurocognitive processes that engender that experience – are just beginning to be explored by neurologists and by some art historians.[84]

The Mithraic tauroctony is an example of a bi-stable image in which a single visual datum alternatively projects two familiar but incongruent possibilities, an image of sacrifice and that of a star-map. Familiar bi-stable images include such parlour-game optical illusions as that of Rubin's vase in which one sees either a vase or two opposing faces in profile. Because of the limits on cognitive resources for visual processing, the visual system is capable of seeing only one of the images of a bi-stable representation at a time as the brain seeks to resolve the mutually exclusive perceptions.[85] Artists have long intuited, and neuroscientists now confirm, that imagery is visually construed more as the product of habits of the mind than of the eye.[86]

The habits of any Roman mind would most certainly have recognized the tauroctony as a depiction of sacrifice, rites that were central to Roman civic religion. However, Jaś Elsner has contended that none of the iconographical elements of the tauroctony reflects 'the actualities of ancient sacrifice or the norms of its representation,'[87] and Richard Gordon has concluded that the Mithraic image of sacrifice was a 'commentary upon civic sacrifice rites' and represented a 'deviant' portrayal of them.[88] For example, the conventional view of sacrifice was as an offering to the god(s) and not an act by the god. Nevertheless, contemporaneous references to Mithras refer to his sacrificial role,[89] and although these classical references are to the Persian Mithras, they most certainly influenced the habits of mind by which Romans viewed the tauroctony. Most modern scholars have followed Roman mental habits to understand the tauroctony to be an image of sacrifice.[90]

But, in addition to sacrifice, the habits of Roman minds would have recognized the patterning of the tauroctony also as a star-map, a pattern

---

[84] Macknik and Martinez-Conde 2010, Lehrer 2007, Kandel 2012.
[85] Martinez-Conde and Macknik 2013: 8, Landry et al. 2014: 10.
[86] Ziamou 2014, Macknik and Martinez-Conde 2010, 4, 12, and 142, Seckel 2004.
[87] Elsner 1998: 207.   [88] Gordon 1996b: 69 and 49; see Clauss 2001: 81–82.
[89] While Herodotus (1.131) and Strabo (*Geogr.* 15.3) refer to sacrifice to Mithra, Plutarch refers to sacrifice *taught by* Mithras (*Is. et Os.* 46); in another place Plutarch refers to sacrifice *in the name of* Mithras (*Pom.* 24–25) as does Pallas (as cited by Porphyry, *de Abstin.* 2.5).
[90] E.g. Bremmer 2014: 130, Clauss 2001: 81, Beard et al. 1998: 179, Turcan 1996: 224 and 226.

unfamiliar to modern minds. The tauroctony is composed of selected astrological constellations, in which the bull corresponds to Taurus, the dog to Canis Minor/Major, the serpent to Hydra, the scorpion to Scorpio, the cup or lion to Krater or Leo (when these two are present from the Rhine and Danube regions, e.g. *CIMRM* vol. 2; 1083), and the wheat emerging from the tail of the bull to the star Spica.[91] (The astrological significance of the figure of Mithras, should there be one, remains contested.)[92] These selected constellations were invariably related to one another by their positioning on the ecliptic, the path of the sun's annual orbit around the earth.[93] Popular knowledge of astrology that informed virtually all religious expressions at the beginning of the Roman Imperial period,[94] and the specifically astrological imagery employed by the cults of the Roman Mithras, would have shaped Roman minds readily to recognize the tauroctony also as a star-map.[95] Neuroscientists have found a cognitive tendency for *H. sapiens* to consolidate such complex visual stimuli as the tauroctony not only in terms of remembered cultural representations, such as sacrifice, but also in terms of patterns,[96] such as a star-map.

The coincidental seeing of two familiar representations in a common image such as in parlour game illusions like Rubin's vase, evokes curiosity and gives rise to attention and, when the ambiguity is fully seen, pleasure. Apart from the parlour, however, such '[d]iscrepant information' can cause stress.[97] Even everyday irritations, like being stuck in traffic, being unable to find a parking place, facing a deadline, or relationship problems, can be stressful. Depending upon individual tolerances, the response to stress stimuli is triggered and elaborated by a complex '*stress system*' that modulates quotidian levels of both physiological and cognitive sentience. Most basically, this system responds to stress with a release of cortisol, the primary

---

[91] Beck 2006: 31–32, 190–200.
[92] Michael P. Speidel, for example, argues that Mithras was equivalent to the constellation Orion (Speidel 1980), David Ulansey contends that Mithras corresponded to Perseus (Ulansey 1989), while Beck identifies Mithras with the Sun (Sol) (Beck 2006: 215).
[93] Beck 2006: 31–32, Fig. 1 and 160.
[94] Cumont 1960 [1912]: 32 and 51–52, Hegedus 2007: 2–11 and notes, Adamson 2015: 195–197. Most recently, Roger Beck has characterized the tauroctony, and Mithraic imagery generally, as a kind of public discourse of representations that he terms 'star-talk', which draws from a 'set of astronomical and astrological concepts' that were familiar throughout the ancient world (Beck 2006: 7, 15, and 39, 153).
[95] Beck 2006, Panagiotidou 2012. Given the profusion of astronomical/astrological imagery in Mithraic art and in the mithraeum itself, I find the interpretation of the tauroctony as a star-map convincing. For questions concerning interpretation of the tauroctony as a star-map, see Turcan 1996: 227–228.
[96] Macknik and Martinez-Conde 2010: 11. Just the recognition of a pattern in complex visual stimuli is, in itself, sufficient for it to be considered meaningful (Heintzelman et al. 2013).
[97] Galen 2017: 230.

stress hormone. Cortisol raises the level of glucose in the blood and brain, causes an increase in heart rate and blood pressure, and results in the well-known fight-or-flight response.[98] The cognitive dissonance presented by the bi-stable image of the tauroctony, in the context of perplexing images of threat such as those in Santa Prisca, and the psychological apprehensions intentionally evoked by the initiation rites, would most likely have triggered stress for the Mithraic initiate with a responsive and affective anxiety.

Resolution of stress stimuli and anxiety might include such cultural responses as dismissals through humour, ritual performances, justifications on the basis of authority, or rationalizations, whether logical or mythological.[99] The cults of the Roman Mithras broadly mirrored a Roman cultural pattern of cosmological descent/ascent. This pattern was born of a Graeco-Roman cosmological revolution, described in the second century CE by the mathematician Ptolemy of Alexandria.[100] The Ptolemaic cosmos depicted a geocentric universe, hierarchically embraced by seven planetary spheres, the realm of the fixed stars, and a domain of deity in the hypercosmic domain beyond. A religio-philosophical understanding of descent/ascent through these cosmic spheres was shaped by a revival of Platonism that was developing from the pseudo-Platonic dialogue of Axiochus in the first century BCE to its full-blown expression in the Neoplatonic philosophy of Plotinus in the third century CE. It is, of course, references by Plotinus' student, Porphyry, that document the Mithraic version of this religio-philosophical pattern.[101]

Fundamentally, the tauroctony as sacrifice of a domestic animal represents Mithras presiding over the existential reality of this mundane life and mortality,[102] the world of descent, and a reminder of the ephemerality of existence that would have been a poignant experience for the predominantly military membership of the Mithraic cults.[103] The initial mortification of initiates ritually replicates this sacrifice. On the other hand, the tauroctony as a star-map represents a promise of *salvus*, a hypercosmic ascent presided over by Mithras' transit through the heavens as *Sol Invictus*.[104] This parallel

---

[98] Godoy et al. 2018. [99] Martin 2013a. [100] Ptol. *Alm.* and *Tetr.*
[101] Porph. *De antr. nymph.* 5–6. [102] Bloch 1992. [103] Galen 2017: 234.
[104] The word *salvus* or 'safe' is rare in Mithraic inscriptions (*CIMRM* vol. 1: 658). Nevertheless, its juxtaposition in this inscription with *invicto*, the eponymous characteristic ascribed to Mithras, suggests a soteriological sense of safety as freedom from the difficulties of mundane existence (Lewis and Short 1879, *s.v.* II. A). Of course, a well-known (if contested) inscription from the north wall of the Santa Prisca Mithraeum (Line 14) reads: 'And you saved us after having shed the eternal blood' (*Et nos servasti eternali sanguine fuso*) (Vermaseren and Essen 1965: 217–221). Beck refers to 'the bull-killing of Mithras … as a mighty act of *salvation*' generally (Beck 1998: 123, italics added). Since Heraclitus, the agency in which the tensions that characterize reality are reconciled could be called 'God' (Fernández-Armesto 2015: 14–15).

convergence, by which the tauroctonous Mithras is simultaneously viewed as both mundane sacrificer as well as transcendent *kosmokratôr*, reflects the Platonic notion of 'harmonious tension in opposition'.[105] This mythological concept of cosmic descent/ascent was increasingly a familiar characteristic of religions in the Imperial era, including early Christianity, for example the descent/ascent framing structure of the Gospel of Mark,[106] or the 'incarnation' pattern, generally.[107]

Whatever local understandings of the bi-stable tauroctonous image the various Mithraic groups may have reached, and whatever their resolution of its attendant anxiety, their experiences would have been understood, within their Mithraic context, as, of course, religious.

The Visual Technology of the Mithraeum

The large numbers of mithraea distributed throughout the Roman Empire are, in addition to the tauroctony (and its elaborative imagistic commentaries), a second visual technology for understanding Mithraic religious experience. 'Mithraeum' is a modern term used by scholars for Mithraic gathering places. Mithraists themselves generally referred to their gathering places as 'temples' (*templa*), while Italian Mithraists referred to these places as 'caves' (*spelaea*).[108] According to Porphyry, these Mithraic 'caves' represented 'an image of the cosmos' (*eikôn ... tou kosmou*),[109] a description confirmed by archaeological evidence. The curved upper vaults of these structures were often painted blue and decorated with stars to represent the arch of the heavens; the seven planets familiar from Ptolemaic cosmology (and from the seven grades of Mithraic initiation) were also often represented. And, of course, the visual focal point of every mithraeum was the tauroctonous zodiacal map, itself an image of the Mithraic cosmos.

The mithraeum was the place where the Mithraic rites of initiation were performed and ritualized meals were consumed by the brotherhood. The benches along the side of every mithraeum, reminiscent of the popular configuration of domestic *triclinia*, intimated for the cults' largely itinerant brotherhoods of merchants, militia, and civil servants a Mithraic promise of 'at-homeness' in the face of the hostile vastness of the Ptolemaic cosmos and the bewildering social disruptions of Empire.[110] Initiatory admittance

---

[105] [Pl.] *Axiochus* 365a-b; Beck 2006: 6 and 79–80.   [106] Ulansey 1991.   [107] 2 Cor. 12: 2–4.
[108] Clauss 2001: 42.   [109] Porph. *De antr. nymph.* 5–6, 9–10, 20.
[110] On mundane *Homo Hellenisticus* as a 'wanderer', see Pachis 2008: 388–405.

into the hospitable structure of the mithraeum offered 'a special case of a cognized environment,'[111] in which the cognitive mappings of the cults' initiates were re-oriented from this-worldly peril into the fraternal security of an astrologically defined Mithraic microcosm, legitimated by the hypercosmic authority of *Mithras Deus Sol Invictus*.

Conclusion

If human 'experience' is itself material, as the prescient novelist of our epigraph portended, then we might expect the symptoms of those experiences to be fossilized in the religious remains of ancient material culture. The ritualized modulations of baseline neurocognitive levels of sentience among the membership of some groups are more suited to provoking cognitive vulnerabilities and personal reflections[112] than they are for documenting abstract concepts or claims to universal truths.[113] Evidence for the technologies and visual primes that engendered those neurocognitive modulations often remains engraved in the stones of their material environment. Reflections on and conjectures about their subjective meaning become encoded in individual memory systems as personally relevant information.[114] Since there is nothing inherently convincing or persuasive in such subjective 'qualia', their inferential – or 'revelatory' – potential is high. When these personal experiences, their emotion-laden associations, and their individual interpretations, are recalled and shared, they engendered locally situated confabulations. The cults of the Roman Mithras, with their dearth of literary attestation but profusion of archaeological remains, provide historians with an exemplary case study for that expectation.

There was among these cults no robust communicative network or any regulatory body (or bodies) to maintain conceptual control that might assure a faithful dissemination of any of their parochial 'revelations' over a wide geographical expanse. However, these cults did share experiences that were common to the broad religious culture of the Roman Empire:[115] (1) an exclusivist sense of group loyalty in the face of the social anonymity of

---

[111] Beck 1996: 141–148.   [112] Levitin 2009:16.   [113] Rubin 1995: 40 and 62.
[114] 'Personally relevant information' is understood here as 'information *identified* as being *about* something specific' and that, consequently, 'justifies representational activity' (Dennett 2017: 111–112 and 117: italics original). 'The *amount* of ... [that] information carried or contained in any delimited episode or item is ... roughly comparable in local circumstances' (Dennett 2017: 128, italics original).
[115] For an extended discussion of religious traditions independently developing analogous traits within a common cultural context, see Smith 1990.

Empire;[116] (2) cognitive evocations of 'harmonious tension in opposition', documented from the first century CE in the growing Platonic revival – in the religious language of the time, death (descent) and rebirth (ascent);[117] and (3) a newly promised and developing awareness of a hypercosmic *salvus* in the face of an incomprehensible cosmic vastness, documented among Roman religions also from the first century CE, a promise still situated, however, in a domestically patterned sense of 'at-homeness'.[118] The principal distinctiveness of cults of the Roman Mithras from other contemporaneous Roman cults was their claim to the authority of the same deity, Mithras, *Deus Sol Invictus*, and the legitimation in his name of the various local interpretations of the personal experiences evoked by cult technologies.

When memorialized in the material culture, specific symptoms of religious experience can be identified from the archaeological (as well as from the ethnographic and textual) evidence of specific religious movements. Those memorializations might serve to give substance to William James' metaphysical characterization of religious experience as a 'consciousness' of 'union' with the 'More', by defining his immaterial 'More' with such materialized symptoms as those of the various cults of the Roman Mithras.

BIBLIOGRAPHY

Adamson, P. 2015. *Philosophy in the Hellenistic and Roman Worlds*, vol. 2. Oxford.
Adrych, P., R. Bracey, D. Dalglish, S. Lenk, and R. Wood. 2017. *Images of Mithra*. Oxford.
Allen, M. R. 1967. *Male Cults and Secret Initiations in Melanesia*. Melbourne.
Beard, M., J. North, and S. Price. 1998. *Religions of Rome*, vol. 1: *A History*. Cambridge.
Beck, R. 1976. 'Cautes and Cautopates: Some Astronomical Considerations', *Journal of Mithraic Studies* 2(1): 1–17 (rpt. in Beck. 2004. *Beck on Mithraism: Collected Works with New Essays*, 133–149. Aldershot).
  1996. *The Religion of the Mithras Cult in the Roman Empire: Mysteries of the Unconquered Sun*. Oxford.

---

[116] The 'social brain hypothesis' (Dunbar 2016) predicts that evolved limits on the neurological capacity for the processing of social information constrain a hierarchical tier of group size differentiated by relations of intimacy. These groups range from conversation groups up to five; close friends, working groups, or sports teams of twelve to fifteen; cliques and clubs with groups of thirty-five to fifty, up to a limit of 150 for groups able to maintain stable groups organized by face-to-face relationships. Most mithraea measure less than ten by ten meters (Clauss 2001: 43), an area that could accommodate between twenty and forty people (Liebeschuetz 1994: 197, Meiggs 1973: 372), or the size group predicted by the social brain hypothesis for clubs. Such clubs or collegia proliferated in Mediterranean cultures following the conquests of Alexander (Martin 2013b).
[117] E.g. Apul. *Met.* 11, esp. 11: 18.   [118] Martin 1987.

1998. 'The Mysteries of Mithras: A New Account of their Genesis', *Journal of Roman Studies* 88: 115–128 (rpt. in Beck. 2004. *Beck on Mithraism: Collected Works with New Essays*, 31–44. Aldershot).

2000. 'Ritual, Myth, Doctrine, and Initiation in the Mysteries of Mithras: New Evidence from a Cult Vessel', *Journal of Roman Studies* 90: 145–180 (rpt. in Beck. 2004. *Beck on Mithraism: Collected Works with New Essays*, 55–92. Aldershot).

2006. *The Religion of the Mithras Cult in the Roman Empire*. Oxford.

Bloch, M. 1992. *Prey into Hunter: The Politics of Religious Experience*. Cambridge.

Bøgh, B. S. ed. 2014. *Conversion and Initiation in Antiquity. Shifting Identities – Creating Change*. Frankfurt.

Boyd, B. 2009. *On the Origin of Stories: Evolution, Cognition, and Fiction*. Cambridge, MA.

Boyer, P. and P. Liénard. 2006. 'Why Ritualized Behavior? Precaution Systems and Action Parsing in Development, Pathological and Cultural Rituals', *Behavioral and Brain Sciences* 29: 595–650.

Brady, T. F., T. Konkle, G. A. Alvarez, and A. Oliva. 2008. 'Visual Long-term Memory Has a Massive Storage Capacity for Object Details', *Proceedings of the National Academy of Sciences* 105(38): 14325–14329.

Brashear, W. M. 1992. *A Mithraic Catechism from Egypt*. Tyche Supplementband 1. Vienna.

Bremmer, J. N. 2014. *Initiation into the Mysteries of the Ancient World*. Berlin.

Budgen, F. 1972. *James Joyce and the Making of 'Ulysses' and Other Writings*. London.

Chalupa, A. 2008. 'Seven Mithraic Grades: An Initiatory or Priestly Hierarchy?' *Religio: revue pro religionistiku* 16(2): 177–201.

Chalupa, A., E. Výtvarová, A. Mertel, J. Fousek, T. Hampeis. 2021. 'The Network(s) of Mithraism: Discussing the Role of the Roman Army in the Spread of Mithraism and the Question of Interregional Communication.' *Religio: Revue pro Religionistiku* 29(2): 107–131.

Chaniotis, A. ed. 2012. *Unveiling Emotions: Sources and Methods for the Study of Emotions in the Greek World*. Stuttgart.

Chaniotis, A. and P. Ducrey, eds. 2013. *Unveiling Emotions II. Emotions in Greece and Rome: Texts, Images, Material Culture*. Stuttgart.

Chaniotis, A., N. Kaltsas, and I. Mylonopoulos, eds. 2017. *A World of Emotions: Ancient Greece 700 BC – 200 AD*. New York, NY.

Clasen, M. 2017. *Why Horror Seduces*. New York, NY.

Clauss, M. 2001. *The Roman Cult of Mithras*. London.

Coarelli, F. 1979. 'Topographia Mithraica di Roma', in U. Bianchi, ed. *Mysteria Mithrae, Atti del Seminario Internazionale su La specificità storico-religiosa dei Misteri di Mithra, con particolare riferimento alle fonti documentarie di Roma e Ostia*, 69–79. Leiden.

Cohen, E. E., R. Ejsmond-Frey, N. Knight, and R. I. Dunbar. 2010. 'Rowers' High: Behavioural Synchrony Is Correlated with Elevated Pain Thresholds', *Biological Letters* 6(1):106–108.

Collar, A. 2013. *Religious Networks in the Roman Empire: The Spread of New Ideas*. Cambridge.

Cumont, F. 1956 [1911]. *Oriental Religions in Roman Paganism*, rpt. of authorized translation with Introduction by Grant Showerman. Chicago, IL.
   1960 [1912]. *Astrology and Religion among the Greeks and Romans*. New York, NY.
Damasio, A. 1994. *Descartes' Error: Emotion, Reason and the Human Brain*. New York, NY.
Daniels, C. M. 1975. 'The Role of the Roman Army in the Spread and Practice of Mithraism', in J. R. Hinnells, ed. *Mithraic Studies*, 249–274. Manchester.
Dawkins, R. 1999. *The Extended Phenotype*. Oxford.
   2006. *The God Delusion*. London.
Dennett, D. C. 1991. *Consciousness Explained*. New York, NY.
   2017. *From Bacteria to Bach and Back: The Evolution of Minds*. New York, NY.
Dunbar, R. I. 2016. 'The Social Brain Hypothesis and Human Evolution', in S. Murray Sherman, ed. *Research Encyclopedia for Neuroscience*, 1–33. Oxford.
Edwards, J. 1960 [1746]. 'Treatise Concerning Religious Affections', in H. S. Smith, R. T.Handy, and L. A. Loetsche, eds. *American Christianity: A Historical Interpretation with Representative Documents*, Vol I: *1607–1820*, 341–349. New York, NY.
Elsner, J. 1998. *Imperial Rome and Christian Triumph: The Art of the Roman Empire AD 100–450*. Oxford.
Fernández-Armesto, F. 2015. *A Foot in the River: Why our Lives Change and the Limits of Evolution*. Oxford.
Fisher, W. R. 1985. 'The Narrative Paradigm: In the Beginning', *Journal of Communication* 35(4): 74–89.
Galen, L. 2017. 'Overlapping Mental Magisteria: Implications of Experimental Psychology for a Theory of Religious Belief as Misattribution', *Method & Theory in the Study of Religion* 29(3): 221–267.
Geertz, A. W. and J. S. Jensen. 2011. *Religious Narrative, Cognition and Culture: Image and Word in the Mind of Narrative*. London.
Godoy, L. D., M. T. Rossignoli, P. Delfino-Pereira, N. Garcia-Cairasco, and E. Henrique de Lima Umeoka. 2018. 'A Comprehensive Overview on Stress Neurobiology: Basic Concepts and Clinical Implications', *Frontiers in Behavioral Neuroscience* 12(127): 1–23.
Gordon, R. 1996a [1980]. 'Panelled Complications', in R. Gordon, *Image and Value in the Graeco-Roman World: Studies in Mithraism and Religious Art*, 9: 200–227. Aldershot.
   1996b [1988]. 'Authority, Salvation and Mystery in the Mysteries of Mithras', in R. Gordon, *Image and Value in the Graeco-Roman World: Studies in Mithraism and Religious Art*, 4: 45–80. Aldershot.
Green, D. G. 2000. 'Visual Acuity, Color Vision, and Adaptation', in D. M. Albert, F. A. Jakobiec, and D. T. Azar, eds. *Principles and Practices of Ophthalmology*, 3 vols. (2nd ed.), vol. 3, 1673–1689. Philadelphia, PA.
Greene, Robert L. 1987. 'Effects of Maintenance Rehearsal on Human Memory', *Psychological Bulletin* 102(3): 403–413.

Harari, Y. N. 2014. *Sapiens: A Brief History of Humankind*. London.
Hegedus, T. 2007. *Early Christianity and Ancient Astrology*. New York, NY.
Heintzelman, S. J., J. Trent, and L. A. King. 2013. 'Encounters with Objective Coherence and the Experience of Meaning in Life', *Psychological Science* 24 (6): 991–998.
Herz, R. S., J. Eliassen, S. Beland, and T. Souza. 2004. 'Neuroimaging Evidence for the Emotional Potency of Odor-evoked Memory', *Neuropsychologia* 42: 371–378.
Hoffecker, J. F. 2011. *Landscape of the Mind: Human Evolution and the Archaeology of Thought*. New York, NY.
Horn, H. G. 1994. 'Das Mainzer Mithrasgefäss', *Mainzer Archäologische Zeitschrift* 1: 21–66.
James, W. 2008 [1902]. *The Varieties of Religious Experience*. New York, NY.
Kandel, E. R. 2012. *The Age of Insight: The Quest to Understand the Unconscious in Art, Mind, and Brain*. New York, NY.
Kosfeld, M., M. Heinrichs, P. J. Zak, U. Fischbacher, and E. Fehr. 2005. 'Oxytocin Increases Trust in Humans', *Nature* 435: 673–676.
Landry, M., K. Appourchaux, and A. Raz. 2014. 'Elucidating Unconscious Processing with Instrumental Hypnosis', *Frontiers in Psychology* 5(785): 7–24.
Ledoux, J. 2019. *The Deep History of Ourselves: The Four-Billion-Year Story of How We Got Conscious Brains*. New York, NY.
Lehrer, J. 2007. *Proust Was a Neuroscientist*. New York, NY.
Lentacker, A., A. Ervynck, and W. Van Neer. 2004. 'The Symbolic Meaning of the Cock. The Animal Remains from the Mithraeum at Tienen (Belgium)', in M. Martens and G. De Boe, eds. *Roman Mithraism: The Evidence of the Small Finds*, 191–200. Brussels.
Levitin, D. J. 2009. *The World in Six Songs: How the Musical Brain Created Human Nature*. New York, NY.
Lewis, C. T. and C. Short. 1879. *A Latin Dictionary*. Oxford.
Lewis-Williams, D. 2002. *The Mind in the Cave: Consciousness and the Origins of Art*. London.
Liebeschuetz, W. 1994. 'The Expansion of Mithraism among the Religious Cults of the Second Century', in J. R. Hinnells, ed. *Mithraic Studies*, 195–216. Rome.
Lindahl, J. R., C. T. Kaplan, E. W. Winget, and W. B. Britton. 2014. 'A Phenomenology of Meditation-induced Light Experiences: Traditional Buddhist and Neurobiological Perspectives', *Frontiers in Psychology* 4.973: 1–16.
Lindahl, J. R., N. E. Fisher, D. J. Cooper, R. K. Rosen, and W. B. Britton. 2017. 'The Varieties of Contemplative Experience: A Mixed-methods Study of Meditation-related Challenges in Western Buddhists', *PLOS One* 12(5). https://doi.org/10.1371/journal.pone.0176239 [accessed 10 January 2020].
MacKay, D. M. 1968. 'Electroencephalogram Potentials Evoked by Accelerated Visual Motion', *Nature* 217: 677–678.

Macknik, S. L. and S. Martinez-Conde. 2010. *Slights of Mind: What the Neuroscience of Magic Reveals about our Everyday Deceptions*. New York, NY.
Malafouris, L. 2013. *How Things Shape the Mind: A Theory of Material Engagement*. Cambridge, MA.
Martin, L. H. 1987. *Hellenistic Religions: An Introduction*. Oxford.
— 2013a. 'The Ecology of Threat Detection and Precautionary Response from the Perspectives of Evolutionary Psychology and Historiography: The Case of the Roman Cults of Mithras', *Method and Theory in the Study of Religion* 25 (4–5):431–450.
— 2013b. 'When Size Matters: Social Formations in the Graeco-Roman World', in C. J. Hodge, S. M. Olyan, D. Ullucci, and E. Wasserman, eds. *The One Who Sows Bountifully: Essays in Honor of Stanley K. Stowers*, 229–241. Providence, RI.
— 2014. *Secular Theory, Deep History: Scientific Studies of Religion, Collected Essays of Luther H. Martin*. Berlin.
Martin, L. H. ed. 2015. *The Mind of Mithraists: Historical and Cognitive Studies in the Roman Cult of Mithras*. London.
— 2018a. 'Light from the Cave: Interdisciplinary Perspectives on a History of Religions Example', in A. K. Petersen, I. Gilhus, L. H. Martin, J. Jensen, and J. Sørensen, eds. *Evolution, Cognition, and the History of Religion: A New Synthesis*, 524–535. Leiden.
— 2018b. 'Was There a Network of Roman Mithraists?', *Religio: Revue pro Religionistiku* 25(2): 167–182.
— 2021. 'Seeing the Mithraic Tauroctony.' *Numen* 68(4): 357–381.
Martinez-Conde, S. and S. L. Macknik. 2013. 'The Neuroscience of Illusion.' *Scientific American Mind* 20(3s): 6–9.
Mastrocinque, A. 2017. *The Mysteries of Mithras: A Different Account*. Tübingen.
McNab, B. K. 1997. 'On the Utility of Uniformity in the Definition of Basal Rate of Metabolism', *Physiological Zoology* 70(6): 718–720.
Meiggs, R. 1973. *Roman Ostia*. Oxford.
Merkelbach. R. 1984. *Mithras*. Königstein.
Nisbett, R. E. and T. D. Wilson. 1977. 'Telling More than We Can Know: Verbal Reports on Mental Processes', *Psychological Review* 84(3): 231–259.
Pachis, P. 2008. '*Hominibus Vagis Vitam*: The Wandering of *Homo Hellenisticus* in an Age of Transformation', in W. Braun and R. T. McCutcheon, eds. *Introducing Religion: Essays in Honor of Jonathan Z. Smith*, 388–405. London.
Packard, V. 1957. *The Hidden Persuaders*. New York, NY.
Panagiotidou, O. 2012. 'The Cognitive Route of 'Star-talk': The Scene of the Tauroctony As a System of Signs', *Pantheon* 7(1): 70–78.
Panagiotidou, O. with R. Beck. 2017. *The Roman Mithras Cult: A Cognitive Approach*. London.
Parks, G. S. and J. Burgess. 2019. 'Hazing in the United States Military: A Psychology and Law Perspective', *Southern California Interdisciplinary Law Journal* 29(1): 1–63.
Plassmann, H., J. O'Doherty, B. Shiv, and A. Rangel. 2008. 'Marketing Actions Can Modulate Neural Representations of Experienced Pleasantness', *Proceedings of the National Academy of Sciences* 105(3): 1050–1054.

Playfair, W. 1786. *The Commercial and Political Atlas: Representing, by Means of Stained Copper-plate Charts, the Progress of the Commerce, Revenues, Expenditure and Debts of England During the Whole of the Eighteenth Century*. London.
Pronin, E. 2009. 'The Introspection Illusion', *Advances in Experimental Social Psychology* 41: 1–67.
Proudfoot, W. 1985. *Religious Experience*. Berkeley, CA.
Ranke, K. 1967. 'Kategorienprobleme der Volksprosa', *Fabula* 9: 4–2. English translation by Carl Lindahl. 1981. 'Problems of Categories in Folk Prose', *Folklore Forum* 14(1): 1–17.
Ridley, M. 2010. *The Rational Optimist: How Prosperity Evolves*. New York, NY.
Rosenberg, A. 2018. *How History Gets Things Wrong: The Neuroscience of Our Addiction to Stories*. Cambridge MA.
Rubin, D. 1995. *Memory in Oral Traditions: The Cognitive Psychology of Epic, Ballads, and Counting-out Rhymes*. New York, NY.
Ruck, C. A. P., M. A. Hoffman, and J. A. G. Celdrán. 2011. *Mushrooms, Myth and Mithras: The Drug Cult that Civilized Europe*. San Francisco, CA.
Ryle, G. 1949. 'Descartes' Myth', in G. Ryle, *The Concept of Mind*, 11–24. London.
Sanders, E. and M. Johncock. 2016. *Emotion and Persuasion in Classical Antiquity*. Stuttgart.
Schnider, A. 2008. *The Confabulating Mind: How the Brain Creates Reality*. Oxford.
Schooler, J. and C. Schreiber. 2004. 'Experience, Meta-Consciousness, and the Paradox of Introspection', *Journal of Experimental Psychology: General* 129: 27–42.
Seckel, A. 2004. *Masters of Deception: Escher, Dali and the Artists of Optical Illusion*. New York, NY.
Shryock, A. and D. L. Smail, eds. 2011. *Deep History: The Architecture of Past and Present*. Berkeley, CA.
Simone, T. 2013. '"Met him pike hoses': *Ulysses* and the Neurology of Reading', in M. Gold and P. Sicker, eds. *Joyce Studies Annual*, 207–237. New York, NY.
Smail, D. L. 2008. *On Deep History and the Brain*. Berkeley, CA.
Smith, J. Z. 1990. *On the Comparison of Early Christianities and the Religions of Late Antiquity*. Chicago.
Speidel, M. 1980. *Mithras-Orion: Greek Hero and Roman Army God*. Leiden.
Stock, B. 1983. *The Implications of Literacy: Written Language and Models of Interpretation in the Eleventh and Twelfth Centuries*. Princeton, NJ.
Strenski, I. 2019. 'Much Ado about Quite a Lot: A Response to Alessandro Testa's Review of Strenski, *Understanding Theories of Religion*', *Studi e Materiali di Storia delle Religioni* 85(1): 365–388.
Tarr, B., J. Launay, E. Cohen, and R. Dunbar. 2015. 'Synchrony and Exertion during Dance Independently Raise Pain Threshold and Encourage Social Bonding', *Biology Letters* 11. https://doi.org/ 10.1098/rsbl.2015.0767. Published on-line 28 October 2015.

Taves, A. 2009. *Religious Experience Reconsidered: A Building Block Approach to the Study of Religion and Other Special Things*. Princeton, NJ.
Turcan, R. (trans. A. Nevill). 1996. *The Cults of the Roman Empire*. Oxford.
Tylor, E. B. 1958 [1871]. *Primitive Culture. Part II: Religion in Primitive Culture*. New York, NY.
Ulansey, D. 1989. *The Origins of the Mithraic Mysteries: Cosmology and Salvation in the Ancient World*. New York, NY.
 1991. 'The Heavenly Veil Torn: Mark's Cosmic "Inclusio"', *Journal of Biblical Literature* 110(1): 123–125.
Vermaseren, M. J. (trans. T. and V. Megaw). 1963. *Mithras: The Secret God*. New York, NY.
 1971. *Mithraica I: The Mithraeum at S. Maria Capua Vetere*. Leiden.
Vermaseren, M. J. and C. C. Van Essen. 1965. *The Excavations in the Mithraeum of the Church of Santa Prisca on the Aventine*. Leiden.
Verplanck, W. S. 1949. 'Night Vision: The Terminal Visual Thresholds', in C. Barens, ed. *The Eye and Its Diseases* (2nd ed.), 203–209. Philadelphia, PA.
White, A. 2015. 'Smells Ring Bells: How Smell Triggers Memories and Emotions: Brain Anatomy May Explain Why Some Smells Conjure Vivid Memories and Emotions', *Psychology Today.Com*. www.psychologytoday.com/us/blog/brain-babble/201501/smells-ring-bells-how-smell-triggers-memories-and-emotions [accessed 10 January 2020].
Whitehouse, H. 1995. *Inside the Cult: Religious Innovation and Transmission in Papua New Guinea*. Oxford.
 2021. *The Ritual Animal: Imitation and Cohesion in the Evolution of Social Complexity*. Oxford.
Whitehouse, R. 2001. 'A Tale of Two Caves: The Archaeology of Religious Experience in Mediterranean Europe', in P. F. Biehl and F. Bertemes, eds. *The Archaeology of Cult and Religion*, 161–167. Budapest.
Winslow, D. 1999. 'Rites of Passage and Group Bonding in the Canadian Airborne', *Armed Forces & Society* 25(3): 429–457.
Wittig, R. M., C. Crockford, T. Deschner, K. E. Langergrabe, T. E. Ziegler, and K. Zuberbühler. 2014. 'Food Sharing Is Linked to Urinary Oxytocin Levels and Bonding in Related and Unrelated Wild Chimpanzees', *Proceedings of the Royal Society B* 281(1778): 20133096. http://dx.doi.org/10.1098/rspb.2013.3096.
Ziamou, L. 2014. '*Where Art Meets Science: A Conversation with Dr. Hank Hine on Marvels of Illusion at The Dali Museum*', *Huffington Post*, August 14. www.huffingtonpost.com/lilia-ziamou/where-art-meets-science-a-conversation-with-hank-hine_b_5709295.html [accessed 10 January 2020].
Zunshine, L. 2006. *Why We Read Fiction. Theory of Mind and the Novel*. Columbus, OH.
Zunshine, L. ed. 2010. *Introduction to Cognitive Cultural Studies*. Baltimore, MD.

PART V
Texts

CHAPTER 10

Bridging the Gap
From Textual Representations to the Experiential Level and Back

Anders Klostergaard Petersen

Moving from Representations of Feelings to Their Emotional Counterparts

Whereas the majority of contributions to this book have focused on the cognitive science of religion, and how it may be used in historical studies, my chapter is slightly different. Traditionally, cognitive science of religion directs its main interest towards mental representations and their underlying neural underpinnings, paying closer attention to the former.[1] In recent years, however, we have witnessed developments in which the cognitive science of religion has begun to draw upon moral and evolutionary psychology and biology. In this chapter, I follow this trend by looking at some of the areas in which we as classicists, ancient historians, and scholars of religion may learn from these fields. In particular, I concentrate on the emotional dimension, which by tradition has not featured largely in the cognitive science of religion, although it plays an increasingly important role in cognitive studies in general.[2] Hence, my focus here is different from the first-generation cognitive science of religion, but I think it is in line with the most recent developments in the field. Additionally, I consider this relatively novel interest in emotions as very promising for the disciplines studying ancient worlds and texts.

A truly tantalizing problem that historians and textual scholars face is how, if at all, to bridge the gap between textual representations of feelings and the underlying experiential, emotional level. In accordance with

---

I want to express my gratitude to three anonymous peer reviewers for the useful commentaries given on my chapter. In particular, I am grateful to the editors for their thorough reading and helpful comments on this chapter.

[1] For a fine overview of the cognitive science of religion from beginning to present, see the contributions in Martin and Wiebe 2017.
[2] See, for instance, the contributions by Carr, Kever, and Winkielman 2018, Hobson 2018, Colombetti 2018, and Stephan 2018, which give a good impression of cognitive science's current attempt to remedy its lack of the emotional dimension.

current literature in cognitive psychology and evolutionary biology, I differentiate between emotions and feelings, referring respectively to unconscious biological reactions on the one hand, and consciously mediated and emotionally triggered effects on the other hand.[3] Whereas the former are instinctive, the latter pertain to the deliberated acknowledgement of the former. In this chapter, I raise the question of the connection between textual references to feelings and their elicited emotional counterparts. Is it possible to study this relationship, and can it be done in the context of ancient texts? What effects are textual representations of feelings likely to have elicited on the *authorial instance* and in the intended audience and their emotional system?[4] Such questions may appear aberrant and impossible to answer with respect to past texts. How could we possibly know anything about ancient audiences and authorial instances' biological reactions to the texts under scrutiny? After all, we are at a considerable distance from the past uses of these texts and, thereby, the effects they may have had on ancient audiences. Concomitantly, we cannot perform functional magnetic resonance imaging of ancient audiences, but even that would not help us very much in accounting more closely for the relationship between the emotions and their acknowledgement as feelings. The distance from the neurobiological to the cultural level is difficult, if not impossible, in present-day research to traverse, as neurophysiologists, researchers on the brain, classicists, and historians well know.

Rather than asserting the connection between emotions and feelings (which, although intrinsic, in practice is seemingly methodologically unbridgeable), in this chapter I shall try to explain the link between the

---

[3] Among some neuroscientists the distinction between emotions and feelings is formulated as, respectively, 'affects' and 'second emotions', with the latter designating what I refer to as 'feelings'. See Smail 2008: 150–151 and Plamper 2015: 271–272. Both refer to Damasio 1994 and 2003 and LeDoux 1996.

[4] I am not speaking about the actual historical author, to whom we have no access. By 'authorial instance', I refer to the author as a textually embedded element. Contrary to the notion of 'implied author', which is an open textual position filled out every time the text is read, 'authorial instance' designates the textually authorial position interpreted in light of the cultural and social conventions of the original situation of communication. Similarly, 'intended audience' does not refer to the actual audience, to whom we likewise have no access. It denotes the textually embedded audience interpreted on the background of the cultural and social conventions characterizing the text's historically operative function (Eco 1990: 62). Contrary to Eco's emphasis on codes (1979: 48–150), I prefer to speak of conventions, since the latter concept is broader by not suggesting a one-to-one relationship between the *repraesentamen* and its relationship to a particular *object* (in the specific Peircean sense). Even in the sign-object relation with respect to a specific ground, there is ample room for different colourings depending on the context in question. Such a broader understanding helps us to perceive the great variability through which the generation of new interpretants takes place. Eco also uses the concept of convention, but he has it overdetermined by the code category, see 1979: 244–258.

two and, in this way, seek to approach ancient religious experience. I begin by discussing the current state of the art regarding the study of feelings in classics, ancient history, and Bible studies; then I will establish the connection between emotions and feelings through a reading of a Pauline text relating to the use of water in the context of ritual cleansing. In the final section, I emphasize the need for greater interdisciplinarity between the humanities and the life sciences. An intensified interaction between the two faculties would not necessarily lead to a completely new outlook, but certainly may develop one that has a greater depth and, potentially, breadth regarding many problems in the disciplines of classics, ancient history, and Bible studies.

Despite the unusual character of this endeavour and the methodological problems involved in it, I shall argue that it is not only possible to study the emotional aspect relating to ancient texts, but also that it is crucial to take it into consideration if we want to acquire a more thorough grasp on past representations of feelings.[5] As strange as this may sound at first, it has an obvious connection to traditional scholarship. In fact, it is a natural extension of rhetorical research.[6]

The study of classical rhetoric amply demonstrates how *ethos* and *pathos* figure prominently in speeches and texts, in order to impress their message on audiences. The speeches of the fourth-century BCE politician Demosthenes, for example, provide ample evidence of this. The construction of the writer's or rhetor's own *ethos* was central in endowing the discursive speaker with such an aura of credibility in the recipients' minds that the speech appeared trustworthy and, ideally, as the only possible outcome to be embraced by the audience. The opening of Demosthenes' famous speech *De Corona* is a telling example (*De Corona* 1–11). Likewise, the continuous appeals to *pathos* (the emotional effects stirred in the

---

[5] Chaniotis and Ducrey reject this view (2013: 10–11) arguing: 'The nature of their [historians and classicists] sources sets certain limits to their quest. They cannot directly study neurobiological processes, and only in some well-documented cases they may have access to psychological reactions or the physiological/somatic aspects of emotion. But they do have access to the external stimuli that generated emotions. They also have information concerning the various factors that determine the manifestation of emotions.' I disagree with this view on the basis that the emotional level triggering representations of feelings is pan-human and, therefore, we may apply current insights from evolutionary and moral biology and psychology on emotions to the study of the representations of feelings. True enough, the representations of feelings are culturally constrained by time and space, but we may, as I shall argue, use emotion research to cast light on ancient representations by turning to their emotional aspect and, thereby, come closer to a fuller grasp of their cultural manifestations. For a different view, see Lateiner and Spatharas 2017.
[6] Konstan (2010: 411) also emphasizes ancient rhetoric as the most obvious field in which to explore ancient discussions of feelings (in Konstan's terminology 'emotions').

intended audience) helped to secure the addressees' adoption of the textual message and the worldview it expressed. Demosthenes' rhetorical scolding of his fellow politician Aeschines in *De Corona* is illustrative of instantiating *pathos* in the intended audience (10–11). Opposing it implied siding with the emotion-arousing castigation of the textually constructed 'villain-other'. In his treatise on *Rhetoric*, the philosopher Aristotle emphasized how stirring an audience's feelings helps to persuade them.[7] Evidently, the use of emotion-arousing elements was not confined to rhetoric proper, but permeated a wider gamut of genres. In fact, references and appeals to feelings are a ubiquitous element of ancient texts, as they are of contemporary literature and social life in general.[8] Given this, it is obvious to examine this dimension further by focusing on the emotional aspects underlying feelings. The rhetorical use of *ethos* and *pathos* is likely not only to affect the feelings of the audience, but also to influence them in a more profound way by triggering their gut emotions of attraction and disgust. This is the more plausible in light of recent research on emotions in evolutionary and moral biology and psychology as well as cognitive science.[9]

In pursuing the question of the relationship between feelings and emotions, I do not claim that the way feelings are conceived in current discussions corresponds to ancient understandings of feelings.[10] Most likely, this is not the case.[11] But regardless of this discrepancy between past and present understandings of feelings, I think we shall be able to see other elements that ancient authors also drew on, although they seldom reflected upon them in their thinking about feelings. The reason for following such a procedure is, as I stated earlier, the fact that past and present understandings of feelings differ considerably, but in terms of their underlying emotions there is no difference. Thus, by directing attention to

---

[7] Arist. *Rh.* 1356a 5. For the problems in reconciling this view with the argument of the first chapter (1354a 5), see Konstan (2010: 414).
[8] Sanders and Johncock (2016: 13) similarly emphasize the prevalence of representations of feelings in ancient Graeco-Roman literature (cf. Cairns and Nelis 2017: 8), but the interest of the various contributors in the volume lies entirely on the side of the cultural representations.
[9] Haidt (2012: 84–108) documents how appeals to gut feelings are decisive in the way we behave in politics. Intuitive feelings precede reasoning and greatly determine our behaviour. See also the studies by Delton, Petersen, and Robertson 2018; Petersen, Giessing, and Nielsen 2015; as well as Westen 2007.
[10] Lateiner and Spatharas (2017: 2–4) regarding ancient notions of disgust emphasize that we may advantageously compare past expressions with current ones and, thereby, get a better grasp of both.
[11] Konstan (2010: 415–416) emphasizes the difference between modern psychological and ancient Greek rhetorical understandings of feelings according to which they were understood as 'the kinds of things that can be roused or assuaged by arguments, or by appeals to the intellect' (416).

the emotional level, we may move beyond the cultural specifics and gain a better understanding of what unites humans across time and space. At the same time, though, I argue that, thereby, we shall also be able to acquire a deeper understanding of the cultural level.

The proof of the pudding, I hope, lies in the example I shall provide from Pauline studies. Here I point to pan-human biological elements, but, more importantly, I argue that by taking them into consideration in light of recent insights from moral psychology and evolutionary biology, we will also get a better understanding of the text in its historical, cultural, and social context. Some may wonder why I have chosen Paul as my case in point and not an ancient Greek or Roman rhetorician. But, in my view, Paul belongs as much to this tradition as do the time-honoured *rhetors* of the classical tradition. In fact, Paul should be reckoned as belonging as much to the tradition of ancient Greek rhetoric as he should be recognized a Judean. Moreover, there is every good reason for selecting Paul as the test-case for my endeavour, since he makes some very explicit references to feelings in connection with his audience's previous religious experiences.

The Neglect of the Emotional Level in Recent Scholarship on Feelings

With the so-called 'emotional turn' three decades ago there has been a steadily growing interest in the way texts of the past represent and evaluate feelings, and in exploring differences between ancient representations and modern ones as well as expressions in non-Western contexts. Classicists and ancient historians in particular have done an excellent job in highlighting an element we traditionally did not discuss extensively, if at all.[12] Bible studies have been considerably slower in following this development,[13] although New Testament studies were quick to engage with and contribute to the cognitive science of religion.[14] Presumably, when it comes to the study of feelings, an Enlightenment bias made it less acceptable to spend time on what had been judged the 'darker' and more 'primitive' aspects of

---

[12] The literature has become so immense that it is difficult to achieve an overview of it. However, some prominent pioneer studies are easy to identify: see Konstan 1997, 2007, and 2015, Kaster 2005, Chaniotis and Ducrey 2013, Caston and Kaster 2016, Sanders and Johncock 2016.

[13] One exception is Kazen who has worked extensively on disgust in connection with notions of purity and impurity (2011) and has also discussed emotions in the context of biblical laws (2011). Lately, Harkins has written several articles especially devoted to the topic of grief in scriptural texts as well as on the relationship between hortatory texts and emotions (2015a, 2015b, 2016a, 2016b, 2017, and 2020).

[14] See, for instance, Luomanen, Pyysiäinen, and Uro 2007, Czachesz 2012 and 2016.

human existence.¹⁵ In line with a Kantian tradition, feelings constituted an element that reason should subdue for human culture to flourish.¹⁶ Moreover, the twentieth century has frighteningly shown what can happen when feelings are unleashed and reason is left behind. All this contributed to a scholarly milieu impeding research on the emotional side of human life.

Pauline scholarship is a telling example. In almost all readings of the Pauline letters during the twentieth century, no-one has been concerned with the fact that his letters strive to hone particular feelings and, even more so, to elicit certain emotions in the audience in order to achieve social cohesion in the communities, compliance to his message, and full loyalty to him. Despite all the merits of the literature on affect in classics, ancient history, and biblical studies during the past decades, two interrelated factors made it less promising than it could have been. First, the analyses are predominantly descriptive, rarely moving beyond an examination of the feelings at stake and the role played by them by virtue of their textual representations.¹⁷

By saying this, I do not mean to downplay the importance of such studies. In fact, they are significant not only in reconstructing the role of different feelings in past semiotic systems, but also in highlighting differences between modern and ancient understandings of feelings and what is accorded to particular feelings. Such studies, however, generally remain at the cultural level and therefore miss much that could be of interest for the analysis of this level as well.¹⁸ Second, and connected to the previous

---

[15] Despite the pervasiveness of representations of feelings in ancient texts, I disagree with Cairns and Nelis (2017: 8, cf. 12), who argue that this ubiquity is the reason that classicists have always had an acknowledgement of and interest in the subject. This pertains to classical rhetoric and much less so to tragedy and comedy. But even in studies on classical rhetoric, it took a long time to positively acknowledge the importance ancient rhetoricians placed on stirring emotions of audiences. This element was also part of the reason why rhetoric for a long period had a culturally poor reputation as intrinsic to sophistry. During the last thirty years, there has also been increasing interest in the role of feelings in the context of the Hellenistic philosophical schools and ancient ethics as is evident in, for example, the work of Annas 1992 and Nussbaum 1994. Similarly, there has been a growing interest in representations of feelings in comedy and tragedy, as is evident from the literature referred to in note 12.

[16] The magic lurking in rhetoric constantly threatening to unleash uncontrollable emotions was already seen in antiquity, see Gorgias' *Encomium to Helen* D24 8.

[17] In the most recent development in classics and ancient history, though, there is a notable and important exception to this trend. A few scholars have, in fact, begun to work seriously on trying to combine emotion studies with examinations of feelings: see Eidinow (2016: 82–101), Cairns and Fulkerson (2015: 1–11), Larson (2016), and Cairns and Nelis (2017: 7–13).

[18] This is also acknowledged in Cairns and Nelis (2017: 11 footnote 25). At the same time, the two authors emphasize that biological and psychological studies on emotions are of value to classicists and historians: 'At all levels, these phenomena reflect the fact that cognition is embodied and that

point, until now little of this literature has made use of insights from evolutionary and moral biology and psychology despite the fact that these disciplines abound with studies of emotions.[19] In the next section, I discuss one strand in current emotion research and seek to show how it may be used in a reading of Paul's references to baptism.

Tracing Emotions Underlying Textual Instantiations of Feelings

Water is a prevalent feature in rituals of purification across the world and across time. In four experiments, Chen-Bo Zhong and Katie Liljenquist have shown how the use of water plays an important role with respect to our basic cognitive notions of cleanness, purity, dirt, moral filth, and impurity.[20] Their experiments garnered considerable attention, since they seem to confirm a relationship between moral and physical purity in human cognition, and that we may use physical purity to induce moral purity. The study builds on older research in experimental psychology priming participants for disgust biases with behavioural consequences.[21]

The experiments, though, have not been replicated.[22] But that is a general problem in experimental studies, which does not, however, necessarily detract from the value of the experiments.[23] A further study has been published suggesting that washing with water not only affects the moral domain but also draws on cleansing from past experiences, thereby reducing the need to justify them in retrospect.[24] Certainly, more work needs to be done before we can discard or verify Zhong and Liljenquist's results,

---

cognition and affectivity are inextricably linked as aspects of the single complex system that is the living organism. If we as Classicists can insist on the extent to which our discipline, too, focuses on embodied, embedded, and enactive aspects of emotion, then we can engage in meaningful dialogue with emotion researchers in a variety of other disciplines, while also seeking to pursue a dialogue within our own discipline in synthesizing the material, visual, *and* textual data that the ancient evidence has to offer' (2017: 18). In Cairns' contribution to the volume, he makes extensive use of cognitive metaphor theory to gain a greater grasp of the ancient Greek notion of *phrikê*.

[19] The studies mentioned in footnote 12 largely remain on the cultural level and hardly make use of contemporary research in biology and psychology on the ground that it is too basic to shed light on culturally specific references to feelings. Lateiner and Spatharas discuss the interrelation between emotions and feelings of disgust and make extensive use of Ekman's and especially Rozin and Nemeroff's work. They emphasize that representations 'of disgust is so effective because it morphs physical dirt into moral dirt, but also because the cognitive background of disgust rests on magical thinking' (2017: 3, cf. 23–34). Despite this promising discussion, Lateiner and Spatharas admit that subsequent studies 'address expressions of disgust (the social texture and interaction) more than ancient humans' (unknowable) interior experiences' (2017: 5).

[20] Zhong and Liljenquist 2006.   [21] See Rozin and Nemeroff 1990 and Nemeroff and Rozin 2000.
[22] Fayard et al. 2009, Earp et al. 2014, and Siev et al. 2018.   [23] Earp et al. 2014: 97.
[24] Lee and Schwarz 2010.

just as we need more experiments to examine the psychological impact of physical cleansing more closely.

That said, however, substantial insights coming from experimental research unequivocally indicate 'a causal relationship between disgust and moral judgement, by showing that experimentally evoked disgust – or its opposite, cleanliness – can influence moral cognition'.[25] Returning to Zhong and Liljenquist's experiments, they found evidence that, in filling out questionnaires, subjects who were asked to wash their hands with soap prior to responding to the questionnaires became increasingly moralistic in values regarding moral cleanness. Once bodily cleansed, the subjects evidently also wished to abstain from becoming morally impure regarding their future. In this way, the experiment demonstrated that experiences of physical and moral disgust are psychologically closely intertwined and exert influence on each other. In another experiment, these researchers demonstrated how subjects requested to recall past moral transgressions in a subsequent word-completing task generated more cleansing-related words than other participants who had been asked to recall a past ethical deed.[26] Zhong and Liljenquist called the close relationship between physical and moral purity 'the Lady Macbeth complex', after Lady Macbeth's obsessive and vain attempt to cleanse herself from her manipulation of Macbeth to assassinate King Duncan: 'Out damned Spot: out, I say.'[27] In summarizing their four studies, Zhong and Liljenquist conclude that 'Threats to moral purity activate a need for physical cleansing, which can assuage moral emotions and reduce direct compensatory behaviors.'[28] By the same logic, they argue, evocations of physical cleansing may trigger notions of moral purity.

I shall leave physical cleansing for the moment and turn to the reverse side of the coin, impurity and disgust. To understand the importance of biologically anchored notions of purity, we also have to consider its opposite. It is unclear what caused a probable evolutionary adaptation for avoiding toxic food to eventually become identified with immoral elements.[29] If vomit and faeces elicit strong emotions of physical disgust, by what means can morally disgusting representations trigger similar reactions? It may be, as Chapman and Anderson surmise, that the moral disgust system represents an evolutionary offshoot of the physical disgust

---

[25] See Chapman and Anderson 2013: 313. [26] Zhong and Liljenquist 2006: 1451.
[27] Shakespeare *Macbeth* V, i, l. 2127. [28] Zhong and Liljenquist 2006: 1452.
[29] See Chapman and Anderson 2013: 317.

system, serving a social rather than a disease-avoidance function.[30] According to this view, we may be able to account for some of the differences that appear in experiments when trying to tease apart the relationship between physical and moral disgust: the latter triggers other negative emotions as well, and it has more lasting effects than physical disgust, but the former may be elicited more frequently.[31] At the same time, though, it may well be that the overlapping of the two disgust systems, with the physical disgust system preceding and underlying the moral system, may account for the fact that elements of physical disgust need to be triggered in order to elicit emotions of moral disgust.[32]

An Emotional Reading of Paul

I now turn to a central Pauline text in which feelings of moral disgust play a role, as do references to ritual physical cleansing: 1 Cor 6:1–11. I shall not provide an in-depth textual study. I use the text as an example of the kind of bridging I envision as a future task both for studies of past religious experience and, not least, for spanning the gap between emotions and feelings. The reading put forward can easily be extended to all other Pauline references to baptism, which are at the centre of Paul's attempt to create a new identity for his audience. His rhetoric effects what it describes, but to this I add a similarly crucial point: Paul's forging of a new identity for his recipients is achieved by evoking strong feelings triggering underlying gut-emotions.

Paul is facing a number of problems with a community he founded, which at the time of the letter presumably consisted of several house churches convening for ritual gatherings in the private homes of more affluent Christ-adherents. Public churches were not found until

---

[30] Chapman and Anderson 2013: 316. In the scholarly literature, there is a debate as to whether or not disgust is a primary emotion. One reason for rejecting it is the argument that it may be a sub-category of anger. Chapman and Anderson, however, point to the fact that whereas anger typically involves taking action and, thereby, paying remedy for the anger-eliciting situation, disgust entails the opposite type of action, implying a withdrawal from the disgust-provoking source and avoidance of it in future action (2013: 317). Although disgust may not be a sub-category of anger, it could be a sub-category of another primary emotion, namely fear, with which it has many overlapping features such as the immediate physical withdrawal from the fear- or disgust-provoking source.
[31] Chapman and Anderson 2013: 316.
[32] Chapman and Anderson 2013: 316. See also Haidt 2012: 71: 'In other words, there's a two-way street between our bodies and our righteous minds. Immorality makes us feel physically dirty, and cleansing ourselves can sometimes make us more concerned about guarding our moral purity.'

considerably later. After Paul's formation of Christ-religion in Corinth,[33] another missionary, Apollos, entered the community. This led to internal tension between a faction adhering to Paul and a faction supporting Apollos. As is evident from chapters 1:18–2:5, 5–7, 8–10, and 15 in particular, economic and educational divisions underlay the tensions. Apollos was supported by a smaller, but socially powerful group, comprising the more affluent and highly educated members of the community, the so-called strong ones, over and against the weak ones.[34] In the eyes of Paul, the disloyal faction had betrayed him in favour of Apollos.[35] Presumably, members of the strong ones were also the ones housing the community gatherings.

By means of a deliberative, symbouleutic writing, Paul in this second letter to the Corinthians intervenes in the situation (in 5:9 he refers to a previous, but no longer extant letter).[36] He enjoins the addressees to renewed unity expressed in total loyalty to him. Thereby, he primes the strong ones to distance themselves from Apollos: 'I admonish you, brothers, through the name of our Lord Jesus Christ that you all (*pantes*) think the same (*to auto*) and that there be no schisms (*schismata*) among you, but that as veins you are united (*ête katêrtismenoi*) in the same mind (*nous*) and the same opinion (*gnômê*).'[37] This *propositio* of the letter has an unmistakable ring of mind control, which is characteristic of any form of sectarian thinking that does not allow deviant forms to exist. The injunction that 'they all think the same' is undoubtedly conducive to complete adherence to Paul's way of construing the world; but Paul is careful to retain the letter's symbouleutic nature and, thereby, avoid any indication

---

[33] 1 Cor 3:1–15. I use formative Christ-religion rather than Christianity to emphasize, first, how early forms of Christ-religion still comprised an integral part of Judaic religion, and second, that the emergence of Christianity, understood as an independent and autonomous form of religion with respect to Judaism, was a late fourth- and fifth-century phenomenon. It was also more or less during the same period (with the Bavli appearing at the beginning of the sixth century) that that which we now dub Judaism came into existence founded on the two Talmuds. For this whole argument, I refer to Becker and Reed 2003, Boyarin 2004, Petersen 2005, and the essay of Schäfer 2010: 1–31, with the programmatic title *Die Geburt des Judentums aus dem Geist des Christentums* ('The Birth of Judaism from the Spirit of Christianity').

[34] See 1:26–28 formulated in traditional class and status terms, cf. Arist. *Rh.* 1360b–1361b.

[35] Martin 1995 excellently demonstrates how class and status distinctions underlie the conflict and Paul's intervention in it.

[36] Translations are my own. A body metaphor – congruent with the symbouleutic discourse of 1 Cor – permeates the letter, culminating in its use in 12:12–31. Mitchell 1991 highlights the symbouleutic nature of the letter and demonstrates how the letter can be read advantageously in light of ancient political discourse as promulgating the avoidance of *stasis*.

[37] 1 Cor 1:10.

of dissent between himself and Apollos, which would undermine his call to unity and emphasis on the concord between himself and Apollos.

At the same time, however, as he accentuates the accord between Apollos and himself, the metaphors that he uses reduce, if not eliminate, Apollos as a fellow missionary. In 3:6–8, Apollos is diminished to assistant of the gardener, while Paul ascribes the latter role to himself (planter vs. waterer), but simultaneously is keen to emphasize that together they constitute a oneness with God as the one who makes the plant grow. At the same time, though, Paul also emphasizes that each of them shall receive reward according to his own labour. Picking up a new metaphor, the subsequent verses continue to disparage Apollos.[38] He is someone, who, presumably illegitimately, adds building material to a foundation Paul has already laid. Again, Paul threatens Apollos and, by extension, the faction in the community adhering to him. At the day of judgement, fire shall try every man's work of what sort it is. To the extent that it is burned, the extra builder shall be able to save his skin only: 'He himself shall be saved, yet as so by fire!'[39] The Corinthians constitute God's temple laid by Paul, and if anyone destroys it, this person (hardly anyone but Apollos) shall be destroyed by God.[40] Having discursively annihilated Apollos by the end of chapter four, Paul can proceed to mould his audience in the form he wants them.

In the large body of the letter, the *pistis* section, consisting of four grand clusters of argument, Paul strives to nudge his community to total loyalty towards his way of looking at things and, through this, to refrain from a variety of practices occasioning the community divisions. The section 6:1–11 is part of the larger second complex of proofs revolving around communal integrity against external threats.[41] Paul counsels his audience in a number of areas that have generated some of the tensions in the group(s). The larger section deals with two main areas of problems, of which the main section 5:1–7:40 relates to matters pertaining to sexual transgression, litigations, and group solidarity. In chapter five, Paul focuses on a specific case of sexual transgression and proceeds in 6:1–11 to chastise Christ-followers for bringing cases against each other before civil and, thus,

---

[38] 1 Cor 3:10–17.   [39] 1 Cor 3:15b.
[40] 1 Cor 3:17b. This metaphorical cluster serving to belittle Apollos is further elaborated in ch. 4, in which Paul describes himself as the male progenitor and father of the community and school master of the Corinthians, while Apollos is indirectly attributed the less flattering role as the servant taking the boy to school (*paidagôgos*). For the demeaning significance of the school metaphor, see Martin 1995: 66.
[41] 1 Cor 5:1–11:1.

pagan courts. Subsequently he sharpens the argument to say that it is on the whole a problem that they have court cases among each other. Alan Mitchell plausibly suggests that underlying this discussion is the fact that the Corinthian strong ones have made use of civil litigation to settle cases in the community. He sharpens the argument by surmising that the strong have exploited the weaker by bringing them to court.[42]

Paul opens the section by scolding all of them, although in actuality it refers exclusively to the strong ones: 'Does any one of you having a court case against another dare (*tolma*) to bring it before the unrighteous and not the holy ones?'[43] As holy ones, Christ-adherents ought to know (*ouk oidate*) that they shall pass judgement on the world. Yet, they disregard their own status by showing themselves unworthy in the minutest of matters (*anaxioi kritêriôn elachistôn*).[44] In fact, they shall judge angels, wherefore their behaviour in life matters appears utterly ridiculous. The more so, since they appoint as judges those who are despised (*tous exouthenêmenous*) in the community.[45] Emphatically, Paul states how he has to cast shame upon the community (*pros entropên humin legô*), since they are not able to provide one wise man who can pass judgement among brothers. In this way, they fall short of embodying the epistemological structure to be adhered by Christ-followers.[46] In effect, they prove how they have not yet reached the level of perfection.[47] Whereas the 'pneumatic' person (i.e. in Paul the category for the perfect Christ-adherent filled by the spirit and cognizing according to the spirit) shall judge all things, but not himself be judged by anyone, Corinthian Christ-followers fail on this account.[48] Paul, however, has achieved the mind of Christ and, therefore, is capable of teaching the Corinthians, teaching of which they are in urgent need, since they lack both cognitive and behavioural transformation.[49] Contrary to the ideals and norms of the Christ-community, brothers raise cases against each other and, even more so, they bring them before the unfaithful.[50]

In 6:7–8, Paul sharpens the rebuke by accentuating how it is already a total failure (*êdê holôs oun hêttema*) that they have raised lawsuits against one another rather than accepting the wrong done to them and suffering themselves to be defrauded. The Corinthians, however, unremittingly promote their own interests, and even do so against brothers. Thereby,

---

[42] Mitchell 1993.   [43] 1 Cor 6:1.
[44] 1 Cor 6:2, cf. 3:17c: 'For God's temple is holy, which you are.'   [45] 1 Cor 6:3–4.
[46] See 1 Cor 1:18–2:5.   [47] 1 Cor 1:26.   [48] 1 Cor 2:15.
[49] Cf. 1 Cor 1:17, 1:23–25, 2:16, cf. the use of the school teacher metaphor in 4:16–21.
[50] 1 Cor 1:5–6.

community boundaries disappear and there is no difference between the surrounding culture and community behaviour. To drive the argument home, Paul appeals to the ideal or hoped-for knowledge of the recipients. They ought to know that the unrighteous shall not inherit the kingdom of God. Therefore, he enjoins them not to be deceived.[51] A catalogue of people embodying different vices sets the argument in relief.[52] I would argue that the juxtaposition of sexual and social transgressors serves to induce a disgust bias in the recipients. There is, as we have seen, a fairly strong experimental basis for thinking that evocations of moral dirt provoke physical, emotional reactions. Both Ekman and Rozin argue that representations of disgust are very effective because they not only morph physical dirt into moral impurity, but also because the cognitive background of disgust rests on magical thinking. Calling to the audience's mind people engaging in sexually illicit actions, characters exploiting the possessions of others as well as other socially deviant roles, Paul induces physical disgust in his audience. His audience is not only rhetorically led to distance themselves from the social worst-case scenario, which Paul's list of people committing vices exemplifies, but also to transfer their physical revulsion to these characters. Viewed against this background, Paul's subsequent move is even more shocking to the audience, when he claims that some of his addressees (in light of the previous rhetoric, presumably the strong ones in particular) belong to these groups of people committing vices. Yet, the vices have been washed away from them (*apelousasthe*), just as they have become holy (*hēgiasthēte*) and righteous (*edikaiōthēte*) in the name of the Lord Jesus Christ and in the spirit of their God.

In the text at this point, Paul's tripartite use of the adversative particle *alla* ('but') serves to underscore the irrevocable change that happened to his audience at their baptism. The irreversibility of the baptismal change is obviously of an ideal nature only. The recipients have not been precluded biologically from being able to sin, in Augustinian terms formulated as a *non posse peccare*. The idea is that the addressees have been transferred to a modal situation of 'principally not sinning', although they are still capable of it. The rhetorical push implies the sense of *posse* ('to be able') [*non posse peccare*]. In semiotic modal terms, this difference signifies the contrast between the actualized (being able to not sin) and the realized stage of being able to do (not being able to sin). Whereas the former state refers to 'living in this world', the latter state denotes the future eternal life, where Christ-adherents are precluded from being able to sin by having obtained eternal life.[53]

[51] 1 Cor 6: 9b. [52] 1 Cor 6:9c–10. [53] See Petersen 2004: 284–286.

The renewed evocation of the name of the Lord Jesus Christ serves to inculcate in them the foundational emblem uniting them as a distinctive community, while also awakening in them a memory of their baptism as a transfer into the name of the Lord Jesus Christ. The emphasis on their becoming holy enforces the cultural boundaries of the community and the recipients' sense of 'having been taken out of the world', and, thus, partaking in a counter-cultural, enclavistic life.[54] Underlining the addressees' righteous stance emphasizes to them how their distinctive behaviour is contrary to the one governing the ordinary world, just as it highlights their categorical difference from the life represented by the depraved characters of the previous verses. The preposition expressing how the actions have taken place '*by means of*' or '*in the spirit of*' 'our God' similarly conveys Paul's essential message that the recipients, in fact, are spiritual and, therefore, need to manifest it in practice.

Psychologically, the section primes the addressees to change their current behaviour by aiming to evoke in them a strong sense of community-belonging and sectarian identity. It evolves an enclavistic argument: Christ-adherents have separated themselves from ordinary culture to constitute a community located on a vertical axis between the heavenly world and the earthly one. In the current world, they begin to realize celestial life by adhering to the norms and values defined by the life of Christ. A catalogue of dissolute characters, a strong emphasis on now and the past, continuous emphasis on the incongruity between community life and cultural existence in general, evocations of possible failure and, therefore, ultimate judgement, strong use of shaming vocabulary, and a corresponding iteration of attraction biases as well as recollection of the foundational group's emblems serve to hammer home the message. The language is performative. It effects what it describes: identity-formation is achieved by evoking strong feelings triggering underlying gut-emotions. The fact that many of Paul's addressees, ultimately, did not accept his textual transformation of them, as we know from 2 Corinthians, does not diminish his attempt to accomplish this effect. Paul pushes them back into an emotional situation of shaming and guilt from which he subsequently liberates them by rhetorically re-performing baptism for them. The textual, redundant repetition of threats to moral purity in the minds of the intended addressees cognitively triggers a need for physical cleansing. In this way,

---

[54] Cf. the previous uses of the term emphasizing the audience's special status as having been separated from the remaining world. Already in the letter's prescript, the audience is rhetorically moulded as 'having been sanctified in Christ Jesus, and called as sacred'.

Paul then provides the yearned-for physical cleansing by rhetorically re-invoking their previous physico-cultural cleansing in baptism.[55]

To what extent did Paul succeed in what he tried to accomplish? We do not know, although we have, as I indicated, a suspicion of failure, insofar as problems continue in 2 Corinthians (in actuality, the Third Letter to the Corinthians, cf. 1 Cor 5:9). Yet, one has to acknowledge that the difficulties confronting Paul in Second Corinthians are different. The question of whether Paul succeeded or not is not, however, so decisive for what is at stake in the letter. As Durkheim astutely understood, any cultural group is in continuous need of reloading the symbolic storage battery so as to have group feelings reinvested, lest the emblem slowly but unremittingly fade away.[56] While resetting and reaffirming group norms, ideals, and values, Paul infuses the community with symbolic effervescence. Paul textually has his addressees undergo a psychological re-transformation through the text by recalling before them their previous baptismal experience.

Paul and Lady Macbeth in Dialogue

Although results relating to the Lady Macbeth complex are moot, it is very plausible that a causal relationship exists between disgust and moral cleanness. I have taken this research as a point of departure for trying to tease apart the question of whether it is possible to bridge the gap between textual instantiations of feelings and underlying emotions. We can easily adduce examples other than 1 Cor 6:1–11, but the primary aim has been to demonstrate how a cognitive, emotional reading provides us with a better grasp of past texts. I have focused on the question of possible priming effects on past audiences. The approach is not revolutionary, since we already know from rhetoric how evocations of feelings are crucial in driving one's message home to the recipients. Yet I think that we can and should do more in the service of understanding the means by which past texts achieved this goal. To accomplish that, we also need to take into consideration insights from emotions research. By doing so, we also bridge the gap between the life sciences on the one hand, and the social sciences and the humanities on the other.

Paul and Lady Macbeth do not have much in common, but there is one point at which they interconnect. They are both anxiously concerned with moral impurity. Paul's Lady Macbeth complex is obviously of a different

[55] Cf. Petersen 2019 and 2022.　[56] Durkheim 1912: 330–331.

nature than Lady Macbeth's. Yet his absorption with keeping his communities morally clean and himself as their indisputable leader also testifies to an obsession, as it should for anyone concerned about cultivating and maintaining culture over time. Much recent moral psychological research explores the causal relationship between moral purity and disgust. We may use it to cast light not only on Paul and the rhetoric he develops, but also on the likely rhetorical effects on his intended audiences. That is the point at which Lady Macbeth and Paul meet. Lady Macbeth strives in vain to free herself from the guilt originating from her perfidious connivance in King Duncan's murder. Paul strives to have his recipients progress towards becoming unblemished and spotless on the day of judgement. Both, however, witness a close relationship between basic emotions of disgust and deliberate attempts to achieve moral stainlessness or perfection. To fully grasp that, we need to bring to bear insights from cognitive, emotional, and evolutionary approaches. This may, as I have sought to argue, give us some access to past religious experiences, since underlying textual representations of feelings convey an emotional side that is much the same as we find in modern human beings.

Conclusion

Is it possible to take insights from evolutionary biology, moral biology, and psychology and apply them to the textual analysis of feelings? Is there a chance of bridging the gap between textual instantiations of feelings and the underlying emotional level? I have striven for a bridging at three different levels. The first one is of a general character. I aspire to the ongoing bridging of the gap between the natural and social sciences and the humanities. Today, we are in an extraordinary situation – seen with the hindsight of the previous fifty years of scholarship – that allows us to engage in new research in which we join hands with colleagues across fields and faculties in a truly interdisciplinary way to pose anew the grand questions pertaining to evolution and to human predicaments. Contrary to some humanists, I do not see this situation as a threat to the humanities. It is a unique opportunity that will not only restore the humanities to the centre of research, but also enable us to take up again some of the core ideas of the Enlightenment with regard to a joint scientific endeavour. Daniel L. Smail puts it nicely: 'What do we gain from a deep history centered on the neurophysiological legacy of our deep past? Well, one benefit is a new kind of interdisciplinarity that joins the humanities and social sciences with the physical and life sciences. This is, I hope, something we would all like to aim for.'[57] Similar to Smail's support of this development, it has been my ambition in this chapter to show what we can gain by interpreting past texts in light of recent research in evolutionary biology and moral psychology and biology.

The second level of bridging concerns how we can tie together the experiential and the textual levels in the analysis of ancient texts and, thereby, acquire a better grasp not only of the texts, but also of the experiential dimension underlying the textual discursivity.

The third type of bridging relates to the commonly held assertion of a vast difference between ancient and modern people, but on this point care is needed. Feelings are obviously very different dependent upon historical contexts, but in terms of underlying emotions they are hardly different. To bridge the gap between ancient emotions and their textual instantiations as feelings, it is crucial to realize that as regards the deep biological level, most likely there is no significant difference between ancient and modern people.

Film-makers are ingenious in scaring the wits out of us, producers of commercials in effectively priming us to buy their products, and politicians, unfortunately, in using a rhetoric that works on our gut-feelings rather than on reason. By the same means, it should be possible to uncover how ancient texts adopt some of the same mechanisms to exert influence on our basic emotional system. Obviously, we cannot say anything about the influence on the actual ancient audience, but that is not different from textual interpretation in general, which only allows us to offer arguments regarding the intended recipients. When in historical interpretation we seek to examine a text or a social group in light of certain cultural and social conventions dominant in a specific past context, we reconstruct the perceptual habits in the most plausible way we can think of. However, by answering the question of a possible relationship between representations of feelings and their eliciting emotions, we come to deepen our understanding of past texts. This is not an aimless academic exercise. It is taking what we are already acquainted with from classical rhetoric an important step further by examining what, for instance, the *ethos* and *pathos* dimensions may have evoked in the intended addressees when using present-day knowledge of underlying emotions. It is one thing to say that a given ancient author evokes disgust in his audience; however, if we can deepen this claim by including insights from emotion psychology on disgust biases, and how they work on our deep biology, we are, in fact, reaching a greater and more comprehensive understanding. To exemplify this,

[57] Smail 2008: 8–9.

I have used emotion research to show that in analyzing Pauline references to baptism, with 1 Cor 6: 1–11 as case-study, we may, in fact, move from representations of feelings to the underlying emotional level, and from there back again to the textual level. I think we can and should do more in this regard in using insights from evolutionary and moral biology and psychology to cast light on ancient texts and on past religious experiences.

BIBLIOGRAPHY

Annas, J. 1992. *Hellenistic Philosophy of Mind.* Berkeley and Los Angeles, CA.
Becker, A. and A. Y. Reed. eds. 2003. *The Ways that Never Parted: Jews and Christians in Late Antiquity and the Early Middle Ages.* Tübingen.
Boyarin, D. 2004. *Borderlines. The Partition of Judaeo-Christianity.* Philadelphia, PA.
Cairns, D. 2017. 'Horror, Pity, and the Visual in Ancient Greek Aesthetics', in D. Cairns and D. P. Nelis, eds. *Emotions in the Classical World: Methods, Approaches, and Directions,* 53–78. Stuttgart.
Cairns, D. and L. Fulkerson. 2015. 'Introduction', in D. Cairns and L. Fulkerson, eds. *Emotions between Greece and Rome,* 1–22. London.
Cairns, D. and D. P. Nelis. 2017. 'Introduction', in D. Cairns and D. P. Nelis, eds. *Emotions in the Classical World: Methods, Approaches, and Directions,* 7–18. Stuttgart.
Carr, E. D., A. Kever, and P. Winkielman. 2018. 'Embodiment of Emotion and Its Situated Nature', in A. Newen, L. De Bruin and S. Gallagher, eds. *Oxford Handbook of 4E Cognition,* 529–551. Oxford.
Caston, R. and R. A. Kaster, eds. 2016. *Hope, Joy, and Affection in the Classical World.* Oxford.
Chaniotis, A. and P. Ducrey. 2013. 'Approaching Ancient Emotions in Greek and Roman History and Culture: An Introduction', in A. Chaniotis and P. Ducrey, eds. *Unveiling Emotions II. Emotions in Greece and Rome. Texts, Images, Material Culture,* 9–14. Stuttgart.
Chapman, H. A. and A. K. Anderson. 2013. 'Things Rank and Gross in Nature: A Review and Synthesis of Moral Disgust', *Psychological Bulletin* 139(2): 300–327.
Colombetti, G. 2018. 'Enacting Affectivity', in A. Newen, L. De Bruin, and S. Gallagher, eds. *Oxford Handbook of 4E Cognition,* 571–587. Oxford.
Czachesz, I. 2012. *The Grotesque Body in Early Christian Discourse: Hell, Scatology, and Metamorphosis.* London and New York, NY.
    2016. 'Religious Experience behind the Account of Isaiah's Ascent to Heaven: Insights from Cognitive Science', in J. N. Bremmer, T. N. Karmann, and T. R. Nicklas, eds. *The Ascension of Isaiah,* 235–257. Leuven,
    2017. *Cognitive Science and the New Testament: A New Approach to Early Christian Research.* Oxford.

Damasio, A. 1994. *Descartes' Error: Emotion, Reason, and the Human Brain*. New York, NY.
   2003. *Looking for Spinoza: Joy, Sorrow and the Feeling Brain*. London.
Delton, A. W., M. B. Petersen, and T. E. Robertson. 2018. 'Partisan Goals, Emotions, and Political Mobilization: The Role of Motivated Reasoning in Pressuring Others to Vote', *The Journal of Politics* 80(3): 890–902.
Durkheim, É. 1912. *Les Formes élémentaires de la vie religieuse. Le système totémique en Australie*. Paris.
Earp, B. D., J. A. C. Everett, E. N. Madva, and J. K. Hamlin. 2014. 'Out, Damned Spot: Can the "Macbeth Effect" Be Replicated?', *Basic and Applied Social Psychology* 36(1): 91–98.
Eco, U. 1979. *A Theory of Semiotics*. Bloomington, IN.
   1990. *The Limits of Interpretation*, Bloomington and Indianapolis, IN.
Eidinow, E. 2016. *Envy, Poison and Death: Women on Trial in Classical Athens*. Oxford.
Ekman, P. 2003. *Emotions Revealed. Understanding Faces and Feelings*. London.
Fayard, J. V., A. K. Bassi, D. M Bernstein, and B. W. Roberts. 2009. 'Is Cleanliness Next to Godliness? Dispelling Old Wives' Tales: Failure to Replicate Zhong and Liljenquist (2006)', *Journal of Articles in Support of the Null Hypothesis* 6(2): 21–29.
Haidt, J. 2012. *The Righteous Mind. Why Good People Are Divided by Politics and Religion*. London.
Harkins, A. K. 2015a. 'The Emotional Re-experiencing of the Hortatory Narratives Found in the Admonition Section of the Damascus Document', *Dead Sea Discoveries* 22(3): 285–307.
   2015b. 'A Phenomenological Study of Penitential Elements and Their Strategic Arousal of Emotion in the Qumran Hodayot (1QH cols. 1[?]-8)', in R. Egger-Wenzel and S. C. Reif, eds. *Ancient Jewish Prayers and Emotions: A Study of the Emotions Associated with Prayer in the Jewish and Related Literature of the Second Temple Period*, 297–316. Berlin.
   2016a. 'Ritual Mourning in Daniel's Interpretation of Jeremiah's Prophecy', *The Journal of Cognitive Historiography* 2(1): 14–32.
   2016b. 'The Pro-social Role of Grief in Ezra's Penitential Prayer', *Biblical Interpretation* 24(4–5): 466–491.
   2017. 'How Should We Feel about the Teacher of Righteousness?', in A. Feldman, M. Cioata, and C. Hempel, eds. *Is There a Text in this Cave? Studies in the Textuality of the Dead Sea Scrolls in Honour of George J. Brooke*, 493–514. Leiden.
   2020. 'Emotion and Law in the Book of Baruch', in B. Schmitz and K. De Troyer, eds. *The Early Reception of the Torah*, 49–69. Berlin.
Hobson, R. P. 2018. 'Thinking and Feeling: A Social-Developmental Perspective', in A. Newen, L. De Bruin, and S. Gallagher, eds. *Oxford Handbook of 4E Cognition*, 553–569. Oxford.

Kaster, R. A. 2005. *Emotion, Restraint, and Community in Ancient Rome*. Oxford.
Kazen, T. 2011. *Emotions in Biblical Law: A Cognitive Science Approach*. Sheffield.
Konstan, D. 1997. *Friendship in the Classical World*. Cambridge.
  2007. *The Emotions of the Ancient Greek: Studies in Aristotle and Classical Literature*. Toronto.
  2010. 'Ancient Rhetoric and Emotion', in I. Worthington, ed. *Companion to Greek Rhetoric*, 411–425. Oxford.
  2012. *Before Forgiveness. The Origins of a Moral Idea*. Cambridge.
  2015. 'Emotions and Morality: The View from Classical Antiquity,' *Topoi* 34: 401–407.
Larson, J. 2016. *Understanding Greek Religion*. London.
Lateiner, D. and D. Spatharas. 2017. 'Introduction: Ancient and Modern Modes of Understanding Disgust', in D. Lateiner and D. Spatharas, eds. *The Ancient Emotion of Disgust*, 1–42. Oxford.
LeDoux, J. 1996. *The Emotional Brain: The Mysterious Underpinnings of Emotional Life*. New York, NY.
Lee, S. W. S. and N. Schwarz. 2010. 'Washing Away Postdecisional Dissonance', *Science* 328 (7 May): 709.
Luomanen, P., I. Pyysiäinen, I., and R. Uro, eds. 2007. *Explaining Christian Origins and Early Judaism*. Leiden.
Martin, D. B. 1995. *The Corinthian Body*. New Haven, CT.
Martin, L. H. and D. Wiebe, eds. 2017. *Religion Explained? The Cognitive Science of Religion after Twenty-Five Years*. London.
Mitchell, A. C. 1993. 'Rich and Poor in the Courts of Corinth. Litigiousness and Status in 1 Corinthians 6.1-11', *New Testament Studies* 39: 562–586.
Mitchell, M. M. 1991. *Paul and the Rhetoric of Reconciliation: An Exegetical Investigation of the Language and Composition of 1 Corinthians*. Tübingen.
Nemeroff, C. and P. Rozin, 2000. 'The Makings of the Magical Mind: The Nature and Function of Sympathetic Magical Thinking', in K. S. Rosengren, C. N. Johnson, and P. L. Harris, eds. *Imagining the Impossible: Magical, Scientific, and Religious Thinking in Children*, 1–34. Cambridge.
Nussbaum, M. 1994. *The Therapy of Desire. Theory and Practice in Hellenistic Ethics*. Princeton, NJ.
Petersen, A. K. 2004. 'Paraenesis in Pauline Scholarship and in Paul – An Intricate Relationship', in J. Starr and T. Engberg-Pedersen, eds. *Early Christian Paraenesis in Context*, 267–295. Berlin and Boston, MA.
  2005. 'At the End of the Road: Reflections on a Popular Scholarly Metaphor', in J. Ådna, ed. *The Formation of the Church*, 45–72. Tübingen.
  2019. 'Ritual and Texts', in R. Uro, J. J. Day, R. E. DeMaris, and R. Roitto, eds. *The Oxford Handbook of Early Christian Ritual*, 370–387. Oxford.
  2022. 'The Ritual Efficacy of Water and Imposition of Hands in the Context of Rituals of Initiation', in P. Urizzi, ed. *Nati due volte: segreto e iniziazione*. Turin (forthcoming).

Petersen, M. B., A. Giessing, and J. Nielsen. 2015. 'Physiological Responses and Partisan Bias: Beyond Self-reported Measures of Party Identification', *PLoS ONE* 10(5): e0126922.

Plamper, J. 2015. *The History of Emotions. An Introduction*. Oxford.

Rozin, P. and Nemeroff, C. 1990. 'The Laws of Sympathetic Magic: A Psychological Analysis of Similarity and Contagion', in J. W. Stigler, R. A. Shweder, and G. Herdt, eds. *Cultural Psychology: Essays on Comparative Human Development*, 205–232. Cambridge.

Sanders, E. and Johncock, M. 2016. 'Introduction', in E. Sanders and M. Johncock, eds. *Emotion and Persuasion in Classical Antiquity*, 13–24. Stuttgart.

Schäfer, P. 2010. *Die Geburt des Judentums aus dem Geist des Christentums*. Tübingen.

Shakespeare, W. 1996. *The First Folio of Shakespeare. Based on Folios in the Folger Shakespeare Collection* (2nd ed.). New York, NY and London.

Siev, J., S. E. Zuckerman, and J. J. Siev. 2018. 'The Relationship between Immorality and Cleansing: A Meta-Analysis of the Macbeth Effect', *Social Psychology* 49(5): 303–309.

Smail, D. L. 2008. *On Deep History and the Brain*. Berkeley, CA and London.

Stephan, A. 2018. 'Critical Note: 3E's Are Sufficient, but Don't Forget the D', in A. Newen, L. De Bruin, and S. Gallagher, eds. *Oxford Handbook of 4E Cognition*, 607–619. Oxford.

Westen, D. 2007. *The Political Brain: The Role of Emotion in Deciding the Fate of the Nation*. New York, NY.

Zhong, C.-B. and K. Liljenquist. 2006. 'Washing Away Your Sins: Threatened Morality and Physical Cleansing', *Science* 313(5792): 1451–1452.

CHAPTER 11

A Relevant Mystery
Intuitive and Reflective Thought in Gregory of Nyssa's Representations of Divine Begetting in the Against Eunomius

Isabella Sandwell

Gregory and the Problem of the Material Aspects of the Language of Begetting for the First Two Persons of the Trinity

Gregory of Nyssa's three books *Against Eunomius* (*Contra Eunomium*) were written between 380 and 383/4 CE in response to Eunomius of Cyzicus' *Apology for the Apology*.[1] One of their aims was to justify the use of the language of begetting, father and son for the first two Persons of the Trinity, that was found in the creed formulated at the Council of Nicaea in 325. This refers to 'God, the Father almighty' and 'Jesus Christ, the Son of God', language found in the New Testament, and to the Son being 'only-begotten' and 'begotten not made', language not found in scripture. In this work, I want to explore how Gregory defends the continued use of this language and, in particular, will show that he does so by resorting to material images of begetting that might seem surprising given the Christian emphasis on God as an immaterial, eternal being who could not suffer. I will argue that turning to the cognitive science of religion can help us see that these material images of begetting were useful to Gregory precisely because they made the Trinity more comprehensible by presenting it in human terms that made it more intuitive and so easy to grasp. We can thus even suggest that the reason Nicene Christianity eventually ended up becoming accepted as orthodox in the later fourth century, despite some periods where it was not obvious this was going to be the case, was precisely because of its reliance on the language of fatherhood, sonship, and begetting for Trinitarian relations and that the very features of this language that made it problematic, and so debated at the time, were also the features that made it useful as a way to comprehend the divine.

[1] For English translations of the *Against Eunomius*, see Stuart G. Hall in Mateo-Seco and Bastero 1988, Karfíková, Douglas, and Zachhuber 2007, and Leemans and Cassin 2014. For the Greek text, see Jaeger 1960. For an introduction to the *Against Eunomius*, see Lootens 2015.

For Gregory and other supporters of Nicaea, the term 'begetting' was useful because it showed how the second Person of the Trinity was caused by/derived from the first Person without imputing any sense of being 'created' in time or a lesser divinity to the second Person because of the oneness of essence (*ousia*) and nature (*natura*) of Father and Son. In the *Apology for an Apology* Eunomius had attacked the use of the language of begetting by the supporters of Nicaea as unsuitable for the divine because of its material associations. In his view the term 'begotten' could only be used in the much more general sense of 'created' and so could support his understanding of the second Person of the Trinity as being less divine than the first Person. While the first Person was uncreated in nature or essence, and so without beginning, timeless and fully divine, the second Person was created in nature or essence and so of a different ontological order and less divine, a position sometimes known as Neo-Arian because of its continuity with the ideas of Arius of Alexandria (250/6–336 CE), which had prompted the council of Nicaea to be called in the first place.[2] The standard reading of the *Against Eunomius* is that Gregory responds to Eunomius' arguments about the problems of applying the analogy of material begetting to the divine by saying that all human language is limited in what it can tell us about the divine anyway. As Lewis Ayres puts it, '[p]ro-Nicenes argue that we can have no knowledge of God in which we can rest as if we have finally understood' because 'God's existence does not fit in the categories that characterize the created order'.[3] This approach to language is thus connected to apophatic theology, in which the divine can only be known by negatives, which was becoming common in the fourth century among the Eastern fathers.

This approach can be seen at the beginning of the second chapter of book three of the *Against Eunomius*. Here, Gregory quotes a passage in which Eunomius summarizes some of the key problems of using the analogy of earthly begetting for the divine. Eunomius concedes that 'those who beget naturally pass on their own essential being to those begotten, and those begotten participate in the same [essential being as their begetter]', which is what thinkers such as Gregory wanted to take from the analogy. However, Eunomius goes on to say that this is only possible because the begetter and the begotten 'share the same material origin, and the sustenance which comes to them from the outside',

---

[2] On Eunomius see Vaggione 2000 and Lootens 2015: 31–44. See also Ayres 2004: 144–149. The term 'Arians' for a united group is now discredited by scholars of the period.
[3] Ayres 2004: 284 and also 279, 282, 286, 341.

referring to the fact that the food that the mother eats is used to feed the fetus.[4] At the same time, Eunomius characterizes the bodies which 'beget and are begotten' as 'subject ... to action and passivity' and says that 'the begotten are born in the course of passion (*pathos*)'.[5] For Eunomius these material and passible aspects of begetting, that as well as being enacted through fleshy bodies also involves pain, suffering, and other passions, make it an unsuitable analogy for the divine. In response, Gregory berates Eunomius for 'scrupulously' examining 'terrestrial bodies and material origins and the passion of begetting and being born' when this was inappropriate for the divine.[6] Gregory in contrast argues that there are two types of begetting, one human and earthly and one divine, and that we must keep the two distinct 'since the fleshly coming into being is a physical thing and proceeds through passion, while what is incorporeal, intangible, invisible and free from material contamination, is incompatible with any passible condition'.[7] Here we see the language of begetting coming face to face with the apophatic understanding of God so that most of the features of earthly begetting are negated. This leads Gregory to ask why Eunomius constantly dwells 'upon this bodily physiology, staining nature with his disgusting compilation of words, advertising the passionate elements in human generation'.[8] In any case, says Gregory, there is no need for Eunomius to remind people that human begetting involves passion and suffering because it is obvious to anyone who 'observes his own humanity'.[9]

Gregory then ridicules Eunomius for claiming to know 'the intangible' and to be able to explain the 'ineffable begetting' by using analogies drawn from human begetting that involve 'flux, passion, material cause, activity not free from filth, sustenance flowing in from outside'.[10] As Gregory points out, Eunomius tries to 'use the slander of passion to circumscribe the begetting of the Lord'[11] and to deny that the term Begotten can be applied to the second Person of the Trinity in any other way than as a title that distinguishes it from the first Person of the Trinity, who is unbegotten and so uncreated.[12] In response, Gregory argues that if we do away with all its material associations, the analogy of human begetting instead tells us about the 'community of essential being' and 'authentic sonship' between

---

[4] Quoted at 3.2.1 (Jaeger 2:52).
[5] Quoted at 3.2.1 (Jaeger 2:52). The Greek word *pathos* translated as 'passion' actually means any emotional or physical state that overwhelms a person, including suffering.
[6] 3.2.2–4 (Jaeger 2:52–53). [7] 3.2.4 (Jaeger 2:53). [8] 3.2.5 (Jaeger 2:53).
[9] 3.2.6 (Jaeger 2:53–54). [10] 3.2.8 (Jaeger 2:54). [11] 3.2.11 (Jaeger 2:55).
[12] 3.2.11–12 (Jaeger 2:55–56).

Father and Son.[13] Finally, Gregory argues that the reason the Gospel of John does not at first use the titles 'Father' and 'Son' and the term 'begetting' is precisely because John is worried that our 'habituation to lower nature' might make us apply unwanted material implications of these terms to the divine, such as the presence of a mother or the role of suffering in childbirth.[14] Gregory then uses this as evidence to prove that Eunomius is wrong to bring in all the material associations of begetting saying '[b]ecause I heard "Son," I was not of course dragged down by the word to the terrestrial meaning of "son," but I both learn from the father and do not learn from passion.'[15]

In the above passage Gregory seems to be suggesting that people's own experiences of begetting and parent-child relations cannot really be used for understanding the divine and that people need to do away with many of their habitual associations with the terms 'father,' 'son', and 'begetting'.[16] As such, Gregory would be following in a tradition of supporters of Nicaea arguing that Arians are only able to mock the language of begetting for the divine because they rely too much on actual, human experiences of childbirth in their understanding of what begetting is. As Athanasius of Alexandria (296/7–373 CE) suggested, it was Arius and his followers who asked women about their experiences of childbirth, and the fact that they did not 'have a son before giving birth', to support their doctrinal position that the second Person did not exist before he was created by the first Person.[17] In this essay, I will question this normal picture of Arians drawing on people's experiences of childbirth and supporters of Nicaea avoiding doing so. Virginia Burrus has noted that in the *Against Eunomius* Gregory keeps repeating what Eunomius says about begetting and thus keeps invoking the material aspects of begetting before negating them. As Burrus puts it, 'the generative body is initially invoked, disciplined, and then ... translated into the upper region of the intellect' and it seems that for Gregory 'the irreducible physicality of sexual generation can be neither openly embraced nor completely ignored'.[18] I want to explore why Gregory might have kept evoking the material aspects of begetting in this way in his representations of Nicene doctrine.

---

[13] 3.2.15 (Jaeger 2:56–57).   [14] 3.2.16–23 (Jaeger 2:57–59).   [15] 3.2.24–25 (Jaeger 2:59–60).
[16] See Widdicombe on the Greek Fathers generally (Widdicombe 1994: 258). See Burrus 2000: 48.
[17] Athanasius, *Orations Against the Arians* 1.22.   [18] Burrus 2000: 99. See also 97, 107, and 209.

The *Against Eunomius* and the Popularizing and Dissemination of Nicene Doctrine

I think we can better answer this question if we first understand that one of the goals of the *Against Eunomius* might have been to make Nicene doctrine disseminate more easily among ordinary Christians. Scholarship on the supporters of Nicene Christianity usually characterizes them as having a strong interest in mystifying the divine and preventing ordinary Christians from comprehending it for themselves.[19] Concomitantly it is usually Arius and Eunomius who are associated with popularizing their understandings of Christian doctrine.[20] Gregory has described the effect of the Neo-Arians' approach to popularizing theological discussion in another work where he describes how:[21]

> [t]hroughout the city … *If you ask about small change, someone would philosophize to you about the Begotten and Unbegotten. If you inquire about the price of bread, the reply comes: "The Father is greater and the Son is a dependent." If you should ask is the bath prepared?" someone would reply, "The Son was created and did not exist before."* I don't know what to call this evil; an inflammation of the brain, or a mania, or some epidemic that destabilizes the mind.

Much has been made of this passage in previous scholarship, and the veracity of the situation described here has been questioned.[22] What matters for my purposes is Gregory's representation of the Arians and his awareness that some doctrinal ideas might be 'contagious'. As we see, Gregory criticizes the way Neo-Arian ideas, such as 'the Father is greater and the Son is dependent', were like an epidemic that took hold of people's minds and spread. At first, it might indeed look like Gregory had an entirely negative view towards doctrinal ideas spreading like an epidemic in this way, but is this really likely to have been the case? Could Gregory really have afforded to take such a negative stance to the 'catchiness' of doctrinal ideas given that he wanted Nicene Christianity to become dominant in the Roman Empire? Might it not be that Gregory was only so negative about religious ideas being contagious when they were not his own religious ideas? Rather than wanting to mystify the Nicene

---

[19] Lim 1995: 149–181. But an underlying assumption of work on the Greek Fathers of this period.
[20] On Arius' popularizing, see Drake 2000: 399–400 and Lim 1995: 13–48 and 149–151.
[21] Gregory of Nyssa, *Oration on the deity of the son and of the Holy Spirit* (PG 46:557.25–31 Migne).
[22] Lim 1995: 149–151, Drake 2000: 289, and Gregory 1979: 3–4. Imperial legislation forbidding money-changers from engaging in theological discussion supports Gregory's picture (Theodosian Code 16.4.5 with Lim 1995: 150).

understanding of the divine might he, to some degree at least, also have been interested in making it 'catchy' and cognizable by ordinary Christians in order to give it some chance of being talked about by ordinary people and thus of being disseminated more widely?[23]

Lootens has shown, in his recent dissertation on the *Against Eunomius*, that there is evidence that Gregory was 'not a reclusive mystical theologian, but a bishop actively involved in his text's promotion and carrying out sustained efforts to cultivate a readership of the *Contra Eunomium*'.[24] Gregory circulated all three books of the work widely and this contributed to him becoming established as a leading defender of Nicaea.[25] Of particular significance is the fact that the first two books of the *Against Eunomius* were read aloud during the Council of Constantinople in 381, which reaffirmed the doctrine of Nicaea on the Father and the Son and provided extra clarification on the Holy Spirit.[26] Ramsey MacMullen's thoughtful analysis of church councils has shown that appeal to what 'everyone believed', to 'the universal', and to what was 'general' or standard' was crucial to the way fourth-century councils reached agreement about doctrine.[27] For MacMullen, church councils thus had a concern with finding language for the Trinity that fitted with the usage of words found among ordinary people as well as theologians. I have shown elsewhere that Gregory had an explicit concern in the *Against Eunomius* with drawing on the ordinary, generally shared meanings of the terms 'father', 'son', and 'begetting' to support his conception of the divine.[28] Here I would like to argue that this concern could have had the goal of helping those involved in the council of Constantinople to see how the language of begetting for the Trinity could fit with ordinary usage. Similarly book three of the *Against Eunomius*, which was written a year or two after the council of Constantinople, could have contributed to the justifying of the choice of language by the council after the fact.

MacMullen talks of the attempt by church councils to find a universal language for the divine as the 'cognitive factor', but then shows that what he means is acculturation to Christian ideas as he talks of lay Christians becoming 'educated in a new style of theological analysis'.[29] He thus equates cognition with culture and education and suggests that it is at

---

[23] On the role of popular opinion in doctrinal conflicts see Gregory 1979. [24] Lootens 2015: 61.
[25] Lootens 2015: 44 and 60. [26] Lootens 2015: 55–56. See also Jerome's *On Illustrious Men*.
[27] MacMullen 2006: 69. [28] Sandwell 2019: 113–119.
[29] MacMullen 2006: 29 and more generally 24–41. On education into Christianity, 26–30.

the level of culture that the 'universal' or 'general' operates.[30] This approach is typical of scholars working in the arts and humanities, who see culture as determining how people think. However, cognitive science proposes an alternate approach. Dan Sperber in his *Explaining Culture: A Naturalistic Approach* has argued that such culturally determinist approaches are misguided because they assume that 'mental representations result from the internalization of public representations' when in fact the opposite can be just as true.[31] As Sperber puts it, '[c]ultural phenomena are ecological patterns of psychological phenomena. They do not pertain to an autonomous level of reality.'[32] Sperber talks of this as an epidemiological model of culture because it tracks how ideas move in and out of human minds, from private, mental representation to public representation and back again, and shows that cultural ideas are those that disseminate widely in more or less the same form either because they are more attractive to human minds or because there are material and environmental factors that enable their dissemination in more or less the same form.[33] In this chapter I want to suggest that approaching culture from such a cognitive point of view can give us a new way to look at the concern with finding a universal and commonly agreed language for the Trinity. I would argue that we should think of this language for the Trinity not just in terms of what was culturally agreed or shared, but also in terms of a language that was appealing to human minds more generally. I will also suggest that the epidemiological model of culture gives us a much more positive way to interpret Gregory of Nyssa's accusation that Neo-Arian ideas spread like an epidemic that took hold of people's minds. In Sperber's view, all this would mean is that these Neo-Arian ideas had the best chance of becoming widespread and thus part of what constituted culture at the time, and surely this is precisely what Gregory would have wanted for Nicene doctrine? In the next section, I will thus explore the kinds of religious ideas that cognitive scientists propose are most likely to be contagious in human populations. In the final two sections I will then show how this theory can be applied to Gregory's use of the language of begetting for the relationship between the first and second Persons of the Trinity in the *Against Eunomius*.

---

[30] See also Lewis Ayres on Christian culture at 2004: 274–278 and also Drake 2000: 289 on popular participation in theological debates in this period.
[31] Sperber 1996: 78–79 and also 113 and 65. See also Pyysiäinen 2004b: 139.
[32] Sperber 1996: 60.   [33] Sperber 1996: 5, 23, 28, and 92.

Cognitive Science of Religion and Conceptualizing Successful Religious Concepts

One line of thinking in the cognitive science of religion makes a clear distinction between religious concepts that are a good fit with the human mind and those that are not. The former are referred to as 'cognitively optimal' because they are a 'by-product of the processes of ordinary human cognition', employ 'tacit, noncultural knowledge about the world', and so 'fit rather closely with certain evolved features of human cognitive architecture'.[34] These evolved features of the human mind are thought to have arisen as adaptations in early humans to help people categorize, understand, and make inferences about the world around them; they can now be observed developing in all humans in early childhood.[35] Together they constitute what can be labelled as intuitive, natural, or implicit – the processes that happen automatically below the conscious level.[36] The first feature is a set of distinct mental systems that include a 'naïve physics' for understanding the 'movements of an inert solid object'; a 'naïve biology' for understanding the 'appearance of an organism'; and a 'naïve psychology' for understanding why people act as they do.[37] The second feature is a set of 'ontological categories', ANIMAL, PERSON, TOOL, NATURAL OBJECT, NUMBER, and PLANT, that act as templates to which new information can be mapped so that people can easily categorize, and so 'understand', it.[38] Thus categorizing incoming information as a TOOL will activate the 'naïve physics' system, and with it intuitive ideas about how structure relates to function.[39] Or matching incoming information to the ANIMAL category will activate the naïve physics and biology systems, as well as intuitive ideas about goal detection (the ability to have goals and pursue them).[40] Or categorizing incoming information as a PERSON will activate the naïve biology and physics systems, intuitive ideas about goal detection, and also the naïve psychology system that allows one to generate inferences about how a person thinks.[41]

According to cognitive science, cognitively optimal religious concepts will mostly conform to these ontological categories as this makes them easy

---

[34] For the first quote, see Slone 2004: 47. For the second quote, see Whitehouse 2004: 2 and also 29–48.
[35] Sperber 1996: 113 and also 66–67, McCauley 2011: 31–82, Boyer 2002: 122 and 1996, and De Cruz 2014.
[36] See Boyer 2002 and 1996 and Sperber 1997.   [37] Sperber 1996: 123.
[38] Boyer, 2002: 46–51, 69–70, 70–75, and 114–115.   [39] Boyer 2002: 115.
[40] Boyer 2002: 115.   [41] Boyer 2002: 115.

to process. As Sperber puts it, concepts that 'excite more inference systems, fit more easily with their expectations and trigger richer inferences (or all of these) are more likely to be acquired and transmitted' because they 'produce the richest set of inferences with the lowest cognitive effort'.[42] However, cognitively optimal concepts will also violate one or two intuitive features of the ontological category to which they are assigned because 'people recall descriptions of artefacts or persons or animals that include violations of intuitive expectations much better than descriptions that do not include them'.[43] This might include denying something we would normally categorize as a person, animal, or plant a feature of intuitive physics or biology or, conversely, attributing an inanimate object with a feature of intuitive biology or psychology.[44] In Pascal Boyer's formulation such concepts are labelled minimally counterintuitive.[45] An example is a ghost, a concept that is based on the category of PERSON and adheres to most of the intuitive properties of a person, but violates some physical properties of a person in that it lacks a material body and so can walk through solid objects.[46] For Boyer this 'combination of one violation with preserved expectations is probably a cognitive optimum, a concept that is both attention-grabbing and allows rich inferences'.[47]

The problem is that such cognitively optimal concepts are usually ones that we associate with popular religions, such as ghosts and ancestors. What about the concepts of mainstream world religions such as Christianity that have also become widespread in human populations? Harvey Whitehouse has argued that these mainstream religions favour, 'much more complex otherworldly forces ... that are hard to understand and demand enormous cognitive resources to manage and transmit'.[48] These concepts are described as 'cognitively costly' because they violate many of the intuitive properties of a particular ontological category at once, for example being described as 'immortal, all-knowing, all-powerful, nontemporal, nonspatial, a trinity and so forth'.[49] They are thus difficult

---

[42] Sperber 1996: 186–188.   [43] Boyer 2002: 92 and 92–95. See also Pyysiäinen 2003: 20–21.
[44] Boyer 2002: 70–82.
[45] Boyer 2002. For summaries of Boyer's thought see Whitehouse 2004: 31, Barrett 2004: 21–30, and Luomanen, Pyysiäinen, and Uro 2007: 7–8, Pyysiäinen 2003: 20–21. For further discussion see Barrett and Nyhof 2001, Boyer and Ramble 2001, Lisdorf 2004, and Purzycki and Willard 2016.
[46] Boyer 2002: 84–85 and also 186–188.   [47] Boyer 2002: 100 and also 98.
[48] Whitehouse 2004: 51 and also 3 and 46. See also Sperber 1996: 82–83, Barrett 2011: 139, and Pyysiäinen 2003: 219. See also Bowden, Chapter 1, in this volume.
[49] See Barrett 2004: 29. See also Whitehouse 2004: 49–62, Barrett 2011: 47–48, 105–106, and 138, De Cruz and De Smedt 2015: 34, Pyysiäinen 2004b, Luomanen, Pyysiäinen, and Uro 2007: 7–8, and De Cruz 2014.

'to think with' because it is very hard to make inferences from them. As Barrett put it, theological concepts do not act as 'full-blown concept[s] in the sense of providing a set of causal relations between various features of God, that generate predictions, explanations, and inferences. Theologically, God might be represented as ... a list of decontextualized properties like omniscient, omnipotent, loving, etc,' but will not constitute 'a robust, developed concept of God'.[50] Because such concepts cannot be grasped intuitively, they are thought to operate instead at the level of explicit or reflective thought.[51] Because cognitively costly religious concepts operate at the level of explicit or reflective thought in this way, the cognitive science of religion has struggled to propose explanations for how they become widespread.[52] Instead, figures such as Harvey Whitehouse have argued that we can only explain the success of these 'doctrinal' religious concepts by turning to external structures of support such as authoritative leaders, teaching and preaching, and constant repetition and rote learning.[53]

From what we have said so far it would seem that the cognitively costly ideas of mainstream theological religions and the cognitively optimal ideas of popular religion operate at two distinct levels: the former that of reflective, explicit thought; the latter that of intuitive, implicit thought. The latter is thus the domain of cognitive science, the former that of cultural studies. However, others working in the cognitive science of religion have challenged the dichotomy between cognitively optimal and cognitively costly concepts and have argued that 'there is more continuity between theological concepts and ordinary religious beliefs than cognitive science of religion authors have hitherto recognized'.[54] The work of Ilkka Pyysiäinen is particularly significant here. Pyysiäinen challenges any simple attempt to equate folk religion with intuitive reasoning and theological religion with explicit reasoning and instead argues that we need to understand how 'the two systems of reasoning work together'.[55] He argues that, when people process theological concepts, they do so by oscillating between implicit/intuitive thought processes and the explicit/reflective ones that are more typical of theology. In contrast to Whitehouse, he

---

[50] Barrett 1998: 616–617. Pyysiäinen 2004a: 177 versus Whitehouse 2004: 18–19, 58–60.
[51] Sperber 1997: 75–76.   [52] On this see De Cruz 2014 and Pyysiäinen 2004b: 143.
[53] See Whitehouse 2004: 46 and 22–23. See also Pyysiäinen 2003: 197–236.
[54] De Cruz 2014. See also Pyysiäinen 2004b. For summaries of the approaches, see De Cruz and De Smedt 2015: 34–39, Barrett 2011: 47–54, Barrett and Keil 1996: 219–221, and Pyysiäinen 2003: 11. On cognitively costly concepts, see Whitehouse 2004: 49–59 and Pyysiäinen 2009: 95–136.
[55] Pyysiäinen 2004b: 127.

argues that people do not simply learn theological concepts by rote, but rather, in the first instance at least, submit them to normal intuitive processes.[56] Thus, when one first hears a complex theological idea, one will start by processing it according to implicit or intuitive thought as one does with any incoming information. As Pyysiäinen explains, when the system of implicit thought processes theological concepts, it acts as 'a pattern recognition system' by trying to match the concepts with, and assimilate them to, existing intuitive knowledge. As such, implicit thought 'tries to combine all features of counter-intuitive agents into a coherent representation so that apparent contradictions are harmonized ... simple cues often trigger representations of larger wholes and ... some counter-intuitive features tend to drop off.[57] As Barrett and Keil show, when people process 'reflective theological concepts', there is a strong tendency for them to think of 'God as having human properties in contradiction' to the normal theological ones.[58] As a result, Pyysiäinen has argued that '[w]ritten theologies ... cannot be used as indicators of what those subscribing to the religion in question actually believe' but are just 'artefacts that serve as cues directing people's inferences'. They can trigger certain inferences in people's minds but cannot control what people do with those inferences.[59]

For Pyysiäinen, if 'explicit theology' does not maintain its 'connection with intuition' in this way it can become impotent because the theological concepts it contains can become cut off 'from their real-life context, making them more abstract and reducing their inferential potential'.[60] This 'means that theological concepts merely complement intuitions; they cannot replace them'.[61] However, according to Pyysiäinen, intuitive thought about religion also needs theology. This is because, Pyysiäinen argues, the system of explicit thought is brought into play 'when the [implicit system] fails to provide a satisfactory treatment of religious issues', such as when 'the output of the [implicit system] is felt to be doubtful', or when 'someone calls into question one's religious views'.[62] In such cases, triggering the explicit system of thought then allows one to adopt a more 'reflective stance towards one's own thoughts' and so to correct the perceived problem.[63] One of the functions of the reflective/

---

[56] Pyysiäinen 2004b: 127–136.   [57] Pyysiäinen 2004b: 134–136.
[58] Barrett 2004: 10–11, summarizing Barrett and Keil 1996. See also Pyysiäinen 2004b: 125 and 2003: 11. For a critique of Barrett and Keil's work, see van Slyke 2011: 61–90. See also Eidinow, Chapter 3, in this volume.
[59] Pyysiäinen 2009: 52 and 2004b: 124–125.   [60] Pyysiäinen 2004b: 141.
[61] Pyysiäinen 2004b: 143.   [62] Pyysiäinen 2004b: 134–136.   [63] Pyysiäinen 2004b: 134–136.

explicit system and of theology thus might be to restore counterintuitiveness and so mystery to people's thinking about the divine and so make it more 'theologically correct' again.[64] Sperber has argued that the most 'addictive' religious concepts are ones that are 'relevant mysteries' because they find a balance between triggering implicit/intuitive thought process, and never being fully explainable by these and so remaining at the level of reflective thought. As he put it: 'The most evocative representations are those which, on the one hand, are closely related to the subject's other mental representations, and on the other hand, can never be given a final interpretation.'[65] This model of relevant mysteries differs from Boyer's minimally counterintuitive concepts because it allows for cognitively costly theological concepts to be appealing to the human mind. As Sperber suggests, it is precisely the inability of such concepts ever to be completely understood, so that 'you are never through interpreting them', that makes them so addictive.[66] One could thus argue that it is the job of reflective, theological thought to keep reminding people of the 'element of mystery' of doctrine and so to maintain their addictive nature in the face of the tendency of implicit thought to draw them towards the intuitive end of the spectrum.

In such a view, a thinker like Gregory will have had much to gain from engaging with both ways of thinking about the divine because it was precisely by doing so that he could create the kind of relevant-mysterious concepts that were a good fit with the human mind and that thus would become widespread in human populations and so part of what constitutes 'culture'. In the next two sections, I will argue in more detail how we can see this oscillation between implicit/intuitive and explicit/reflective thought in Gregory's approach to the analogy of begetting for the Trinity.

Intuitive Understandings of Divine Begetting

Let us now come back to the question of why Gregory kept returning to the 'generative body' and the irreducible physicality of sexual generation.[67] First, we can note that the language of father, son, and begetting can be described as intuitive in the sense that people's understanding of them would, according to cognitive science, have been built up from people's own experiences of parents, children, and the various processes involved in bringing a child into existence.[68] Even if people have not experienced or

---

[64] Pyysiäinen 2004b: 140.   [65] Sperber 1996: 73.   [66] Sperber 1996: 90 and also 73.
[67] Burrus 2000: 99.   [68] On this see Turner 1987.

seen childbirth first-hand, they are likely to have heard about it from others. It is thus language that is likely to generate a rich set of inferences in those hearing and using it and would thus have the impact of making conceptions of the divine more relevant to people and so easier to cognize. We can see how this works if we turn back to the example of Gregory of Nyssa and his use of the language of father, son, and begetting for the Trinity.

We saw in the previous section that one of the highly counterintuitive features of the Nicene creed is the way it conceives of the divine as both one and three. The creed states that 'we believe in one God' and then goes on to mention the three distinct entities: God, Son of God, and the Holy Ghost. It also both speaks of God and the Son of God as distinct entities and states that the Son of God was of one substance with the father. The problem at the heart of many of the Trinitarian debates of the fourth century thus ultimately revolved around the question of how God could simultaneously be a single unified being and three distinct persons.[69] By Gregory's time, in the Greek speaking world, this problem was being posed as one of the relationship between the unity of essence (*ousia*) or nature (*natura*) and the distinction of the three 'persons' or 'existences' (*hypostases*).[70] The difficulty in resolving the contradiction involved in this has led cognitive scientists of religion to see the Nicene creed as a classic cognitively costly concept. As De Cruz puts it, the creed's claim that God is both three and one, both distinct persons and simple and undivided, 'far exceeds the minimal counter-intuitiveness that makes ordinary religious belief memorable' and easy to make inferences from.[71] The Nicene conception of the Trinity is thus an example of the 'impotence of explicit theologizing' that needs to be reconnected with intuitive thought to make it relevant to ordinary life again.[72]

One of the ways that pro-Nicene theologians like Gregory try to reconnect their conception of the divine with intuitive thought, and so to restore relevance to it, is by finding analogies from the earthly world that make some sense of it.[73] Scholars of Gregory have in recent decades most often presented him as favouring two kinds of analogies for the Trinity: either those such as a flame and its light or a perfume and its scent, as in the work of figures such as Ayres and Barnes; or that of individual humans

---

[69] See Ayres 2004: 207 and Anatolius 2011: 235.
[70] On nature and *ousia* being interchangeable for Gregory, see Cross 2002.
[71] De Cruz 2014. See also Sperber 1997: 75–76. [72] Pyysiäinen 2004b: 143.
[73] See Sandwell 2019.

acting as coordinate realities, as in the work of Zachhuber, following trends originally established by von Harnack, if in a rather different form.[74] However, favouring one or other of these analogies also means placing emphasis on either unity of essence at the expense of distinction of hypostases, in the case of analogies such as a flame and its light, or distinction of persons at the expense of unity of essence, in the case of analogies of three coordinate realities. According to Ayres, Gregory prefers analogies for the 'indivisibility of natures' that imply an ontological or cosmological conception of natures in general, such as the relationship between a grape and wine or a flame and its light, rather than those of 'three people sharing a common nature'.[75] The problem is that, as Anatolius has pointed out, the kind of 'ontological or cosmological' conception of natures and their indivisibility seen in Ayres' work fails because it 'tends not to involve the particular intense evocation of unity-within-distinction articulated by the combination of *ousia-hypostasis* and kindred pairings'.[76]

I would argue that this difficulty of finding an appropriate analogy for the Trinity arises from the fact that many of the scholars above ignore or play down Gregory's interest in analogies of begetting for the Trinity.[77] They thus miss the fact that what Gregory finds so useful about this analogy is that it does allow equally both for unity of nature/essence, because father and son share the same nature of the species to which they belong, and for distinction of persons, because the son is a distinct entity from the father.

If we turn back to what Gregory actually says, we can see how this worked for him. In an example from book one of the *Against Eunomius*, in response to Eunomius' argument that the second Person took his essence from his title Begotten and thus that he was begotten and so created in essence, Gregory uses a vivid image of earthly begetting. Gregory first tells us that it 'is reasonable and apparent in nature, that the begotten is like its begetter'[78] and then says:[79]

> What is born does not resemble the form or mode of its birth. In animal generation birth is the bodily separation, which brings into open the animal

---

[74] For the former, see Barnes 1998 and Ayres 2004: 205, 292, 350. For the latter, see von Harnack's proposition that Gregory and the other Cappadocian fathers represented a shift from essentialist to personalist understanding of the Trinity (von Harnack 1958: 84–85). For a more recent version of this argument, see Zachhuber 2000. For a summary of the tradition following von Harnack, see Ayres 2004: 237–239 and Hanson 1988: 696–699. On the problem of opposing 'essentialist' and 'personalist' models of the Trinity, see de Halleux 1986: 129–155 and 265–292.
[75] Ayres 2004: 350.   [76] Anatolius 2011: 233.   [77] See Barnes 2002: 483.
[78] 1.450 (Jaeger 1:157).   [79] 1.453–454 (Jaeger 1:158).

that was perfected by formation in the entrails, but what is born is human or horse or calf or whatever it is that arises by the generative process. How then the mode of likeness of what is born follows the mode of generation, let Eunomius tell us, or someone trained by him in obstetrics. Birth is one thing, the result of birth another.

Let us first note that here it is Gregory who prompts people to draw on actual experience of childbirth. This is particularly clear when he asks Eunomius to think about what 'someone trained in obstetrics' would say about birth. Clearly, he wants to use the knowledge of those who have direct experience of childbirth to counter Eunomius' view of childbirth. Gregory's point in using this analogy is to make it clear that what a creature is, its nature or essence, is determined not by the way it is born but by the species to which it belongs, whether a 'human, a horse or calf or whatever'.[80] But at the same time, we see the bodily separation and distinction involved in childbirth as the infant animal emerges from the mother's body being used to emphasize that the baby and mother exist as distinct physical entities. This can be seen in such phrases as 'the animal that was perfected by formation in the entrails' and then was 'brought into the open' in an act of 'bodily separation' and 'the result of the birth', which implies a baby. We thus have an image that balances distinction and separation of a physical, embodied child and the essence or nature of belonging to the same species that unites parent and child. To show what he means, Gregory then uses Adam and Abel as an example of how two beings could have been brought into existence in different ways, the former created by God and the latter by the 'coupling' of Adam and Eve, and yet have exactly the same human nature.[81] As he says, on the one hand they are 'both believed to be two' and, on the other hand 'in terms of their essence (*ousia*), they are not split from each other'.[82] This provides a very easy-to-grasp image of two distinct physical individuals who are one in nature which could then be used as analogy for the Trinity that people could relate to their own experience, and knowledge of childbirth, whether first- or second-hand, and could easily make inferences from.

Further evidence that Gregory was concerned with this balance between unity and distinction in human begetting in this passage can be seen from the fact that he next tells us that this is what the biblical usage of the terms Father and Son means. He says, '[w]hen we heard from the Truth about

---

[80] See Zachhuber 2000 on the importance of the idea of species in Gregory.
[81] 1.496–497 (Jaeger 1:170). [82] 1.496 (Jaeger 1:169).

Father and Son, we learned the unity of nature in the two subjects – *tois hupkeimenois* – the relation to each other being signified naturally, first by the names and secondly by the very voice of the Lord.'[83] He then uses a phrase found in the Gospel of John, 'I and the Father are one',[84] to support his view of the balance between distinction and unity in the first two Persons of the Trinity and tells us that it fights off both the followers of Sabellius (third century CE), who emphasize the unity and singularity of God at the expense of the distinction of the persons because they see the three Persons of the Trinity just to be different manifestations of the one Godhead, and the followers of Arius, who emphasize the distinction of the three Persons of the Trinity to the extent that they deny that the second Person of the Trinity shared the same full divine nature/essence as the first person.[85] Instead, for Gregory, 'having heard therefore that "I and the Father are one," we have been taught by his voice both that the Lord has a Cause and that the Son and the Father are indistinguishable in nature, not blurring together our conception of them into one hypostasis'.[86]

In another passage in book three, chapter one, Gregory again tackles Eunomius' misuse of the analogy of begetting when he takes it to mean that the first two Persons of the Trinity are 'divided by begottenness and unbegottenness into difference of nature' because the second Person is begotten and so created by nature while the first Person is unbegotten and so without beginning, timeless, and uncreated in nature.[87] Gregory argues that this is not at all what can be seen in childbirth in the human world and in so doing he provides another vivid image of birth:

> The Lord said in the Gospel that as childbirth approaches the woman suffers pain, but afterwards rejoices exceedingly, because a human has been born into the world.[88] Just as in this passage we learn from the Gospel of two distinct ideas, first the birth, which we perceive in the child-bearing, and secondly that which is produced by the child-bearing; the birth is not the human, but the human comes by birth.[89]

The point here is, again, that the process of giving birth is distinct from what is produced during that process, a new human child. For Gregory this provides a useful analogy for the Trinity: begetting is a process by which the second Person was derived from the first Person, not something that defines his essence. However, that act of giving birth, of causing another being to come into existence, leads to there being two distinct

---

[83] 1.498 (Jaeger 1:170).   [84] Jn 10.30.   [85] 1.499 (Jaeger 1:170).
[86] 1.503 (Jaeger 1:171–172).   [87] 3.1.68 (Jaeger 2:28).   [88] Jn 16.21.
[89] 3.1.70–71 (Jaeger 2:29).

Persons or existences: Father and Son. So, again, note the focus on the separation that occurs between mother and baby in phrases such as 'a human being has been born into the world' and 'that which is produced by the childbearing'. Gregory then cites Adam and Abel again as an example of two men who shared the same 'definition of the human *ousia*' and the 'same defining character of human nature', despite the fact that they came into existence in different ways: Adam was made by God while Abel came into existence 'in accordance with the principle of human begetting'.[90] However, as before, this is also an example involving two clearly distinct, embodied individuals. Again, we have a familiar image of distinction in unity, one that is again based in human experience of childbirth and relatively easy to grasp and make inferences from.

In another example from book three, chapter six, Gregory tells us that begetting is one of the types of causation that can be used to understand how the first Person causes the other two Persons of the Trinity. He describes begetting as causation by 'material and nature' in which 'nature constructs the generation of living things from each other' so again emphasizing the role of matter and the way new distinct, embodied living things are created during begetting.[91] Gregory explicitly tells his audience that the purpose of using models for causation from the human world is precisely that they make 'accessible to us [the Holy Spirit's] teachings about things beyond our understanding'.[92] From what Gregory goes on to say, it is clear that he wants this model to tell his audience something both about the individual Persons of the Trinity and about unity of essence and nature that made them one. At one point he says, 'when it expounds the ineffable existence (*hypostasis*), beyond description, of the Only-begotten from the Father, because human poverty cannot attain to doctrines beyond word and thought, there it also accommodates to our position and calls him "Son," which is a word ordinarily applied by us to things coming to birth by material and natural processes'.[93] Just as a son is derived from his parents and gains his distinct existence from the material and natural processes of childbirth, so the same is true of the way the Only-begotten, the second Person, derives his existence/personhood (*hypostasis*) from the first Person in the Trinity. At the same time, though, begetting can also tell

---

[90] 3.1.73–75 (Jaeger 2:29–30). For Zachhuber this passage does not suggest that Gregory thinks that Abel derives his human nature from Adam via generation, nor that he thinks the second Person of the Trinity derives his divine nature from the first Person (Zachhuber 2000: 99–101 and 265). For a critique of this argument, see Ayres 2004: 205–207.
[91] 3.6.27–29 (Jaeger 2:195–196). On this passage see Hanson 1988: 728 and Barnes 2014: 371–377.
[92] 3.6.32 (Jaeger 2:197).   [93] 3.6.36 (Jaeger 2:198–199).

us, Gregory says, about the 'affinity of nature' between father and son.[94] For Gregory there are two elements involved in the 'generation of living things': matter and nature. Nature provides the affinity and so the implication is that it is matter that brings the distinction of persons just as it did in the passages we explored earlier where the bodies of mothers and babies were emphasized.

In each of these examples we have very vivid reminders of the physicality and materiality of begetting and that such images are particularly useful for conveying the idea of a distinct individual. It is the mother's body that provides the matter for the creation of the fetus, and the baby when it is born appears as a new distinct material entity; or when fathers and sons are referred to, they are clearly embodied individuals. But at the same time, the image of human begetting can help us see how two distinct individuals can have the same essence/nature if we think of this as essence/nature of the species, which is then instantiated in different material existences. This makes it much easier to grasp how the first two Persons of the Trinity could be two but still one. I would thus argue that Gregory did, to some degree at least, want to push people to think of their own knowledge and experience of childbirth when they thought about how the terms 'father', 'son', and 'begetting' applied to the divine in the Trinity, and that this did sometimes involve bringing in the material and physical aspects of begetting so that people could begin to cognize the divine begetting as akin to the way a mother gave birth to a material baby. In the passages from this section, as in the passage from book three, chapter two, that I discussed at the beginning of this chapter, we see Gregory emphasizing the body of the mother with its role in conception and childbirth and the body of the baby as it grows in the mother and then emerges from her body as a distinct entity. In conjuring up these vivid images of childbirth, Gregory could submit the Trinity to intuitive thought. In Pyysiäinen's terms, first we see 'pattern recognition' and the 'triggering' of the representation 'of a larger whole', in that Gregory uses earthly begetting with all its material elements as a model that can encompass and hold together the seemingly contradictory elements of the Trinity.[95] This then allows Gregory 'to combine all features of' the Trinity 'into a coherent representation so that apparent contradictions are harmonized' because it is possible to show how two individuals could both share the same human nature and yet be distinct persons.[96] As this happens 'some counterintuitive features' of the Trinity

---

[94] 3.6.48 (Jaeger 2:202) and 3.6.37 (Jaeger 2:199).   [95] Pyysiäinen 2004b: 134–136.
[96] Pyysiäinen 2004b: 134–136.

'drop off', as there is no longer such a contradiction or mystery in how three can also be one.[97] In so doing, Gregory made the Nicene conception of the Trinity, in which the divine was both three and one, more easily relatable to people's own lives and so easier to make inferences about: the 'relevance' part of Sperber's relevant mysteries.

Reflective Thought and Conceptualizations of Divine Begetting

Unsurprisingly, a move towards an intuitive understanding of the Trinity could cause many problems from a theological perspective. As Gregory tells us, it can lead people to make all kinds of unwanted inferences about the divine such that the second Person of the Trinity was born in time like an actual baby,[98] or that divine begetting might involve change in the same way that a fetus grew into a baby,[99] or that God could suffer in the same way that the mother suffered during childbirth.[100] For this reason, the reflective system of thought and theology have to take over and reassert that the divine is immaterial by negating the material aspects of begetting. This is the case in a number of the passages that we discussed in the previous section. Thus, at 3.6.36–37 (Jaeger 2:198–199), just after Gregory has invoked causation by 'material and nature', in which nature constructs 'the generation of living things from each other,'[101] he then argues that 'in saying "Son", it rejects all those other things which human nature associates with earthly birth (*gene-sis*)' and that '[n]o such material and temporal thinking being implied by the designation "Son", the nature alone remains.'[102] Or in the example from book three, chapter one, discussed in the previous section, just after he has introduced the example of Adam and Abel, Gregory goes on to say that to make this analogy work for the divine we need to remove all 'material' and 'temporal associations' and all 'pollution of the flesh' so that 'we shall have, in the thought that remains, when it is purified of such elements, the surest possible guide to sublime and unapproachable things'.[103] What is this 'nature alone' or 'thought' that remains once you remove matter from begetting? We saw from earlier that for Gregory, nature and essence are nature and essence of the species; that is, what unites distinct individual examples of the species.

---

[97] Pyysiäinen 2004b: 134–136.
[98] See 3.6.42–45 (Jaeger 2: 200–202) and 3.1.79–82 (Jaeger 2: 31–32). [99] 3.2.65.
[100] 3.2.65 (Jaeger 2:73) and 3.6.36–37 (Jaeger 2:198–199). [101] 3.6.27–29 (Jaeger 2:144–145).
[102] 3.6.36–37 (Jaeger 2:198–199). [103] 3.1.76 (Jaeger 2:30–31).

However, we also suggested, in the previous section, that it was matter that allowed for mother and child to exist as distinct individuals. What happens to that idea if we remove matter from begetting and leave only the nature or essence of the species that unites parent and child? We can see an example of Gregory struggling with this if we return to our discussion of the start of chapter three, book two, with which we opened this essay. There we saw Gregory combatting Eunomius' constant reference to the material aspects of begetting and his own assertion that we had to remove all material aspects of begetting from the analogy before we could apply it to the divine.[104] A little later Gregory continues these arguments by combatting those who 'associate passion with divine begetting' and instead arguing for the special, spiritual nature of divine begetting.[105] In so doing, he tackles Eunomius' accusation that the analogy of begetting in the human world will always imply an active parent acting to create something, which is then by definition passive because it has been formed by another, because talking of the divine as passive would be inappropriate.[106] In so doing, however, he concedes that Eunomius is right on one issue, that begetting involves two distinct individuals: parent and child. As he says:[107]

> in the nature of beings he [Eunomius] knows how to observe the truth accurately, so as to distinguish the one who gives a share of essence (*ousia*) [the parent] from the one who receives it [the child], and to say that each of them exists in itself as something other than the essence (*ousia*); for the one giving or receiving a share is surely distinct from what is shared or given, so that one must first have some idea of something envisaged in its own particular entity (*hypostasis*), and only so to go on to speak about its giving what it has, or receiving what it has not.

Gregory clearly wants to maintain the idea that the material entities involved in childbirth, the parents who begot and the child who was begotten, existed 'in their own particular entities' without also bringing in any of the other material associations of them as 'subject to ... activity and passivity' and without bringing in anything we might learn about 'flux', change, and suffering from 'observing pregnancy and foetal formations'.[108] How can he manage this?

If we return to the example from book three, chapter one, which we have already discussed in the previous section, where Gregory used the

---

[104] 3.2.1–25 (Jaeger 2:52–60). [105] 3.2.58–61 (Jaeger 2:71–72).
[106] 3.2.1 (Jaeger 2:52) and 3.2.66 (Jaeger 2:74). [107] 3.2.67 (Jaeger 2:74).
[108] 3.2.65 (Jaeger 2:73).

example of Adam and Abel, we can see that Gregory struggled with the unity of nature of the species and distinction of persons in a father and his son when he says that Adam 'begot from himself another self'.[109] Adam and Abel are two distinct people but are exactly the same because they are both humans. We can again see a similar attempt to capture the contradiction between unity and essence a little later after Gregory had claimed that once you have removed matter from earthly begetting you have only the 'thought that remains'.[110] Here Gregory makes clear that by removing matter from the analogy of earthly begetting he does not in any way mean to do away with the sense of distinction of persons that the role of matter in earthly begetting implies. After emphasizing that the second Person shared the same essence as the first Person despite coming into existence in a different way from him, because the son was begotten while the father had always existed, he says:[111]

> having come forth from the Father and being in the Father, as the Gospel says (Jn 8.24), but is, in accordance with the simple and specific definition of our faith, 'Light from Light, true God from true God'; the one being all that the other is except for actually being him.

So, just as before we had the phrase 'begot from himself another self', here we have 'the one being all that the other is except for actually being him'. In both phrases he tries to capture the sense of unity within distinction. However, I would argue that these enigmatic phrases only work to their full effect because Gregory has first conjured up images of material begetting in which one distinct material entity is born from another, before negating them. I would thus argue that the distinct, material bodies of parent and child haunt Gregory's portrayal of the Trinity and are essential to it. Gregory pushes people to start processing all the inferences of earthly begetting and to start applying them to the divine so that they conceive of the divine persons as both distinct and as also sharing the same nature. However, as the problematic aspects of these inferences become clear, Gregory teaches people to revert to the reflective system of thought by negating all the material aspects of begetting. This puts a brake on their intuitive processing of divine begetting and instead leaves them in a situation where they are wondering how the first and second Persons can be distinct from one another like a human parent and child when they are immaterial, a-temporal beings. This prompts them to come up with their

---

[109] 3.1.75 (Jaeger 2:30). Burrus (2000: 80–133) discusses the gender issues involved in such passages.
[110] 3.1.79–82 (Jaeger 2:78–80).   [111] 3.1.84–85 (Jaeger 2:80–81) quoting the creed of Nicaea.

own formulations along the lines of 'another self' or 'being all that the other is except for actually being him'.

In so doing, Gregory maintains a balance between the relevance and the mystery of his conception of the divine, and the Nicene conception of the Trinity can thus be presented as a relevant mystery in Sperber's terms. Phrases such as begetting 'another self' or begetting an entity that is 'all that the other is except for actually being him' are good examples of representations of the divine that, in Sperber's words, one is 'never through interpreting'.[112] We can have some understanding of what these words mean by thinking about the example of Adam or Abel or the way a child is born from its mother, but we can never quite pin them down or grasp them completely. As we saw in the second section, the benefit of such ideas is that they both hold off the 'impotency' of purely theological ideas and keep them in touch with ordinary life, while also maintaining sufficient mystery to make them catchy and addictive.[113] As such, they have the potential to be a very good fit with human minds and so are the most likely kind of concepts to become 'cultural', that is, to count as what people think of as a universal, general, standard and what everyone believed. We can then suggest that one reason the supporters of Nicaea generally, and the Council of Constantinople in particular, continued to use and defend the language of begetting for the relationship between the first two Persons of the Trinity was because this language allowed them to present the Trinity in a way that fit, to some degree at least, with ordinary human concepts and thus with meanings that could, more or less, be agreed upon by all because they were based in human embodied experience or second-hand knowledge of that experience, but were not fully explainable by it. It is this that made them universal (*katholikos*). In this way, using the language of begetting for the divine could actually have assisted the dissemination of Nicene Christianity in the Roman world by helping some of its key ideas become a better fit with human minds, and so more likely to be disseminated widely and to become cultural.

BIBLIOGRAPHY

Anatolius. K. 2011. *Retrieving Nicaea: The Development and Meaning of Trinitarian Doctrine*. Grand Rapids, MI.

Ayres, L. 2004. *Nicaea and Its Legacy: An Approach to Fourth-Century Trinitarian Theology*. Oxford.

---

[112] Sperber 1996: 73.   [113] Sperber 1996: 90–91 and Pyysiäinen 2004b: 124–125 and 2009: 52.

Barnes, M. R. 1998. 'Eunomius of Cyzicus and Gregory of Nyssa: Two Traditions of Transcendental Causality', *Vigiliae Christianae* 52: 59–87.
  2002. 'Divine Unity and the Divided Self: Gregory of Nyssa's Trinitarian Theology in Its Psychological Context', *Modern Theology* 18: 475–496.
Barnes, M. R. 2014. '*Contra Eunomium III.6*', in J. Leemans and M. Cassin, eds. *Gregory of Nyssa: 'Contra Eunomium III': An English Translation with Commentary and Supporting Studies*, 371–377. Leiden.
Barrett, J. L. 1998. 'Cognitive Constraints on Hindu Concepts of the Divine', *Journal for the Scientific Study of Religion* 37: 608–619.
  2004. *Why Would Anyone Believe in God?* Lanham, MD.
  2011. *Cognitive Science, Religion and Theology*. West Conshohocken, PA.
Barrett, J. L. and F. C. Keil. 1996. 'Conceptualizing a Nonnatural Entity: Anthropomorphism in God Concepts', *Cognitive Psychology* 31: 219–247.
Barrett, J. L. and M. Nyhof. 2001. 'Spreading Non-natural Concepts: The Role of Intuitive and Intuitive Conceptual Structures in Memory and Transmission of Cultural Materials', *Journal of Cognition and Culture* 1.1: 69–100.
Boyer, P. 1996. 'What Makes Anthropomorphism Natural: Intuitive Ontology and Cultural Representations', *Journal of the Royal Anthropological Institute* 2.1: 83–97.
  2002. *Religion Explained: The Human Instincts that Fashion Gods, Spirits and Ancestors*. London.
Boyer, P. and Ramble C. 2001. 'Cognitive Templates for Religious Concepts: Cross-cultural Evidence for Recall of Counter-intuitive Representations', *Cognitive Science* 25: 535–564.
Burrus, V. 2000. *'Begotten not Made.' Conceiving Manhood in Late Antiquity*. Stanford.
Cross, R. 2002. 'Gregory of Nyssa on Universals', *Vigiliae Christianae* 56.4: 372–410.
De Cruz, H. 2014. 'Cognitive Science of Religion and the Study of Theological Concepts', *Topoi* 23.2: 487–497.
De Cruz, H. and J. De Smedt. 2015. *A Natural History of Natural Theology: The Cognitive Science of Theology and Philosophy of Religion*. Cambridge, MA.
De Halleux, A. 1986. 'Personalisme ou essentialisme Trinitaire chez les pères Cappadociens', *Revue Théologique de Louvain* 17: 215–268.
Drake, H. A. 2000. *Constantine and the Bishops: The Politics of Intolerance*. Baltimore, MD and London.
Gregory, T. E. 1979. *Vox Populi: Popular Opinion and Violence in the Religious Controversies of the Fifth Century A.D.* Columbus, OH.
Hanson, R. P. C. 1988. *The Search for the Christian Doctrine: The Arian Controversy 318-381 AD*. Edinburgh.
Jaeger, W. ed. 1960. *Contra Eunomium libri*. (Revised ed.) 2 vols. *Gregorii Nysseni Opera 1–2*. Leiden.
Karfiková, L., S. Douglas, and J. Zachhuber, eds. 2007. *Gregory of Nyssa: "Contra Eunomium II": An English Version with Supporting Studies*. Supplements to Vigiliae Christianae 82. Leiden.

Leemans, J. and M. Cassin, eds. 2014. *Gregory of Nyssa: 'Contra Eunomium III': An English Translation with Commentary and Supporting Studies*. Supplements to Vigiliae Christianae 124. Leiden.

Lim, R. 1995. *Public Disputation, Power, and Social Order in Late Antiquity*. Berkeley and Los Angeles, CA and London.

Lisdorf, A. 2004. 'The Spread of Non-natural Concepts', *Journal of Cognition and Culture* 4.1: 151–174.

Lootens, M. R. 2015. 'Gregory of Nyssa's *Contra Eunomium*: Context, Method, and Theology', PhD dissertation, Fordham University.

Luomanen, P., I. Pyysiäinen, and R. Uro. 2007. *Explaining Christian Origins and Early Judaism. Contributions from Cognitive and Social Sciences*. Leiden.

MacMullen, R. 2006. *Voting about God in Early Church Councils*. New Haven, CT and London.

Mateo-Seco, L. F. and J. L. Bastero, eds. 1988. *El 'Contra Eunomium I' en la produccion literaria de Gregorio de Nisa: VI Coloquio Internacional sobre Gregorio de Nisa*. Pamplona.

McCauley, R. N. 2011. *Why Religion Is Natural and Science Is Not*. Oxford.

Purzycki, B. G. and A. K. Willard. 2016. 'MCI Theory: A Critical Discussion', *Religion, Brain and Behavior* 6.3: 207–224.

Pyysiäinen, I. 2003. *How Religion Works: Towards a New Cognitive Science of Religion*. Leiden.

2004a. 'Corrupt Doctrine and Doctrinal Revival. On the Nature and Limits of the Modes Theory', in H. Whitehouse and L. H. Martin, eds. *Theorizing Religions Past. Archaeology, History and Cognition*. Lanham, MD.

2004b. 'Intuitive and Explicit in Religious Thought,' *Journal of Cognition and Culture* 4.1: 123–150.

2009. *Supernatural Agents: Why We Believe in Souls, Gods and Buddhas*. Oxford.

Sandwell, I. 2019. 'Gregory of Nyssa's Engagement with Conceptual Metaphors: The Analogies of "Father," "Son," and "Begetting" in the Against Eunomius', *Religion and Theology* 26.1–2: 112–146.

Slone, J. D. 2004. *Theological Incorrectness: Why Religious People Believe What They Shouldn't*. Oxford.

Sperber, D. 1996. *Explaining Culture: A Naturalistic Approach*. Oxford.

1997. 'Intuitive and Reflective Beliefs', *Mind and Language* 12.1: 67–83.

Turner, M. 1987. *Death is the Mother of Beauty: Mind, Metaphor, Criticism*. Chicago.

Vaggione, R. P. C. 2000. *Eunomius of Cyzicus and the Nicene Revolution*. Oxford.

van Slyke, J. A. 2011. *The Cognitive Science of Religion*. Farnham–Burlington, VT.

von Harnack, A. (trans. N. Buchanan). 1958. *The History of Dogma*, vol. iv. New York, NY.

Whitehouse, H. 2004. *Modes of Religiosity: A Cognitive Theory of Religious Transmission*. Walnut Creek, CA.

Widdicombe, P. 1994. *The Fatherhood of God from Origin to Athanasius*. Oxford.

Zachhuber, J. 2000. *Human Nature in Gregory of Nyssa: Philosophical Background and Theological Significance*, Supplements to Vigiliae Christianae 46. Leiden.

Index

Page numbers in italics are figures; with 't' are tables.

absorption 122
Acharaca cave, 61n77
actors 97–100, 105–106
   and *mimesis* 148–149
   and ritual 146–147
Aegina 193
Aeneid (Virgil) 135
Aeschylus, *Prometheus Vinctus* 79–80
Against Eunomius (Gregory of Nyssa) *see* Gregory of Nyssa
Agamedes 47, 49
agency, sense of 122
agency detection theory 99, 108
   and maenadic ritual 157–159, 161
alma sacerdos 174
altars, and animal sacrifice 24–32
ancilia (shields) 124, 131
Andersen, Marc 157
Anderson, A. K. 253n31
Andromache (Euripides) 111
anger 253n31
animal sacrifice
   Greek 19–23, 34–37, 39–40
      cult of Demeter and Kore 198
      examples 23–29
      rituals of 29–35
   Roman
      Bona Dea 170–171, 173–174
      Mithraic 230–231, 233–234
Annaeus Lucanus, L. *see* Lucan
anthropomorphism
   gods in ancient Greek culture 69–70
   concepts of 74–76
   divine appearances 70–74
      divine smellscapes 83–85
      divinities smelling 85–88
   and smell 79–83, 88–90

grounded cognition 76–79
antistites (chief priestesses) 174, 180
aparchê 29
   see also sacrifice
Aphaia 193
Aphrodite 71
Apollo
   and animal sacrifice
      in Homer's *Iliad* 23–24, 26, 28, 39
      sacred calendar 25–26
   and belief/trust 110–111
   and Croesus' test of the oracles 85–87
   appearance of 71
   temple at Delphi 47
Apollos 254–255
Apology for the Apology (Eunomius of Cyzicus) 266–267
apophatic theology 267
Appian 136
Apuleius 132
Aristophanes
   mimesis 149
   smell 83–85
   and the Trophonius cult 61n78
Aristotle
   on feelings 248
   on initiation at Eleusis 201
   on mimesis 149
Arius of Alexandria/Arians 267, 269–270, 281
   see also Neo-Arians
Artemis
   Agrotera, animal sacrifice 27
   and the Brauronia 83
   in Euripides' *Hippolytus* 80–81
Arts and Humanities Research Council (AHRC) 6
'as if' 104, 106
Asclepius 113, 193

Index

astrological constellations 231–232
Athanasius of Alexandria 269
Athena, in Homer's *Odyssey* 28, 39, 71
authorial instance 246
authority *see* religious authority
awe 55, 73, 209n78
Ayres, Lewis 267, 278–279

Bacchae (Euripides) 110–111, 145, 150, 156, 160
Bacchanalia 176
Bacchants 119, 123–124
  see also oreibasia
bakchai 146
baptism 257–259
Barrett, Justin 75, 275–276
Barsalou, Lawrence 69, 76–78, 89
Beard, Mary 167
begetting
  and the Trinity 266–270, 277–284
  and reflective thought 284–287
belief 11–12, 159
  and make-believe 99–105
  modes, *deus ex machina* 109–113
Bembo, Pietro 182–184
Bernabé, A. 45
bi-stable images 231, 233–234
Bible studies 249
  see also Paul the Apostle
biology
  evolutionary 245–246, 247n6, 249, 260–262
  moral 247n6, 251, 260–262
birth *see* childbirth
Black Demeter of Phigalia 70–71
blood, smearing altars with 29–30
body techniques 121–123
Bona Dea
  damiatrix 173–177
  December festival 170–179, 182
  May celebration 172–173, 180–183
  origins 168–170
  and social classes 177–178
  socio-cognitive approaches to 178–184, 179t, 180–181t, 182–183t, 182t
bottom-up processes 2–3, 45, 195, 202, 206–207
Bourdieu, Pierre 3
Boyer, Pascal 22, 69, 75, 274
brain 10–11, 22, 58, 77
  and body 121–122
  see also predictive coding; predictive processing
Brauron/Brauronia 83
bread, Mithraic meal 225
Bremmer, Jan 29, 147, 155
  Greek Maenadism Reconsidered 154

Brouwer, Hendrik H. J. 173, 175n54, 176
bulls, and Mithras 224
Burkert, Walter 20
burning 33
  and sacrifice in the Hebrew Bible 35–37
Burrus, Virginia 269

Cairns, D. 250–251n19, 250n16, 250n19
calendars, sacred, and animal sacrifice 25–27
Canis Minor/Major, constellation 232
Capua Vetere Mithraeum 227–228
carmen Arvale 118
carmen Saliare see vocal techniques/Salian chant (*carmen Saliare*)
Catullus 127–128
Censorinus, *On the Birthday* 131
Chaeronea 72
Chaniotis, A. 247n6
Chapman, H. A. 253n31
Characters (Theophrastus) 34
chief priest of Eleusis *see hierophant*
childbirth, Gregory of Nyssa and 269, 278–285
Christianity
  historical documents 223n30
  and relating to God 102–103
  and wild dance 126–127
Cicero 130–131
Circe 132
clairvoyance 57
Claros 49, 53, 61
Claudia (gens) 178
Clauss, Manfred 222, 230n83
cleanliness/cleansing 251–252
  and Paul's letters to the Corinthians 253, 257–260
Clodius Pulcher, P. 176
clothing
  special
    Demeter and Kore initiation 199
    Salian rite 135
    and Trophonium 52
Clouds (Aristophanes) 61n78, 83
cognition 2–4
  embodied 76, 130, 202
  grounded 69, 76–79 *see also* situated conceptualization
cognitive anthropology 20
Cognitive Approaches to Ancient Religious Experience (CAARE) network 6–8
cognitive psychology 20, 246
cognitive science of religion (CSR), and Ancient Greek animal sacrifice 19–20
collegia 225–226
concepts, religious 273–277
Connor, W. R. 99–100

consciousness
  altered states of 180–181t
    and Euripides' *Bacchae* 151
    and maenadic ritual 153, 160
    ritual form hypothesis 179t, 180–181t
    and the Salians 124, 128–130
    and the Trophonium 54, 56–57, 61–62
Constantinople, Council of 271, 287
1 Corinthians 253–260
cortisol 232–233
couches, dining 224
Council of Constantinople 271, 287
Council of Nicaea *see* Nicene
Cratinus, on music in the Trophonium 49
Croesus 85–87
Csordas, Thomas 3
cultural knowledge, and predictive processing 154–156
culture 271–273
Cumont, Franz 226n48
Curetes 127, 132
Cyclops (Euripides) 151
Cyropaedia (Xenophon) 27

Daedalus 52
Daimonion of Socrates, The (Plutarch) 55–58
Damia 177
  cult of 173–175
damiatrix 173–177, 179–180, 184
dance, and the Salii 123–130
darkness
  and the descent to Trophonius 50, 53–58
  and the initiation at Eleusis 201–207, 209–210
  in Mithraic initiation 227–228
Datis (Persian general) 33
de Corona (Demosthenes) 247–248
De Cruz, H. 278
De' Guidobaldi, Domenico 173, 178
de Hemmer Gudme, Anne Katrine 39
death
  and initiates at Eleusis 201, 210–211
  Platonic revival 236
  see also Trophonius
dedication 24, 48, 159, 197
deiknymena (things shown) 199, 207–208
delirium 146
Delphi, Apollo's temple 47
Demeter
  Homeric Hymn 81–83
  and smell 81–83
Demeter and Kore cult (Eleusis) 196–197, 223n30
  initiation ritual 197–200
    prior expectations 200–201

post-ritual understanding 209–212
religious authority 206–207
Telesterion walls 207–209
temenos walls 201–202
emotional contagion 205–206
and the initiates' engagement with ritual 204–205
and the initiates' sense of self 202–204
Demosthenes, *de Corona* 247–248
Dennett, Daniel 229n74
depersonalisation 122
Detienne, Marcel 34
deus ex machina 96–99, 113–115
  belief and make-believe 99–105
  and modes of belief 109–113
  and ritual impersonation 105–109
Deus Sol Invictus 223, 235–236
Didyma 49, 61
dinê see vortex
dining, Mithraic communal meals 224–226
dining couches 224
dining rooms 224, 234
Diodorus Siculus 32–33
  maenadic ritual 145–146, 148–149
Dionysia 32
Dionysius of Halicarnassus, *Roman Antiquities*, on the Salii 124–125, 130–131, 135
Dionysus
  Homeric Hymn 156
  and libation 32–33
  and maenadic ritual 145–152, 155–156, 159
  Theatre 107
  see also oreibasia
disgust (moral/physical) 251–253
  and Gregory of Nyssa 268
  and Paul's letters to the Corinthians 257, 259–260
dissociation 121–123
  and the Salian priests 118–120
  body techniques 123–130
  and the mimicry of Mars 134–136
  vocal techniques (*carmen Saliare*) 121–122, 130–134
dissociative techniques 122
  body 121–130
  vocal (*carmen Saliare*) 121–122, 130–134
divination
  and animal sacrifice 27–28, 31–32
  and the descent to Trophonius 49
  extispicy 26, 32
  and the Hebrew Bible 36
  omen 31, 160, 179n80
  see also oracles
divine impersonation 99–105
doctrinal mode 21, 33, 181, 182t

Dodds, Eric 153, 156, 161
domestic violence 171
domitrix, 175n58
drink-offering (*loibê*) 37
dromena (things done) 199,
  204–205
drugs 121–122, 129
Ducrey, P. 247n6
Durkheim, Emile 259

eating, and animal sacrifice 33–34
Echetleus 72
Eco, U. 246–247n5
ecstasy 147, 153
Ekman, Paul 251n20, 257
Electra (Euripides) 110–111
Eleusis *see* Demeter and Kore cult (Eleusis)
Elsner, Jas 231
embodied cognition 76, 130, 154–155,
  157–159, 202
emotion
  anger 253n31
  and feelings defined 246
  studies 211–212
  see also feelings
emotional contagion 205–207, 210
the emotional turn 249
endorphins 224–225
engodedness 61
environment, VR experiment 157, 159
Epidauros, sanctuary of Asclepius 193
epinephrine 227
epiphany
  and *deus ex machina* 103–109
  and divine appearances 72–73
  in maenadic ritual 155–160
episodic ('flashbulb') memory 21–23
Epizelus 72
epoptai 198–200, 204, 208–209
Erichtho 132–133
essence (*ousia*) 267, 278–283
ethos 247–248
Eunomius of Cyzicus 270
  Apology for the Apology 266–267
Euripides
  dance ritual 160
  and *deus ex machina*
    Andromache 111
    Bacchae 110–111
    Electra 110–111
    Helen 110–111
    Hippolytus 110–111
    Ion 110, 113
    Iphigenia in Tauris 110–111, 113
    Orestes 110–111

Supplices 110
and Dionysus 156
maenads 145, 150–151, 157
  sparagmos 150
  smell/odour 80–81
Europa, rape of 83
Eurynome sanctuary (Arcadia) 193
evolution 20, 22
evolutionary biology *see* biology, evolutionary
expectation, prior
  and the initiation at Eleusis 195, 200–201,
    205–207
  maenadic ritual 157
  and the Salian ritual 123
  and Trophonius 59
  see also top-down processes
experience, defined 220–222
extispicy 26, 32

faith (*pistis*) 112–113
Fauna 168–170, 177
Faunus 168–170
feelings 4
  and emotions defined 246
  scholarship on 249–251
  textual representations 245–249,
    260–262
  and emotions 251–253
  Pauline studies 250, 253–260
Festus *see* Pompeius Festus
fiction, paradox of 101
flashbulb memory *see* episodic ('flashbulb' memory)
flutes, in ritual 131
forest experiment 157, 159
Fortuna Muliebris (cult) 171
Foucault, M. 171
Frontisi-Ducroux, Françoise 72
functionalism 115, 159

Galloi 119, 123, 127, 129, 134
gathering, initiation at Eleusis 208–209
Glossaria Latina (Placidus) 174
glossolalia 122, 132
goal detection 273
God
  concepts of 275
  and the Nicene creed 278
god concepts 69–70, 74–78,
  275
  and smell 82–83, 88–89
gold tablets, Bacchic 51–52
Good Goddess *see* Bona Dea
Gordon, Richard 69,
  230–231

Gospel of John, Gregory of Nyssa on 269, 281, 286
Gospel of Mark 234
grain-offerings 35–36
  importance of smell 37–38
Greater Mysteries *see* Demeter and Kore cult (Eleusis)
Gregory of Nyssa
  Against Eunomius (*Contra Eunomium*) 266–269
    and begetting 277–284
    and the Nicene doctrine 270–273
    and reflective thought 284–287
grounded cognition 69, 76–79
guilt-offerings 35–36
Guthrie, Stewart 74

Habinek, Thomas 119
Hades 45
  Odysseus' visit 50
  see also Trophonium (sanctuary)
hallucination, in Trophonius' grotto 54, 56, 60
hallucinogens, in Trophonius' grotto 54
Harris, Paul L. 101
Harrison, Jane Ellen 152–153, 156
Harrison, Thomas 104
head-tossing/-shaking 127–129, 158–160
Hebrew Bible
  Leviticus 22–39
  Numbers 37
Helen (Euripides) 110–111
Henrichs, Albert 152
Hercules 135
  and Bona Dea 169
Hercyna (river) 50
Hermes
  animal sacrifice 24–25
  Homeric Hymn 87–88
  Psychompos 50
  smelling the sacrificial meat 87–88
Herodotus
  and animal sacrifice 30
  on the cult of Demeter and Kore 198n18
  divine presence 72–73
  on Pisistratus and Phye 99–100
  and the test of the oracles 85–87
Herz, Rachel 38–39
Hesiod
  Fr. 140 83
  Theogony 34, 88n98
Hesychius 146
hierophant (chief priest of Eleusis) 199, 204, 207–210
Hippolytus (Euripides) 80–81, 110–111
Hoffecker, John 229

Hollinshead, M. 208
Homer
  Iliad 23–24, 27, 37
  Odyssey
    animal sacrifice 24–26, 28, 32
    divine presence 73
    Odysseus' visit to netherworld 50
    smells 88
Homeric Hymn to Apollo 71
Homeric Hymn to Demeter 81–83
Homeric Hymn to Dionysus 156
Homeric Hymn to Hermes 87–88
homicide, and the Fauna/Bona Dea myths 168–170
Horace, *Odes* 123
Huxley, Aldous 171
Hydra, constellation 232
hymns, and animal sacrifice 33
hypnotism/hypnotizability, and sanctuary of Trophonius 48, 59
hysteria 147, 153, 161

identity, dissociative 123
Iliad (Homer) *see* Homer, *Iliad*
imagery
  Mithraic 229–235
  and the tauroctony 230–234
imagination 96–98
imagistic mode 21, 181–182, 184
immersion 54, 102
impersonation 99–109
implicit thought 275–277
incubatio 180–181
inhibition 221
initiates (*mystai*)/initiation *see* Demeter and Kore cult (Eleusis); Trophonius
intoxication 146
intuitive processes 273–277
  and divine begetting 277–284
Iobakchoi 99, 103
Ion (Euripides) 110, 113, 157
Iphigenia in Tauris (Euripides) 110–111, 113
Isocrates 201

James, William 236
Jerome 226
Jerusalem 35
Joyce, James 218–220
Jupiter Dolichenus, cult 223n30
Justin 169, 225–232

katabasis
  defined 45
  see also Hades; Trophonius
Keil, F.C. 75, 275–276

Keuls, Eva 148
killing, and animal sacrifice 27–30
knisê 37
  see also animal sacrifice; smells
knowledge 9–11, 22, 70n4
  cultural, predictive processing 154–156
  and grounded cognition 77–78
  secret 58
Kore *see* Demeter and Kore cult (Eleusis)
Krater/Leo, constellation 232

Lady Macbeth complex 252, 259–260
Larson, Jennifer 39, 100, 107
Larsson, Maria 78–79
Lateiner, D. 251n20
laughter 60
Lawson, E. Thomas 20–23, 28, 33–35, 38–39
Lebadeia 44, 46n12, 46
legionary units, Roman 223
legomena (things said) 199–200, 204–205
Lenaea vases 156
Lethe (water of Forgetfulness) 50–52
Leviticus, Hebrew Bible 22–39
libation, and animal sacrifice 24–32
light
  burst of, initiation at Eleusis 209
  in Mithraic initiation 227–228
Liljenquist, Katie 251–252
Lindsay, Dennis R. 112
livers, and divination 31–32
Livy 132, 135
loibê 37
  see also libation
Lootens, Matthew 271
Lowell, Francis Cabot 229n74
Lucan (Annaeus Lucanus, L.) 128–129, 132–133
Lucretia, rape of 167
Lucretius 126
Luhrmann, Tanya M. 105
  When God Talks Back 102–103

McCauley, Robert N. 20–23, 28, 33–35, 38–39
Macedonia 87n88, 147
Macknik, Stephen 221
MacMullen, Ramsey 271–272
McNamara, Patrick 122, 135–136
Macrobius
  on the Bona Dea 173–174, 175n58
  on Fauna 168n12
madness, maenadic 152–154
Maenads
  and the *tripudium* 127–129
  see also oreibasia
magical thinking 251n20, 257
Magnesia-on-the-Maeander 147, 151, 156

Maillard reaction 37–38
Mainz, mithraeum 227
make-believe 97–105, 114–115
Marathon 27, 72
Mars, and the Salii 134–136
Martines-Conde, Susana 221
masculinity
  Roman 125
  and the Bona Dea 167
masks, and Dionysus 156
Mastrocinque, A. 169n18, 230n83
Mauss, Marcel 121
medial orbitofrontal cortex (mOFC) 227–228
memorability 221
memory 78–79, 211, 229n74
  Aristophanes' *Clouds* 61n78
  and the Bona Dea cult 179t, 180–184, 180–181t, 182t
  and emotion 211–212
  semantic/episodic 21–23, 38–39
  and smell 22–38, 228n64
  and Trophonius 51–53, 58–59
  Mnemosyne 50
  see also schema/-ata; situated conceptualization
mental maps 122, 130
Merkelbach, Reinhold 223n33
Merleau-Ponty, M. 3
metacognitive gaps 211
metempsychosis, and the Trophonium 57
Miletus 147–148
Mimallones 148
mimesis, and the *oreibasia* 148–149
mimicry, and the Salii 134–136
minimally counterintuitive (MCI) features 74–75n33, 96, 99
mirthless rock 199
misogyny 167, 170–171
Mitchell, Alan 256
Mithraeum/mithraea 224–225, 234–235, 236n116
  Capua Vetere 227–228
  of Felicissimus (Ostia) 226–227
  Santa Prisca 228, 233n104
Mithraism/Mithras
  historical documents 222–224, 235
  iconography/imagery 229–235
  ritual practices 224
    communal meals 224–226
    initiation 226–229
Mnemosyne 50–51, 59
modes of religiosity 21
  and the Bona Dea cults 180–184, 182–183t, 182t
monumental architecture 193–195, *196*, 196–197, 202, 208

moral biology *see* biology, moral
moral disgust 252–259
moral judgement 252
mountains
    and maenadic ritual 147–148, 150, 157, 161
    and the Trophonium 47
multimodal simulation 77
music, in the Trophonium 49
mystagogoi see sponsors of initiates
mystai see initiates
mysteries *see* Bona Dea; Demeter and Kore cult (Eleusis); *oreibasia*; relevant mysteries model; Trophonium (sanctuary)
mystical experience 2–8

Naiden, Fred 29, 32, 34, 37
naïve biology 273
naïve physics 273
narrative 123, 219–220, 222
    pre-established 211
    and the tauroctony 230
    see also god concepts
Natural History (Pliny the Elder) 133
Natural Questions (Seneca the Younger) 123
Nelis, D. P. 250–251n19, 250n16, 250n19
Neo-Arians 267, 270, 272
neural networks 184
neurotransmitters 172, 225–226
Nicaea
    Council of 266
Nicene
    doctrine/creed 266, 270–273, 278, 284, 287
    dissemination/popularizing 270–273
Nilsson, Martin 69
nomizein 112
    see also belief
Nonius Marcellus 120, 132
Numbers, Hebrew Bible 37

obedience 110–111
Odyssey (Homer) *see* Homer, *Odyssey*
Oedipus at Colonus (Sophocles) 193
Oedipus Tyrannus (Sophocles) 113
omens, and divination 31, 160, 179n80
On the Birthday (Censorinus) 131
On the Civil War (Lucan) 128–129
On the Nature of Things (Lucretius) 126
Onatas 70
oracles 49, 160
    and the cave of Trophonius 45, 49–50
    Croesus' test of the 85–86
    Delphi 26
    fees for 46n12
    in Leviticus 36n81

oreibasia 145–147, 161
    cultural knowledge of maenads and predictive processing 154–156, 161
    epiphanic experience 157–160
    maenadic madness 152–154
    Maenads 149–151
    sources for 147–149
    see also mountains
Orestes (Euripides) 110–111
Origen 226
Orphic/Bacchic mysteries *see* Demeter and Kore cult (Eleusis)
Orwell, George 171
Osborne, Robin 160
Oscan 175–176
ousia see essence (*ousia*)
out-of-body experience, in Trophonius' grotto 57, 60

Packard, Vance 221n21
pagan religions 112, 223n30
paradox of fiction 101
Parker, Robert 30–31
pater familias 170
pathos 247–248
patriarchy 167–169, 172
Paul the Apostle 249–250
    and 1 Corinthians 253–260
Paulus Diaconus 174–175
Pausanias
    and the Black Demeter of Phigalia 70–71
    and Echetleus 72
    and Poseidon 72–73
    on Trophonius 47–52
        the grotto 53–55, 57–58
        return from the grotto 58–59
Peace (Aristophanes) 84–85
perceptions 2–3
performance *see deus ex machina*; Salian priesthood
Persephone 56
    see also Demeter and Kore cult (Eleusis)
Phaedrus (Plato) 73, 132
Philoctetes (Sophocles) 110–111, 113
Phye 99–100, 107
physical disgust 252–253
Piaget, Jean 101
pilgrimage 46–47
Pisistratus 99–100, 107
pistis
    section of 1 Corinthians 255–259
    see also faith (*pistis*)
placebo treatment 46, 48, 122
Placidus 174

Plato
  divine appearances 73
  mimesis 148–149
  vocal techniques 132
Platt, Verity 103–104
Playfair, William 229
Pliny the Elder, *Natural History* 133
Plotinus 233
Plutarch
  on the cult of Demeter and Kore 209n78
  madness of ritual performers 152
  on the *oreibasia* 146–147
  on the Salii 124–125, 131, 135
  on the Thyiades 157
  on the Trophonium 55–58
polis religion 7, 159n84
Pompeius Festus, Sextus 126, 174–175
Porphyry 233–234
porticoes 194n4
Poseidon
  and animal sacrifice 25–26
  and the Mantineans 72–73
possession 128, 133–134, 136
prayer, and animal sacrifice 29, 33
predictive coding 11, 195–196, 210, 212
predictive processing 3, 122–123n33
  and cultural knowledge 154–156
presence
  divine 72–73, 98, 103–104
  deus ex machina 105–109, 114
pretend-play 101, 114–115
  see also make-believe
priestesses, chief *see antistites* (chief priestesses); *damiatrix*; Vestal virgins
priestesses *see oreibasia*
priming 48–49
processions 29
  cult of Demeter and Kore 198
Prometheus Vinctus (Aeschylus) 79–80
Propertius 169, 174
prophecy *see* divination; omens
prosopon 146
  see also masks
psychology, cognitive 20, 246
psychosomatic reactions 121–122
Ptolemaic cosmos *see* Ptolemy of Alexandria
Ptolemy of Alexandria 233–234
pudicitia see sexual modesty
Pudicitia/*Pudicitia plebeia* (cult) 178
purification of worshippers 29
  and the cult of Demeter and Kore 197–198
  and the Trophonium 49–51
  see also cleanliness/cleansing
Pythia 60
Pyysiäinen, Ilkka 275–277, 283–284

qualia 218n3, 235
Quintilian 126, 130–133

rape
  Europa 83
  Fauna 168–170
  Lucretia 167
Rapp, Adolph 152, 156, 161
relevant mysteries model 277, 284
religio 5
  see also religion
religion (term) 6, 223n32
religious authority 4, 206–207, 210
  sponsors of initiates (*mystagogoi*) 197–201, 207, 210–211
religious experience (defined) 1–6, 218
Remoria 172
Remus 172
Republic (Plato) 148–149
revelation 58, 182t
  see also epiphany
rhetoric 247–249, 250n16, 250n17
Rhetoric (Aristotle) 248
ritual 20–22
  and animal sacrifice 29–35
  dance 118–120
  special agent 21, 39
  special patient 21, 28, 33–35
ritual form hypothesis 21–22, 28, 34, 179t, 180–181t
robots 108
Rodaway, Paul 78–79, 85
Rohde, Erwin 152–153
role-play 115
Roman Antiquities (Dionysius of Halicarnassus) 124–125, 130–131, 135
Romanness 125
Rome, and Bona Dea 172–173
Romulus 168
Rozin, P. 257
Rubin's vase 231

Sabellius 281
Sabine women 167
sacred language 133
sacred objects, cult of Demeter and Kore 199–200, 209
sacrifice, animal *see* animal sacrifice
sacrificial meal 225–226
sacrilege 176
saffron 83–84
Salian priesthood
  and ritual dance 118–120
  body techniques 123–130
  mimicry of Mars 134–136

Salian priesthood (cont.)
    vocal techniques/Salian chant (*carmen Saliare*) 130–134
Santa Prisca Mithraeum 228, 233n104
schema/-ata 154–155, 161
Scipio Africanus 132
Scorpio, constellation 232
Scott, Joan 5
seclusion 49
secrecy 52, 58
    and the sanctuary at Eleusis 197n14
self-consciousness 98, 101–103, 106–107
Seneca the Younger 123–126
sensation 38, 51, 58, 85
sensory confusion 158
sensory deprivation
    and the initiation at Eleusis 210
    in Trophonius' grotto 56–57, 60
sensory pageantry 21, 33, 38
    and the Bona Dea cults 179t, 179
sensory-motor processes 76–77
serotonin 225
sexual modesty (*pudicitia*) 168
    and *Pudicitia plebeia* (cult) 178
Sharf, Robert 5
shields (*ancilia*) 124, 131
Sibyl 128–129, 132
silence
    Bona Dea myth 168–170
    and sensory deprivation 56
    and the *Telesterion* 209n78
Silk, Michael 84–85
sin, and baptism 257
sin-offerings 35–37
Sinos, Rebecca 100
situated conceptualization 69–70, 77–79, 83, 89–90
Smail, Daniel Lord 171–172, 224, 260–261
smells
    and animal sacrifice 34–37
    and embodied religion 88–90
    and Mithraic initiation 228
    and situated conceptualization 78–79
Smith, Jonathan Z. 5
snakes
    and Bona Dea 173
    and Faunus 168
    and the *oreibasia* 148
    Sosipolis 71
    in Trophonius' grotto 54
social brain hypothesis 236n116
social power 171–172
somatosensory processing 158
song see *carmen Arvale*; *carmen Saliare*
Sopatros 201, 205n59

Sophocles
    deus ex machina 110–111, 113
    temenos 193
Sørensen, Jesper 19
Sosipolis 71
Sounion, and animal sacrifice 26
Sourvinou-Inwood, Christiane 106
sparagmos 150–152
Spatharas, D. 251n20
speaking in tongues (glossolalia) 122, 132
special agent rituals 21, 39
    and the Bona Dea Cults 179–181, 179t
special instrument ritual 28, 179–180
special patient rituals 21, 28, 33–35
    and the Bona Dea cults 179–180, 184
Sperber, Dan 272, 274, 277, 284, 287
Spica, constellation 232
spondai 32
sponsors of initiates (*mystagogoi*) 197–201, 207, 210–211
star maps 231–232
Statius, P. Papinius 132
story/story-telling 115, 172
    see also narrative
stress 232–233
Suda 149–150n32
superstimuli 221
Superstitious Man (Theophrastus) 72
Supplices (Euripides) 110
suspension of disbelief, and *deus ex machina* 104–105, 107
Symposium (Xenophon) 73
symptoms 4, 8–10, 220
    and Mithraism 222–224, 236

Tambiah, Stanley 133
tauroctony 230–234
Taurus, constellation 232
Taves, Ann 2–4
the *Telesterion* 197, 199–200, 202n46, 207–209
temenos, sanctuary of Demeter and Kore 193–199, *196*
temple walls see walls
Tertullian 127, 225
Theatre of Dionysus 107
Thebes 147–148, 150, 156
Theogony (Hesiod) 34, 88n98
theology 75, 275–277
    apophatic 267
    and divine begetting 284
    Neo-Arian 270
Theophrastus 34, 72
theôria 33
theory of mind 75, 99

thiasoi 148, 161
  see also ritual
things done see *dromena*
things said see *legomena*
things shown see *deiknymena*
Thorikos, and animal sacrifice 25–27, 34
Thucydides, trust 113
thuein 33, 39–40
thusia 30, 39–40
Thyiades 148, 157, 158n78
thyrsoi 145, 148, 150, 158n73
  see also Maenads
Timarchus, and the Trophonium 55–57
Tomlinson, R. 193–194
top-down processes 2–3, 45, 155, 184, 195, 200, 205–207, 209–211
  and the initiation at Eleusis 210
tortoise meat 86–87
tossing of heads 127–129, 160
transgression, ritualized 171
treaty, and libations 32
the Trinity 266–269
  and begetting 266–270, 277–284
tripudium 123–124
Trophonium (sanctuary) (Boeotia) 44–45, 60–62
  preparation for the *katabasis* 45–50
  route/descent to the grotto 50–53
  in the grotto 53–58
  return from the grotto 58–60
Trophonius
  myth 44, 47
  see also Trophonium
trust 109–111
Turner, Victor 119
Tylor, E. B. 223n32

ululatio 132–134
uncanny valley 108
understanding, intuitive 277–287
Underworld see Hades; *katabasis*
unity 254–255, 278–283, 286
universalization 2

van Gennep, Arnold 119

Varro 130
Vedic ritual, as special patient ritual 22
Vegetius 226n48
Vernant, Jean-Pierre 20, 34, 81–82
Verrius Flaccus 126n53, 174, 176
Versnel, Henk 73–74, 88, 172
  Coping with the Gods 104
Vestal virgins 170, 173, 179, 180–181t, 182–183t
vestibular system 158–159
violence
  domestic 171
  sexual 167
Virgil, *Aeneid* 135
vocal techniques, Salian chant (*carmen Saliare*) 121–122, 130–134
volition 109, 122, 128
vortex (*dinê*), and the Trophonium 54, 56–58, 60

walls, Sanctuary of Demeter and Kore at Eleusis 193–197, *196*
water 52–53, 251–252
well-being offerings 35–36
Westh, Peter 76
Whitehouse, Harvey 20–23, 274–275
wine
  and Bona Dea 170, 172
  and Mithraism 224–225
  and Roman women 168–169

Xenophon
  animal sacrifice 26–27, 30
  divine appearances 73
  on Socrates 113
Xenophon of Ephesus 99–100

Zachhuber, J., 282n90
Zeus
  animal sacrifice 26
  Ctesius 71
  and Europa 83
  Meilichius 71
Zhong, Chen-Bo 251–252

For EU product safety concerns, contact us at Calle de José Abascal, 56–1°, 28003 Madrid, Spain or eugpsr@cambridge.org.

www.ingramcontent.com/pod-product-compliance
Lightning Source LLC
LaVergne TN
LVHW011801060526
838200LV00053B/3651